WHAT THE BRITISH DID

Two Centuries in the Middle East

PETER MANGOLD

I.B. TAURIS

LONDON · NEW YORK

Published in 2016 by
I.B. Tauris & Co. Ltd
London • New York
www.ibtauris.com

ISBN: 978 1 78453 194 2
eISBN: 978 0 85772 909 5
ePDF: 978 0 85772 704 6

A full CIP record for this book is available from the British Library
A full CIP record is available from the Library of Congress

Library of Congress Catalog Card Number: available

Typeset by Freerange
Printed and bound in Sweden by ScandBook AB

FSC
www.fsc.org

MIX
Paper from
responsible sources
FSC® C007584

Peter Mangold is a Visiting Academic at the Middle East Centre, St Antony's College, Oxford. He is a former member of the Foreign and Commonwealth Office Research Department and the BBC Arabic Service. He has written extensively on British foreign policy and is the author of *The Almost Impossible Ally: Harold Macmillan and Charles de Gaulle* and *Britain and the Defeated French: From Occupation to Liberation 1940–1944*, winner of the 2013 Edith McLeod Literary Prize (both I.B.Tauris).

'*What the British Did* is an enjoyable and profitable read'
– **Wm. Roger Louis, Professor of History, University of Texas, Austin**

'This book is a major contribution to the existing literature on Britain's encounter with the Middle East. It is unique in offering a comprehensive survey of over two centuries of history. And it has the added merit of exploring many different aspects in Britain's relationship with this complex, volatile, and endlessly fascinating region.'
– **Avi Shlaim, author of *The Iron Wall: Israel and the Arab World***

For Meridel Holland

Contents

List of Maps and Illustrations

Acknowledgements

My thanks to Clare Brown, Professor Raymond Cohen, John Eidinow, Roger Hardy, Dr Meridel Holland and Valerie Yorke for taking the time and trouble to read all or parts of the manuscript (though, needless to say, responsibility for the final text is my own). At St Antony's College, Oxford I am most grateful to the librarian the Middle East Centre, Mastan Ebtehaj, for her patience as I discovered more and more relevant volumes, and to the archivist, Debbie Usher, for guiding me through the Centre's fascinating collection of photographs. I am also grateful to Lester Crook at I.B.Tauris for his support for the project. I should also acknowledge one other considerable debt, to the late Philip Windsor of the London School of Economics, who supervised the thesis which many years later led to this book.

Abbreviations

AIOC (previously APOC)	Anglo-Iranian Oil Company
APOC	Anglo-Persian Oil Company
BJMES	*British Journal of Middle Eastern Studies*
EEC	European Economic Community
EU	European Union
INS	*Intelligence and National Security*
IPC	Iraq Petroleum Company
ISIS	Islamic State in Syria and the Levant
JIC	Joint Intelligence Committee
JICH	*Journal of Imperial and Commonwealth History*
MECA	Middle East Centre Archive, St Antony's College, Oxford
MES	*Middle Eastern Studies*
MI5	Security service
MI6 (also SIS)	Britain's external intelligence-gathering service
RUSIJ	*Journal of the Royal United Services Institute*
SAS	Special Air Service
UAE	United Arab Emirates
UAR	United Arab Republic

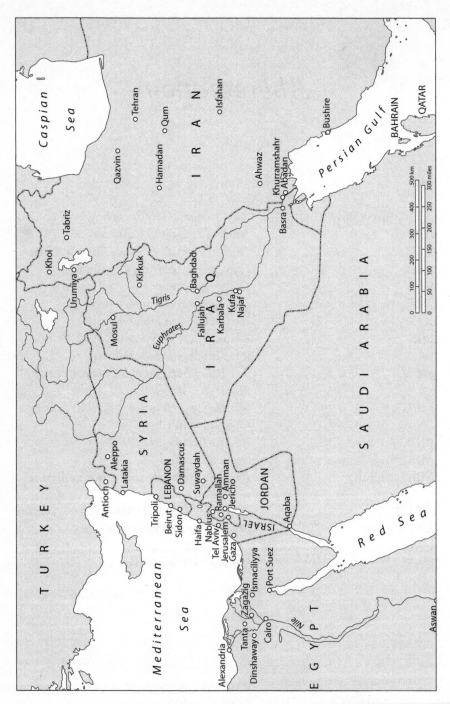

Map 1. The Middle East before 1967

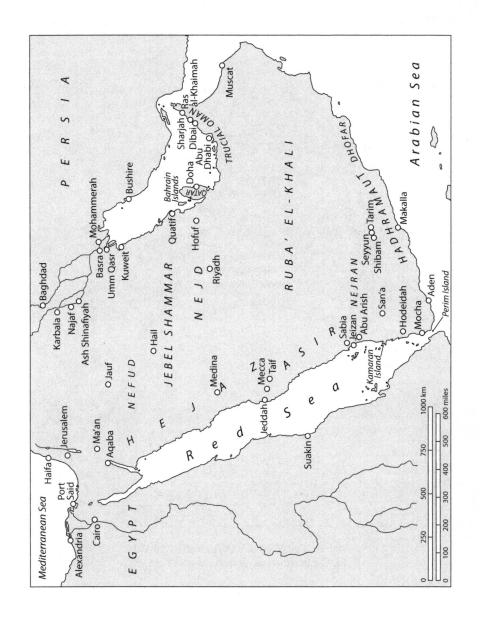

Map 2. Arabia and the Persian Gulf, 1916

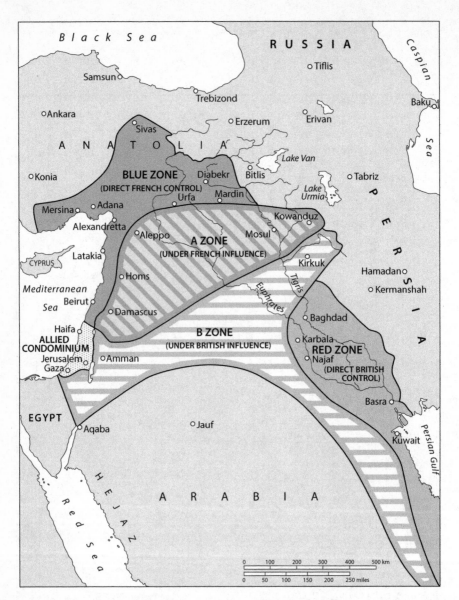

Map 3. The Sykes–Picot Agreement of 1916
for the Partition of Arab Inhabited Territory

Introduction

'The Pedigree of a White Stallion'

Huree Babu: 'You sit tight, Master O'Hara [...] It concerns the pedigree
of a white stallion.'
Kim: 'Still? That was finished long ago.'
Huree Babu: 'When everyone is dead the Great Game is finished. Not
before.'

Rudyard Kipling, *Kim* (London, 1944 edn, p. 316)

A t South Shields on the estuary of the Tyne and Wear are the outlines of
a Roman fort. Its name is surprising – Arbeia, 'The Place of the Arabs',
an apparent reference to one of the Roman units stationed there. This may
have been an irregular unit of bargemen from the River Tigris, but archers
from Syria were also known to have been stationed along Hadrian's Wall.[1]
The Roman Empire provides the earliest link between England, then its
most northerly possession, and what is today known as the Middle East.
Egypt, modern-day Syria and Israel, along with Mesopotamia, were also
Roman provinces.

The first English soldiers to go to the Middle East went during the
Crusades, the two-century conflict for the control of the Holy Land between
Christianity and Islam, beginning at the end of the eleventh century AD;
Richard I took Acre in 1191. Thirty years later, a Palestinian soldier, St
George, was adopted as England's patron saint. English traders were going
to the Middle East in the fifteenth and sixteenth centuries. 'Her husband's
to Aleppo gone, master o' th' *Tiger*' intones one of the witches in *Macbeth*,
the *Tiger* being the name of a ship.[2] The Levant Company had in 1581 been
granted a monopoly of trade with the Ottoman Empire, and for the next
240 years appointed all the commercial and diplomatic representatives in
the Levant. The East India Company, established in 1600, opened its first

1

'factory' or trading station at Jask on the Persian side of the Gulf of Oman in 1616. Its first commercial foray to Bussorah, today's Basra, took place in 1635.

It was not, however, until the Napoleonic wars that the expanding British Empire began to take a serious interest in the Middle East, understood here as the region between the Libyan desert in the west and Persia's eastern border with Afghanistan. Outside Europe, Britain's major eighteenth-century wars had been fought primarily in India, America and the Mediterranean. The combination of the growing British presence in India and French intervention in Egypt in 1798 first drew in the British to the Middle East. 'The possession of Egypt by any independent power', declared the Secretary of War, Henry Dundas, 'would be a fatal circumstance to the interests of this country.'[3] Two British expeditions to Egypt followed, along with treaties with Persia and Muscat, and a brief occupation of Perim Island at the mouth of the Red Sea. Around the same time the East Indian Company sent a naval expedition to the Persian Gulf, to deal with what it viewed as piracy.

Over the next two centuries, the Middle East held an importance to Britain, unmatched by any other region of the world. An expanding European world power, the heart of whose empire lay in the Afro-Asian world, was bound to concern itself with the control of the strategically critical crossroad region linking Europe, Asia and Africa. The Middle East became the 'swing door of empire', or more colloquially, the 'Clapham junction' of imperial communications.[4] It was also an important piece of strategic real estate, the point at which the Empire could be severed, from which power could be projected, which thus needed to be denied to rivals and enemies. In the first half of the twentieth century came the discovery of oil. Today regional violence threatens to spill over onto the streets of Britain. Twenty-first-century politicians are as conscious as their nineteenth-century predecessors that the holy sites of Islam, as also of course of Christianity and Judaism, lie in the Middle East.

In a classic study published in 1963, Elizabeth Monroe coined the notion of Britain's 'moment' in the Middle East. Forty years, she wrote, 'is only a moment in the life of a region with a recorded history of four millennia. Britain's time of dominance will seem short in the eyes of later centuries.'[5] Monroe was writing at a time when British power across the globe was in very visible retreat. Disillusioned by the 1956 Suez fiasco, she focused on the very brief period of British paramountcy beginning in World War I when British power expanded into Palestine and Iraq, which lasted only until the decade after World War II and the disastrous

Suez operation. A second edition of *Britain's Moment in the Middle East*, published in 1981, took the story on until the formal British withdrawal from the Gulf in 1971. The last chapter was entitled 'Nightfall'.[6]

Seen from the early twenty-first century, what seems striking about British engagement with the Middle East is its continuity rather than its brevity. Monroe had little to say about the nineteenth century, during which the *Pax Britannica* was established in the Persian Gulf, Britain became involved in rivalry with Russia in Persia, and only 13 years after the opening of the Suez Canal in 1869, British troops occupied Egypt. And Monroe, like most observers in the 1960s and 70s, had little inkling that Britain would subsequently still fight two wars with Iraq in 1990 and 2003, take part in 2014 in a campaign in Iraq against ISIS – the Islamic State in the Levant – and help precipitate the overthrow of Colonel Qadaffi of Libya. 'We're back' read the 2014 headline in the *Economist* announcing that Britain was to re-establish a permanent base in Bahrain as part of a 'sustained commitment east of Suez'.[7] Huree Babu's admonition regarding the remarkable persistence of the 'Great Game' in Asia, with its recurring patterns of behaviour which had seemed to have faded into history, thus seems more apposite than the idea of a British 'moment'.

Taking this long view of Britain's engagement with the Middle East has other advantages. It provides a wide-angle lens, which allows us to identify patterns of success and failure, and see parallels and continuities. It highlights consequences. Diplomacy, as Eden once noted, 'is a continuing process. The consequences travel on.'[8] Seemingly minor decisions can have major long-term effects, curtailing the freedom of action of subsequent British governments, illustrating the law of unintended consequences, and shaping political geography and ordinary lives in the Middle East. And it brings out the shifting kaleidoscope of British rivalries and alliances in the region, most notably the way in which Britain and France have morphed from enmity to rivalry and alliance.

Until the middle of the twentieth century, Britain's external relations centred around the twin poles of Europe and empire. The preference of a global trading power was to look beyond Europe to empire and the open sea. Its security, however, was ultimately dependent on Europe and the European balance of power. At the beginning of the nineteenth century there was a debate between Dundas and the Foreign Secretary, Lord Grenville, over what to do about Napoleon's forces in Egypt. Dundas belonged to the 'blue water' school, which saw Britain's role primarily in global and naval terms. His immediate concern was with the potential threat to Britain's growing empire in India, and he therefore wanted the French expelled from Egypt. Grenville, who viewed Britain as first and foremost a European power, preferred to allow Napoleon's army to stay in Egypt, rather than cause havoc elsewhere on the Continental mainland.[9] Dundas won, but by the twentieth century events in Europe rather than India determined British policy in the Middle East. The first of the two great wars against Germany precipitated the final expansion of British power in the region; the second precipitated the end of empire. Nevertheless it was India which provided the frame of reference within which the Middle East was normally discussed.

The Middle East came relatively late in the imperial day. The apogee of British power lay between Waterloo in 1815 and the 1860s.[10] By the time it gained paramountcy in the Middle East, the trajectory of British power was well into decline. As Commander Hogarth of the Arab Bureau remarked in 1920, 'the Empire has reached its maximum and begun the descent. There is no more expansion in us [...] and that being so we make but a poor Best of the Arab Countries.'[11] The importance of the Middle East to Britain, however, only peaked in the middle decades of the twentieth century. With the expulsion of British forces from Continental Europe in June 1940, the Middle East and the Mediterranean became central to British strategy until the expulsion of German forces from North Africa in May 1943. After the war came Britain's heavy dependence on Middle East oil in terms both of its energy security and of the parity of sterling, which was seen in Whitehall as underpinning its residual claim to Great Power status. The fact that this dependence coincided with the growing power of Arab nationalism, which Britain was decreasingly able to counter, was to cause major problems.

This points to another peculiarity of British Middle East policy. The Middle East was the scene of some major military victories – the battles of the Nile in 1798, Tel-el-Kebir in 1882 and El Alamein in 1942. But since the British surrender at Kut al-Amara in Mesopotamia in 1916 and the difficulties resulting from the wartime attempts to partition the Ottoman Empire, British policy in the region has seemed remarkably accident-prone. Some of the biggest controversies and worst failures of modern British imperial and foreign policy have centred on the region. Writing of domestic policy, Anthony King and Ivor Crewe distinguish between mistakes and blunders, the latter being defined as mistakes which are stupid and careless – driven by some combination of hubris, laziness, wilful ignorance or sheer incompetence.[12] Blunders also resulted from what might be termed an overriding imperative, a motive so pressing that it overrides all other considerations and distorts assessment of cost and risk. Suez, the promotion of the ill-fated South Arabian Federation which collapsed in 1967 and the 2003 Iraq war all fall into this fascinating category, fascinating precisely because the outcomes were foreseeable and hence, theoretically at least, avoidable.

Middle East policy making was never easy. There was a myth prevalent in parts of the Middle East that British policy was all-powerful, omni-competent and far-seeing.[13] The reality was rather different, The region defied attempts to establish a single, or even coherent policy. Already in the nineteenth century there were frequent differences between the Bombay Presidency which had immediate responsibility for the Persian Gulf, the Indian government in Calcutta and Whitehall. By World War I, with new power centres emerging in Cairo and Baghdad, the decision-making machine had become hydra-headed. Officials and allies alike were at times frustrated and perplexed. Decisions were more likely to get bogged down in inter-departmental disagreement than be made in a timely fashion or carefully thought through. Some order was created in 1921 when the Colonial Office gained responsibility for the newly acquired League of Nations mandates over Palestine, Transjordan and Iraq, but this did not prevent continued overlaps of responsibility or departmental rivalries.

The problem was not simply the lack of an effective system of coordination, or that of departments looking after their own interests. Different views also reflected different perspectives on complex problems. Military planners thought in terms of worst-possible-case scenarios and demanded a large and accordingly expensive margin of security. The Treasury demanded economy. The Foreign Office took a political perspective, and placed problems within the wider framework of British foreign policy. Views were at times passionately argued.

Those held in London or India were not necessarily shared by the men on the spot. They made mistakes, and their outlook could be narrow. George Brown, Foreign Secretary in the 1960s, once accused Political Officers in South Arabia of having a 'worm's eye view'.[14] But their understanding was frequently more acute than that of officials in India and London, who were often dealing with countries they had never visited, and issues which they had only assimilated intellectually from files and despatches.[15] Particular dangers arose where prime ministers, who have considerable power in foreign policy, got bees in their bonnets about the Middle East. Prior to the 2003 Iraq war, the Foreign Office sent an official with considerable experience of the Middle East, Dr Michael Williams, to brief Tony Blair about the ethnic and religious tensions in Iraq, and why an occupation might not be popular. 'That's all history, Mike,' came the reply. 'This is about the future.'[16]

Other than Aden, the British eschewed direct colonial control, relying either on ad hoc interventions, notably in the nineteenth and again in the late twentieth and early twenty-first centuries, or on informal empire. Although informal empire was widely practised in China, south-east Asia and Latin America, historians, like officials at the time, disagree as to how it should be described.[17] This is hardly surprising since its essence was its flexibility. In the Middle East, where it variously took the forms of actual or quasi-protectorates, treaty relationships and, in the twentieth century, League of Nations mandates, it was primarily a matter of indirect rule. As Lord Cromer put it in the late nineteenth century, 'We do not govern Egypt, we only govern the governors of Egypt.'[18] Rather than giving instructions, the British tendered 'advice', although the distinction between offering advice and ordering might be little more than a vocal inflection.[19] Constraints were imposed on the foreign, and sometimes also domestic, policies of nominally independent states or rulers. These were variously aimed at keeping Great Power rivals out, maintaining local order and stability, ensuring 'friendly' (i.e. pro-British) governments, and in the twentieth century, securing strategic facilities and oil on favourable terms. Most of the British policy debates centred on the form and extent of the controls it seemed desirable or politic to impose.

By the 1920s, with traditional imperialism under attack, informal empire became the only option available. This did not unduly worry British policy makers. Informal empire had long proved adequate to the protection of their Middle East interests. And it was cheap. The British were parsimonious – some would say miserly – imperialists. They had to be. A small group of islands with a population of some 16 million in 1800, rising to 37.4 million in 1890, running an empire which at its height covered nearly a quarter of the globe, needed to husband its resources.[20] At the same time governments were well aware that the public did not take kindly to heavy imperial expenditure, let alone expensive imperial and post-imperial wars. During the brief period of British paramountcy in the 1920s and 30s, there were only some 20 British officials and officers in Transjordan. In Palestine in 1929 there were 397.[21]

Empire, whether formal or informal, was underwritten by military power. With the exception of the Persian Gulf, where the *Pax Britannica* relied on sea power, control of dissident tribal activity and the suppression of revolts and insurgencies was primarily the responsibility of the RAF, locally recruited levies, and only where necessary, the army. But the recourse to force was regarded as a failure of policy. This could be best avoided by the maintenance of prestige – the confidence of allies and clients in, and the respect of adversaries for, imperial power. This was a major preoccupation of policy makers, who tended to be hyper-sensitive to any developments which seemed likely to impair it. The skills of imperial management were also important in this respect. Wise and self-confident ministers and officials knew how to pre-empt trouble, whether by nipping it in the bud, or by making judicious concessions. They knew when and when not to intervene, when to be firm and when to show restraint.

This required good intelligence, as well as a knowledge and understanding of language, local history and custom. The widespread use of Arabic made it relatively easy to create a corps of experts capable of serving across the region. The Levant consular service, founded in 1877, recruited native-born British subjects to fill the more important consular posts in Persia and part of the Ottoman Empire. After World War II the Foreign Office trained six or seven Arabists a year, who could expect to spend most of their careers in the Middle East. The larger British missions had long had an Oriental Counsellor, who was responsible for providing insights from the Arab rather than British perspective, and information on local politicians and personalities. They also provided continuity of expertise, staying, unlike regular diplomats, in posts for many years.[22]

Local allies and collaborators were essential to the operation of informal empire. Ideally they would be educated in Britain. Harrow and Sandhurst seemed particular favourites. (Though this didn't always work. Sir Anthony Parsons, who was in Iraq in the early 1950s, found that some Iraqi officers who had been to Sandhurst or Woolwich Military Academy would not forgive the humiliating treatment they had received either in terms of racial arrogance or gross horseplay.[23]) There might even be a short spell of service with a British regiment. A few were genuine Anglophiles, such as the Iraqi Regent, Abdulillah, of whom a diplomat reported that 'his cars, his aircraft, his clothes, his hunters, his foxhounds, even his swans are British, and so are many of his closest friends'.[24] Others collaborated because it was advantageous for them personally or for their countries to do so. Perhaps the largest group collaborated because the British were powerful, and it seemed wiser to accommodate the interests of the local paramount power than to oppose it.

Whatever the motive, it was preferable from the British perspective that informal empire should be amicable, and that however uncomfortably unequal the relationship, the local parties should benefit enough to want to continue with it. Where, however, consent could not be obtained, a Khedive tried to assert himself, or nationalist sentiment was hostile to British privileges and the interventions in domestic affairs which secured them, the British had few qualms about prioritising their interests over those of local parties and enforcing their demands. At least until the 1950s, the British approach to the Middle East reflected a sense of entitlement. They took it for granted that they had a right to demand bases or economic advantages, and to impose the constraints that these were deemed to require.

Apart from the two world wars, when several million British and imperial troops descended on the region, relatively few of the people of the Middle East had direct contact with Britons. Those that did often met men with a genuine interest in, and affinity for, the region. British officials came with a belief in fairness and good administration. They thought that they were there not simply to serve their own country's interests, but to do good. As one former officer in the Arab Legion put it, 'I didn't try to assimilate Jordan or anything like that but my spirit was with this country and I felt I was living to a purpose and creating something.'[25]

The romantic image of the Arab projected by writers like Richard Burton, which made them appear as English gentlemen 'translated into another idiom', was, however, very much a minority affair and strictly limited to the Arabs of the desert.[26] By no means all of the Britons who came or lived in the Middle East were respectful. The prevailing official perspective saw the region in terms of strategic real estate and oil, rather than of the people who lived there. Moreover, as so often when living abroad, the British kept themselves socially apart. A document produced by the Anglo-Iranian Oil Company in the 1930s noted a 'peculiar disinclination of the average Britisher to meet on a pleasant social basis with foreigners'.[27] At times they were blunderingly ignorant. Sir Anthony Parsons, recounts meeting the wife of a senior officer on a base in Iraq, who thought she was in Egypt.[28]

Where they did come into contact with the Arabs, Britons could be patronising and condescending. As their empire expanded, so did the British sense of ideological mission and self-righteousness. The British saw themselves at the apex of a hierarchy of civilisations, followed by the Americans and Germans, the Roman Catholic French and then the other Latin nations. Much lower down, the historian Ronald Hyam notes, 'came the Asian and African communities, with the Irish about on a par with them. All Orientals from Cairo to Canton were despised as barbarians and, ignorant and insolent', although the historian and philosopher James Mill was prepared to concede that the nations of western Asia 'the Persians, the

Arabians, and even the Turks possessed an order of intellectual faculties rather higher than the nations situated beyond them to the East'.[29]

Here, of course, lay some of the roots of the eventual breakdown of informal empire. The greatest threat came not from Great Power rivals, whom the British knew how to deal with, but rather from local nationalists opposed to what one Arab writer describes as 'the introduction of a foreign people whose aim was to dominate and exploit'.[30] Their objection derived not simply from the fact that they lost out. As important, if not more so, was a sense of humiliation at the imposition of inferior social and moral status and being dictated to or occupied by outsiders. 'A people ruled by foreigners has no life', says the young Fahmy in Naguib Mahfouz's novel, *Palace Walk*, set in Cairo during and after World War I.[31] What motivated nationalist opposition to the British was the desire for dignity and self-respect, as much as for independence.

By the 1920s and 30s increasingly large numbers of groups in Egypt and Iraq, ranging from students to professional bodies and some army officers, were opposing informal empire. The nationalist message spread, thanks first to newspapers and then, in the 1950s, to Cairo radio. Once popular sentiment was aroused, the balance of power quickly shifted against the British. Although they still had the firepower, the political and economic costs of imposing empire after 1945, when the British economy was constantly under strain and social welfare had become a domestic priority, proved prohibitively expensive. Informal empire, like formal empire elsewhere, was abandoned. That made British interests more vulnerable, but not critically so.

What follows is a study in the exercise of power. Elizabeth Monroe sought to address three main questions: the establishment of British power, the uses to which it was put, and why it declined after 1945.[32] The aim 50 years on is to assess the effectiveness of British policy and the ways it adapted to change. How was power exercised and how did this change over time? How do we explain the patterns of success and failure? How well were the British served by informal empire? How did the Middle East fit into the larger picture of British imperial and foreign policy? Why was the end of empire in the Middle East so much more painful than elsewhere, and why, contrary to all expectations, did British forces return? In seeking answers, extensive use is made of what was said and written at the time. The documents convey mood and mindset. They are also the language of power.

Some element of short-hand is inevitable. If the policy was British, policy making was in the hands of a tiny elite, with only intermittent parliamentary and public interest, usually when something went wrong. 'Britain' or 'the British' therefore refers to the British government or its policy makers, as well as to the actions of the British state. Similarly the term Middle East embraces a series of bilateral relationships with states or rulers. These, however, are at least as, if not more important as chapters in the history of the countries of the region, as in the history of British imperial and foreign policy. For a good deal of the period, Britain loomed much larger in the consciousness of Middle Eastern states than vice versa. Several owed their existence to the British.

To Arabs or Persians, this was a melancholy reversal of history. Addressing the leaders of the victorious Great Powers at the Versailles peace conference in 1919, Emir Feisal, who had led the 1916 Arab Revolt, and went on to become the first king of Iraq, declared that 'my nation has a great civilisational legacy, and when it was at its height of civilisation, the nations that you represent were in a state of chaos and barbarism'.[33]

The first human development of urban centres took place in the fourth millennium BC in Mesopotamia, today's Iraq. Baghdad, established in AD 762, became the world's most important centre of knowledge and learning, and with a population of more than one million was said to be the world's most populous city. Until the construction of the Eiffel Tower in 1889, the Great Pyramid, built around 2250 BC during the Old Kingdom, was the tallest building in the world. Egypt was the world's first unified state. The Arab Empire established in the seventh and eighth century AD stretched from the Pyrenees to the Pamirs in central Asia. As late as the sixteenth century, Persia under the Safavid dynasty was undergoing dynamic, political, artistic and religious development.

Since the imposition of Ottoman control in the sixteenth century, however, most of the Middle East has ranked among the shaped rather than the shapers of the world. The very term Middle East, first used by British and American commentators around 1900, defined the region in geographic location to the then locus of world power, namely Europe.[34] In the nineteenth century just Persia and Egypt counted as independent states, the latter only nominally so. Most of the region was poor, sparsely populated and inhospitable. Outside Egypt and a few urban centres, society was predominantly tribal, and by British standards, seriously underdeveloped. And not even Egypt proved a match for the pioneer of the Industrial Revolution, with its mastery of railways, the telegraph and Gatling gun.

The informal nature of its empire, and the unwillingness to spend money, nevertheless imposed limits on Britain's impact on the region.

France exercised much greater cultural influence in Egypt, even though from 1882 the country was firmly under British control. The British did not invest much in education. They did not build, either physically or institutionally. Despite advocacy of reform and good government, there were few sustained constitutional British initiatives.

That said, British fingerprints are to be found in every country in the Middle East, even when, like Syria, Yemen or Saudi Arabia, they were never part of Britain's informal empire. From the early nineteenth century until the formal British withdrawal from the Persian Gulf in 1971, and for part of the time elsewhere in the region, the British were the key arbiters of Middle Eastern politics. They determined who could hold power, and what policies were permissible. They decided how far an Ibn Sa'ud or Muhammad 'Ali could expand, and where they must stop. They established borders, resolved disputes and determined the fate of minorities. The British initially complemented and then replaced the Ottomans as the main source of order in the region. They did so not simply through their overt roles as policeman and arbitrators but by virtue of the fact that an imperial order was able to contain the tensions inherent in the ethnic, sectarian and tribal divisions in the region in a way that the later independent state system has found increasingly difficult.

Two hundred years of often dramatic change in British, Arab, Jewish and Persian history breaks down into four distinct periods. The creation of Britain's informal empire during the nineteenth and early twentieth centuries was a piecemeal, sometimes accidental, sometimes opportunistic affair. High noon, the period of British paramountcy between the latter part of World War I and the aftermath of World War II, was astonishingly brief. The subsequent unravelling of informal empire proved difficult, and was partially mismanaged. And yet there was, and remains, a lengthy post-imperial coda, the result of residual links with the region, especially the Gulf, an activist British foreign policy, and the instability which gripped the Middle East once empire had ended. Together these make for an eventful, and at times puzzling, journey.

Part One

Lines of Incursion, 1798–1922

1

Persia's Doubtful Friend

1800–1914

Every September since the British Empire began to disintegrate in the mid-1950s, a curious ritual has been enacted at the Royal Albert Hall in London. At the end of the last night of the Proms, broadcast on the BBC World Service and televised in 2013 to some 20 countries, an enthusiastic but largely unjingoistic audience sings some of the most stirring patriotic songs of the imperial era.[1] They include the paean to British sea power, 'Rule Britannia', and the setting of William Blake's visionary 'Jerusalem', beginning

> And did those feet in ancient time,
> Walk upon England's mountains green?

Composed during World War I, this equation of England with the Holy Land has come to trigger a nostalgic image of Englishness, of school chapel, cricket and tradition.[2] Then there is Elgar's imperial threnody, the 'Pomp and Circumstance' (March No. 1), composed for the coronation of King Edward VII. 'Wider still and wider', sing the Promenaders,

> shall thy bounds be set;
> God who made thee mighty, make thee mightier yet.

When these words were written in 1902, the British Empire was already the largest the world had ever seen, and with the exception of the Middle East, would expand little further. The original line of British imperial expansion had been westward across the Atlantic to North America and the Caribbean. But following the loss of the American colonies in 1783, imperial attention shifted east. British power in India was consolidated in the decades between the battle of Plassey in 1757 and the defeat of the Maratha confederacy in 1818. India was the platform from which British business advanced across Asia, as well as into East Africa.[3]

To Victorian statesmen the British Isles and India were 'the twin centres of their wealth and strength in the world'.[4] Britain, wrote one Viceroy, Lord Mayo, was 'determined as long as the sun shines in heaven, to hold India. Our national character, our commerce, demand it, and we have, one way or another, 250 millions' English capital fixed in the country.'[5] By the 1880s India took 19 per cent of British exports, and nearly one-fifth of British overseas investment. Following the abolition of slavery in 1833, cheap Indian labour provided a substitute elsewhere in the Empire. More important, the Indian army, paid for by the Indian not the British government, provided the Empire's central strategic reserve for use from China to the Western Front in World War I. If India went, so it was feared, Britain would cease to be a Great Power.[6]

India was regarded as an empire in its own right. Following the dissolution of the East India Company in the wake of the 1857 Mutiny, India had its own government in Calcutta, responsible for its own foreign policy, while a Secretary of State for India sat in the Cabinet in London. An empire on this scale had its own sub-empire. 'Greater India' extended from Aden to Burma, with its own sphere of interest in the Persian Gulf, Persia, Afghanistan and Tibet.[7]

India's interest in the territories on its western flank was three-fold. Prior to the advent of steam in the nineteenth century, shipping from Britain had been routed around the Cape, with only some despatches going by way of Syria, Mesopotamia and the Persian Gulf.[8] But already some 30 years before the opening of the Suez Canal in 1869, travel times were being cut by steamship services to the port of Suez, with passengers transferred overland to Port Said on the Mediterranean. The Anglo-Persian war of 1856–7 and the Indian Mutiny underscored the need for better communications between the imperial capital and its most important colony, and in 1865 London and India were linked by electrical telegraph, running via Mesopotamia, Persia and the Persian Gulf. Until the end of the 1920s, this was Britain's most important asset in Persia.[9]

A second Indian concern, which became more acute in the wake of the Mutiny, and the growing British involvement in the Middle East, was the potential impact of British policy on India's Muslim minority. Experience of various nineteenth-century *jihad* movements in India had created an image of Muslims as fanatics prone to holy war against non-Muslims and thus difficult to rule. By the beginning of the twentieth century more than half the Empire's population were Muslim. Of these almost

70 million lived in India, with a disproportionately high number in the Indian army.[10] This also meant that Britain was concerned with the safe organisation of the *Haj*, the pilgrimage to the Holy Places of Mecca and Medina in Arabia.

Concern with subversion underlay the third, and most important, Indian interest in the Middle East. The formidable Himalayan mountain boundary did not extend as far as the north-west of the country, at which point India was, at least theoretically, vulnerable. At the beginning of the nineteenth century the main threat was seen as coming from Britain's hereditary enemy – France. The longer-term concern was Russia. The 'Great Game' in Asia, whose ultimate goal, or so the British feared, was India, might be no more than a tournament of shadows, in which the British at times tended 'to see connections between a number of seemingly disparate facts', but it was none the less real for that.[11] Behind the vague talk of invasion lay the more insidious danger of a European rival subverting India from within. This threatened to increase the costs of holding India to the point of making it unprofitable; alternatively the need to buy off such a danger could impose constraints on British policy in Europe.[12]

Apart from Afghanistan, the western country of most concern to India was Persia. Although diplomatic and trading contacts went back to the sixteenth century, until the very end of the eighteenth century, Persia was, in Sir Denis Wright's words, regarded as 'a remote, fabulous country, difficult of access, of some commercial but minor political importance'.[13] During the nineteenth century this weak, sparsely inhabited country of 628,000 square miles came to be seen by the government of India as a buffer state, whose independence needed to be protected, but without incurring significant costs. There was no disposition, certainly in London, to turn Persia into a British dependency.

This had both advantages and disadvantages for the Persians. British interest offered the only available counterweight to the power of Persia's great northern neighbour. The Persians had lost two wars with Russia in the early part of the nineteenth century, and towards the end of the century the Persian army had effectively ceased to exist. But, as the Persians would discover, British support was not something they could rely upon. British policy was very much a function of the twists and turns of European power politics. Tehran, the Duke of Argyll noted, was the capital where Indian and European politics met, but the centre of interest was Europe. European considerations, along with the problems of coordinating the various government departments responsible for policy making – the

Foreign Office, the India Office, the Indian Government, the War Office, and at times also the Admiralty and Treasury – help explain why British policy tended to vacillate between what one historian describes as 'active interference and passive contemplation'.[14]

The modern British relationship with Persia began with some ceremony during the Napoleonic wars, when the Persians found themselves repeatedly courted and then abandoned. In 1800 a British mission under Captain John Malcolm was sent from Bombay. Seeking to make an impression, he arrived with a retinue of some 400 soldiers, servants and camp followers, 137 horses, 27 camels and 345 mules, at a cost of £100,000, equivalent to nearly half that of the Mediterranean Fleet. It was the largest mission ever sent to Persia by a European power.[15]

There were several reasons for this lavishness. In addition to seeking to thwart Napoleon's planned invasion of India in cooperation with Russia – a secret French mission had been sent to Tehran to request the passage of troops – the government of India was concerned about a threat to Punjab by the Afghan ruler, Zeman Shah.[16] The result was a commercial and political treaty, whereby the Shah undertook to attack Afghan territory should the Afghans invade India, and prevent the French settling or residing in Persia. Britain was to provide Persia with military equipment and aid in case of a French or Afghan attack. But the French threat disappeared almost immediately afterwards with the Anglo-French Treaty of Amiens of 1802. When the Persians appealed for British help against Russian attack on their Caucasian provinces, the British refused. Never ratified, the treaty did not cover a Russian attack, but this did not stop the Shah from feeling betrayed.[17]

The Anglo-French peace was short-lived, and in 1803 Napoleon, who was planning another invasion of Egypt, was again showing interest in Persia.[18] A Franco-Persian treaty of May 1807 was aimed primarily against Russia; nevertheless the Shah agreed to break all political and commercial links with the British and declare immediate war on them. French naval vessels in the Gulf were to receive support in Persian ports. When this treaty almost immediately fell victim to Franco-Russian rapprochement in July 1807, the Persians turned again to the British. They now sent no less than two rival missions, the one from India, the other from England. The 1809 Preliminary Treaty of Friendship and Alliance claimed to establish the basis for 'a sincere and everlasting definitive Treaty of strict friendship and union' between the two countries. The Shah declared the Franco-Persian treaty null and void and promised to do nothing to endanger India. Britain promised to send either forces or a subsidy, plus arms and training personnel, should Persia be attacked by a European power, i.e. Russia, even if Britain had concluded a treaty with that power.[19]

A British military mission duly arrived in Persia and became engaged in renewed fighting between Persia and Russia in the Caucasus. While the immediate aim was to divert Russia from Europe, the extent of Russian inroads into Persia was also beginning to raise fears that the real threat to British interests in Asia came from Russia.[20] Britain's role caused some controversy. One diplomat expressed doubts about placing weapons in the hands of 'these barbarous Mussulmans and even fighting their battles against our brothers in Christianity'.[21] Any embarrassment on this score was removed with Napoleon's 1812 invasion of Russia. The British envoy in Tehran, George Ousley, now helped broker a peace agreement between Russia and Persia. He got little thanks, as the terms were a humiliation for the Persians. This didn't prevent the signature in 1814 of a definitive Anglo-Persian treaty, though from the British point of view, it was already almost obsolete. The Persians, however, remained anxious for any support against Russia they could get. Earlier promises to train their armed forces were now omitted – the British military mission was largely withdrawn in 1815 – but the British promised military assistance, or alternatively an annual subsidy and arms and ammunition, if, but only if, Persia was attacked. This treaty provided the basis of Anglo-Persian relations until 1838.[22]

Just how little the British were prepared to help became evident when war once again broke out between Persia and Russia in 1826. Unfortunately for the Persians, this coincided with British efforts to reach an accommodation with Russia to secure Greek autonomy and prevent Russia from dismembering the Ottoman Empire. To avoid the risk of war with Russia in Asia, the Foreign Secretary, George Canning, declared that Persia was technically guilty of being the aggressor and thus not eligible for British aid. Two years later, in an agreement described by one British official as of 'extraordinary rigour, and even of doubtful honesty', the aid clause was removed from the Anglo-Persian treaty in return for a cash payment.[23]

The 1830s mark two new departures in Anglo-Persian relations. In 1834, in the first major intervention in Persian affairs, the British helped avert an extended succession struggle, when the British Minister, John Campbell, advanced £20,000 to pay the Persian forces, thereby securing the throne for Muhammad Mirza.[24] Four years later, Britain and Persia came into conflict when, encouraged by Russia, the Shah laid siege to Herat, which had previously been Persian territory. The westernmost of three Afghan states, Herat was regarded by the British as a gateway to India. They responded by occupying Kharq Island in the Persian Gulf, where they remained until

1842. Consideration was given to an invasion of Persia, but rejected. 'If we were to march on Shiraz', wrote the Foreign Secretary, Lord Palmerston, 'we should either succeed or fail. If we failed, it is needless to say, we should cut a very sorry figure; and, if we succeeded, we might shake the throne and the power of the Shah more than would be for our interest.'[25]

Besides, there was the risk of war with Russia, should the Shah appeal to Moscow for help. Though the Persians gave way, the matter was far from resolved. They occupied Herat in 1852, were forced out by a British threat to reoccupy Kharq, but then retook Herat in 1856. Despite some unease in the Cabinet, a Persian Expeditionary Force of some 5,720 men was despatched from India. By the spring of 1857 one-third of the Bombay army was in Persia.[26]

The immediate object was once again Kharq, but this time troops were also landed on the Persian coast at Bushire. Better armed and disciplined, the British had little difficulty in defeating the Persians and the war was over in less than six months. Like some later British wars in the Middle East, this one was unpopular – the public mood was against military adventures. In a leading article, *The Times* declared, 'Where Herat is we neither know nor care.'[27] Politicians complained of the government's failure to consult parliament, with Conservative leader, Lord Derby, arguing that the failure to issue a declaration of war and to rely instead on a proclamation by the Governor-General of India, raised a fundamental constitutional issue. Under the terms of the Treaty of Paris, the Persians relinquished 'all claims to sovereignty over the territory and city of Herat and countries of Afghanistan'. This effectively ended the matter, though it again left a lingering sense of Persian resentment.[28]

Behind this acute British sensitivity towards Herat lay fear of the Bear – 'those detestable Russians, horrible, deceitful cruel', as Queen Victoria referred to them.[29] 'Persia was for many years', as Palmerston, by then prime minister, had written in 1856, 'deemed our barrier of defence for India against Russia [...] We must now look upon Persia as the advanced guard of Russia.'[30] British distrust of Russian intentions had a long history. 'The route by which Alexander and other conquerors arrived in India, is still open', General James Stuart noted in 1800. In the late 1820s and early 1830s two books, respectively entitled *The Designs of Russia* and *On the Practicability of the Invasion of British India*, enjoyed a considerable vogue in Britain and India. Indian anxiety was fuelled by uncertainty as to Russian intentions, and lack of intelligence.[31] The threat may have been exaggerated, but hostility to the British, regarded in the Russian military as 'the energetic, pitiless and harmful enemy', was a dominant element of

Russian political life. The idea of a march on India persisted for decades, extending beyond extreme Russian nationalist circles.[32]

British concerns were increased by the Russian advances in central Asia, which began in the 1860s. In 1863 nearly 1,700 miles of desert and mountain separated the Russian from the Indian border. Twenty years later the distance had halved. By the mid-1880s the Russians were sharing a border with northern Persia, as well as Afghanistan. Where, British military planners wondered, would all this stop? Even if the Russians did not currently intend to invade, an advanced Russian position in central Asia would allow them to bring pressure on India in the event of an Anglo-Russian war. The two countries had fought in the Crimea in the mid-1850s and in 1885 an Anglo-Russian war over Afghanistan briefly seemed inevitable. At this point the British military authorities examined the use of Persian territory as a means of reaching Russia.[33]

If the Shah found it difficult to maintain a balancing act between Britain and Russia, his inclination was to rely on the more distant, and thus less dangerous of the two powers. But the Persians were accumulating a series of grievances against the British, not least resentment against what they felt was an arrogant and overbearing attitude.[34] To make matters worse, when the Persians asked for support, all they got was good advice and honeyed words. In 1882 the retiring Persian ambassador in London acidly complained that he could get similar assurances of friendship and support from the American, Belgian or Brazilian governments. Platonic sentiments were not enough.[35]

It was all, however, the Persians would get, given the conflicting British views as to whether India should be defended in Persia in Afghanistan, and whether it was more advisable to pursue what Rose Greaves describes as policies of masterly inactivity or mischievous activity. British ministers, moreover, were all too well aware that the areas of likely Russian encroachment in the north of the country lay beyond easy British military reach. But there was also a political factor. As the prime minister, Lord Salisbury, explained to the Persian prime minister in 1888, it was impossible for a government answerable to parliament to pledge itself regarding eventualities which could only be vaguely foreseen, or to undertake a war against a Great European and Asian Power.[36]

On the ground Anglo-Russian competition in Persia took a variety of forms. One was in an increasing consular presence. The Persians had initially been reluctant to grant Britain consular rights, for fear of having their country partitioned between the two rivals, and only gave way under pressure. The first two consulates were established as part of an 1841 commercial treaty, in Tehran and Tabriz; by 1921 there were 23. The most important British consulate was in Mashad, the holiest city in Persia, and capital of the strategically important province of Khorasan, bordering Transcaspia and Afghanistan. Having been pressurised by the Russians to open a consulate there, the Shah, who wanted to counter the Russian presence, invited the British to follow suit. The British Consul-General's main task was collecting intelligence on Russian military activities across the border. By the early twentieth century this task required an additional defence attaché.[37]

Quarantine stations, doctors at court and bank branches were also used as part of the Great Game in Persia.[38] There were the military escorts who accompanied the British and Russian ministers and their consuls, and who aroused a good deal of Persian ill-feeling. The Russians employed Cossacks, the British Indian *sowars*, whose turbans and pennoned lances were intended, in the words of one British Minister, to impress the Persians 'with the might and majesty of the British Empire'.[39]

Then there was the quest for economic concessions and development. British engineers involved in the construction of the telegraph line in the mid-1860s faced a formidable task. As one later wrote,

> A line of 1,250 miles, through an extremely difficult and troublesome country, had, by hook or by crook, to be made with Persian materials, at Persian expense, by a handful of foreigners whom every man in the Kingdom, from the Shah downwards, then regarded as pestilent interlopers. Looking back with the knowledge of subsequent experience, the writer is astounded at the cool impudence of the whole undertaking.[40]

The new line strengthened the authority of the central government, as well as bringing it closer to Europe, which the Shah visited in 1873. A year earlier he had made a major concession to a naturalised British subject, Baron Julius de Reuter, which Curzon described as 'the most complete and extraordinary surrender of the entire industrial resources of a kingdom into foreign hands, that has probably ever been dreamed'. So extraordinary in fact that the Shah was quickly forced to cancel it. Part of the thinking behind this had been the hope that by giving the British an important economic stake in Persia, they would become more committed to its independence.[41]

But it was the Russians who seemed to be gaining the upper hand. Their power became increasingly suffocating in the late 1880s, with the arrival of a new Russian Minister, Prince Dolgorauki, who sought to bring the country more closely under the Russian embrace. The Russians sought gradually to subject Persia to its dominant influence, and make the country 'an obedient and useful, i.e. sufficiently powerful, instrument in our hands, and economically, to preserve for ourselves the large Persian market for a free application of Russian labor [sic] and capital'.[42] Russia's attitude was similar to that of the British – *we* maintain our rights; *they* intrigue and meddle.

The British responded by sending an energetic new Minister in Tehran, Sir Henry Drummond Woolf, a Conservative MP who moved in high political and City circles. He sought to strengthen the country by urging reform, of which the Shah had a mortal dread, and by opening it up to desperately needed economic development. When the young George Curzon had visited Persia in 1889, he had had to travel by mule and horse, since there were only two carriageable roads in the country. The previous year, however, the Shah had agreed to open up the Karun river in the south-west to international navigation, as well as granting a concession for the Imperial Bank of Persia to British interests. The bank would become Britain's most successful tool for penetrating Persian markets.[43]

The 1890s were, nevertheless, a period of growing Russian influence, Persian disintegration and British impotence. Salisbury had noted that the British were powerless until there was a railway concession to the coast. But in 1889 the Russians had succeeded in getting the Shah to agree not to grant any railway concessions, a commitment renewed in 1900 as part of a Russian loan intended to give them control over Persian finances. Under its terms the Shah was precluded from accepting money from any other country until Russia had been paid off.[44]

During the Boer war at the turn of the century, which tied up some 400,000 British troops in South Africa, the Kaiser told the Tsar that he would protect Russia against a British attack in Europe, if Russia marched on India. With Britain internationally isolated, opinion about Persia became increasingly pessimistic. Sooner or later, Salisbury noted in 1901, Persia would become a Russian protectorate, and there was nothing Britain could do about it. The logic of this position pointed to the abandonment of the idea of Persia as a buffer state in favour of tighter control of the southern end of the Persian Gulf and also the province of Seistan, which lay at the point of junction of the Persian, Afghan and Balochistan frontiers.[45]

The imperious Curzon, who by now was Viceroy, took a typically more robust approach. He would 'undertake in half an hour with the Shah to say a few necessary things to him that would produce a most salutary revolution in Persian policy and in Anglo-Persian relations during the next twenty years'.[46] The invitation was not taken up, but under Lord Lansdowne, who became Foreign Secretary in 1902, the buffer policy was reaffirmed. The

Figure 1. The Shah returning to Tehran from a European visit, 1904

Shah was invited to London, and awarded the Order of the Garter (albeit after a tussle with Edward VII, who objected to conferring it on a Muslim). Britain supported the construction of roads, which were of particular importance in the absence of railways, and helped with the negotiation of concessions for British companies, most notably the D'Arcy oil interests. An important innovation in British policy was the provision of loans, some of which came from the secret service fund, which was the only source available without questions being asked.[47]

All this bolstered the British position and gained time. In 1905 the Russians suffered a major military reverse at the hands of the Japanese. Partly facilitated by the 1902 Anglo-Japanese alliance which the British had hoped would divert the Russians from the Middle East, this was the first occasion since the Middle Ages that a non-European power had defeated a European state. The news, as Curzon put it, reverberated 'like a thunderclap through the whispering gallery of the East'.[48] In Russia the result in 1905 was revolution.

The Russians were now forced to consider an idea which they had previously rejected – an Anglo-Russian understanding in Persia. Against the background of the rise of Germany, which from the turn of the century had been engaged in a naval arms race with Britain, the British Foreign Secretary, Sir Edward Grey, was anxious to see Russia re-established as an important factor in European politics. Britain had already reached an imperial *modus vivendi* with the Anglo-French *Entente Cordiale* of 1904. The Anglo-Russian Convention of 1907 sought to remove Asia as a source of tension between London and St Petersburg. It covered Afghanistan and Tibet as well as Persia, and from the government of India's perspective, the Persian section was the least satisfactory part of the agreement. While it claimed to recognise the independence and integrity of Persia, the country was effectively divided into a Russian sphere of influence in the north and a much smaller British sphere in the south-east bordering India, including the crucial Seistan triangle. Between the two was a neutral zone, open to both Russian and British commerce.[49]

In terms of strategic *realpolitik*, the convention was readily justifiable. Since northern Persia was effectively lost to Britain, it seemed wise to gain recognition of British predominance in the area most crucial to Indian security, even if this amounted to a strategic minimum.[50] But these were lines drawn on maps, by men who knew – and cared – little of the people of whom they were disposing. The Persians had long feared such an Anglo-Russian carve-up. It nevertheless came not simply as a deep shock, but also as a betrayal. They had looked to the British as protectors, and were tired of the moralising tone of British diplomats who lectured them about Persian probity and honour. It was another Persian black mark against the British. From here on, the Persians were prepared to believe the worst of them.

By now, however, a classic tale of Great Power rivalry had become interlinked with domestic Persian politics, in which the British become players, albeit by their acts of omission as much as commission. Britain was already closely involved in Persian internal affairs, interfering, as Salisbury noted in 1899, to a greater extent than it did in Siam, China or the South American republics, giving advice on the appointment and dismissal of governors, even where no British interests were involved.[51] The new element was the emergence of a constitutional movement which was both nationalist and anti-autocratic. Although the Shah was forced in 1906 to establish an elective assembly, he did not reconcile himself to this loss of power and in 1908 the Majlis building was shelled by his Cossack forces. The following year, however, he was forced to abdicate.

The Persian constitutionalist movement evoked sympathy among British diplomats. An oppressed people struggling for liberty appealed to their sense of justice, especially if it worked to their advantage. It also appealed to the British public. The story was widely covered in the British press, including some of the smaller provincial papers. In 1906 the grounds of the British Legation had provided asylum and protection to some 14,000 constitutionalists, and it was from the grounds of the Legation that the first successful constitutionalist movement had been launched. It looked to British institutions as models to emulate, and the belief that they enjoyed British support helped give their leaders courage.[52]

These hopes were partially realised. The British Minister, Sir Cecil Spring-Rice, pressed the Shah to grant a constitution and implement political reforms, and the Shah was denied access to British or sizeable Russian capital, without which he had no prospect of putting down the nationalist movement. The British dissuaded the Russians from providing military relief to the Shah in 1909, as rebel armies were converging on Tehran.[53]

But as so often in such cases, British interests were contradictory. As Spring-Rice noted, this nationalist movement would give

> a very bad example to other nations, who should be justified in playing the same game in our gardens. But if we take sides against the popular party, we cannot hope that the Mussulmans [sic] all over the world who are watching affairs here with greatest interest will fail to take note.[54]

Grey, moreover, was all too well aware that support for the movement would place the Anglo-Russian agreement at risk. The spread of democratic ideas so close to the Russian border could not fail to concern the Tsarist autocracy. There was no effective British reaction when in 1912 Russian troops subdued Azerbaijan and the Caspian provinces. In April 1912 the Russians bombarded a Muslim shrine at Meshed, outraging Indian Muslim opinion. They also began to penetrate Isfahan province in the neutral zone. The British remonstrated, but failed to back this up with any real pressure. Hardly surprisingly they were ignored. By 1914 the Russians were even pushing British commercial interests aside in the zone allotted to Britain under the 1907 convention.[55]

By then Persia was close to disintegration. The central government, which existed only in name, was bankrupt, civil servants and troops were unpaid and there was widespread disorder, which spread to the south of the country, where Britain's main interests now lay. An indication of the measure of the authority the British enjoyed in the affairs of the Bakhtiari tribes, who in 1909 had captured Tehran, can be seen from a 1912 despatch from the British Minister, informing the Foreign Office that he had ordered some of the younger khans to behave themselves, at the requests of 'the khans here who say they will pay attention to the orders of the British

Minister although they would snap their fingers at the commands of the Persian Government'.[56] Unwilling, however, to police the area, the British proposed the establishment of a Persian *Gendarmerie*, which they would finance, but which would be commanded by Swedish officers, deemed more acceptable to the Russians.

By far the most important of the economic activities the British continued to promote as a means of asserting political influence proved to be oil. By 1905 the D'Arcy concession, which had been awarded four years earlier and covered some 480,000 square miles, an area five times the size of Britain, was running out of money. Anxious to develop sources of supply in British-controlled territory, the British government stepped in and persuaded Burmah Oil to help the company out. The discovery of oil in 1908 marks both a turning point in Anglo-Persian relations, and the beginning of a new and critically important element in British interests in the Middle East. Over and above economic considerations, oil was immediately recognised as a vital strategic commodity. Against the background of a naval arms race with Germany, the Royal Navy was in the process of converting from coal to oil. In the words of the First Lord of the Admiralty, Winston Churchill, 'The use of oil made it possible in every type of vessel to have more gun-power and more speed for less size and less cost.'[57]

While Britain had ample stocks of coal, oil would have to be acquired from abroad. Britain needed a secure as well as an economical source of supply. When alternative methods of financing proved impractical, the government decided to acquire a 51 per cent interest in the Anglo-Persian Oil Company for £2.2 million. The government would place two directors on the board, who would have a veto on questions involving Admiralty fuel contracts and political but not commercial matters. The only precedent for such a stake was Disraeli's acquisition of shares in the Suez Canal Company. The deal was widely criticised both at home by liberal supporters of free enterprise and abroad, most notably by the Russians, but the Royal Navy got a very good bargain.[58]

By 1911 a pipeline had been constructed to take the oil to a refinery being built on the sweltering mudflats at Abadan on the Shatt-al-Arab waterway, the confluence of the Tigris and Euphrates rivers at the head of the Persian Gulf. This had involved negotiations not with the central government in Tehran, but with Sheikh Khazal of Mohammerah, one of the most independent and powerful of the country's tribal chiefs, who enjoyed the allegiance of the predominantly Arab population of Khuzistan. The negotiations proved difficult. As Sir Percy Cox, the Political Resident in the Persian Gulf, later wrote, the Sheikh foresaw that the enterprise would eventually overshadow all other commercial and other interests and would inevitably cause the Persian Government to seek to extend their administration (hitherto delegated to him) to every part of Arabistan – a country as different from Persia as is Spain from Germany. As an Arab he hated and feared such a prospect as did his people. Could he rely upon us to protect him? Without a guarantee that we would assist him to the utmost of our power in maintaining his hereditary and customary rights and his property in Persia it would be suicidal for him to meet our wishes.[59]

The assurances were given, albeit reluctantly, and to the displeasure of Tehran. Cox subsequently steamed up to Mohammerah in his official launch, where, with much ceremony, he bestowed the insignia of a Knight Commander of the Most Eminent Order of the Indian Empire on the Sheikh.[60]

Persia can be seen as the prototype of Britain's unequal relations with the Middle East, a weak and backward state in a strategically sensitive location, caught up in the slipstream of imperial rivalries. If Persia might hope to look to liberal Britain for support both against Russian encroachment and for constitutional change, imperial Britain often treated it with disdain and disregard. The balance of power in Europe increasingly overrode concerns about Indian security, which were in any case often exaggerated by the government of India. Britain did not need to maintain the whole of Persia as a buffer state; its strategic interests were adequately served by a sphere of influence. Such a policy could only be pursued at Persia's expense, but this was not a consideration to worry men like Salisbury, Curzon or Grey.

2

Toeholds in Arabia

The Gulf and Aden, 1798–1914

The establishment of the *Pax Britannica* in the Persian Gulf during the nineteenth century reflects the incremental, essentially reactive nature of the expansion of Britain's informal empire in the Middle East. It was driven not by the prospect of gain, but by the need to establish order, maintain prestige and keep others out. 'We don't want Koweit' [sic], one senior India Office official noted in 1899, 'but we don't want any one else to have it.'[1] Prior to the days of oil, the Gulf was not a tempting prize. One official described it as

> an area of bleak coasts, torrid winds and pitiless sunshine. The amenities of life are few and far between. Nature is in her fiercest humour and man has done little to improve upon her handiwork. The population is scanty, the standard of living low. Towns are few and insanitary; villages little more than clusters of mud huts.[2]

The Gulf, along with south-west Arabia, lay at the outer reaches of empire, minor territories of concern to India but of only intermittent interest in London. At issue were relations with tribal leaders of tiny, poor territories with a tradition of looking to more powerful protectors.[3] It was not a place to become too deeply involved, and the government of India was always anxious to confine itself to the Arabian periphery.

British officials were, nevertheless, proud of their work in the Gulf, believing that the eradication of piracy, the assaults on the slave and arms trades, their role in surveying the coasts, building lighthouses and laying buoys, had benefited the common good.[4] They acquired detailed knowledge of the dialects, tribes, flora and fauna of the region and expressed an admiration for its inhabitants, which stands in marked contrast to British attitudes in Persia and Egypt. 'Meeting these Arabs', Lewis Pelly, Political

Resident in the mid-nineteenth century, told the Royal Geographical Society, 'you readily comprehend how they once stormed across the world.'[5] But the impetus behind all this activity lay in self-interest. Britain's objectives in the Gulf were the creation and maintenance of order along the eastern maritime approaches to India and trade. As the network of treaties evolved, so too did a further objective – the protection of its client rulers and sheikhdoms, in the first place from external, but also in some cases internal enemies.

It was done remarkably cheaply, with the help of a small naval squadron, five to seven ships-of-war in the age of sail, three to four gunboats from the 1860s, originally provided by the Bombay Marine and later by the Royal Navy. True, there were constant complaints that insufficient ships were available, while the harsh climate took its toll. In one 15-year period, four commanders of the squadron died in post.[6] But the Gulf was an environment in which a little power went a long way. The mere appearance of a gunboat could induce rebels or rulers to comply with British demands. Prestige, of course, had to be upheld. 'Every action, every step we take in these parts,' one official noted in 1879, 'is closely scrutinised by those around us.'[7] The British conceived their position in the Gulf as akin to a seamless web. 'If we admit exceptions', another official noted, 'I do not see how we can stop in our retreat till we reach the narrow ground covered by our Treaties. We shall never make the exceptions intelligible to those who are not admitted to the benefit of them.'[8]

The tiny size of the sheikhdoms, and the absence of any significant local power or European rival, also meant that the *Pax Britannica* could be enforced by a very small number of Political Officers, along however with a much larger number of native agents. These were usually affluent Gulf merchants with considerable influence with the local rulers, as well as extensive knowledge of local culture, language and politics. They were much cheaper to employ than British Political Officers, who were often reluctant to go to the Gulf for climatic reasons.[9] Their task was to gain the confidence of the tribal rulers and to deal quickly and effectively with crises, sometimes without, and sometimes exceeding their instructions. Tact and respect for local customs were as important as firmness and the maintenance of prestige. The Political Officers in turn were responsible to a Political Resident based at Bushire on the Persian coast, who, in Curzon's phrase, was the Uncrowned King of the Gulf. He was responsible for enforcing the treaties the British signed, and arbitrating in local disputes, although the British refused to get involved in the execution of any settlement. Similarly they sought to avoid being drawn into internal administration. From 1887 the Resident had his own paddle steamer, which took him on an annual tour of the sheikhdoms, where he was received with the pomp and ceremony due to the representative of the paramount power.[10]

The Resident was appointed by, and was answerable to, the government of India, which until 1873 meant the Presidency of Bombay, acting under the supervision of Calcutta. But, and this is typical of the complicated division of responsibilities in the Middle East, as Consul-General in Bushire, he answered to the Minister in Tehran, who in turn was answerable to the Foreign Office. The India Office, established in 1858, also had its finger in the Gulf pie. The Residency was run on Indian lines. Other instances of Indian influence included the rupee, which was the Gulf currency, and British-Indian post offices. Gulf trade with India more than trebled between the 1830s and 1860s, from some £700,000 to £2,770,000.[11] There was also a British Resident in Baghdad, who, thanks to his retinue of sepoys, the grandest steamer on the Tigris, and an ample budget for dispensing largesse to tribal leaders, was normally able to outclass the French.[12]

Until the Portuguese discovery of the sea route to India in the late fifteenth century, the Gulf had been one of the great highways of Asiatic trade, with mercantile city states flourishing on its shores. The Portuguese were the first Europeans to establish themselves there in the sixteenth century, but their ascendency was broken by a combined Persian and English assault in 1622.[13] In the mid-seventeenth century the British and Dutch competed for commercial supremacy, while the French had made an unsuccessful attempt to gain a foothold. Sporadic British military activity was already taking place in the mid-eighteenth century. Following the French invasion of Egypt in 1798, the Sultan of Muscat entered into an agreement which ensured Britain of his support at the expense of the French. A British Political Agent was appointed under a further agreement in 1800 so that 'the friendship between the States may exist unshook to the end of time, and till the sun and moon have ended their revolving career'.[14] Aware of his dependence on trade with India, the Sultan scrupulously kept to these agreements. Muscat, which also ruled Zanzibar, was the only organised state in maritime Arabia, and its port and proximity to India gave it particular importance in British, and potentially also French eyes. The flowery rhetoric was prescient. The British connection with Muscat would remain uniquely durable.

The first significant British military incursion in the Gulf occurred at the beginning of the nineteenth century. The Strait of Hormuz was then controlled by the al-Qawasim family of Sharjah and Ras-al-Khaimah (part of today's United Arab Emirates), much of whose revenues came from tolls which they levied on ships entering the Gulf. The British refused to pay, out of a combination of misunderstanding and arrogance. When the al-Qawasim then raided shipping not just in the Gulf but also in Indian waters, the British regarded this as piracy, a view which the al-Qawasim family still dispute. Three naval expeditions were sent from India in 1806, 1809 and 1819 against the raiders. On the last occasion the town of Ras al-Khaimah was razed to the ground, and ships were burnt or captured. As part of a treaty signed the following year, the sheikhs of Abu Dhabi, Dubai, Ajman, Amm al-Qaiwain, Sharjah, and Ras al-Khaimah agreed to 'a cessation of plunder and piracy'. Other articles sought to impose on the tribes what one British historian describes as 'a more humane code of conduct towards their fellow men', forbidding the slaughter of prisoners and the carrying of slaves.[15]

This, however, was the beginning rather than the end of the matter. In a report written in 1823, the British Resident in the Gulf, Lieutenant John Macleod, argued that Britain's great object was

> to keep down hostilities at sea, if possible, and to prevent their quarrels amongst themselves from leading to a renewal of disorders; at the same time we must not interfere too far, and must observe great caution to avoid giving offence. Much may be done by persevering in the system of steady control, combined with friendly intercourse, which Government has adopted.[16]

Raiding could not be finally eradicated without first dealing with the maritime warfare which was the curse of the Gulf. There was hardly a state along the Arabian shore of the Gulf which was not feuding with at least one of its neighbours. In 1835 the Political Resident, Colonel Samuel Hennell, persuaded the rulers who had signed the 1820 treaty to agree to a one-year maritime truce which stipulated penalties for infringement. The British had previously been reluctant to take on formal responsibilities. They did not want to be drawn into the unstable affairs of the sheikhdoms or become the arbiters of endless disputes. They also feared losing political leverage and encouraging local despotism, as had occurred in some Indian states.[17] But the rulers were anxious for British protection and the new peace proved sufficiently successful to be renewed on an annual basis, until in 1843 a ten-year truce was agreed. Ten years later, the truce became perpetual. Bahrain was brought within the ambit of what became known as the Trucial system in 1861. All this owed much to Hennell's tact and perseverance, supported by the British naval presence. But the rulers were also quick to recognise the economic benefits which the peace conferred, and the protection against external attack which Britain could afford. This was a mutually profitable arrangement.[18]

With maritime warfare largely ended by the 1840s, the Persian Gulf squadron was better able to focus on the elimination of slavery in the region. African slaves were imported into the Gulf primarily by Omani and Qawasimi Arabs, for sale on both the Arab and Persian shores. The first agreement was concluded with Muscat in 1822, and by 1873 all the littoral states of the Gulf, including Persia, had signed treaties banning the trade. British motives were essentially humanitarian. There was little or no political gain; on the contrary the policy served to strain some bilateral relations. More would probably have been achieved, however, if the Royal Navy had concentrated on suppressing the trade at its point of origin in East Africa rather than in the Gulf.[19]

Britain's third contribution to the establishment of law and order in the Gulf came at the turn of the century, by which time gun-running from Europe to tribes both in Persia and on the north-west frontier had replaced slave trading as a lucrative local business. Originally run from Bushire, once British and Persian controls had been strengthened, the operations moved to Muscat, from where arms were smuggled into small harbours on the Mukram coast.[20]

By the middle of the nineteenth century, the policy of trying to avoid being drawn into internal affairs of the sheikhdoms was breaking down. Bahrain and Muscat became wracked by internal instability, as pretenders sought to wrest power from established rulers. This opened the way for outside powers – the Wahhabi emirate of Najd in the case of Muscat, Najd, Persia and the Ottoman Empire in that of Bahrain – to threaten their independence and integrity. As so often, growing British intervention was a reaction to events, compounded here, however, by what the historian J.B. Kelly describes as

> the inability of those responsible for the formulation and execution of British policy to see clearly where their actions were leading them: even when they did see it they were confident that they could turn aside at any time they wished. When the critical moment came, they found they could not.[21]

Following the death in 1856 of Sa'id Ibn Sultan, who had ruled Muscat since 1807, a dispute arose among his sons over the inheritance of Zanzibar. The British arbitrated, awarding Zanzibar to one son and thereby dismembering the sultanate. This was unwise, for the government of India now found itself effectively responsible for subsidising and upholding both the Sultanate and the Al Bu Sa'id dynasty, lest the French and Persians step in. With the subsequent overthrow of Imam Syid 'Azzan, and the accession under British auspices in 1871 of Turki ibn Sa'id, the imperial power found itself drawn into a succession of dynastic struggles. Turki's obvious dependence on the British stirred up tribal feeling. Two attempts to overthrow him narrowly failed, in part because of British sea power. His son, Faisal, tried hard but unsuccessfully to free himself of British control. When Curzon visited Muscat in 1903, he described Faisal's demeanour as that of 'a loyal feudatory of the British Crown, rather than of an independent sovereign'.[22]

The first major challenge to the British position in the Gulf came from Egypt. The British had not objected when, in 1811, Muhammad 'Ali had moved against the Wahhabis in Arabia. But a second Egyptian expedition to central and eastern Arabia in 1837 caused sufficient concern in London for Palmerston to warn Muhammad 'Ali against extending his authority towards the Persian Gulf and the *pashalic* of Baghdad. The following year three iron steamers were sent from India to Basra to discourage any Egyptian incursion into the Shatt-al-Arab. This did not, however, prevent the Egyptians from garrisoning the chief coastal ports of Hasa north of Bahrain, and briefly obtaining Bahrain's submission. In the event, revolts in central and eastern Najd resulted in the withdrawal of Egyptian forces.[23]

A more serious and sustained challenge came in the early 1870s from the Turks, who, taking advantage of the newly opened Suez Canal, re-established their authority along the Hasa coast after a two-century-long absence. Turkish pressure led Britain to the conclusion of a new treaty with Bahrain in 1880, precluding the emirate from entering into relations with any foreign governments, or establishing a coaling station without British agreement. Similar agreements with the Trucial States followed in 1887. Britain also blocked Turkish attempted expansion into Qatar and neighbouring areas. It was not until 1913 that Britain and Turkey resolved their Arabian differences.[24]

Intensifying imperial rivalries at the end of the nineteenth century led other European powers to take an interest in what had previously been very much a British-dominated backwater. In 1899 Curzon listed the proliferation of French, Russian, Ottoman and German 'agents, spies, survey parties, quarantine teams, military advisers, naval patrols, merchant steamers and trading companies' all of whom were deemed to be actively undermining British political and commercial influence.[25] To counter these menaces, Muscat had been persuaded to follow Bahrain and the Trucial

States in signing an exclusive foreign representation agreement with Britain. 'We subsidise its ruler,' Curzon wrote, 'we dictate its policy; we should tolerate no rival influence.'[26]

A French Vice-consul had been appointed in Muscat, and in 1898, the year of the Fashoda incident when the British Mediterranean fleet was reinforced, the Sultan was reported to have granted the French a coaling station in Muscat. This clearly would not do. Possession of Muscat by a foreign power would, in the words of the Political Resident, 'be a menace to our prestige and influence not only in the Persian Gulf, but in India itself'.[27] A British ultimatum, backed up by a naval demonstration, during which the British admiral exceeded his instructions, forced the Sultan to cancel the lease. The French, for whom Muscat was in any case of peripheral interest, were, however, allowed a coal depot. Lord Salisbury maintained a sense of proportion over the affair, which complicated more important Anglo-French negotiations over Africa. While the Political Resident 'was pluming his own feathers,' the Prime Minister tartly observed, 'it should have occurred to him that he was possibly ruffling ours'.[28]

As, if not more, alarming was the growing Russian activity at the turn of the century, which coincided with the most assertive phase in Russian policy in Persia and British isolation during the Boer war. A visit by a Russian surveyor to Hormuz in 1895 is described by a leading British authority on the region as the first 'attack on the political predominance in the Persian Gulf'.[29] In 1900 a Russian naval ship visited the Persian port of Bandar Abbas, where its captain was reported to have requested a coaling station. In 1903 there was a joint Russo-French visit to Kuwait. The Foreign Secretary, Lord Lansdowne, responded with the blunt public warning that Britain would regard the establishment of a naval base, or of a fortified port, in the Persian Gulf by any other power as 'a very grave menace to British interests, and we should certainly resist it with all the means at our disposal', a declaration dubbed by *The Times* as a 'Monroe Doctrine of the Persian Gulf'.[30]

German interest in the region met with a more ambivalent response, if only because it represented a potential counterweight to the more worrisome Russians. The Kaiser, along with a number of German soldiers, diplomats and bankers, was attracted by the idea of creating a bridgehead into the Middle East, in order to exploit the region's natural resources. The German proposal for a railway from Constantinople via Syria and Mesopotamia to the Persian Gulf worried the government of India far more than it did London. The prime minister, Arthur Balfour, warned of the futility of British opposition to the scheme. But a combination of vested commercial British interests, along with anti-German sentiment, helped defeat the government. Construction of part of the Baghdad railway went ahead, observed by British intelligence using the cover of archaeological excavations, including the young T.E. Lawrence. It was only in April 1914 that an Anglo-German agreement was reached. The railway terminus would now be Baghdad, and, of particular importance to Britain, there would be no line to the Persian Gulf without British approval.[31]

The earlier prospect of both German and Russian railway interests terminating in Kuwait had drawn British attention to the sheikhdom at the head of the Persian Gulf. Fearing tightening Turkish control – Kuwait was under nominal Turkish jurisdiction – the Ruler, Sheikh Mubarak al-Sabah, made overtures for British protection. In 1899 he signed a non-alienation bond agreeing not to lease any of his territory to a foreign power, nor enter into negotiations with any foreign power without British consent. Mubarak received a payment of £1,000. His brothers were so incensed by this lack of generosity that they refused to witness the signature of the document. Nevertheless when in 1911 a German envoy attempted to wean Mubarak away from the British, he was sent packing by the Sheikh, who told him that 'at a critical juncture in my affairs the British government interfered to protect me and landed soldiers who threw up entrenchments, and owing to their kindness and firmness the danger passed away'.[32]

This unique period of active Great Power rivalry in the Gulf coincided with Curzon's tenure as Viceroy. Curzon saw international politics as a zero-sum game. His anxieties were not always shared in London, where officials had a wider international perspective, and were less sensitive to what they regarded as pinpricks in the Gulf.[33] But this did not prevent Curzon maintaining and extending the British position in the Gulf. In 1903, accompanied by a naval escort including the largest warship ever to have entered Gulf waters, he toured the region to warn off interlopers and demonstrate British power to the local rulers. Much of this was political theatre, which on at least one occasion – a camel ride in Kuwait – dissolved into farce. But the tour gave the Royal Navy the chance to inspect strategic conditions in the Gulf, and the official view was that prestige had been enhanced.[34] In a further sign of growing British interest, the *Gazetteer of the Persian Gulf, Oman and Central Arabia*, comprising more than five thousand pages, was produced between 1908 and 1915.[35]

By the early twentieth century all the sheikhdoms of the Persian Gulf except Qatar were in some form of treaty relationship with Britain. Their exact legal status was ambiguous; they were 'protected states' rather than protectorates. According to the scholar and diplomat, Glen Balfour-Paul, the indeterminate status of the Gulf shayhkdoms wears in retrospect all the marks of that scrupulous imprecision characteristic of so many of Britain's imperial contrivances. Britain may be said to have made up the rules of the game as she went along, with the result that no one really knew what they were. Perhaps for that reason Britain's right or obligation of protecting them was never seriously questioned, any more than was her right or obligation of representing their interests in the outside world.[36]

★★★

The situation in Aden, Britain's only colony in the Middle East, was very different. When occupied in 1838, Aden was little more than a village of some 200 mud houses. But with its large deep-water harbour, well protected from all winds and seas, Aden occupied a key strategic position at the mouth of the Red Sea. A British force had briefly occupied Aden in 1799, when the Sultan had asked to be taken under British protection, a request which, following debate within the Indian government, was refused.[37] The advent of steam navigation in the 1830s made a coaling station in this part of the world essential, since vessels were unable to carry sufficient fuel for the journey from India to Suez. The immediate background to British action included the ever-present Anglo-French rivalry and Muhammad 'Ali's activities in South Yemen. According to the records of the Secret Council, meeting in Bombay in 1838,

> Since first obtaining possession of Egypt by an act of shocking perfidy and cruelty, his ['Ali's] career has been uniform. By treason to his acknowledged sovereign, he has extended his sway over the heart of Africa [...] His next adventure will be on Baghdad, and on the western shores of the Persian Gulf; and, if once permitted to the Straits of Bab al-Mandib, he will never rest till he has stretched his power along the whole coast of Arabia. The object of Mohamed Ali is evident in the plans to erect Egypt, Syria, and Arabia, into an independent Kingdom; and, whenever it suits the views of France or of Russia to abet him in accomplishing that purpose, he will gladly league with either of those powers against England.[38]

The occupation of Aden was very much the result of pressure from a few energetic men, including Commander Stafford Haines of the Indian Navy, the Governor of Bombay, Sir Robert Grant, and the Chief Secretary of the Bombay government, James Farish. Their task was by no means easy. In R.J. Gavin's words, 'much correspondence and hesitation preceded the final decision. Counsels were divided on the matter and even when the occupation had been affected there were many in high places who urged withdrawal.'[39]

The British brought prosperity to Aden. In the early 1850s its total trade amounted to between 5 and 8 million rupees. Twenty years later it stood at between 22 and 35 million. By the beginning of the twentieth century, thanks to the opening of the Suez Canal, it was a bustling port, with a powerful, modern-minded commercial community, as well as an important telegraph junction.[40] Its importance in strategic thinking fluctuated. For some time the authorities in India regarded Aden as nothing more than a coaling station, but its use as the main base in the Abyssinian campaign of 1867–8, and the subsequent opening of the Suez Canal, focused attention on what propagandists of empire now ranked among the most important British possessions. Once, however, the strategists began speculating on the relative ease with which the canal might be blocked in war, that importance declined, with Aden now seen as a second line of defence, important only if the whole British position in the Middle East collapsed.[41]

Aden became responsible for a wide area stretching from the Kuria Muria islands off the South Arabian coast, to Socotra off Cape Guardafui, with the two Hadhrami ports of Mukalla and Shihr also under the eye of the Aden Resident. In addition to the strategic value of these two ports in the hands of a rival power, there was a significant Indian connection, since the Nizam of Hyderabad drew on the Hahramaut for his personal guards. Conflict at the Nizam's court in the 1870s therefore drew the British into Hadhramaut affairs. A Protectorate treaty of 1888 fenced off a large section of the South Arabian coast from other powers.[42] Two years previously a protection treaty had been negotiated with the Sultan of Qishn and Socotra.

Aden depended for water, supplies and security on the tribal hinterland, primarily Lahej, some 20 miles away, where intrigue and conflict were constant. The challenge facing the Aden authorities was to ensure the security of the port without getting dragged into tribal politics, as the government in India was strongly opposed to further commitments. Much depended on the abilities of the men on the spot, and here the British were initially lucky in Haines's uncanny ability to outwit the tribal chiefs. His diplomacy was based on a combination of imagination, bluff and the exploitation of inter-tribal dissension – a classic case of divide and rule. But he also believed that 'goodwill, kindness and respect' were more useful in Arabia than bayonets.[43]

Over time, however, the British nevertheless found themselves drawn deeper into the hinterland's affairs. Their preferred instruments were money and arms. But by the end of the 1860s a small force had been established for operations in the tribal areas, and Britain was frequently interfering to settle tribal disputes.[44] Suggestions for a protectorate were strongly opposed. 'If we protect these tribes', the Assistant Secretary for Foreign Affairs, Lord Teneterden, warned, 'we must see to their good behaviour and sooner or later we shall have to govern them altogether and annex them.'[45] The prime minister, William Gladstone, was even more vehemently opposed to the idea. Yet by 1904, and still much to the dislike of officials in London, protectorate agreements had been signed with most of the tribes. The accompanying dispensing of presents and award of subsidies led sceptics to complain that those tribal leaders who signed were motivated simply by greed.[46]

Britain's hand had in large measure been forced by the expansion of Ottoman rule in Yemen. With Turkish forces soon encroaching on Lahej, the British had to decide how much of the hinterland was in fact essential to Aden's security. A list of nine tribes, whose independence Britain wanted the Ottomans to respect, was forwarded to Constantinople. When Turkish forces nevertheless continued to advance to within twenty miles of Aden, London warned the Turkish government that unless they restrained their local subordinates, war would ensue. Subsequent Ottoman religious claims to the whole of Arabia as the 'cradle of Islam' led to fears that a Turkish presence in South Arabia could represent a threat to India.[47]

Tensions continued intermittently over the following decades, with India, Aden and London by no means always in step, as policy makers sought to juggle the needs of Aden's security and the very parochial tribal politics this now entailed with larger policy considerations. Following a major uprising in the Yemen, Britain turned down a proposal in 1898 by the Imam to partition his territory in return for British protection. The preference was for the maintenance of Ottoman authority, if only because the Turks were more amenable to British pressure. A stand-off between British and Turkish troops in 1903 brought the two countries close to war, but at the last moment the Cabinet shied away from a conflict in an area so remote to the main centres of British power. It was the Turks, however, who evacuated the disputed area. A *procès-verbale* on the frontier was signed in 1905. The subsequent success of Imamic forces in Yemen against the Turks was not welcomed by the British authorities, who feared the emergence of a Mahdi – an Arabic term meaning guide or leader, with religious overtones – who would threaten the British-protected chiefs.[48]

The exercise of British power around the fringes of Arabia was, for the most part, economic, judicious and welcomed. The British were more successful in limiting their engagement in the Gulf than in Arabia. But local rulers needed security, and in providing it, the British were careful to leave existing institutions intact. They succeeded not only in breaking the previous cycle of protection-seeking, raiding and invasion among the rulers, but in increasing prosperity and beginning a slow process of modernisation. English became the language of trade, technology and administration in the Gulf; indeed the very notion of the Gulf as a region was of British rather than Arab origin.[49] This was informal empire at its most mutually beneficial and constructive.

3

Mediterranean Approaches

Egypt, Syria and Palestine, 1798–1882

The lines of British incursion into the Middle East ran not just west from India but east from the Mediterranean, and in the nineteenth century British interests were as often linked to the balance of power in Europe as to the security of imperial communications. Unlike Arabia, the Levant (Constantinople, Asia Minor, Syria, Egypt) was a part of the world with whose affairs Palmerston, Disraeli, Gladstone and Salisbury were all at least intermittently familiar. Britain's concern for most of the nineteenth century was essentially watchful. The Levant was not part of its empire, formal or informal, and Britain would intervene temporarily only when events threatened its interests. Reliant in the first place on sea power, until 1882 Britain remained an offshore power.

The Royal Navy had begun operating in the Mediterranean in the eighteenth century. By the following century it could control the Mediterranean from both ends, through the Strait of Gibraltar and the Dardanelles; indeed the Mediterranean, like the Persian Gulf, came to be known as a British lake. 'From their accustomed haunts there', writes Robert Holland, 'the British could watch events, control their exposure to any major war in Europe, and bring their influence to bear when they really needed to.'[1] Their main interest in the eastern basin was the integrity of the Ottoman Empire, which by the nineteenth century was in manifest decline. While they occasionally toyed with partition, nineteenth-century British statesmen always rejected the idea. Ottoman Turkey was too valuable as a barrier to Russian expansion into the Mediterranean. They themselves had no ambitions in Turkey's remaining European, or indeed its Asiatic empire, but once partition became imminent, there would be a scramble for spoils. Its outcome was unpredictable, but carried a serious risk of war. This was all too prescient. The Balkan crises of 1912–13, connected to the loss of Turkey's last European provinces, played a crucial role in the events precipitating World War I.[2] In addition the Indian government feared that acquiescence in any scheme of partition would alienate its Muslim subjects. In the Duke of Wellington's words, 'The Ottoman Empire stands not for the benefit of the Turks but of Christian Europe.'[3]

The second key interest was Egypt, an autonomous province within the Ottoman Empire. Britain was successively concerned to keep the French out, to prevent Egypt itself becoming too powerful, and later to prevent the country collapsing into anarchy. Egypt's strategic importance in Britain's emerging imperial system had been underscored when Napoleon led the first European army to invade the Middle East since the Crusades; at more than thirty-six thousand men, it was also the largest force France had ever sent overseas. This was a world war. Having abandoned the idea of a cross-Channel invasion, the French sought an alternative means of striking at British power. 'Truly to overthrow England', Napoleon told the French Directory, 'we must occupy Egypt.'[4] From here he hoped to link up with the Sultan of Mysore, Tipu Sultan, who had been fighting the British in India since 1782. This threat was taken seriously by Dundas and his advisers, who believed that an attack on India, either via the Red Sea or overland through Syria and Iraq, was perfectly feasible. With Britain in control of less than a third of the subcontinent, the intervention of even a small European force could tilt the balance of power against her. Egypt also offered the French economic advantages, including compensation for the earlier loss of the Caribbean sugar islands to Britain, through the capture of Levant trade and the prospect of controlling North African food production.[5]

Nelson's overwhelming victory in August 1798 against the French Fleet, negligently moored at Aboukir Bay, 20 miles north of Alexandria, was the single most dramatic British demonstration of sea power in the Middle East. Enthusiastically celebrated in Britain, it gave the Royal Navy supremacy in the Mediterranean and helped coalesce a new European coalition against Napoleon. Turkey declared war on France, the Russians sent a squadron from the Black Sea to cooperate against France, and in 1801 a 15,000-strong British force was landed in Egypt.[6] Napoleon's army was now cut off and unable to receive reinforcements; his advance into Syria was halted by Sir Sydney Smith at Acre. 'Acre once taken,' Napoleon lamented in exile on St Helena, 'I would have reached Constantinople and India. I would have changed the face of the world.'[7] But he also acknowledged that he had made a mistake, and would have done much better to attack Ireland than Egypt.[8]

In 1801 a two-pronged British attack was launched from the Mediterranean and the Red Sea, and by September the French occupation was over. Two years later British forces were evacuated. Following a shift in alliances in the wake of the French victory at Austerlitz, which saw the Turks join with France, a second British expedition was sent to Egypt in 1807. It achieved nothing, and was soon withdrawn.[9]

Having thwarted a would-be French conqueror of Egypt, the British next found themselves exercised by the emergence of a powerful Egyptian ruler. Muhammad 'Ali was an Albanian officer who had arrived with the Turkish expedition of 1801. After a prolonged period of stagnation and misrule under the Mamluks, whose power had been broken by the French, he transformed Egypt into a significant regional power. An innovator and reformer, he was ready to draw on European ideas and technology, undertaking one of the first industrialisation programmes outside Europe, and the only one in the Middle East. During his reign, which lasted until 1847, the Egyptian population grew from about two and a half to four and a half million, while there were substantial increases in government revenue, land under cultivation and trade. By the mid-1830s, the Egyptian army numbered some 130,000. It had defeated the Wahhabi movement which had emerged in Arabia at the turn of the century, and gained control of the Arabian Red Sea province of the Hejaz. Egyptian forces subsequently conquered the Sudan, and then cooperated with the Ottomans in the 1820s to try to put down a nationalist revolt in Greece.[10] These military successes took Muhammad 'Ali and his son Ibrahim Pasha, a highly successful general, onto the European political stage.

The scale of Muhammad 'Ali's ambitions, however, eventually brought him into conflict with the British. At the very least he wanted control of the three Syrian *pashaliks*; ideally he wanted not just independence from the Sultan, but to take over the latter's leadership of the Muslim world. But he was acutely conscious that these objectives could not be achieved in conflict with the European powers, of whose military superiority he was well aware. 'With the English as my friends I can do anything; without their friendship I can do nothing,' he once remarked. He was usually careful therefore to keep the British informed of his intentions, and try to seek their support.[11] The British had raised no objection to his Sudanese operations. Determined to uphold the integrity of the Ottoman Empire, they were, however, strongly opposed to Egyptian secession, and by 1827 were also anxious to see the end of Turkish and Egyptian intervention in Greece. In October the Egyptian and Turkish navies suffered a major defeat at the hands of the combined British, French and Russian fleets at the battle of Navarino, Britain's first major military engagement against a Middle Eastern country. The Egyptian army was now trapped in Greece, and Muhammad 'Ali had to negotiate directly with Britain for its repatriation.

In 1832 Muhammad 'Ali made his next move. He had tried for an anti-Russian alliance with Britain, arguing the Ottoman Empire was a broken reed, and that the British would do much better to rely on him, but Palmerston refused. Ibrahim Pasha's army then invaded Syria, where it defeated the Turks, and proceeded into Anatolia to within some 150 miles of Constantinople. The advice of a local British official was an important factor in preventing an Egyptian advance on the Ottoman capital.[12] Palmerston feared that the Sultan might be so weakened as to become a Russian vassal. Russia would then come to terms with Muhammad 'Ali, 'Persia would probably be nibbled at by both, and their union might produce inconvenient consequences to our Eastern possessions'. But with the British Fleet depleted by expenditure cuts, the distractions of events in Iberia and the Netherlands, plus the domestic agitation surrounding the 1832 Reform Bill, the Cabinet refused a Turkish request for support.[13] The Turks turned to the Russians, who took the opportunity, through the Treaty of Unkiar Skelassi, of establishing an informal Russian protectorate over Turkey.

For Palmerston, this was a major defeat, and he now developed a strong personal animosity against the Egyptian leader, whom he described as 'an ignorant barbarian, who by cunning and boldness and mother wit has been successful in rebellion [...] I look upon his boasted civilisation of Egypt as the arrantest humbug, and I believe that he is as great a tyrant and oppressor as ever made a people wretched.'[14]

The 1830s saw constant friction between Britain and Egypt over Syria, the Yemen and the Persian Gulf, with London also nervous over Muhammad 'Ali's relations with both Russia and France. The latter's policy, according to the Consul-General in Egypt, Patrick Campbell, writing in 1837, was 'strongly directed towards obtaining a preponderance in Egypt', with Frenchmen holding a whole series of key military as well as civil appointments.[15] When in 1839 hostilities between Egypt and Turkey were resumed, with the Turks again suffering land defeat and the Turkish Fleet defecting to Egypt, a major European crisis erupted. The Mediterranean Fleet was now ordered to cut communications between Syria and Egypt. Palmerston had multiple targets in his sights. Apart from Muhammad 'Ali, who might move from Syria to Mesopotamia and threaten the British route to India, there were the Russians, as well as France whom he believed had over the last 50 years laid down to herself 'a systematic plan of aggrandizement in the Levant, to the intended detriment of England'.[16]

In July 1840, Britain, Austria, Prussia and Russia signed the London Convention with Turkey, issuing an ultimatum for the Egyptian evacuation of Syria. The French press, parliament and public opinion were outraged at the humiliation of France's exclusion from this agreement, and there was talk of war.[17] The problem of how to remove Egyptian forces from Syria was solved by the outbreak of local revolts, stirred up by Turkish agents. The British provided arms and the Royal Navy, in cooperation with a small Austrian flotilla, bombarded Beirut and Acre. British marines were landed. It was, the British commander, Charles Napier, later remarked, 'rather a new occurrence for a British Commodore to be on the top of Mount Lebanon commanding a Turkish army and preparing to fight a battle which would decide the fate of Syria'.[18] Napier then sailed on to Alexandria. Unlike Palmerston, Napier was fascinated by the old military adventurer, Muhammad 'Ali, negotiating an agreement on his own authority. In return for surrender of the Turkish Fleet and acceptance of the Convention of London, Napier agreed to evacuate Egyptian forces from Syria, and undertook that the hereditary *pashalik* of Egypt would be conferred on Muhammad 'Ali and his family. It would be more than a hundred years before another Egyptian leader mounted a comparable regional challenge.[19] One French historian lamented that all the advantages in the crisis had fallen to Britain, which was now pre-eminent in the Levant.[20]

In the incessant game of European rivalries, few advantages, however, are permanent. In 1860 news emerged of a massacre in Lebanon of Christian Maronites by the Druzes, who had played a leading role in the revolt against Muhammad 'Ali 20 years earlier. Palmerston sought to prevent the French sending troops, fearing that once in Syria they would stay. But his position became untenable, and in an early instance of humanitarian intervention, the European powers gave French troops a six-month mandate in Lebanon.[21] Britain vetoed a subsequent extension, but the French had nevertheless succeeded in greatly increasing their influence in the country, while British influence with the Druzes had declined. France's subsequent attempts to establish cultural and financial dominance were interrupted by their defeat in the Franco-Prussian war of 1870, after which the main threat to Britain's position in the Middle East came from Russia rather than France.[22]

At one point during the 1839 crisis, Palmerston encouraged the Sultan to allow the Jews back to Palestine, leading the social reformer, the Earl of Shaftesbury, to declare that Palmerston 'had already been chosen by God to be an instrument of good to his Ancient people'.[23] In fact Palmerston acted out of considerations of *realpolitik* as much as idealism. He wanted to strengthen the Ottoman Empire by providing it with Jewish support; to foil Muhammad 'Ali and the French by creating a British-backed Jewish homeland which would block their advance; and to provide Britain with a client in the Levant as an excuse for intervention in Ottoman affairs. That said, the idea of a Jewish return to Palestine as the fulfilment of Scriptural prophecy, which dated back to the Puritan ascendency of the seventeenth century, was enjoying a revival in Victorian England. With the future of the Ottoman Empire in doubt, Shaftesbury had in 1840 presented documents for 'the recall of the Jews to their ancient land', an idea supported by *The Times*.[24]

Here lay the seeds of the Palestine mandate which Britain would acquire some 80 years later. The immediate result, however, was confined to the opening of a British consulate in Jerusalem. A quarter-century later came the establishment of the Palestine Exploration Fund, which brought together an unusual coalition of clergy and the military. The Archbishop of York, William Thomson, declared that 'this country of Palestine belongs to you and me. It was given to the Father of Israel. It's the land whence comes news of our redemption. It's the land where we look with as true a patriotism as we do this dear old England.'[25] The Fund, to which Queen Victoria contributed, was intended to open the Holy Land not just to archaeology, but also to mapping and surveying. It was heavily dependent on the War Office for support, and provided cover for intelligence activities. Palestine had acquired strategic significance for Britain as a result of the opening of the Suez Canal in 1869.[26] Army officers, including a future Field Marshal, the young Lieutenant Herbert Kitchener, surveyed the territory and the maps they produced were later used in Allenby's 1917 Palestine campaign. The year 1876 saw the publication of George Eliot's *Daniel Deronda*, the story of a young man who discovers his Jewish origins, and determines to devote himself to 'restoring a political existence to my people, making them a nation again, giving them a national centre, such as the English have, though they too are scattered over the face of the globe'.[27] The book had a considerable effect on the emerging Jewish national movement.[28]

Britain's main preoccupation, however, remained Egypt, where *The Times* had had a correspondent since 1849, earlier than anywhere else outside Europe. Visiting the country in 1850, the French novelist, Gustave Flaubert, prophesied that 'it seems to be almost impossible that within a short time England won't become mistress of Egypt', thereby repeating a similar prophecy made by Muhammad 'Ali 35 years earlier.[29] This was not the British view, and proposals by both Napoleon III and later the German Chancellor, Otto Bismarck, for a British take-over were rejected.

In Palmerston's words, 'We want to trade with Egypt and to travel through Egypt, but we do not want the burden of governing Egypt.'[30]

Britain was Egypt's main trade partner. Between 1862 and 1872 the number of British ships visiting Alexandria doubled, the value of their cargoes being more than twice that of all Alexandria's other cargoes combined.[31] In 1880 Britain took 80 per cent of Egypt's exports – mostly raw cotton, and provided 44 per cent of its imports.[32] There was substantial private investment in the country. Travel to Egypt had begun in the 1870s, when the British tour operator, Thomas Cook, opened a Cairo office. But this was not of course what Palmerston had in mind. The advent of the steamship in the 1830s had cut the journey time from London to India from five months via the Cape, to forty days including an overland transit route from Alexandria to Suez. Until the opening of the Suez Canal, however, the high cost of transhipment meant that the carriage of heavy goods by this route was uneconomic. Palmerston had vehemently opposed the canal's construction by a French company, which to quote A.D. Farnie, he saw as 'another lance in the hand of France to pierce the armour of England'. The Prime Minister was against any change in the balance of power in the Levant that might compel Britain to take out territorial guarantees for the security of her empire. The integrity of the Ottoman Empire and the security of India seemed again at stake. The fear was that France would seize the canal in wartime. French warships could then reach India from Toulon in five weeks, while British warships having to sail around the Cape would take ten.[33]

Sections of French opinion did indeed believe that 'in piercing the isthmus of Suez', they were 'piercing the weak point in the British armour'.[34] But Palmerston was playing Canute. As Gladstone warned, he had engaged in a conflict in which in the end he would have to give way. The canal was duly opened with great ceremony in 1869, but with the British conspicuously absent. 'The Queen of England', the *Saturday Review* sardonically noted, 'has opened the Holborn Viaduct, and the Empress of the French is going to open the Suez Canal.'[35] Having dwelled on the strategic disadvantages, while meanwhile taking a number of precautions to secure the route to India, the British were quick to appreciate the great commercial potential of the new waterway. Once again the French had been responsible for focusing British interest on Egypt, this time on a much more lasting basis.

By the mid-1870s just over half of Indian trade was being carried via the new canal.[36] Suez was also being used for military transit, cutting the costs (paid by the government of India), by some 25 per cent per head.

During the Russo-Turkish war of 1877–8, the canal was used for the first time to send some 8,000 Indian troops to the Mediterranean. The Foreign Secretary, Lord Derby, declared it to be a vital British interest and the Russians were warned not to interfere with it. Three years earlier the prime minister, Benjamin Disraeli, had jumped at the opportunity to purchase the Khedive's shares in the canal in 1875, a decision which was warmly welcomed in the British press. The price was four million pounds, and proved an excellent long-term investment.[37]

From the Egyptian point of view this was dangerous, since the world's leading imperial power was now likely to take a much closer interest in their affairs. What precipitated permanent intervention, however, was the extraordinary growth in Egyptian debt. In the 13 years following Sultan Ismail's accession in 1863, it had risen from £3.3 million to £91 million.[38] While this owed much to the Sultan's improvidence, it also reflected his desire to modernise the country and its infrastructure, and to turn it into a great power which could take its place in the 'civilised' world. Ismail had declared Egypt to be part of Europe. Egypt established telegraph and rail networks decades before China and Japan, and Cairo became the cultural and financial capital of the Arab world.[39]

In the process, however, he had exposed Egypt to the power of its European creditors, who had little respect for her culture and people. The local English population had the reputation of despising everything not connected to their own race. The Portuguese novelist, Eça de Queiroz, noted in 1883 that they 'never integrate or de-Anglicize themselves'.[40] 'What chokes me', wrote Lady Duff Gordon, who lived there, 'is to hear English people talk of the stick being "the only way to manage Arabs" as if anyone could doubt that it is the easiest way to manage any people where it can be used with impunity.'[41] In Alexandria, with its large foreign community, it was said that the watches of foreign consuls 'controlled the sun'.[42]

By 1876 Egypt was effectively bankrupt, with the Sultan having to borrow at 30 per cent. Were Egypt to default, European bond-holders would lose heavily, while Egypt would only be able to acquire future funding on ruinous terms.[43] This left the country on the slippery slope to foreign control. The British were anxious to keep in step with the French. Egypt had after all been a contested sphere of influence between Britain and France in their global contest for dominance since 1798.[44] As Salisbury remarked of the system of dual Anglo-French financial control which was imposed on Egypt, 'You may renounce – or monopolize – or share. Renouncing would have been to place the French across our road to India. Monopolizing would have been very near the risk of war. So we resolved to share.'[45] It was also a means of restraining the French. But financial control, even if it was in the Egyptians' own long-term interests, was inevitably resented. The Egyptian Ministry of Finance and Public Works came under British and French supervisors, who were in effect the real rulers of the country. The army was halved, officials were sacked. This was too much for the Khedive, who in 1879 responded by sacking his foreign controllers. Retribution quickly followed, with the British and French persuading the Sultan to depose the Khedive in favour of his more pliable son, Tewfiq.[46]

Salisbury had preferred for the British to act indirectly, more as 'wire-pullers than as ostensible rulers', partly in order not to inflame Muslim sentiment, but also to avoid becoming too closely involved in Egypt. But as the Foreign Secretary realised, 'after having a khedive deposed, the character of non-intervention is not easy to retain'.[47] This became increasingly clear with the emergence of a nationalist revolt, led by an army officer, Colonel 'Urabi. With the slogan of 'Egypt for the Egyptians', this was a protest movement against both the country's Turco-Circassian rulers and its foreign debt collectors, which affected almost every segment of society. Having forced the resignation of the Minister of War, at the end of 1881 the native Egyptian officers in the army brought down the government. Its successor, dominated by the 'Urabi faction, refused to collect taxes and pay interest to the foreign bond-holders. The French were particularly alarmed. 'Urabi's actions threatened to provoke a nationalist movement in Tunisia, which France had occupied earlier in the year. And just as the British suspected French designs in Egypt, so the French in turn suspected British ambitions. In January 1882 they persuaded their ally-rivals to issue a tough and undiplomatic joint statement in support of Tewfiq's authority. The effect was akin to lighting a candle in a mine. Seen in Egypt as an unprovoked threat, it led the Egyptian Chambers of Notables and moderate intellectuals to close ranks with the army.[48]

The Liberal prime minister, William Gladstone, now found himself in an awkward position. Hitherto he had been squarely in the long-standing British tradition of opposing British intervention in Egypt. When in 1877 the writer and journalist Edward Dicey had proposed British occupation of the Suez isthmus and the Nile valley in an article entitled 'Our Route to India', the Prime Minister had warned of the effect on relations with France, and asked 'whether to protect a few square miles of canal, we are to take charge of two thousand square miles of territory?'[49] At the same time he had a personal interest in Egypt, since some 37 per cent of his wealth was invested in Egyptian bonds. How far this influenced his actions can only be a matter of speculation. What is clear is that Gladstone now saw 'Urabi as crossing a line between seeking Egyptian autonomy and independence, and began to portray the Egyptian leader not as a worthy Garibaldian nationalist, but rather as a military dictator akin to Cromwell. The contradictions between the Prime Minister's anti-militarist conscience and his increasingly interventionist approach was reflected in a cartoon of Gladstone in civilian dress belabouring an Egyptian with his umbrella.[50]

Against the background of talk of the landing of Turkish troops, the British and French decided on a naval demonstration to try to strengthen the Khedive and safeguard law and order. Once again, the result was to play into 'Urabi's hands. An attempt by Tewfiq to dismiss the 'Urabist ministers failed and patriotic feeling across Egypt rose. On 11 June, there was serious rioting in Alexandria in which some 50 Europeans died, and hundreds were injured.[51] With the European press playing up the riots as a massacre of Christians and Europeans, the next step on the escalatory ladder, in which the French refused to participate, was the bombardment of Alexandria on 11 July. The city, in the words of a British consulate official, was turned into 'a Dantesque Inferno, alight from end to end'.[52] 'Urabi responded by declaring holy war against Britain and anti-British riots spread into the interior. The British government now decided to intervene onshore. They did so unilaterally only because nobody else was prepared to act with them.

It is easier to evoke the increasingly tense atmosphere in which the decision for the first major British military intervention in the Middle East was taken, than to disentangle its exact motives. The Cabinet would seem to have shared the belief of one of the senior British officials on the spot, Sir Auckland Colvin, that European interests in Egypt were 'too various and important to permit of the engagements contracted by the Khedive being placed at the mercy of Egyptian soldiery, or of inexperienced native administrators'.[53] Such generalised concerns seem – the evidence has been disputed – to have weighed more heavily than specific fears about the security of the Suez Canal, even though the latter were publicly cited to justify intervention.[54] But at least two other subsidiary factors came into play. Hard-liners in the Cabinet, notably the Secretary of State for India, the Marquess of Hartington, were concerned that concessions to 'Urabi would involve a loss of face, thereby undermining the British position not just in Egypt and the Near East, but even in India. They also saw the crisis as a useful opportunity to demonstrate that Liberals could act decisively to defend the national interest.[55]

To this extent the action was highly successful. While the Liberal press was hostile, parliament was in a jingoistic mood. 'They want very badly to kill somebody', Sir Charles Dilke, the Under-Secretary at the Foreign

Office and another hard-liner, recorded in his diary on 15 June, 'but they don't know who.'[56] The value of Egyptian bonds jumped 32 per cent at the news that Britain would be sending troops. With bond-holders, shipping and trade interests all in favour of military action, parliament voted the necessary funds with 275 votes in favour and only 19 against. Sixty-five MPs had investments in Egypt.[57] Albert Hourani's verdict that the real reason for intervention 'was that instinct for power which states have in a period of expansion, reinforced by the spokesman of European financial interests', seems close to the mark. Between 1874 and 1902, the British added 4.75 million square miles and some 90 million people to their empire.[58]

Military intervention is always a tricky operation, in which risks are easily underestimated and the law of unintended consequences readily comes into its own. It tends to be undertaken in an atmosphere unconducive to clear thinking, tinged either by hubris or driven by a desperate sense that something must be done to try and rescue a deteriorating situation. Much depends on reliable information from the men on the spot, as well as the ability of the decision makers in far-off capitals to think through both the military and political elements of the operation. The latter requires a knowledge of local politics, language and culture which few politicians possess, and which they are not necessarily interested in being briefed about.

In the summer of 1882 reliable information was in short supply. Colvin, who had only rudimentary knowledge of Arabic, and scant knowledge of Arabs beyond the stereotypes of the day, was inclined to see events through the eyes of worried investors. The reporting from Cairo, which suggested that the country was on the verge of anarchy, was unduly alarmist.[59] A divided Cabinet, distracted by an Irish crisis, failed to set any clear political objective for military action.[60] Ministerial thinking was both inconsistent and ill-considered. On the one hand the government repeatedly, and quite sincerely, declared this was a purely temporary operation. At the same time Gladstone had told parliament that 'we shall not fully discharge our duty if we did not endeavour to convert the present state of Egypt from anarchy and conflict to peace and order'. He had, however, no idea of what this would involve. When Hartington, trying to prepare the necessary financial estimates, had asked how long the expedition would stay, nobody knew the answer.[61] The government might not have gone into Egypt with their eyes shut and fingers crossed, as a later British government is said to have gone into Afghanistan, but they had done so with an inadequate appreciation of the risks, and without an exit strategy.[62]

Figure 2. 'British Triumphalism, 1882'

Yet the military operation, which, had it gone wrong, could have proved politically fatal, was a resounding success. A 40,000-strong force from both Britain and India was assembled under General Sir Garnet Wolseley, who arrived off Alexandria on 15 August. The canal was quickly seized and on 13 September 'Urabi was routed at the battle of Tel-el-Kebir. The British lost a mere 57 men, with another 380 wounded and 22 missing. Estimates of Egyptian losses vary between 'in excess' of 2 ,000 and 10,000.[63] Church bells were rung in Britain, and guns fired in Hyde Park to celebrate the most impressive British military victory since Waterloo. There was no further opposition and in consequence no need to conquer. For the Egyptians, however, it meant the end of their ambitions to join the modern world as an independent state. The country's constitutional development towards representative government had been thwarted, as had the first attempt by a subject oriental people to throw off the domination of a privileged minority.[64] Egypt, wrote Eça de Queiroz the following year, 'is now in that giant Anglo-Saxon grasp which no human force, once it has seized a foreign land, whether it is a rock like Gibraltar, a point of sand like Aden, an island like Malta, or an entire world like India, can ever again dislodge or remove'.[65]

4

Unintended Consequences

Egypt, 1882–1914

Tel-el-Kebir marks the first watershed in Britain's engagement with the Middle East. Hitherto the region had lain at the outer edges of empire. The territories which the British had thus far allowed themselves to be drawn into had been valuable not in themselves, but only in relation to more important territory elsewhere. In 1882 the British suddenly found themselves masters of the most populous, economically advanced and strategically important country in the region.

More than any other Middle East territory, Egypt fits into the mainstream of British imperial history, occupied in the heyday of imperial expansion, and run for 24 years by that most imperial of proconsular figures, Evelyn Baring, ennobled as Lord Cromer. It was also a country which people back home knew about. Thomas Cook had opened its first Middle East office in Cairo in 1872, and its Nile tours received wide coverage in the popular press, with Egypt increasingly regarded as a British asset.[1] The Nile, as David Gange writes, was

> firmly written into British self-conception. Its outflow, the Mediterranean, was conceived as a pleasure ground for British steamers; its twin sources had been anglicized as Victoria and Albert Nyanza; the whole length of the river was accessible to British vessels; figures as iconic as the Prince of Wales and General Gordon had made widely publicised journeys. The battle of the Nile remained only a little less richly evocative of British naval prowess than Trafalgar. But, equally important, Egypt was the scene in which Israelite history began, the point at which the Hebrews became a nation – given a biblical rather than classical rendering, the progress of modern civilization that was assumed to culminate in Britain began by the Nile.[2]

And of course there was Suez, which Kipling promoted to the status of an imperial icon, as the meeting point between East and West and a stage on the road to Mandalay. He described Port Said as one of the 'three great doors in the world where, if you stay long enough, you shall meet anyone you wish'.[3]

It was not what the government had intended. But as soon as withdrawal was contemplated, the dangers of the original policy of 'Rescue and Retire' became apparent. The problem, to quote Lord Dufferin, who was sent out to report, was that it was 'absolutely necessary to prevent the fabric we have raised from tumbling to the ground the moment our sustaining hand is withdrawn'.[4] The Khedive's authority had been seriously undermined by British actions, and there was no reason to believe that the friendliness of either the government, army or population could be relied on. If Britain went, leaving chaos behind, the French might well step in. Besides, as Gladstone's successor, Lord Salisbury, remarked in 1887, 'the national, or acquisitional feeling has been aroused, it has tasted the fleshpots and it will not let them go'.[5] By staying, however, the government found itself subjected to attacks both from within the Liberal Party and from the opposition. Public opinion, which had not been prepared for a lengthy intervention, proved, in the words of one imperial commentator, 'fickle, impatient, wholly uninformed'. Egypt became the football of English politics.[6]

There was also an international cost for staying. Intervention broke the informal understanding between Britain and France, and Egypt now became a significant element in the incessant manoeuvrings by the European Great Powers for security and advantage. Although France had originally egged Britain on, the Chamber of Deputies had decided against joint intervention, and the government had fallen. Only 11 years after their defeat in the Franco-Prussian war, fears for their security on the Rhine outweighed the highly unwelcome prospect of seeing Britain triumph alone on the Nile.[7] Despite, if not because of their refusal to take part, the French felt humiliated by their exclusion, and the subsequent British refusal to continue Dual Control, and the Egyptian question came to dwarf everything else in French policy.

Salisbury blamed the French for 'pouring out upon us the hatred they dare not show to Germany'.[8] Unwilling to go to war over Egypt, France nevertheless wanted the British to honour their commitment to withdraw. Failing this, they wanted to demonstrate that they had rights in Egypt, and should be paid for surrendering them. To this end they were willing to make cause with other European powers as a means of exerting pressure, thereby playing into Bismarck's hands. Gladstone spoke of being 'tortured' by the German Chancellor over Egypt.[9] Salisbury complained of German blackmail. Bismarck was

> perpetually telling us of the offer France is making of reconciliation on the basis of an attack upon England in Egypt and of the sacrifices which Germany makes by refusing these proposals, sacrifices for which, he adds, England must make some return, and then he demands this and that. I heartily wish we had never gone into Egypt. Had we not done so we could snap our fingers at all the world.[10]

Even more alarming to Britain was the prospect of Egypt fuelling an alliance between its two most dangerous rivals. In 1887 the French and Russians persuaded Constantinople not to back an agreement which would have provided for British withdrawal within three years, but with the right of return should conditions again became unsettled. This time Salisbury complained about the French being 'the most unreasonable people I have ever heard or dreamed of'.[11] A Franco-Russian alliance followed in 1894. British defence planners had for some time been concerned that they could no longer block Russian expansion at the Straits. The new Franco-Russian treaty meant that they must now also take account of the potential threat from the French Fleet at Toulon. Under these circumstances Egypt gained a new strategic importance for Britain. It provided a counterbalance to the French in the Mediterranean, as well as a fall-back position from which to defend British influence in the Levant and communications to India, should Russia gain access to the Mediterranean. In the early years of the twentieth century, the First Sea Lord, Admiral Sir Jack Fisher, described Alexandria, along with Singapore, Cape Town, Gibraltar and Dover, as one of the five strategic keys which locked up the world.[12]

In 1898, however, the British had scored a signal victory over their rival. A French expedition had been despatched from the west coast of Africa to cross to the east, partly to claim territory for France *en route*, but also in the hope that its presence on the Upper Nile would force a Great Power conference resulting in British evacuation of Egypt. What instead ensued was a confrontation at Fashoda, an abandoned mud-built fort some 700 miles south of Khartoum. The Mediterranean Fleet was reinforced, and the French, who were outnumbered on the ground, gave way. The humiliation, coming on top of their exclusion from Egypt, ran deep in France. Yet six years later the Franco-British quarrel over Egypt, likened by Wilfrid Scawen Blunt, a persistent critic of British policy in Egypt, to two highwaymen quarrelling over a stolen purse, was over.[13]

Anxious to check the danger from Russia and the Franco-Russian alliance, the Britain acknowledged France's special interests in Morocco in return for French acknowledgement of Britain's position in Egypt. The latter thus finally ceased to be as complicating a factor in European power politics.[14]

Fashoda points to another cost which the British Cabinet had not anticipated in 1882. By assuming responsibility over Egypt, they had also assumed responsibility over the Sudan (where Egyptian authority had been established in 1820). In 1881 a revolt had broken out, led by the so-called Mahdi, who called for a religious war against Christianity and corrupted Egyptian Muslims. Egypt seemed threatened. The Cabinet, already smarting over the repercussions of invading Egypt, was unwilling to commit further troops to adventures in Africa. Instead they sought to persuade the Egyptians to evacuate all territory south of Wadi Halfa or Aswan, a demand which led to the resignation of the Egyptian prime minister, Sherif Pasha. Although his successor, Nubar Pasha, acquiesced, there remained the problem of withdrawing the Egyptian garrisons. The scene was now set for one of the great political dramas of the 1880s. An ill-conceived expedition by the Egyptian army under Colonel William Hicks was overwhelmed, losing its rifles, machine guns and modern artillery; a second expedition under General Charles Gordon then got into trouble. The Cabinet prevaricated over sending a relief force. By the time it finally arrived in Khartoum at the end of January 1885, Gordon was dead. Public opinion, which had originally clamoured for him to be sent, was outraged, and the second Gladstone administration became 'a holed hull'. It fell in June. Gordon's death would haunt Gladstone and members of his Cabinet for the rest of their lives, as well as etching itself deeply into British views of Islam.[15]

This was by no means the end of the matter. During the mid- and late-1880s, defensive actions proved necessary in the face of threats to invade Egypt by the Khalifa, who had succeeded the Mahdi, but with the exception of the Red Sea coast, the whole of the Sudan south of Wadi Halfa was abandoned. The opportunity 'to plant the feet of Egypt rather further up the Nile' and gain credit in Berlin came in 1896, following the heavy Italian defeat at Adowa by the Abyssinians.[16] Germany then asked Britain to save the Triple Alliance, and thereby demonstrate the value of its friendship to Germany. By now the Egyptian army had been turned into an effective fighting force, and the Egyptian government was in a position to finance the operation. Transported by Thomas Cook, Kitchener's army used railways, telegraph and the Maxim gun, an early machine gun, to reassert European military domination.

At the battle of Omdurman on 2 September 1898, the Khalifa's force was routed by an Anglo-Egyptian force just over half its size. Of the Khalifa's forces, 9,700 were killed, 10,000–16,000 wounded and 5,000 taken prisoner. Total British casualties were just under 500. The young Winston Churchill, who participated in the battle, described Omdurman as 'the most signal triumph ever gained by the arms of science over barbarians.[17] Gordon had been avenged and the moustache of the victor, Kitchener, quickly became 'the personification of empire, emblazoned on biscuit tins, buttons and postcards'. An Anglo-Egyptian condominium, a device of doubtful international legality, was established, in which the two countries held theoretically equal powers. The reality was rather different. The Governor-General was appointed by the Khedive, on British 'advice', and was therefore always British. The Egyptians paid for the administration. Egypt and the Sudan formed a customs union, but remained politically separate, and no Egyptian law applied to the Sudan unless specifically proclaimed by the Governor-General. Egyptian nationalists denounced the British for staking a claim to Egyptian territory.[18]

By the time of the Condominium, the permanency of British rule in Egypt itself was well established. By the last two decades of the nineteenth century, British power was in relative terms in decline thanks to the rapid industrialisation of Germany and the United States, and a good deal of the mid-century Victorian optimism had gone.[19] Cromer, however, seemed oblivious to these trends. A highly efficient and energetic administrator, who had served both as one of the two Anglo-French financial controllers of Egypt before 1882 and as finance member of the Viceroy's Council in India, Cromer exuded a self-confidence which others saw as arrogance. The Consul-General's personality seemed to carry all before it. Edgar Vincent, who worked for Cromer, described him as possessing 'that curious combination of character which lends authority even to doubtful decisions, and makes those who possess it respected in counsel and obeyed as rulers'.[20] He certainly enjoyed the confidence of governments in London, which allowed him an unusual degree of latitude. His approach to the Egyptians was one of condescending paternalism. According to Ronald Robinson and John Gallagher,

Like the 'Guardians' of India, he felt too much personal responsibility for the subject peoples' welfare to hand them over to a corrupt and incompetent class of native leaders. For him British rule and influence were ordained by Providence for the progress of the Orient. This faith made him detest nationalism in Egypt as in India. He judged backward

Egypt by the standards of a progressive Europe and found it stunted and degenerate. Both on moral and on practical grounds, the old regime seemed past praying for.[21]

Cromer belonged to a generation of British officials who, as a much later British ambassador to Egypt wrote, 'would never have dreamt of speaking Arabic. He would simply have expressed his wishes in English, and, if not at once understood, would have raised his voice.'[22] The imposing new Agency building into which he moved in the winter of 1893–4 was known locally as *Bait-al-lurd* – the house of the lord. It quickly became the centre for a highly personalised system for ruling Egypt.[23] 'It is a most amazing business', one official commented, 'this one-man government of an immense territory.'[24]

Britain's formal position in Egypt, as in the Persian Gulf, was in fact anomalous, an attempt to gain the benefits of imperial control without paying its costs. Ultimate suzerainty remained with Turkey. Egypt, in the words of Harry Boyle, Cromer's influential Oriental Secretary, was 'ours and not ours'.[25] Alfred Milner coined the more sonorous 'veiled Protectorate of uncertain extent and indefinite duration for the accomplishment of a difficult and distant object'.[26] The veil – fig-leaf is perhaps a better metaphor – was intended to disguise the reality both from other European powers and from domestic opinion. What was indisputable was that British rule was indirect, a matter of governing the governors, in other words the Khedive and his ministers. A key channel of influence was that of the 'advisers', mostly from India, inserted into strategic ministries. They were far from welcome, despite their relatively small numbers. In 1891 366 Britons were employed by the Egyptian government, 39 in senior positions. They were also there to ensure good government and to reform the Egyptian government machine. The ideal, as stated by Milner, was to Anglicise the Egyptian bureaucracy 'in spirit, to infuse into its ranks that uprightness and devotion to duty which is the legitimate boast of the Civil Service of Great Britain'.[27]

The most important figure was the British Financial Adviser, who was responsible for framing the budget, ensuring the country's solvency and meeting Egypt's international obligations. No financial decision could be taken without his consent. As the occupation became more permanent, advisers were introduced into other ministries, including Justice and the Interior, where the British adviser provided the Residency with vital intelligence on what was going on in the country. Nominally subordinate to Egyptian ministers, they were often in virtual command of the departments, and by the mid-1890s, had seats in Cabinet Council. Egyptian authority was bypassed even at the local level.[28] The advisers required a combination of tact and firmness, which they by no means always possessed.

The British garrison ensured that their 'advice' was something more than a mere recommendation. The mostly Indian force, paid for by the Egyptians, was sometimes less than five thousand strong, but could be readily augmented from the constant rotation of some twenty to thirty thousand British troops a year through the Suez Canal to and from India. Cromer took care to see that the regular garrison's presence was noticed. His carriage always had a military escort, and there were frequent military parades in the main towns. 'Any picture of Cairo that does not include the soldier', wrote the American Consul-General at the end of the 1890s, 'cannot be considered complete, for the military aspect is in almost aggressive evidence.'[29] There was a large military display in Cairo on the Sovereign's birthday, reviewed by Cromer and attended by Egyptian officials. Cromer augmented the garrison whenever there was a serious attack by nationalists.[30]

In key respects Egypt benefited from the occupation, indeed in exile 'Urabi admitted that the British were doing most of things he had wanted to do.[31] Cromer was not only implementing much of the nationalists' programme of administrative and financial reforms, but he was doing so in a way which gave confidence to foreign investment. His immediate priority had been to sort out Egyptian finances, a task made more complicated by French obstructionism; the French retained considerable financial influence by virtue of their position on the *Caisse de Dette*. Nevertheless, by the late 1880s, Cromer had succeeded in bringing the budget back into surplus, and by the 1890s, Egypt was enjoying prosperity. While reducing the burden of taxation, he also managed substantially to increase revenue and lower the percentage of debt devoted to redemption.[32]

This required more than good financial management. Egypt's long-term prosperity required both agricultural reform and the renovation and improvement of the country's lifeblood, its decaying irrigation system. The Delta Barrage was restored and the first Aswan dam built. The *corvée*, a system of forced labour which had been used in the construction of the Suez Canal, was abolished, as was the use of the *kurbaj*, a whip made of hippopotamus hide. British irrigation inspectors became arbiters of Egypt's agricultural life, settling disputes over the division of water and where private canals could be constructed, and determining how often the land could be irrigated. They helped ensure the water was distributed equitably to large and small landowners alike. The results could be seen in the increase in land under cultivation, which rose nearly 10 per cent between 1896 and 1914.[33]

Within ten years there was a trebling of cotton yield and sugar production. The population increased from 7.6 million in 1880 to 12.3 in 1914.[34] The downside was that Cromer's agricultural reforms left the country dangerously exposed to fluctuation in the price of cotton, while the perennial system of irrigation led to increased waterlogging of land and pest attacks.[35]

There were, however, clear limits to the extent of reform the British were willing to implement. This had to do not only with money, but also with concern not to undermine social cohesion, and hence the political stability which the occupation sought to maintain. While British officials believed that they had a responsibility for good government, they did not believe that they should transform Egypt on Western lines, or indeed that it could be reformed. British neglect was particularly evident in rural public health and education.[36] Like most Victorian liberals, Cromer did not believe that it was the state's responsibility to provide education, but there was also a more political motive. 'Whatever we do', Cromer wrote to a colleague, 'education must produce its natural results, and one of those natural results, both in India and Egypt, will be the wish to get rid of the foreigner.'[37] Between 1882 and 1902 the amount spent on education came to less than 1 per cent of the Egyptian budget. Although the figure subsequently rose it was never more than 3.4 per cent.[38] There was no attempt to create new political institutions or move Egypt forward on the road to self-government.

This was not an oppressive occupation. The British provided a relatively free atmosphere for Egyptian intellectual life, and under Cromer there was no attempt to prevent criticism of the occupation. Nor was there any interference in religious life. But while the rhetoric was one of public service and altruism, there was often a coldness, which, according to Boyle, needed to be softened by kindliness, patience and courtesy.[39] It did not come naturally to the representatives of a Great Power whose navy ruled the waves. This arrogance was not confined to Cromer. The attitude of English teachers towards their students was often one of contempt and ill-will. Egyptians were effectively barred from the two most exclusive social clubs in Cairo – the Gezira and Turf clubs.[40] Such behaviour was partly a technique of rule – a means of instilling fear and respect. As Ronald Hyam notes, the British 'could only have ruled subject peoples, especially when hopelessly outnumbered, by honestly believing themselves to be racially superior'.[41] But it also reflected the narrow insularity, already noted, of the British abroad, which the novelist E.M. Forster later attacked in *A Passage to India*. Either way it was deeply resented.[42]

One Egyptian particularly conscious of British paternal arrogance was the young Khedive Abbas II, who had succeeded his father in 1892, and quickly came to resent the way Cromer humiliated and belittled him.[43] To Cromer he was 'a self-willed boy of arbitrary disposition'.[44] 'I am riding my new colt with the lightest of snaffles', he had written in February 1892. 'By degrees he will gain confidence in the English government, and, I hope and believe, in me.'[45] This was over-optimistic. The first crisis occurred in 1893, with Abbas's dismissal, without consulting Cromer, of the pro-British Mustapha Pasha Fehmi and replacement by Hussayn Fakhri, a well-known Anglophobe. Cromer, who viewed this as a decisive blow to British influence, believed that 'the young man clearly had to be taught a lesson', and Abbas was duly warned that if he failed to yield, matters might take 'a more serious and complicated turn'.[46] Troops were sent to stop the *Journal Officiel* from publishing the decree appointing Fakhri. What one British minister described as a 'tumultuous storm of sinister telegrams' rained down now from Cairo onto the Foreign Office. The garrison was duly increased, the new infantry battalion being ostentatiously marched into Cairo. In the end a compromise was reached, in part, Cromer claimed, because he did not wish to humiliate the young man unduly. But, as Cromer realised, public opinion had clearly been on Abbas's side.[47]

Worse, from Cromer's perspective, Abbas had not learned his lesson. Egyptian officials dependent on the Khedive continued to be obstructive, while he himself encouraged anti-British agitation in the local press. Cromer bided his time until he could find an issue which would be comprehensible to the British public, and which could not be construed in Egypt as intervention by a foreign power. The opportunity soon arose during the so-called 'Frontier Incident' in January 1894 when the Khedive publicly criticised British officers. Aware that too public a humiliation risked playing into French hands, as well as causing political difficulties in Britain, Cromer contented himself with demanding an apology and the removal of the Under-Secretary for War. But he had sounded out London about dismissing Abbas. The incident marked the end of Abbas's role as public leader of the opposition to the British occupation, and Cromer now stood revealed as what one British journalist described as 'the ultimate ruler of Egypt'.[48]

Cromer subsequently kept the young Khedive in constant fear that he would be deposed if he caused any more disturbances. Abbas's hopes of using the French, whom he had sought to cultivate against the British, were destroyed first by Fashoda and then by the *Entente Cordiale*. A few months later, in November 1904, Abbas reviewed British troops on Edward VII's birthday for the first time. But he was never reconciled to Cromer. In his memoirs Abbas wrote that Cromer 'did not know how to formulate a comprehensive policy for Anglo-Egyptian understanding', but also said that 'when one worked constantly with him, one became aware that he was not a terrible adversary'.[49]

Cromer also had difficulties with Egyptian prime ministers. At the outset of the occupation, the Foreign Secretary, Lord Granville, had made it clear that ministers who failed to carry out British policy would be removed. The three principal Egyptian survivors of the pre-occupation period all collided with the British and were duly ousted.[50] One, Nubar Pasha, in the words of an Egyptian historian,

> saw the necessity of the British army of occupation to maintain order, but, as Prime Minister, he resented the fact that the administration of the country was not in his own hands. He liked the personnel of the British army, but he was constantly opposed to Lord Cromer and the British civilians in the Egyptian service, whom he regarded as intruders in what he viewed as his own preserve.[51]

Cromer described Nubar as being 'as Orientals go, a statesman', which seems to damn with extremely faint praise. In fact he regarded Nubar as too emotional, while Nubar saw Cromer as too unimaginative.[52] Mustapha Pasha Fehmi (1895–1908) by contrast proved much more amenable, to the point that his administration was known in Egypt as the 'ministry of dummies'. Cromer advised Milner of the need to be more respectful of ministers. 'The public tell them they were puppets – we must try to make them think they are not. The result will be just the same but they will be pleased and the whole machine will work much more smoothly.'[53] Here the contempt is undisguised.

Yet at no stage during this period did resentment develop into sustained violent opposition. British rule was generally accepted in a country where two millennia of foreign rule had bred submission and defeatism. Shortly after the battle of Tel-el-Kebir, the crowd at a British military review in Cairo had shown intense curiosity, but no sign of ill-will. The magnitude of the Egyptian defeat demoralised and dispersed the nationalists, while the failure of the 'Urabi revolution had created a more general sense of insecurity and despair. For a time, a strong hand promising stability and security was welcome.[54] In so far as the *fellahin* thought of the occupation, they considered it a punishment by the Almighty for their iniquities, and this acquiescence was deliberately encouraged by the concern which Cromer and his successors showed for their welfare. At a more elevated social and political level, the British were useful. They had allowed Tewfiq, who had welcomed their intervention in 1882, to keep his throne. They allowed members of the alien ruling class of Turkish, Circassian and Armenian administrators and landowners to counterbalance the nationalists. When Boyle left Cairo, *Al Ahram* complained that much of his influence had been due to the way the country's elite had been drawn to him like bees to honey.[55]

By its very nature, however, the British occupation was sooner or later bound to reignite nationalist sentiment. There were specific grievances, such as exclusion from the higher reaches of the administration, which increased with the growing number of British advisers. But Egyptians, notably those from the professional classes, including lawyers and students who were particularly active in nationalist circles, were also affronted by the disrespect and discrimination they experienced. Cromer could see none of this. He described the Egyptian nationalist as 'a demoslemised Moslem and an invertebrate European' trying 'to adapt garments whether of the political or industrial type, made on the banks of the Thames [...] to the unreceptive bodies of the inhabitants of Egypt'.[56] He blamed the nationalist movement not on resentment at British, including his own, behaviour, but on an impression of weakness created by divisions and uncertainty in domestic British politics.[57]

Then there was an incident. In 1906 a British soldier out pigeon shooting died following a fight with local villagers. In a trial whose outcome shocked Egypt, as well as opinion in Britain, four villagers were hanged, and others received harsh punishments. The Dinshawi incident has been ascribed to panic, but according to John Marlowe, the court's verdicts reflected the extent to which the British had lost touch with the people. British officials had surrounded themselves over the previous decade with 'a protective covering of subservient Egyptian opinion' which effectively insulated them from what the Egyptians were really saying and thinking.[58] This was in line with other indications of a growing sense of hubris and carelessness – a decline in Anglo-Egyptian social contacts and an increasing tendency to domineer. The Dinshawi incident thus became a catalyst, bringing latent anti-British feeling to the surface, uniting for the first time all shades of Egyptian opinion against the occupation.[59]

The year after, the first political parties were formed. The Umma, or People's Party, composed of wealthy landlords, and strongly represented in the Egyptian Legislative Council and General Assembly, pursued a generally moderate policy, and was encouraged by Cromer. The more popular National Party appealed to the new generation of professional and middle classes, as well as students. Their demands included a government responsible to an elected parliament, which would receive genuine advice, as opposed to orders from the British advisers. The Constitutional Reform Party represented the interests of the Khedive. All three were in varying degrees opposed to the British occupation, with the National Party regarding military evacuation as their first priority. Nationalism had reached a new level of organisation and articulation, and was making its appeal to increasingly sizeable audiences.[60]

It was at this point that Cromer finally retired. He had stayed too long. The autocratic streak in his temperament had become more pronounced over the years, but perhaps more serious was his inability to appreciate that Egypt would outgrow British tutelage. Boyle feared a hostile demonstration on his departure; in the event the route to the railway station was through streets lined with soldiers with fixed bayonets, behind which stood silent crowds.[61] His successor, Sir Eldon Gorst, tried to make significant changes to his predecessor's policy. There was an urgent need to lower the political temperature and divide the three forces of the Palace, the notables and the middle-class nationalists, who were converging against Britain. Besides, London was anxious to keep Egypt quiet.

Gorst sought to render British rule 'more sympathetic' to the Egyptians, confining himself to pulling the strings in the background, while others did the shouting. Moderate nationalists were wooed – the more extreme element clamped down on. The Egyptians were thus given greater responsibility in governing themselves. Ministers gained more independence, the prospects for Egyptian civil servants were improved, and there were significant advances in local government. Gorst also mended British relations with the Khedive, whom he treated with respect. But this did not of course stop him making the Agency the arbiter of the dislike between the Khedive and his former nationalist allies, who now became suspicious of him.[62]

Gorst's efforts to improve relations with the Khedive succeeded, to the point that Abbas, who was in Paris at the time, visited Gorst on his deathbed in England in 1911. Politically, however, Gorst failed to take the wind out of the nationalist sails, indeed the changes he had instituted in the functioning of the Legislative Council and General Assembly led to these bodies becoming instruments of National Party agitation. Government schools were also providing an increasingly vocal nationalist platform. The nationalist movements increased support among the non-professional classes, while developing new means of resisting British rule. In 1910 the prime minister, Boutros Ghali, was assassinated; two years later there was a plot against Kitchener, Gorst's successor.[63]

It had been the opinion of the Turf Club that Kitchener would succeed where Gorst had failed. He had a soldier's preference for administrative improvement rather than political reform. He paid particular attention to the wellbeing of the *fellahin*, made concessions to the moderate Umma Party, while taking harsh measures against the more extreme National Party, whose leaders were imprisoned or exiled. The Khedive was deprived of some of his powers and threatened with enforced abdication. The overt features of the nationalist movement were duly suppressed, but Kitchener was deeply unpopular.[64]

From the Egyptian perspective the occupation was both a blessing and a curse. As Abbas wrote in his memoirs, 'We have appreciated the real value of the material progress that England was able to bring to Egypt. But we are convinced that the English have made us pay dearly for these advantages with our liberty.'[65] The British had done rather better. If the occupation came close to blurring the limits between informal and formal empire, that scarcely worried officials. The key thing from their viewpoint was that by dint of a combination of skill and determination, the British administration in Egypt had managed to recover from the miscalculations made in London in 1882. Their immediate objectives had been fulfilled. The Egyptian economy had been turned round; and British interests – along with other European financial ones – had been safeguarded. Almost as an added bonus, Britain had placed itself in a position to ensure the long-term security of the Suez Canal. The price it had had to pay in terms of European power politics had proved more of an irritant than a burden. No subsequent British administrator had as much power, or did so much to improve the running of a Middle East country, as Cromer. Nor would any of his successors have quite such an easy task.

5

The Battle for the Middle East

On the Defensive, 1914–16

In the summer of 1914 Kitchener went home on leave. He did not return. At the end of July, a European crisis, which had been simmering since the assassination of the Hapsburg Archduke Ferdinand four weeks earlier, suddenly escalated. By the beginning of August Europe was at war, with Britain, France and Russia pitted against the central powers – an expansionist Germany and a declining Austro-Hungarian Empire. Kitchener, who was appointed Secretary of State for War, was one of the relatively few people to foresee that the conflict would not be over by Christmas.

The Great War, as it was originally known, determined much of the bloody history of the twentieth century. The raw statistics are mind-numbing. Sixty-five million troops were mobilised. Of these 21 million were wounded, while there were some 20 million military and civilian deaths.[1] The war brought about the collapse of three empires, revolution in Russia, and within twenty years of the Versailles peace settlement, a second great conflict. It also marks the second watershed of the Anglo-Middle Eastern story. Flanking Europe and India, the Middle East became the most important non-European theatre of a world war. The Middle East provided an opportunity for the victories which eluded the generals on the Western Front. Those victories brought territorial gains to compensate for the appalling human losses in Flanders and to provide negotiating chips for the peace talks.[2] Hitherto the British had confined themselves to regulating politics in various parts of the Middle East. Now they began to shape its political geography.

This final phase of British expansion in the Middle East was a helter-skelter affair, the result of often chaotic reactions to opportunities and events. Policies and ideas emerged from a disorderly process of competition between institutions and individuals in London, Delhi, Cairo and, in 1917, Baghdad. The previous year, when some degree of rationalisation of the decision-making process was attempted with the creation of the Arab Bureau in Cairo, 18 different authorities needed to be consulted about decisions on the Middle East.[3] Few officials appreciated the way in which the war was setting the scene for the transition of the Middle East from empire into a modern state system. Nor did they appreciate the truth grasped by Field Marshal von der Golz, who commanded the Turkish army in Iraq in 1916, and prophesied that the war was 'only the beginning of a long historical development, at the end of which will stand the defeat of England's world position. The hallmark of the twentieth century must be the revolution by the coloured races against the colonial Imperialism of Europe.'[4]

The main short-term losers, the Turks, had brought about their own misfortune. In the immediate aftermath of the outbreak of war in Europe, Grey's primary Middle Eastern concern was to ensure Turkish neutrality. A war against Muslim Turkey threatened the loyalty of Egyptian and Indian Muslims. It would also mean the closure of the Dardanelles to Russia, thereby blocking the important grain trade from the Black Sea, and making it difficult to keep one of Britain's key allies supplied.[5] Writing to the British ambassador in Paris on 15 August, Grey described the proper course as to

> make Turkey feel that, should she remain neutral and should Germany and Austria be defeated, we would take care that the integrity of Turkish possessions as they now were would be preserved in any terms of peace affecting the Near East, but that, on the other hand, if Turkey sided with Germany and Austria and they were defeated, of course we could not answer for what might be taken from Turkey in Asia Minor.[6]

And yet surprisingly little effort was made to pursue this policy, with at least one minister, Churchill, spoiling for a fight. The British government drifted into the Turkish war relatively casually.[7]

Whether a more determined policy could have kept the Turks neutral is a moot point. Turkey had its own good reasons for staying out of the conflict. It was poor, technically backward and had inadequate communications. War involved an existential risk for an ailing empire, which had only very recently lost its remaining Balkan territories. German victory could not be taken for granted.[8] The majority of the Turkish Cabinet and public opinion favoured neutrality *vis-à-vis* Britain and France, though Turkey's historic enemy, Russia, was another matter. But the opponents of hostilities were outmanoeuvred by the Defence Minister. A former military attaché in Berlin,

Enver Pasha was impressed by Germany's military power. He hoped not just to regain the lost territories in the Balkans, but to liberate Turks under Russian rule in the Caucasus and central Asia, as well as Egypt and Cyprus, which Britain had annexed in 1879. And he wanted to use the Caliphate to make the Ottoman Empire dominant in the Muslim world.[9] What he failed to realise was that by opting for war at the beginning of November, he was bringing the Eastern question, which had been successfully shelved over the previous century, to a head. Unlike the Napoleonic conflicts, this would be a war not so much *in*, as *for* the Middle East, with Britain and Turkey the main protagonists.

Britain initially found itself on the defensive against two enemies. The Kaiser's interest in the Middle East had already been evident during visits in 1889 and 1898, when in a speech in Damascus, Hajii Wilhelm, as he subsequently became known, declared himself the protector of the world's Muslim population. It was subsequently rumoured in the bazaars that he actually converted to Islam.[10] With the outbreak of war in 1914, Germany embraced a revolutionary agenda, aimed at breaking up both the British and Russian Empires. Their 'secret' weapon, which had long fascinated German officials, was the supposed power of pan-Islamic sentiment, which Berlin believed that Turkey, as the seat of the Caliphate, could mobilise. On 30 July Wilhelm noted that German consuls and agents in India and Turkey 'must inflame the whole Mohammedan world to wild revolt against this hateful, lying, conscienceless people of hagglers; for if we are to be bled to death, at least England shall lose India'.[11] Three days later, the German commander, General Helmuth von Moltke, described revolts in Egypt, India and the Caucasus as being of the highest importance.[12] The German strategy was outlined in a 136-page paper entitled *Memorandum on the Revolutionizing of the Islamic Territory of Our Enemies*.[13] Following the Turkish declaration of war, the Caliphate in Constantinople duly declared *jihad* on 14 November, invoking believers throughout the Muslim world to fight Britain, France, Russia, Serbia and Montenegro as enemies of Islam.

It was the British who felt most vulnerable. A hundred million out of the world's 270 million Muslims lived in the British Empire and the threat from a pan-Islamic movement was one of those simple and emotive ideas which touched a raw nerve of imperial insecurity. Before the war, the Permanent Under-Secretary at the Foreign Office, Sir Arthur Nicolson, had referred to the threat from a pan-Islamic movement as 'one of our greatest dangers in the future' which was more of a menace than the 'Yellow Peril'.[14] In his 1916 popular novel, *Greenmantle*, the plot of which revolves round the threat of the German *jihad*, John Buchan's spymaster declares that 'The war must be won or lost in Europe. Yes; but if the East blazes up, our effort will be distracted from Europe [...] The stakes are no less than victory and defeat.'[15] (The novel, which captured Europe's fascination with the latent power of Islamic fanaticism, retained a surprising potency. In July 2005, transmission of a BBC dramatisation of the book was postponed following Islamist terrorist bombings in London.[16])

The reality, however, as Gerald Lowther, the British ambassador to Constantinople, had advised in 1911, was more complicated and less threatening than the Kaiser hoped, and the British feared. The pan-Islamic war cry took no account of Arab unwillingness to cooperate with the Turks or of divisions between Sunni and Shi'a, let alone of the multitude of tribal hostilities among those to whom it was supposed to appeal. As to India's Sunni Muslims, they viewed the Young Turks, who had seized power in Constantinople in 1908, as sacrilegious revolutionaries who had deposed the rightful caliph and replaced him with a puppet. The German ambassador in Turkey, Baron Hans von Wangenheim, appears to have concurred, predicting that the holy war would probably 'coax only a few Moslems from behind the warm stove'.[17]

Events vindicated this judgement. A special pan-Islamic bureau was established in Berlin and Damascus to capitalise on the regional appeal of the Turkish Caliphate. This propaganda effort was accompanied by the despatch of a series of German missions to stir up religious unrest in Egypt, Arabia, the Sudan, Abyssinia, Afghanistan and Persia. They proved singularly ineffective. Over and above the politico-cultural problems Lowther had pointed up, the Germans were unable to provide the one thing which would really have mattered, namely arms and war material. The Berlin to Baghdad railway had not yet been completed, while the Royal Navy dominated the Persian Gulf and Indian Ocean. All prospects of a *jihad* against the Raj ended with the successful Russian offensive against Erzurum launched in January 1916, a battle which provides the climax in *Greenmantle*.[18]

In two areas, however, the Germans did succeed in causing the British difficulties, albeit on a much smaller scale than they had hoped. Their immediate goal was an attack on the Suez Canal, which the German high command hoped would constitute 'a mortal blow against Britain's position'. Turkey provided the troops, while the Germans supplied arms, funds and training. But the operation was premised on the assumption of an Egyptian uprising, as well as a mutiny among Muslim elements in the British forces. If the Turks appeared on the canal, one German Middle East expert optimistically prophesied, they would be 'joined by 70,000 Arab nomads'.[19]

Britain had tightened its hold on Egypt in late 1914, formally declaring a Protectorate; officials in Cairo had successfully deflected an earlier suggestion from London that Egypt be annexed. It had also deposed the Khedive, at whose disposal the Germans had placed four million gold francs. But if educated Egyptians admired Germany, cheering German victories in cinemas in Cairo in February 1915, this did not mean that they welcomed the return of the Turks. There was no revolt when some 20,000 Turkish soldiers reached the canal in February 1915. Defended by British and Indian troops – Egyptian troops had been sent out of the way to the Sudan – the attack was easily repulsed. The Turks, however, remained in control of much of Sinai, forcing Britain to maintain substantial forces in Egypt until the Turkish defeat at the battle of Romani in August 1916. It was from around 1916 that Britain began to treat the canal as a British territorial possession, although German submarines in the Mediterranean reduced traffic through Suez.[20]

The war also turned Egypt into a major British military base. This was used in support of the ill-fated 1915 Gallipoli expedition aimed at seizing the Straits and knocking Turkey out of the war, as a supply base for operations in Salonika and as a transit point for Indian, Australian and New Zealand troops bound via Suez for the Western Front. At one point in early 1916, there were some thirteen divisions and three general headquarters in the country. It was from Cairo that the Arab Revolt would be run from 1916, and it was the Egyptian Expeditionary Force that fought the successful Palestine and Syrian campaigns of 1917–18.[21]

Having failed to raise Egypt, the Germans were no more successful in the Sudan or in Arabia, where their main target was Sherif Hussein of the Hejaz, the keeper of the Holy Places of Mecca and Medina, although the Senussi tribes of Libya did create difficulties for Britain along Egypt's western border.[22] More effective were German activities in neutral Persia. German agents began operating in south Persia in 1914, where anti-British tribes succeeded in penetrating the outskirts of Bushire and cutting the oil pipelines. In the spring of 1915, some 12,000 British and Indian forces drove the Turks and their Arab allies out of Khuzistan province. But there was a good deal of support for the central powers. There was sympathy for Turkey as a Muslim power. Germany was fighting Persia's great enemy Russia, while Britain remained the subject of suspicion and resentment due to the Anglo-Russian 1907 spheres-of-influence agreement.[23] When in 1915 the Germans attempted to bring Persia into the war, the Russian and British ministers in Tehran gave Ahmad Shah to understand in what the British minister described as 'unmistakable language that if the Persian government did not act against the Germans, then Russian troops would undertake the task, and that if Persia allowed herself to be drawn to war against us, the results to Persia and to himself would be disastrous'.[24]

Although the German bid failed, German influence remained. British efforts to control the often chaotic situation in the country were constantly frustrated. Attempts to deal with the government foundered over the political price which the Persians demanded, while the loyalty of tribal leaders whom the British courted was always in doubt. Neither the government of India nor the War Office were prepared to provide troops, even though local levies, including the South Persia Rifles, proved more trouble than they were worth.[25] Nevertheless, Britain's interests survived the war.

To the west of Persia, Britain had quickly gone on the offensive. Contingency planning for a possible war against Turkey had begun in India as early as 1911, and the decision to send troops to the Persian Gulf was taken a month before the Turks declared war. Numbering only some 5,000 men, Force D, made up of troops regarded as unfit for the Western Front, was to have an importance completely out of proportion to its size, a classic example of the phenomenon known today as 'mission creep'. Its initial role was defensive – to show the Turks the British meant business, and to reassure Britain's two key allies at the head of the Gulf, the sheikhs of Kuwait and Mohammerah.[26] Yet no sooner had Basra, a major commercial centre with a population of 60,000, been taken in late November 1914, than there was talk in both India and London that it should be kept. 'Another Red Patch on the Map', read the headline in the *Daily Mail*.[27]

Although the prime minister, Herbert Asquith, warned of the disadvantages of taking Mesopotamia, as Iraq was then known, the initiative lay with India and the military. Commanders deprecated the idea of inactivity, while Sir Percy Cox, who was Political Adviser to the expedition, found it 'difficult to see how we can well avoid taking over Baghdad. We can hardly allow Turkey to retain possession and make difficulties for us at Basra; nor can we allow any other Power to take it.'[28] Initial advances north of Basra proved deceptively easy, thereby facilitating the argument for advancing yet further, put forward by a gung-ho commander, General Sir John Nixon, and the Viceroy, Lord Hardinge. The government of India was anxious to show that they were not being overshadowed by the Western Front.[29]

Their case was reinforced by the trouble in Persia, which placed British prestige on the line, and the Cabinet's desire for victories to offset difficulties in Gallipoli and on the Western Front. As one officer put it, 'Baghdad, like Jerusalem, stood out enticingly in the perfect map of the imagination.'[30] This was not an environment in which warnings that the expedition was becoming dangerously overextended were heeded. The Indian government, which had hitherto only fought frontier wars, had no experience of planning for an operation on this scale. Basra port was overwhelmed and there were insufficient riverboats essential for the supply of the advancing troops. Nor did questions such as how the troops would hold Baghdad, let alone the political implications of what they would do if they got there, receive proper attention.[31] As the subsequent commission of enquiry noted, 'the scope of the objective of the mission was never sufficiently defined in advance, so as to make each successive move part of a well thought-out and matured plan'.[32]

In the event, the troops only got to Ctesiphon, some 25 miles south-east of Baghdad, and then retired to the small village of Kut-al-Amarah. Here, after three failed attempts to break the 145-day siege, which had involved pulling men out of France, and a desperate attempt to airdrop food to the besieged garrison, 13,000 British and Indian forces surrendered at the end of April. The military campaign in Mesopotamia had cost 40,000 British and imperial lives. Kut was Britain's first major military disaster in the Middle East and one of the worst humiliations ever suffered by the British army.[33] Fortunately for Britain the Turks were unable to exploit this defeat, being hard pressed by Russia in the Caucasus and Persia.

Kipling wrote an angry poem,

THEY shall not return to us, the resolute, the young,
The eager and whole-hearted whom we gave:
But the men who left them thriftily to die in their own dung,
Shall they come with years and honour to the grave?[34]

The commission of enquiry duly apportioned blame, forcing the resignation of the Secretary of State for India, Austen Chamberlain. The commander-in-chief of the Indian army, Sir Beauchamp Duff, committed suicide.[35]

It was the Gallipoli campaign which first focused British thinking about a post-Ottoman future in the Middle East. With British forces approaching the Straits in 1915, the Russians had in March reiterated their long-standing claim on Constantinople, while the French put in a bid for Syria. Britain had no claims on the Ottoman Empire, and both Grey, and the prime minister, Herbert Asquith, as well as some senior officials believed that Britain already held enough territory in the world. In the words of Maurice Hankey, Secretary to the Committee of Imperial Defence and the War Council, 'we have not the men to make new countries out of savage deserts'.[36] But Asquith was also on record in 1915 as saying that were Britain 'to leave the other nations to scramble for Turkey without taking anything for ourselves, we should not be doing our duty'.[37] This was a widely shared view. The Middle East offered one of the last opportunities for ambitious young Englishmen 'to fiddle with substantial pieces of history'.[38] Officials in both Cairo and Delhi had for some time been toying with ideas for an extension of British power. There was talk in Cairo about establishing some form of nominally independent federation of Arab states under British protection. Delhi had quickly warmed to the idea that Mesopotamia might provide a breadbasket for India, as well as an outlet for Indian emigration.

The Ottoman succession, however, was fraught with difficulties. Quite apart from deciding what Britain wanted, there was the challenge of reconciling the competing claims not only of the French and Russians, but also of the Italians, Arabs, and the one potential wild card, the Zionist movement. There was a lack of expertise or readily available information about the Middle East and confusion about political nomenclature. The Ottoman Empire was divided into *vilayets* or districts. The Bunsen Committee, which was set up in London in April 1915 to consider British *desiderata* in the region, employed terms used by Hellenistic geographers two thousand years previously. They referred to Syria and Mesopotamia without any clear indication of the geographic limits of these territories. They spoke of Palestine to denote the area of southern Syria once occupied by the Philistines. Palestine, however, had never been a country, and when Lloyd George, making use this time of biblical geography, later referred to Palestine stretching from 'Dan to Beersheba', nobody knew where Dan actually was. At one point during the Versailles peace conference, officials telephoned two Christian publishers in London to find out how biblical authorities defined Palestine.[39]

All this suggests that very careful consideration was required, if serious complications were to be avoided. But this was wartime, and the series of promissory notes which Britain issued between October 1915 and November 1917 reflected the perceived requirements of this peculiarly dreadful and desperate conflict. It is hardly surprising therefore that the outcome of the preliminary division of the Ottoman spoils over which the British presided should prove both embarrassingly and dangerously messy.

The only regional claimant to engage British attention was Sherif Hussein of the Hejaz. A few months before the war, an emissary of the Sherif had approached officials in Cairo to sound out the possibility of British support for a revolt against the Turks. At the time the idea was turned down: British policy was still to support the integrity of the Ottoman

Empire and avoid being drawn into Arabian affairs. But officials were quick to try to re-establish contact following the outbreak of war. The Hejaz might be desolate and uninviting, and the Sherif a much less impressive leader than Ibn Sa'ud of Najd, who had for some years been angling for British support. But the Sherif was in a position to cause difficulty for the Turks in Asir and the Yemen. More important, as the Germans had already realised, the Sherif enjoyed unique prestige in the Muslim world by virtue of his claim to be a descendant of the Prophet Mohammed, and keeper of the Holy Places. Here was a potentially vital counterweight to the Caliphate in Istanbul.[40]

During the summer of 1915 the Sherif sounded out other Arab figures, notably in Syria, where a prewar Arab nationalist movement had emerged in secret societies in Damascus. He then put forward an audacious claim not just to the Arabian Peninsula, but also to Mesopotamia, Syria and Palestine. In return he would start a revolt against the Turks. Cairo was seriously tempted, not least because of what proved a misleading report, which had not been subjected to adequate critical examination, that a large-scale revolt was in the offing in Syria. The British needed help. Their advance north of Basra had recently been repulsed, the Gallipoli campaign was in trouble, while reports suggested that German plans for a *jihad* might be making serious headway. Longer term there was the thought that the Sherif might be a potentially biddable proxy for the spread of British influence in the Middle East.[41]

It was against this background that the High Commissioner in Cairo, Sir Henry McMahon, warned that without immediate assurances, the Arabs would go over to the Germans. McMahon may have deliberately overstated the case; Cairo had for some time been trying unsuccessfully to get instructions from London. If so, the warnings served their purpose. Grey duly authorised McMahon to give assurances to the Sherif. Given the apparent urgency of the matter, details were left to Cairo.[42]

The result was a letter from McMahon to Hussein on 24 October 1915, whereby Britain pledged to 'recognise and support' Arab independence within territories proposed by the Sherif and to guarantee the Holy Places against aggression.

When the situation admits, Great Britain will give to the Arabs her advice and will assist them to establish what may appear to be the most suitable forms of government in those various territories.

On the other hand, it is understood that the Arabs have decided to seek the advice and assistance of Great Britain only, and that such European

Advisers and officials as may be required in the formation of a sound form
of administration will be British.[43]

McMahon's letter marks the beginning of an Anglo-Hashemite alliance,
which would survive, albeit in increasingly diluted form, for much of the
century; it was also a formal British acknowledgement that the Arabs would
be key beneficiaries in any division of the Ottoman Empire. But the letter
proved the cause of much misunderstanding and controversy. At issue
was the wording about the areas to be excluded from Arab control, which
happened to be two of the most fertile areas in the region.

McMahon faced a dilemma. He did not know the extent of either
French claims to Syria or Indian claims to Mesopotamia, and could not
afford to spell out what he did know, for fear of bringing the negotiations
to an end.[44] The main difficulty arose from the language used to protect
French claims in the Levant. 'The districts of Mersina and Alexandretta
and portions of Syria lying to the west of the districts of Damascus, Hama,
Homs and Aleppo' were described as not purely Arab, and therefore to
be excluded from 'the proposed limits and boundaries'.[45] There was no
specific reference to Palestine.

Jeremy Wilson suggests that while McMahon had no intention of
offering complete Arab independence for Palestine, he also realised that to
make a specific reservation might endanger a deal. Jerusalem was after all
one of the holiest cities of Islam, and Hussein saw Palestine as an integral
part of Syria and the heart of a future Arab state. Whether or not the
reference to the areas west of the *vilayet* of Damascus included Palestine
was thus deliberately left ambiguous.[46] McMahon, as Wilson puts it, had
sought to solve his problem by sending a message which 'contained such
subtle reservations that the document could be interpreted differently by
each party. A reply in this time-honoured diplomatic style might save the
immediate situation and allow breathing space to discuss a full settlement.'[47]
Ambiguity, however, held its own longer-term dangers, particularly when it
was compounded by dubious translation and unrecorded verbal messages.
The risk, overlooked under the pressures of war, was not simply that it
would confuse the Sherif, but that it would lay the British open to the
charge of having acted in bad faith.

Having come to an understanding of sorts with the Sherif, it was time
to reach an understanding with France. The 1916 Sykes–Picot agreement
was named after François Georges-Picot, a former French consul in Beirut,
and leading proponent of the expansion of French influence in the Middle
East, and the influential Conservative MP, Sir Mark Sykes. A restless man

with a reputation as an expert on the region, Sykes had a taste for grand, if not always well-considered schemes.[48] It was a classic imperial spheres-of-influence agreement, designed to limit postwar Anglo-French rivalry in the Middle East.

Unlike the Hussein–McMahon correspondence, the Sykes–Picot agreement had, quite literally, been a matter of drawing straight lines on a map (see map 3). There was a red zone consisting of the provinces of Baghdad and Basra, which were to be subject to purely British control. A blue zone, made up of the long coastal zone of what is today Lebanon and Syria, was to come under exclusively French control. Like the Hussein–McMahon agreement, Sykes–Picot envisaged an Arab Arabia and provided for the independence of the Arab peoples, albeit of a distinctly qualified kind. In addition, Britain was to exercise informal influence across northern Arabia from Kirkuk in central Mesopotamia to Gaza. Known as Zone B, this effectively gave Britain a corridor from the Mediterranean to the Persian Gulf, thereby protecting imperial communications from India to Egypt. The comparable French zone A covered a large triangle from Mosul to Aleppo and Damascus. (Kitchener had wanted the French to have Mosul, in order to avoid the risk of Britain sharing a frontier with Russia.)[49]

Unlike in the Hussein–McMahon agreement, specific reference was made to Palestine, which under a compromise solution designed to overcome rival Anglo-French claims, as well as Russian Orthodox interests in the Holy Land, was to be under an effective Anglo-French-Russian condominium. These agreements were subsequently endorsed by the Russians, who were in turn allotted Constantinople and the Straits, Turkish Armenia and Persian Azerbaijan. The preparatory carve-up of the Ottoman Empire was almost complete. Nobody seemed concerned that, in the words of Emir Feisal's biographer, the agreements

> mixed the implausible and unsustainable together with the downright stupid. Relatively advanced populations on the Syrian coastlands, and to a lesser extent in Baghdad and Basra, were placed under direct rule, while desert lands with nomadic populations were given a semi-independent status.[50]

The Sykes–Picot agreement was negotiated in full awareness of what had just been promised to the Sherif.[51] The terms were, however, rather less generous to the Arabs than anything envisaged in Cairo, in regards both to the Basra and Baghdad *vilayets*, but more importantly, in the light of subsequent events, to Syria. The interior of Syria was now to fall under

French influence, something Arab leaders had specifically emphasised they did not want. Moreover, the concessions to the Arabs would lapse unless they themselves took Damascus, Aleppo, Homs and Hama. These discrepancies can be explained in terms of the relative vagueness of McMahon's commitments. But they also reflect the hard strategic reality that France, currently bearing the main brunt of the fighting on the Western Front at the great battle of Verdun, was a vital British ally, whereas the Sherif was an unproven military figure in a remote theatre of the war.[52] Besides, in 1916 all these promises seemed rather hypothetical. In the words of British military intelligence, 'we are rather in the position of the hunters, who divided the skin of the bear before they had killed it'.[53] It would take another two years before the Turkish bear was finally brought down.

6

The Battle for the Middle East

Onto the Offensive, 1916–18

On 5 June 1916, three and a half weeks before Field Marshall Douglas Haig launched his great offensive on the Somme, Britain's new Arabian ally, Sherif Hussein, launched the Arab Revolt. This was the only active Arab contribution to the war, and would have a significant impact on postwar peace making and the future political shape of the Middle East. Unlike the fighting on the Western Front, this imperial operation, described by one French observer as British imperialism in Arab headdress, played very much to British strengths. It was a sophisticated exercise of power, based on a close knowledge of tribal politics and an understanding of guerrilla warfare. The British played an enabling role, with the fighting, other than some naval and air support, left to local forces. Christian troops, as the Arab Bureau recognised, would have been highly unwelcome near the Holy Places. Instead they provided food and substantial amounts of money, some £11 million, by which the Sherif ensured the loyalty of the tribes. In 1916, monthly consignments of gold were shipped to Jeddah in 14 wooden iron-bound boxes. In addition there were supplies of arms and equipment, plus training – the Arab forces had no experience of modern warfare. The operation was supported by a very modern British intelligence operation, including photo reconnaissance and the cracking of both German and Turkish codes. Indeed, according to Priya Satia, intelligence played a greater role in the Middle East than in any other campaign in World War I.[1]

The most famous of the small group of British officers attached to Feisal's forces was, of course, the prewar archaeologist and part-time intelligence agent, T.E. Lawrence. This small, gifted, complex and enigmatic figure, the subject of innumerable biographies and David Lean's classic film, *Lawrence of Arabia*, was one of the few romantic heroes to come out of World War I. He had a unique capacity to get beneath the skin of the participants of the Arab Revolt, developing a personal affinity with one of Hussein's sons and the key Arab commander, Feisal, and gaining his trust.[2] The two men

> complemented one another in many ways. Lawrence's knowledge of the workings in Cairo and ability to get things done there were matched by Feisal's rank and persuasive power among the Arabs. They each had a romantic vision of the Arab national movement, strong enough to transcend everyday setbacks, and they both knew they were helping to shape momentous events.[3]

The revolt was controversial. It was disliked by the Indian government, which was building up Ibn Sa'ud as a counterweight to the Sherif. Delhi feared the potential impact on Muslim opinion, and preferred a policy of divide and rule to one of encouraging Arab unity along India's lines of communication. The Indian government also had a jaundiced, though by no means unrealistic opinion of the calibre of future Arab government. The French, who had established a military mission in the Hejaz commanded by Colonel Edouard Brémond, aimed at denying Britain an exclusive foothold in the region, were even more suspicious. They were anxious not just to prevent the Revolt expanding into Syria, but about its potential impact in North Africa and throughout their empire.[4]

The ill-will was mutual. There was a good deal of what Sykes described as 'Fashodism' on the British side. 'Damn Brémond and his nasty ways,' Colonel Wilson, his British counterpart, once complained, 'he creates more beastly situations for me than one would have thought possible.'[5] Lawrence wanted to 'rush right up to Damascus, and biff the French out of all hope of Syria'.[6] For their part the Hashemites were uneasy with their total dependence on a very powerful ally, which, as they gradually realised, had not been entirely straight with them. In the spring of 1918, by which time the terms of the Sykes–Picot agreement were known, and with Ludendorff having broken through on the Western Front, Feisal was in contact with the Turks.[7]

Any assessment of the military value of the revolt in the Middle East campaign must be set within the wider context of the war. Russian engagement of the Turks on the Caucasian front, where Turkey lost some 300,000 men, played an infinitely larger role in ensuring Britain's victories in the Middle East. Moreover it was only after the capture of Aqaba in July 1917 that Feisal's forces could be integrated into British planning. That said, the revolt denied Germany the use of the Red Sea coast as a stepping stone to promote subversion in East Africa.[8] It protected British forces in Sinai from attack on their right flank, severed Turkish communications with the Yemen, and undermined the loyalty of the Arabs of southern Syria to Turkey. Feisal's forces stopped some 20,000 Turkish troops between Ma'an and Medina participating in the battle for southern Palestine in the autumn of 1917, and in the summer of 1918, before British forces could launch a new offensive against Syria, helped keep up pressure on the Turks.[9]

By the time Aqaba was taken, there had been an important change in the premiership in London. David Lloyd George plays a brief, but critical part in British Middle East policy. A liberal imperialist, quick, ambitious and cynically unscrupulous, he was once described by the French premier, Georges Clémenceau, as a cheat. In contrast to Asquith, Lloyd George shared Gladstone detestation of the Ottoman Empire as oppressively cruel and a blight on subject people, although this did not prevent him from continuing secret peace negotiations with the Turks.[10] More importantly, he was anxious to shift more of the burden of the war towards the Middle East, not because he believed that it could be won there, but because he feared it might be lost in France. The year 1917 was the worst of the war for Britain, with continuing very heavy casualties in Flanders, unrestricted submarine warfare in the Atlantic, and failure in Salonika. And it was the year of the Russian Revolution, which Lloyd George feared would lead to labour unrest in Britain. The premier badly needed a victory; the Middle East seemed the obvious, indeed the only place to look for it.[11]

The first British military success was the taking of Baghdad in March 1917. The fabled city of the *Arabian Nights*, which had caught the imagination of Lloyd George, scarcely lived up to expectations. One general described it as 'not much of a place to look at [...] filthy, dirty place'.[12] Nor had its capture any obvious strategic rationale – the Chief of the Imperial General Staff, General Sir William Robertson, considered the action pointless. The new local commander, General Stanley Maude, however, refused to allow his army to vegetate in its trenches and camps, and wanted to efface the shame of the Kut surrender.[13] It was only once Baghdad had been taken that the War Cabinet set up a Mesopotamia Administration Committee under the chairmanship of Curzon, by now a member of the War Cabinet. It decided that the Basra *vilayet* should come under British control, while the Baghdad *vilayet* should join an Arab political entity under British protection. But no proper plans had previously been drawn up for an occupation. Nor does London appear to have been aware of – and it had certainly not given proper consideration to – the implications of the complex population mix of the Mesopotamian provinces. The antipathy between the Sunni minority and the Shi'a majority, tribal and clan rivalries, and the historic and geographic divisions of the provinces and the commercial Jewish predominance in Baghdad, all meant that the creation of unified government that was also representative, effective and widely supported, was all but impossible.[14] This was an instance in which the principle of first take your territory, and only then start thinking of how to deal with it, would come badly unstuck. In 1917 it contributed to a series of political muddles in Baghdad, which boded ill for any further extension of British power in the Middle East, and would plague Iraq's future.[15]

An even worse problem would confront the British in Palestine, which here was entirely of their own making. Lloyd George had ordered General Sir Archibald Murray's Egypt Expeditionary Force, which the previous year had been halved to provide forces for the Western Front, onto the offensive. When he failed to break out of Gaza, Murray was replaced by General Edmund Allenby. For Allenby, who had blotted his copybook in Flanders, this was a demotion. The Middle East offered him an opportunity to redeem his reputation. Nicknamed 'the Bull' he brought drive, discipline and professionalism, which became dramatically evident when in August the War Cabinet ordered him to take advantage of the capture of Aqaba to attack the Turks.[16]

The Palestine campaign marks the second prong of the British advance in the Middle East, complementing the advance up the Tigris and Euphrates valleys to the east. It was unique in World War I in having a strong emotional resonance for a generation brought up on the Bible; this religious element appeared regularly in correspondence of both officers and men. One soldier wrote of 'a sense of being on familiar ground'. Allenby himself is described as having studied the Bible with the 'passionate absorption of one of Cromwell's Ironsides' and he based his plans on a study of Joshua's wars in the Old Testament.[17] He scored a major victory in September at the battle of Megiddo (the modern Armageddon), took Jaffa on 16 November, and Jerusalem on 9 December.

A painting entitled *Allenby before Jerusalem* foregrounds the General mounted on a very fine large horse, with the Holy City in the background. It's a victory picture, redolent of imperial power. In fact Allenby's entry into the world's most fought-over city, filmed for the widest possible audience, was carefully choreographed. The General went on foot, in deliberate contrast with the Kaiser, who on his 1898 visit had ridden into the city wearing a white cloak and plumed helmet. It also helped downplay the fact that, as a *Punch* cartoon underlined, this was the first time Christian forces had taken Jerusalem since it had been lost to Saladin in AD 1187.[18] Georges-Picot, who had accompanied Allenby's force, immediately announced his intention to set up a civil government in Jerusalem. It provided one of the rare comic moments of the war. According to Lawrence,

> A silence followed, as when they opened the seventh seal in heaven. Salad, chicken mayonnaise and foie gras sandwiches hung in our wet mouths unmunched, while we turned to Allenby and gaped. Even he seemed for a moment at a loss [...] But his face grew red: he swallowed, his chin coming forward (in the way we loved) whilst he said, grimly, 'In the military zone, the only authority is that of the Commander-in-Chief, myself.'[19]

The fall of Jerusalem prevented a Turkish counterattack in Mesopotamia and established a base from which Turkish forces could be expelled from Syria. But its immediate impact, coming shortly after Passchendaele, one of the bloodiest battles in Flanders, was on morale. As after Tel-el-Kebir in 1882, church bells were rung. 'Te Deums' were sung at St Paul's and Westminster cathedral. Speaking to parliament on 20 December, Lloyd George referred to the 'most famous city in the world' having 'fallen into the hands of the British army, never to be restored to those who so successfully held it against the embattled hosts of Christendom'.[20]

Who then would inherit this emotionally resonant, strategically important, contested land? A month earlier, Arthur Balfour had written a letter to a leader of the Jewish community in Britain, Lord Rothschild. In it the Foreign Secretary had declared that His Majesty's Government 'view with favour the establishment in Palestine of a national home for the Jewish people and will use their best endeavours to facilitate the achievement of this object'. The Balfour Declaration, as it became known, is the third and final document in the preliminary wartime division of the Ottoman Empire. It differs in several respects from the two other British wartime promissory notes. It was public rather than secret, and covered a relatively small, if ill-defined area. It provided for something unique in the Middle East, namely the creation of a European settler colony.[21] One of the great markers of Jewish history, it was perhaps the most audacious, and certainly the most disruptive British initiative in the Middle East, an act of historical imagination and political myopia. Lloyd George's biographer, John Grigg, describes it as 'one of the most fateful decisions' of the Lloyd George premiership, which for Britain proved an 'unmitigated curse'.[22]

Historically and geographically, the Zionists were outside claimants to the Ottoman succession. They were a European movement, born of a combination of European nationalism and anti-Semitism, whose claim dated back to biblical times. The motives which now turned the nineteenth-century dreams of Lord Shaftesbury and George Eliot's Daniel Deronda into a political promise were complex. David Gilmour writes of 'those strange combinations of romanticism and strategic reasoning, zealotry and altruism, pro-Jewish sympathy and professed anti-Semitism that were converting so many leading politicians – Balfour, Lloyd-George and Milner above all – into champions of the idea of a Jewish homeland in Palestine'.[23]

Balfour himself, like Lloyd George, had been brought up with the Old Testament. A lifelong study of Jewish history had created a sense of remorse about Christianity's treatment of the Jews, whom he regarded as 'the most gifted race in the world'. And yet as prime minister he had restricted Jewish immigration to Britain, and had once told the Zionist leader, Chaim Weizmann, that he shared Cosima Wagner's 'anti-semitic postulates'.[24]

Sentiment, however, especially at a time when the war was expected to continue into 1919 or 1920, with Britain bearing the brunt of the fighting, was inevitably eclipsed by calculation, or rather in this particular case, miscalculation. The immediate wartime advantage which the Balfour Declaration was hoped to confer was that of propaganda. British ministers and officials, like those in other belligerent countries, had an exaggerated view of Jewish financial and political influence, notably in the United States and Russia. Lloyd George shared a widespread belief that, following US entry in April 1917, several powerful Jewish leaders were inhibiting the United States from pulling its weight in the war. Even more important was presumed Jewish influence in Russia in the wake of the February Kerensky coup. Russian defection from the war threatened to release German troops to fight on the Western Front and Turkish troops to move against the British in the Middle East. Many of the Bolshevik leaders were of Jewish origin, and despite warnings from the British minister in Petrograd that there was no great enthusiasm for Zionism among Russian Jews, ministers hoped that Russian Jewry would keep Kerensky in the war, and prevent the Russian grain trade, which was largely in Jewish hands, being diverted to break the blockade of Germany.[25]

The promise of a Jewish homeland also offered a more tangible strategic advantage. Following the Turkish attack on Suez, Palestine came to be seen as providing an essential strategic buffer for the canal. 'In the long run,' wrote a military commentator in the *Manchester Guardian*, in 1915, 'there can be no satisfactory defence of Egypt or the Suez Canal so long as Palestine is in the occupation of a hostile or possibly hostile Power.'[26]

The international regime envisaged in the Sykes–Picot agreement was regarded in London as unsatisfactory. Far better in Lloyd George's view, to promote the Zionists, who might develop as a prosperous community within the British Empire, bound to Britain, as Leo Amery, who helped draft the declaration, put it, 'by ties of gratitude and interest'.[27] Amery, along with the South African prime minister, General Jan Christian Smuts, saw Palestine as the missing territorial link which would allow the Empire to form a continuous chain from the Atlantic to the middle of the Pacific.[28] The year 1917 was the last time British imperialists thought in such sweeping terms.

All this assumed that a *modus vivendi* could be established between the Jews and the local Arabs, who in 1917 constituted some 92 per cent of the population. This was not a view shared by the Turks, who were well aware of Arab hostility to the existing Jewish population, and believed that further Zionist settlement would inflame the Arabs against the Jews. At least six hundred anti-Zionist articles had appeared in ten leading Arab papers between 1908 and 1914.[29] One minister in London, Curzon, knew the country. In late October Curzon produced a far-sighted memorandum in which he warned that the local Arab population 'will not be content either to be expropriated for Jewish immigration, or to act merely as hewers of wood and drawers of water to the latter'. Curzon went on to point out the difficulties which would arise if Jerusalem were to become a capital of a Jewish state. The most that could be realised, in his view, was the establishment of some kind of European, but not Jewish administration in Palestine; machinery to safeguard Jewish and Christian Holy Places; securing the same civil and religious rights for the Jews as for other elements of the population; and land purchases for Jewish immigrants.[30]

At the subsequent Cabinet meeting, at which, according to the minutes, his warnings were largely ignored, he spoke of the danger of raising false expectations which could never be realised.[31] The Cabinet appears to have assumed that the problem could be taken care of by introducing into the final draft of the declaration the critical rider 'providing that nothing shall be done which may prejudice the civil and religious rights of existing non-Jewish communities in Palestine'. This paper formula glossed over the facts that Britain was making two irreconcilable promises, that the promise to the Jews implied a dramatic change in the balance between the two local communities, and that no formal assessment had been made as to the problems and risks this would create.

Five days after Balfour's letter to Rothschild, one of the most experienced British officials in Cairo, Gilbert Clayton, wrote, 'Experience such as I have gained in this war impels me to deprecate strongly incautious declarations and visionary agreements. We are like men walking through an unknown country in a fog and it behoves us to feel our way and take care of each step we take.'[32] Yet the irony of the Balfour Declaration is not that the government was too imaginative, but that it had been insufficiently so – that it had failed to think through the consequences of policy. Part of the explanation lies in the improvisation and short-term thinking attendant on war.[33] But there was also the fact that as fellow Europeans, the Zionists evoked more sympathy in London than did the Arabs. In Balfour's blunt words, Zionism was 'of far profounder import than the desires and prejudices of the 700,000 Arabs who now inhabit that ancient land'.[34] Perhaps there was a racist element here. Perhaps it had as much to do with the lack of serious historical contact between Britain and the Arab world and the fact that very little was known about the inhabitants of Palestine at the time.[35] What is certain is that none of the ministers or officials had any inkling of the chain of events in Europe which within three decades would render British control of Palestine untenable.

The Balfour Declaration enjoyed an excellent press, but the day it was published news reached London of Lenin's *coup d'état*. Russia then left the war, effectively negating one of the key motives for the Balfour Declaration. The disintegration of Russian armies in Persia caused a degree of panic in London. At a meeting of the War Cabinet on 21 March 1918, as Ludendorff's forces broke through the British lines on the Western Front, Sir Henry Wilson, Chief of Imperial General Staff, spoke of a 'grave menace to the British Empire created by the collapse of Russia in the Middle East'.[36] The Director of Military Intelligence at the War Office warned that the Russians were ready to 'hand over central Asia to the Germans'.[37]

Until the Revolution, the British had relied on their old Russian rivals to guard the northern gateway to India in Persia and protect Mesopotamia's northern flank. Both were now endangered. The Germans had entered the Ukraine, and planned to use thousands of German and Austrian prisoners of war freed in Transcaspia for an invasion of India. The Turks meanwhile launched a campaign towards Baku with the long-term aim of raising *jihad* among Muslims in central Asia and northern India. Indian troops therefore took over the Russian sector of the East Persia corridor, established in 1915 to seal off Persia's eastern border and to prevent German agents moving into Afghanistan. A small expedition under Major-General Charles Dunsterville, the model for one of Kipling's characters, Stalky, was sent from Baghdad to Tiflis and Baku on the Caspian Sea. It met with considerable resistance, but remained in Persia until 1921.[38]

Yet it was the release of German forces for the Western Front, following the Russian defection from the Alliance, which had the greatest military impact in the Middle East. In February, against Wilson's advice, the Supreme War Council, which directed the Anglo-French war effort, had determined that decisive action for 1918 should be on the Turkish Front, with the Western Front remaining on the defensive.[39] Ludendorff's offensive, however, compelled Allenby to surrender a third of his troops to the Western Front. The only significant advance in the Middle East before the autumn was the capture of Kirkuk. It was not until September therefore that Allenby was able to resume the offensive into Syria, reaching Damascus by the beginning of October.

The war ended with the British in control of all former Turkish territories in the Middle East, and a consequent marked increase in Anglo-French tensions. The Sykes–Picot agreement had never been popular in either Cairo or Whitehall, and as British armies, accompanied only by a largely token French brigade, advanced into Syria, Lloyd George became determined to ensure revision in Britain's favour. Allenby was authorised to allow the Arab flag to fly over Damascus, and to hand the administration of the city over to Feisal, which the Foreign Office believed essential to exclude French claims. Anglo-French jockeying for position was again evident when Britain alone negotiated the Mudros armistice, which the Turks signed on 30 October, and in the subsequent entry of a British naval squadron into Constantinople on 12 November. Vice-Admiral Somerset Calthorpe, the British commander in the Aegean, had previously warned that the effect of a fleet under French command would be 'deplorable'. Mosul, which lay in the French zone influence under the Sykes–Picot agreement, was occupied by the British in a last-minute dash at the end of the war. The motive was oil.[40]

To the so-called 'Westerners', the Middle East had always been a sideshow. The war was certainly eventually won on the Western Front, with the Middle East (excluding the Gallipoli operation) tying up two million troops, including 456,000 Indians. This is a substantial figure, not least when compared with the fact that 5.4 million fought on the Western Front, where it is at least arguable that these Middle Eastern forces would have been better employed.[41] Yet as Lloyd George had pointed out when informing parliament about the capture of Jerusalem, the British Empire owed a great deal to sideshows.[42] This one was unique. Britain had never taken such a substantial part of an empire before. In the end, at least, the generals came out with more credit than the diplomats and politicians, although as Bruce Westrate notes, 'one's surprise is not that the men who had to deal with these complexities made mistakes, but that they did not make more'.[43]

The human cost was high. British (i.e. British and Indian) forces had incurred nearly 100,000 casualties in Iraq, 30,000 of whom had died, and some 58,000 in the campaigns in Egypt, Palestine and Syria.[44] The local populations had suffered badly during the conflict. There had been serious devastation in the main areas of fighting, namely Palestine and parts of Iraq. Able-bodied men had been conscripted and draft animals confiscated. In much of Lebanon and Palestine the wooded mountains and hills had been completely deforested, and many fruit and citrus groves lost. Syria and Lebanon had experienced serious famine.[45] One estimate puts the decrease in Palestine's population due to war-related causes at over 80,000.[46]

Politically the Middle East experienced the greatest upheaval since the arrival of the Ottomans in the sixteenth century. The Turks were driven out, and for the first time in their history, important centres of Arab civilisation including Damascus and Baghdad came under European control.[47] Arab nationalism, a very recent movement previously confined to secret societies in Damascus and Baghdad, was significantly strengthened, while Zionism had received a critical boost. But, as the next chapter underscores, the British and French were the most immediate beneficiaries.

7

'Present at the Creation'

Syria, Iraq, Transjordan, Palestine and Persia, 1918–21

The American Secretary of State, Dean Acheson, entitled his memoirs *Present at the Creation*. Acheson held high office at one of the most creative periods in American foreign policy, when American diplomats created a stable new order in Western Europe out of the wreckage of World War II. The same image had previously occurred to British officials trying to establish a new Middle Eastern order after World War I. 'I feel at times like the Creator about the middle of the week. He must have wondered what it is going to be like, as I do', the Oriental Secretary, Gertrude Bell, recorded in Baghdad as she and her colleagues set about the task of state creation.[1] Lawrence wrote of playing with kings and prime ministers.[2] Yet while Bell, Lawrence, Lloyd George and Churchill were all figures of stature, British ministers and officials had much less cause for satisfaction than Acheson. If British interests were safeguarded, at least in the short term, the map of the Middle East which emerged from the peace making of 1918–21 was to prove the cause of much political instability and violence over the following century.

From the British perspective, the most important questions in 1918 were how much they wanted for themselves, and in what form they would take it. Some ministers were opposed to further territorial expansion. Speaking at a meeting of the Cabinet's Eastern Committee in December 1918, Edwin Montagu, Secretary of State for India, complained of drifting into a position 'that right from the east to the west there is only one possible solution to all our difficulties, namely that Great Britain should accept responsibility for all these countries'.[3] Churchill believed East and West Africa offered far better opportunities for imperial development than the Middle East.[4] But these were minority views. Having made such a heavy investment in blood, the majority of British ministers and officials wanted their reward. None more so than Lloyd George. An adviser to the British delegation to the Versailles peace conference overheard the Prime Minister musing aloud: 'Mesopotamia ... yes ... oil ... irrigation ... we must have Mesopotamia; Palestine ... yes ... the Holy Land ... Zionism ... we must have Palestine; Syria ... h'm ... what is there in Syria? Let the French have that.'[5] Other ministers sought to exploit the opportunity created by Turkey's defeat and Russia's implosion to ensure against a recrudescence of the latter's power, and to strengthen the forward defences of India.

This would be the last imperial settlement – some would say carve-up – of the European imperial era. The spirit was that of Curzon and Salisbury. Who got what was determined on the basis of power rather than principle. To the victor the spoils. But the form in which the gains were made reflected the 'new diplomacy' of President Woodrow Wilson, in what was the first significant American challenge to British power in the Middle East. The first British colony to seize its independence, the US had a deep-rooted dislike of imperialism. Outlining his Fourteen Points in January 1918, Wilson declared the days of conquest and aggrandisement to be over. There was to be

> free, open-minded, and absolutely impartial adjustment of all colonial claims, based upon a strict observance of the principle that in determining all such questions of sovereignty the interests of the populations concerned must have equal weight with the equitable claims of the government whose title is to be determined.

As to the Ottoman Empire, the non-Turkish peoples 'should be assured an undoubted security of life and an absolutely unmolested opportunity of autonomous development'.[6]

Although Wilson proved unable to impose his ideas on his European allies, whose behaviour at the peace conference disgusted him, he had struck a powerful international chord. Even Sir Mark Sykes acknowledged in March 1918 that the world had moved on since his agreement with Picot, which could now 'only be considered a reactionary measure'.[7] In November the British and French felt it necessary to declare publicly that the end for which the two countries had prosecuted the war had been 'the complete and definitive liberation of the peoples long oppressed by the Turks and the establishment of national governments and administrations drawing their authority from the initiative and free choice of the indigenous populations'.[8] This was not, as events proved, to be taken at face value, not least because part of the British motive in issuing the declaration had been to try to undermine French claims to Syria. In Curzon's words,

> If we cannot get out of our difficulties in any other way we ought to play self-determination for all it is worth wherever we are involved in difficulties with the French, the Arabs or anybody else, and leave the case to be settled by that final argument, knowing in the bottom of our hearts that we are more likely to benefit from it than is anybody else.[9]

Wilson's main influence, therefore, was reflected in the new concept of League of Nations mandates, designed to square the President's insistence on the principle of self-determination with the European powers' determination to add to their existing empires. To many they were simply a means of draping the crudity of conquest in a veil of morality. That was the view certainly in Baghdad, where in June 1922 *Al-Istiqlal* declared that 'we do not reject the mandate because of its name but because its meaning is destructive of independence'.[10] Nevertheless, mandatory powers were accountable for their administrations of the new territories to the League of Nations. Category A mandates, which included those for the Middle East, were for countries nearly ready to run their own affairs. The prospect for independence, in other words, was explicitly recognised, with the power of the mandatory being only temporary.[11]

Much would depend on the development of Arab nationalism. This could only be exacerbated by the imposition of British hegemony in the place of an Ottoman Empire, which had excited relatively little opposition and had at least the advantage of being Muslim.[12] The time had gone, as Major Hubert Young at the Foreign Office noted in 1920,

> when an Oriental people will be content to be nursed into self-government by a European Power. The spread of Western education, increased facilities of communication, and above all the War, with the resultant emergence of the Wilsonian principle of self-determination, have combined to breed in the minds of Eastern agitators, a distrust for, and impatience of, Western control. We cannot ignore this universal phenomenon without endangering, and possibly losing beyond possible recall, our position in the East.

The problem was not, in Young's condescending view, insoluble, so long as Britain was careful to distinguish between the wild cries of the extremist, anxious to secure for himself and deny to the foreigner what he regards as the spoils of government, and the childish vanity of the masses on which he brings his armoury to bear. If we could but descend to tickling that vanity ourselves, we should deprive the agitator of his most powerful weapon.[13]

Young's solution, which was to work for the next two decades, was the recognition of native governments, and then entering into treaty relationship with them.

There were two more immediate constraints on British policy. The disadvantages of some of the wartime agreements were becoming clear. British ministers and officials believed that they had conceded too much to the French. In the opinion of the General Staff, it was difficult to see how any arrangement 'could be more objectionable from the military point of view than the Sykes–Picot agreement [...] by which an enterprising and ambitious foreign power [i.e. France] is placed on interior lines with reference to our position in the Middle East'.[14] There was talk of confining the French to the narrowest possible limit of Arab land, preferably in the region of Beirut. At the same time there was a belated appreciation of the contradictions between the various British promises as they affected Syria and Palestine and the Zionists and Palestinians.[15]

The other pressing constraint was military overstretch. In 1918 British power in the Middle East was at its apogee. More than a million British and imperial troops now occupied the Ottoman Empire.[16] Forces on this scale could not be sustained for any length of time. The rapid demobilisation of 1919, however, occurred against a background of emergencies across the world, stretching from India, via Egypt and Turkey, to Ireland, all of which were tying up British troops. The press, led by Lord Northcliffe's *Times* and *Daily Mail*, believed they had found a useful stick with which to beat Lloyd George. A *Times* editorial of 18 July 1921 complained that while nearly £150 million had been spent since the Armistice on 'semi-nomads in Mesopotamia', the government could only find £200,000 a year for the regeneration of British slums, and had to forbid all expenditure under the 1918 Education Act.[17]

If these weren't handicaps enough, the continued division of responsibility for the region between government departments was now further exacerbated by the division of government between London and the peacemakers in Paris. This made for endless discussion without resolution. Nor did it help that Lloyd George had a habit of acting without reference to his advisers, departments or prepared positions.[18]

The Middle East was but one of a series of immensely complex problems facing the peacemakers. The broad outline of the settlement in the Middle East was not evident until the San Remo conference of April 1920. Here the British and French effectively awarded themselves mandates over Iraq (as Mesopotamia now came to be known), Palestine and Syria. As Curzon told the House of Lords, the gift of mandates lay not with the League, but 'with the powers who have conquered the territories, which it then falls on them to distribute'.[19] It was only at a conference of British officials and experts held in Cairo in March 1921 and chaired by the Colonial Secretary, Winston Churchill, that the question of rulers was decided, with the award of the Iraqi and Transjordanian thrones to two of Hussein's sons.

Although British policy makers saw linkages between the various ex-Ottoman territories, there was little by way of overview of policy towards the region, and the outcomes are best understood on a country by country basis. Feisal and the French were immediately at odds over Syria. At issue was not simply a territorial dispute between two rival claimants, but the first political contest between a European imperial power and a claimant standing on the rights of self-determination. As Feisal told Lloyd George, he 'could not stand before the Muslim world and say that he had been asked to wage a war against the Caliph of the Muslims and now see the European powers divide the Arab country'.[20]

With Woodrow Wilson reluctant or unable to turn his stirring rhetorical support for self-determination into political reality, Feisal was almost totally dependent on the British. Having committed themselves to both sides, they equivocated and wriggled. The French prime minister, Georges Clémenceau, who was primarily concerned with security against Germany, had little interest in empire. In December 1918 he had been willing to agree to British control of Palestine and Mosul, the latter with the important proviso that French companies would have a share of oil rights there. But he assumed that Damascus and Aleppo would be his *quid pro quo*. Syria was one question he could not politically afford to concede. Strong Catholic interests were determined to ensure that France retained its historic 'presence' in the Middle East, while the war had demonstrated France's vital interest in empire for manpower, money and raw materials. 'No other nation other than France', wrote Maurice Barres in the *Echo de Paris*, in a comment which would certainly not have been approved by any official English reader, 'possesses in so high a degree, the particular kind of friendship and genius which is required to deal with the Arabs [...] If England wishes to give a kingdom to this Amir, let him set up in Baghdad.'[21]

Lloyd George nevertheless seemed determined to try to deny the French their one Middle Eastern prize. His military advisers wanted a rail and air link between Palestine and Iraq across Syrian territory for imperial communications. Allenby warned of the risk that a French mandate would lead to a war between France and the Arabs. Besides, the Prime Minister admired Feisal, and believed that he had been promised at least the interior of Syria, and that French rule would be more oppressive than British rule in Palestine and Iraq. For much of 1919, therefore, the British tried either to reconcile the two parties, or to get the French to change policy, and even withdraw. This led to some furious exchanges between Clémenceau and Lloyd George. It was on one of these occasions that Clémenceau accused Lloyd George of being a cheat.[22]

In the face of French intransigence, by autumn the British opted for France. They could no longer afford to keep an army of occupation in Syria. Moreover, as Sir Arthur Hirtzel, Permanent Under-Secretary in the India Office, put it, 'If we support the Arabs in this matter, we incur the ill-will of France; and we have to live and work with France all over the world.'[23] British troops were withdrawn on 1 November 1919. The garrisons in Homs, Hama, Aleppo and Damascus were handed over to Feisal, those on the Syrian littoral went to the French. Feisal felt deserted. He complained of being handed over 'tied by feet and hands' to the French, insisting that Syria was 'no more a chattel to be used for political bargaining than is liberated Belgium'.[24]

The British advised Feisal to come to terms with the French; he was unable to do so. In March 1920 the Syrian General Congress declared the country independent within its 'natural boundaries' including Lebanon and Palestine. This earned a firm rebuke from Curzon, who pointed out firmly where power lay. 'These countries were conquered by the Allied Armies, and their future [...] can only be determined by the Allied Powers acting in concert.'[25] The French were nevertheless subjected to guerrilla attacks along the coast and denied the use of Aleppo, which was being used in support of French troops in Cicilia fighting Mustapha Kemal. In July 1920, not very surprisingly, the Hashemite leader was expelled. Syria, declared Alexandre Millerand, the new French premier, would henceforward be held by France 'the whole of it, and forever'.[26] British officers who had served with Feisal were deeply embarrassed to see their former comrades 'thrashed and trampled down', as Churchill put it. But there was also a certain relief that the French had extinguished the fiercest source of agitation in the Arab world. French resentment against the British over the affair proved long-lived.[27]

If Syria had been a diplomatic embarrassment, it nevertheless proved much less of a political headache than Iraq, whose future became the source of acute controversy. In 1918 Iraq was 'a ruinously neglected semi-desert, semi-swamp of 171,599 square miles. Its population of some three million inhabitants was a festering agglomeration of sectarian and social rivalries.'[28] It was by far the most expensive British commitment in the Middle East. In September 1919 there were still 25,000 British and 81,000 Indian troops in the country, the size of the garrison partly reflecting the Turkish threat to Mosul. But there were also inefficiencies which the press soon picked up on, with *The Times* running a campaign for withdrawal. Iraq became a prominent issue in the 1922 election; indeed, between 1920 and 1924 something like a national debate was held over whether Britain should remain.[29]

All of this worried ministers sufficiently to come close to a decision for withdrawal. The cost of garrisoning the country seemed out of proportion to its value.[30] But Iraq was one of Britain's few wartime gains, and the Prime Minister was 'on general principles' against a policy of scuttle. Besides, there was the prospect of oil. The British were determined not to continue their heavy wartime reliance on American oil. The Mosul oil fields were regarded as potentially the biggest in the world. Imperial oil consumption was estimated to reach 10 million tons, but Persia and the Empire would only produce 2.5 million tons. It was therefore regarded as imperative that Britain should obtain undisputed control of as much production as possible.[31]

If British power and influence were to be retained therefore, three key issues had to be resolved. Should the three former Turkish *vilayets* of Basra, Baghdad and Mosul be ruled directly by Britain, or indirectly through a nominally independent Arab ruler? If the latter, who should that ruler be? And, most important of all, could all three be welded together as a cohesive, viable state? Historically the *vilayets* had been administered separately, with their own *valis* in direct contact with Istanbul. Iraq had neither a natural capital, a single administrative system nor a ruling class. Mosul looked more to Aleppo and southern Turkey than to Baghdad; Basra had long-established connections with India and the Gulf, while Baghdad was the centre of the Persian transit trade. A unitary state, an awkward creation at best, would have to be imposed against the wishes and traditions of the individual provinces. In addition to the sectarian divisions previously noted, some 600,000 Kurds had been added with the Mosul *vilayet*. The nearest to a common denominator was the Arabic language, which was not however spoken by the Kurds.[32]

Although there had been early talk during the war of annexing Basra, by 1918 it had become clear that, thanks to Woodrow Wilson, taking over the country was no longer a political option. This message had not, however, got through to the man on the spot. The Acting Civil Commissioner, Lt-Colonel Arnold Wilson, was a determined proponent of direct rule. Wilson stands as the Middle Eastern prototype of the British official failing to adapt to changing times in the Middle East. Described by his biographer as a late Victorian, this highly energetic Indian army officer was an unabashed imperialist who wanted to see a protectorate established in Iraq. Like Cromer in Egypt, he had little time or understanding for local nationalism. The country, as Wilson saw it, was neither ready for self-government, nor indeed wanted it. The average Arab, as opposed to the 'amateur politician' in Baghdad, he conveniently believed, saw the future in terms of fair dealing and material and moral progress under the aegis of Great Britain. To install 'a real Arab government' in Mesopotamia was impossible; if Britain attempted to do so, 'we shall abandon the Middle East to anarchy'.[33]

This view was not shared by the more perceptive Gertrude Bell. She was once described as the most powerful woman in the British Empire. The fact that there was little competition does not detract from her real accomplishments. The first woman to take a First in Modern History at Oxford, she was a distinguished traveller and prewar intelligence officer in the Middle East, plus a translator of the Persian poet, Hafez. On her death in 1925, one nationalist Iraqi paper praised 'the true sincerity of her patriotism, free from all desire for personal gain, and the zeal for the interests of her country which illuminated the service of this noble and incomparable woman', citing her as 'an example to all men of Iraq'.[34] Bell, who had her ear much closer to the ground than Wilson, believed that nationalism was gaining an unstoppable momentum. From London, Hirtzel warned that Wilson appeared to,

> be trying impossibly to turn the tide instead of guiding it into the channel that will suit you best. You are going to have an Arab state whether you like it or not [...] it is of no use to shut one's eyes to the main facts. We must adapt ourselves and our methods to the new order of ideas and find a different way of getting what we want.

And again, echoing Young, 'is it not better to do voluntarily what one will sooner rather than later be compelled to do?'[35]

But if more far-sighted officials did not like Wilson's approach, ministers were dangerously slow to impose their more realistic ideas on the Civil

Commissioner. Disagreements between departments, as also between the British and French, along with the delay in making peace with Turkey, all contributed to procrastination.[36] This allowed time for tribal unrest to boil over into a major revolt in 1920. Iraq was a traditionally rebellious society, with a lot of arms left over from the Ottoman era. The immediate causes of this revolt were complex, in part local, in part the result of nationalist propaganda emanating from Syria. In part too this was a reaction against a British administration which failed to take account of local custom, believing rather in the need for the British virtues of order and discipline. And there was also a religious element – Iraq's new masters were Christian infidels.[37] The British response was one of bewilderment. In his memoirs the commander, General Sir Aylmer Haldane, who had insisted on going on leave despite warnings of potential trouble, could only speculate on the 'strangely subtle mind' of the Arab, a being 'so vain, so given to exaggerate, and so susceptible to propaganda' that it was 'extremely difficult for a European to understand him'.[38]

The disturbances lasted seven months, affecting a third of the countryside, but did not spread to the major towns. The police and gendarmerie remained loyal, and fortunately for the British, there was nothing by way of unified tribal organisation. Some 40,000 reinforcements were brought in from India, and the revolt was put down by the time-honoured methods of the Indian frontier, with punitive expeditions, a strong show of force to overwhelm the tribes, as well as a new weapon in the form of aircraft. According to British figures some 2,200 British and Indian troops, and some 8,450 Iraqis were killed or injured. The sheer size of the territory which needed to be retaken and secured meant that the cost was around £40 million. The 'Revolution of 1920', as it became known in Iraq, acquired a special place in the nationalist mythology of the modern state. Generations of Iraqi schoolchildren grew up learning how nationalist heroes stood up to foreign armies in towns like Faluja, Baquba and Najaf. During Shi'a demonstrations against the advance of ISIS in Iraq in 2014, pitchforks, symbols of the 1920 revolt, were brandished.[39] One of the revolt's most lasting damaging consequences was to bring the old differences between Sunni and Shi'a back to the surface.[40]

Wilson left Baghdad in 1920, to be replaced by Sir Percy Cox. A patient, determined and insightful man, Cox could sit through hours of small talk, gradually steering the conversation in the direction he wanted it to go. Feisal's biographer describes him as having an unparalleled knowledge of Arab affairs and 'the rare ability to see into the motives of people from a radically different culture'.[41] His instructions were both to appease the nationalists and preserve British influence. He immediately implemented a policy of handing over control to a provisional Arab government with British advisers, while continuing to exercise an authority over Iraqi ministers which was no less real for being discreet. The British objective, in Hirtzel's inimitably cynical words, was 'some modicum of Arab institutions, which we can safely leave while pulling the strings ourselves, something which won't cost very much'.[42]

The British were looking for a king. Churchill believed that in the Middle East, as elsewhere, British interests 'were best served by friendship and cooperation with the party of monarchy and tradition'.[43] But they wanted an amenable ruler, someone content to reign but not rule. They also wanted to avoid a political system which would provide the majority Shi'a population, who were hostile to the British, with a political majority.[44] The obvious answer seemed to be Feisal, who, according to Wilson 'alone of all Arabian potentates has any idea of practical difficulties of running a civilized government on Arab lines'.[45] There was certainly no local candidate capable of mobilising support to transcend differences in regional loyalty and sectarian affiliation. Choosing Feisal had the additional advantages of easing bad British consciences over his treatment in Syria, restoring Britain's good name in the region, and, by no means the least important consideration, putting him under an obligation to the British.[46] The main problem was the objections of the French, and at least part of the reason for insisting that Feisal should be locally elected, an odd procedure for a monarch, was the need to try to present him to the French as a popular choice.

The authorities did not feel it necessary to be particularly scrupulous in how they went about ensuring the success of his election, which, as Churchill had put it, would require careful study in order to avoid 'confused or meaningless expression of Mesopotamian opinion'.[47] An excuse was found to arrest Sayyid Talib, Feisal's main local rival, and exile him to Ceylon. The new King Feisal, elected by a suspiciously large 96 per cent, was duly crowned on 23 August 1921, flanked by the British High Commissioner, as the band played 'God Save the King'. The official photo underscored where the real power behind the throne lay. As Justin Marozzi writes,

> Feisal, a slight man, is a shrunken figure, dwarfed by the high-backed throne and the towering figures of Cox, Cornwallis and [General] Haldane, who stand around him. The preponderance of military hats, topees and ladies' sunhats in the front row likewise make Britain's driving role unmistakeable.[48]

Feisal's new kingdom comprised all three of the former Turkish *vilayets* which had come under British occupation, following Force D's advance from Basra in early 1915. In Arnold Wilson's prescient view, these would not form a coherent political entity. The Kurds would never accept an Arab ruler, nor would the Shi'a majority accept domination by the Sunni minority. Three-quarters of the country, moreover, was tribal without a previous tradition of obedience to any government. In addition there was the Jewish community which dominated the commercial life of Baghdad, and a substantial Christian community, including the Nestorian-Chaldean refugees from Turkey, the Assyrians, who had gathered in Mosul.[49]

Although alternatives were proposed – Lawrence at one point suggested separate emirates for Baghdad and Basra – the main British debate had been whether to include Mosul in the new state. The problem was its predominantly Kurdish population. Under the Treaty of Sèvres, signed in August 1920, the Kurds had initially been promised autonomy. Opinion at the Cairo conference as to whether to include Mosul was divided, with a strong feeling that Kurdistan should not be brought under an Arab government and should even be made into a buffer between Iraq and a resurgent Turkey. The issue was also hotly contested in parliament and in *The Times*. But if Mosul was to be independent, Iraq's future was economically and strategically compromised. Mosul was essential to Iraq not just for its oil potential, but also as an important grain-growing area, as well as rendering the rest of the country militarily much more defensible. In the end the economic and strategic factors were judged as outweighing this important further addition to Iraqi heterogeneity.[50]

Palestine raised the even more tricky question of whether to confirm wartime policy. The risks were now becoming more evident. In June 1919, the Military Administrator, Sir Arthur Money, warned that fear and distrust of Zionist aims was growing daily and that a British mandate on the lines of the Zionist programme would require the indefinite retention of a military force considerably greater than those currently in the country. When Gertrude Bell visited Palestine in the autumn, she found that Zionism was virtually the only subject of discussion in Jerusalem.

> All the Moslems are against it and furious with us for backing it and all the Jews are for it and equally furious with us for not backing it enough […] I believe that if both [sides] would be responsible they would each of them have not very much to fear. But they won't be reasonable and *we are sowing the seeds of secular disturbance* as far as I can see.[51]

The first riots occurred in April 1920.

Yet neither warnings from those on the spot, nor the calls from the Northcliffe press to drop responsibility for Palestine, nor even the doubts of the Foreign Secretary, Lord Curzon, who believed that Palestine would prove 'a rankling thorn' in the flesh of the mandatory power, led to a reversal of policy. There was still the hope that Jewish–Arab tensions would diminish over time, not least once the economic advantages of Jewish immigration became clear. If Britain gave up the mandate, the French and Italians might step in. Besides, a public commitment had been made, which the government felt honour-bound to fulfil. Any retreat would, in Lloyd George's words in 1921, 'damage Britain's reputation in the eyes of the Jews of the world'.[52]

The Balfour Declaration was duly written almost verbatim into the preamble to the mandate, which alluded specifically to 'the historical connection of the Jewish people with Palestine'. Britain was obliged to secure the new Jewish homeland and use its best endeavours to facilitate Jewish immigration and encourage Jewish settlement of the land. Hebrew was recognised as an official language and a Jewish Agency established to cooperate with the mandatory authorities in the development of natural resources and the operation of public works and utilities. The mandatory award made no reference to the Arabs. In contrast to the Iraqi mandate, the British were invested with full power of legislation and administration. There was, in other words, no obligation for the British to ensure self-government, which could only have been on the basis of an Arab majority.[53]

Geographically, however, the newly mandated Palestinian territory was considerably smaller than the Zionists had hoped. The borders, as agreed with the French in December 1920, cut the country off from all its most important potential water resources, including the Litani, the northernmost sources of the Jordan, the spring of Hermon and the greater part of the Yarmuk rivers. They also left Palestine without natural geographical frontiers, a problem which was to have major repercussions when Israel gained independence in 1948.[54] In addition, the territory to the east of the River Jordan was hived off to an Arab ruler.

Transjordan, paradoxically the most successful of Britain's postwar creations, is the classic case of improvisation in state making, a political entity created to fill a political vacuum; it has been variously described as 'a romantic accident' and a political anomaly.[55] It had been in effect a blank space on the map, situated between Syria and the Hejaz, and Iraq and Palestine, a territory of neither economic nor strategic importance. Since

November 1918 it had come under Feisal's nominal rule from Damascus, but with his expulsion in July 1920, the future of this disorderly area was in doubt. The British feared that the French would use the excuse of some Sherifian officers having fled to Amman to occupy the territory, thereby extending French borders closer to Suez, even though under the San Remo agreement, this was part of the Palestine mandate.[56]

Keen to incorporate the territory into Palestine, Sir Herbert Samuel, the High Commissioner in Jerusalem, wanted to send troops, but this was ruled out in London, where there was no appetite for taking on new military commitments. Instead, six Arabic-speaking political officers and a small number of police were sent to maintain order among the tiny independent statelets which had emerged in the wake of the collapse of Feisal's Syrian kingdom. They had neither money nor troops at their disposal. But at least one British official, Sir Alec Kirkbride, who was sent to Kerak, where he set up the 'National Government of Moab', described the experience as fun.[57]

In early 1921 the situation was complicated by the arrival of Feisal's elder brother. Abdullah had been incensed by the choice of Feisal for Iraq and was now in search of a throne of his own. Welcomed in Transjordan, he quickly established a central administration in Amman. The British decided to make a virtue of necessity by giving him temporary recognition at the same time as Feisal was selected as king of Iraq. Unable to contemplate hostilities with Abdullah, they had no alternative but to cooperate with him. In Lawrence's view, Abdullah had the advantage of being 'not too powerful', was not an inhabitant of Transjordan, and 'relied on HMG for the retention of his office'.[58]

There were some doubts about his character, however, as well as French reaction. There were also questions as to whether Transjordan was not too small for a kingdom and should rather be regarded as 'an Arab province or adjunct of Palestine'. As a compromise it was decided that Abdullah was to stay for six months in Transjordan to prepare the way for the appointment of an Arab governor and British High Commissioner. He would accept British advisers and be given money and troops. In return he agreed not to mount any anti-French or anti-Zionist agitation, to cooperate in the establishment of secure conditions under the British mandate, and to assist in the opening of a trans-desert route to Iraq.[59] This provisional arrangement became permanent, and contrary to expectations the small and exposed kingdom with its Hashemite monarchy survived.

There was one unambiguous failure in British post-Middle East policy. Persia provided a cautionary tale of the dangers of leaving policy in the hands of a powerful expert with a bee in his bonnet, in this case the Foreign

Secretary, Lord Curzon. Perceptive about the dangers inherent in the Balfour Declaration, Curzon now got Persia badly wrong. He thought he saw an opportunity of implementing a long-held dream of protecting the approaches to India with a chain of vassal states from the Mediterranean to the Pamirs. Persia, which had long fascinated him, was an essential link. The security of the oil wells, and of Iraq's eastern border, were other considerations. It was vital therefore to prevent the country being overrun by the Bolsheviks, or becoming, in Curzon's words, 'a hotbed of misrule, enemy intrigue, financial chaos and political disorder'. 'These people', he also said, 'have got to be taught – at whatever cost to them – that they cannot get on without us. I don't at all mind their noses being rubbed in the dust.'[60] In 1919 an Anglo-Persian treaty was negotiated, which sought to reform and revive the country, while effectively giving Britain a free hand to the exclusion of all other powers. Britain would provide expert advisers, train and equip the army, provide a loan for necessary reforms, revise customs tariffs and help build railways.[61]

The fate of the Anglo-Persian treaty provides an unfortunate precedent for later British treaties with countries in the Middle East. It met with widespread opposition not only from the Americans, French and Russians, but more importantly, from all sectors of Persian society. Britain was seen as trying to turn Persia into a protectorate on the lines of Egypt. In the words of one Persian poet:

It is the story of cat and mouse, our pact with Britain,
Once it catches the mouse, how could the cat let it go?
Even if we be lion, she is the fox of our time,
The fox famously deceives the lion.[62]

The British were already unpopular because of their continued military presence in the country, partly intended, in the words of a War Office telegram, 'to support our Minister's policy at Tehran and to induce the Persian Government to subserve British interests'.[63] The secrecy with which the treaty had been negotiated, and knowledge that considerable bribes had been paid, along with a series of other examples of British interference in Persian affairs, increased local opposition. The treaty was never taken to the *Majlis* for ratification.

Despite warnings from the British Legation in Tehran that the country was in a prickly and nationalist mood, and wanted to be left alone and allowed to 'go to the devil in its own way', Curzon was taken by surprise. He had failed to appreciate that with the collapse of Russian power, it was the British who were now seen as the main threat. Moreover, believing, as his biographer David Gilmour puts it,

> that British policy was almost invariably beneficial to backward peoples, Curzon was astonished whenever the British turned out to be unpopular. He did not understand that the advisers might be resented by Persian nationalists, or that the British could conceivably be regarded as more of a threat than the Bolsheviks.[64]

The unfortunate minister, Herman Norman, who had made the mistake of speaking truth to power, was recalled from Tehran, and never subsequently re-employed.[65]

The treaty's failure proved a major turning point in the history of modern Persia, paving the way in February 1921 for a coup by a Cossack officer, Reza Khan (later Shah). The new government denounced the British treaty, while immediately signing a treaty with the Soviet Union. By the end of the year all remaining British troops had been withdrawn, and there was not a single British adviser in the country. Britain's long-term reputation in Persia had taken another serious knock.[66] It was a spectacular example of a British minister drastically overplaying his hand.

The postwar settlement brought to an end some 120 years of British expansion in the Middle East. Over the course of seven years the British had changed the political face of the region. New states and policies had emerged as much by accident as design, with inadequate consideration to their long-term viability. Nevertheless, judged in terms of their own objectives as they had gradually emerged during war and peace making, the British had done reasonably well. They had significantly extended their informal empire, gaining a strategic buffer for Suez and the prospects for access to a new source of oil in Iraq. They had renegotiated the Sykes–Picot agreement to their satisfaction, and compensated the Hashemites for their disappointments in Syria. But the costs – the Iraqi revolt and the quarrel with France over Syria – had been unnecessarily high, while the value of some of the new territory would prove questionable. Jordan was a very minor addition to the British Empire. Palestine would prove an albatross around the imperial British neck.

If the Zionist movement was the most obvious beneficiary of the settlement, the Kurds and the Arabs had good reason for discontent. True, two new Arab kingdoms had been created, and the Arab world was relatively nearer to independence than it had been in 1914. But this was an imposed peace. The British had not come as liberators, as General Maude had declared when taking Baghdad.[67] And, contrary to public Anglo-French promises, as well as Article 22 of the League Covenant, local opinion had scarcely been consulted. The two exceptions were a plebiscite in Iraq in which only the sheikhs, urban notables, religious leaders and educated classes were consulted, followed by Feisal's dubious election victory.[68] Arab territory had been either promised or handed over to outsiders, while the dream of Arab unity had been undermined by the lines the British and French had drawn on the Middle East map. According to George Antonius, author of the highly influential *The Arab Awakening*, published in 1938, the Arabs felt 'betrayed, and betrayed by their best friend'.[69] Feisal's biographer writes of Arab lands having been divided into 'unnatural and potentially adversarial states saddled with different forms of government'.[70]

Like the French, the Arabs were paying the price for their relatively minor contribution to the victory against the Turks. It had been a Hashemite as much as an Arab Revolt. It had never succeeded in mobilising Arab opinion against the Otttomans, and it was the Hashemites, rather than the wider Arab nation, who were the beneficiaries. To some extent, though, the Arabs were also unlucky. The timing of this great upheaval had been unpropitious. Peace had been made in a world still looking backward to the long era of unabashed European imperialism, while only just beginning to look forward to the era of self-determination. Had the Ottoman Empire collapsed after World War II, power might have passed directly to some form of Arab entity or entities, with different consequences for the region's future. Similarly, had Woodrow Wilson proved a more effective diplomat, or had his ideas had more time to establish themselves, the Arabs might have done much better out of the peace.

The long-term weakness of the settlement, evident only once British power went into terminal decline in the 1950s, was structural – the failure, in which the French shared, to provide for a system of viable and stable new states. The settlement, in Mohammed Heikal's words, had an air of 'improvisation and impermanence'.[71] That was in one sense inevitable; declaring new states was only the first stage in a long journey towards a sense of nationhood, whose success would depend more on local effort than on British support. Lloyd George's congratulations to Churchill in 1922, on turning 'a mere collection of tribes' into an Iraqi nation, were distinctly premature.[72] The real difficulty, however, lay in the fact that the Middle East was too much of an ethnic, religious and tribal mosaic to be naturally divided according to the prevailing model of homogeneous West European nation states. To reproduce the security for minorities provided by the Turkish *Millet* system, the new states had to be sufficiently strong and confident to be tolerant. But precisely because they were often heavily divided they proved unstable, insecure and intolerant. Three of the five British- and French-sponsored states into which the Ottoman inheritance was divided – Lebanon, Syria and Iraq – would suffer civil wars within the following century. This, more than the exact placement of the lines of the Sykes–Picot map, constituted the fundamental weakness of the settlement.

With the exception of Palestine, this was not a problem of British making or one which they could have easily resolved. Nor, however, did they make particular efforts to do so. It would prove almost everybody's misfortune that the conditions of Middle East peace making – the improvisation, the piecemeal nature of decision making, the rivalries with the French, the pressure of events and the preoccupations with economy – all militated against thorough consideration of long-term consequences or imaginative solutions. Acheson and his colleagues, albeit with the lessons of the failure of their predecessors, did better. There would be no second chance in the Middle East.

Part Two

On Borrowed Time, 1922–45

8

'*An Inferior Independence*'

Egypt, 1918–39

During the Paris peace conference, Augustus John painted a portrait of T.E. Lawrence, dressed in Arab robes, including a dagger. It resonated with the British public. According to Christine Riding, it distilled a Western orientalist desire for power over the Orient, while suggesting that that power in the figure of Lawrence would be exerted with 'knowledge, understanding and empathy'.[1] Elizabeth Monroe called the interwar period 'the years of good management', when 'the British were powerful, yet their policy was flexible'.[2] The British, Eugene Rogan writes, 'were efficient, inscrutable, orderly, technologically advanced and militarily strong'.[3]

By 1922 Britain's informal empire in the Middle East stretched from the Gulf to Egypt's western border. It was effectively unchallenged. If the French in Syria and Lebanon continued to harbour suspicions of British designs, they posed no threat to their Anglo-Saxon rivals. Of Britain's other former adversaries, the Soviet Union had retired to build socialism in one country, Atatürk was about to transform the defunct Ottoman Empire into the new secular Turkish state, and Germany was coping with the domestic consequences of defeat.

High noon, however, proved to be strikingly brief. British power in the Middle East was only as good as the Versailles peace settlement in Europe, which had left a thoroughly dissatisfied Germany with its power intact. Germany's future ally, Italy, meanwhile had its own grievances. Although wartime promises had been made to them, the Italians had gained nothing in the Middle East from the peace settlement, and from the early 1920s their new leader, Benito Mussolini, was casting a covetous eye across the Mediterranean. In the Middle East, there were the new problems of nationalism and the conflict between an assertive Zionism and a fearful local Palestinian population. Each of these regional and international factors had the potential to create serious difficulties for Britain; on a worst-possible-case scenario, which seemed remote in the 1920s, they might combine and feed off each other.

Until the mid-1930s when Italy became an overt threat, British policy focused around two main issues. One was the consolidation of the state system which had emerged from the Ottoman Empire, including the resolution of border disputes and nation building. The other was negotiation, in response to nationalist pressures, of the terms of an informal empire, which no longer could be simply imposed on the region. This latter lesson had first been learned the hard way in Egypt, which now demanded the end of the occupation. Between 1914 and 1918, Egypt and the Egyptians had been used, and from their viewpoint abused, in the prosecution of a war in which Egyptian interests were not involved. Many Egyptians would have been happy for Britain to have lost.[4] Although the country had suffered far less than Palestine or Iraq, martial law had been declared and hundreds of thousands of British and colonial troops had flooded into the country. Their behaviour frequently scandalised the population. There were also the inevitable price rises and food shortages. Contrary to an unwise early promise that they would not call on Egyptian aid, the British military had begun to make increasing demands, requisitioning food and draft animals, donkeys, buffalos and camels, which were of vital importance to the *fellahin*'s livelihood. In addition they had requisitioned manpower for service in the labour corps. The result was to transform Egyptian nationalism from a mainly educated elite urban movement into one commanding support across a broad cross-section of socio-economic classes.[5]

Having made a significant forced contribution to Britain's military expansion in the Middle East, the Egyptians expected their reward. Only two days after the armistice, a group of Egyptian notables, encouraged by Woodrow Wilson's championship of self-determination and the Anglo-French declaration of 8 November, presented demands for independence. The High Commissioner, Sir Reginald Wingate, was sympathetic, recognising the need to co-opt this new movement before it could harness the underlying anti-British sentiments of both rural and urban workers.[6] London, however, was in no mood to negotiate. Officials were too busy with the impending peace conference to worry about the Egyptians. Besides, allowing nationalist leaders regarded as having placed themselves at the head of 'a disloyal movement to expel the British from Egypt' could only be seen as a sign of weakness. 'There seemed no need to take the movement too seriously.'[7]

Events quickly belied this misjudgement. A new party, the Wafd, was formed under the leadership of a former Minister of Justice, Sa'd Zaghlul, with the aim of achieving independence through peaceful means. It was to become the predominant political party in Egypt over the next three decades, and the first serious political organised opposition movement Britain had encountered in the Middle East. In March 1919 the Acting High Commissioner, Sir Miles Cheetham, made the mistake of deporting Zaghlul and three other Wafdist leaders, without drawing up contingency plans against the possibility of public disorder. Egyptian historians refer to the events which followed as a revolution. Egyptians were no longer afraid of the British, and within a week of the arrests much of the country was paralysed by general strikes and rioting, with European quarters and citizens singled out for attack by angry crowds. Although the violence quickly died down in the countryside, from now on political volatility among students, public servants and some town-dwellers became a permanent feature of the political scene and an important element in British and Egyptian political calculations. The Egyptians suffered most; some 1,000 were killed compared with 36 British and Indian soldiers. It was the worst indigenous violence in British imperial territory since the Indian Mutiny of 1857, and a serious indictment of British policy.[8]

The British response had been bewilderment and dismay. But having mishandled the initial situation, their subsequent decisions were more realistic. A tough new High Commissioner, Lord Allenby, was appointed, who proceeded to release Zaghlul. As a soldier, Allenby recognised the basic sincerity of the emotions which had provoked the explosion, and saw no future in a policy of repression.[9] Nor did a man with equally impeccable imperialist credentials. The Colonial Secretary, Lord Milner, who knew the country well, had been sent out to Egypt to head a commission of enquiry. Despite, or perhaps to some extent because of the fact that the mission was boycotted by the Wafd, Milner came up with a radical solution. 'We have never honestly faced the Egyptian problem', his report stated, 'and our failure to do so is in a measure responsible for the present situation.'[10] British authority, Milner believed, should be confined 'to the narrowest limits possible'. Egypt should gain independence as a constitutional monarchy with representative institutions. Britain's strategic interests would be safeguarded by an Anglo-Egyptian agreement. The recommendations followed logically from the realisation that the status quo had become untenable, that Britain's strategic interests did not require it to 'own' Egypt, and that its interests were best protected by influence rather than domination.[11] Britain should no longer regard herself as being *in loco parentis* and should abandon its imperial mission in Egypt. The claim to represent some kind of higher civilisation was one of the casualties of the carnage of the trenches. As Gertude Bell wrote in 1920, 'The credit of European civilization is gone [...] How can we, who have managed our affairs so badly, claim to teach others to manage theirs better?'[12]

All this came as a considerable shock to imperial opinion, and met with strong opposition from Lloyd George and Churchill. This reaction was partly emotional, with some critics complaining of a surrender to Egyptian nationalism and a loss of imperial nerve. But there were also concerns about the precedent which would be set elsewhere in empire, as well as the distractions of crisis in Ireland.[13] Although negotiations with Zaghlul proved unsuccessful, they indicated that a deal on the lines of the Milner report might be possible, provided the question of Egyptian national status could be satisfactorily resolved. The Egyptians were ready to admit the principle of providing military facilities to Britain as an ally in war, though they bridled at the continuation of a peacetime British military presence. Zaghlul was again exiled in November 1921.

Allenby then proposed that Egypt be given independence without waiting for the conclusion of a treaty. The garrisons in Cairo and Alexandria, along with the Mediterranean Fleet, would, he believed, be sufficient guarantee of British interests. A deal on these lines would be supported by moderate politicians in return for British support for a liberal constitution. When the Cabinet balked, Allenby forced their hand with warnings of renewed violence and the threat of resignation.[14] After eight years, the Protectorate was withdrawn.

The year 1922 represents a milestone in the history of Anglo-Egyptian relations and the first occasion Britain had been forced to negotiate the terms of informal empire. It also represented a triumph of British pragmatism. In Curzon's words:

> Why worry about the rind if we can obtain the fruit? I take it that all we have in view is that Egypt should remain inside rather than outside the British Imperial system. If the best way to do this is to drop the word protectorate and conclude a treaty of alliance with her, as we did with the Indian princes a century or more ago [...] why not do it?[15]

Many Egyptian nationalists viewed independence, rather as Iraqis had viewed League of Nations mandates, as little more than a legal farce providing a camouflage for the continued British Raj. It was a view shared by at least one British official who privately wrote of Egypt getting 'an inferior independence'.[16] More moderate politicians saw it as a step in the right direction which would eventually lead to de facto recognition of

Egyptian rights. Both had a point. Egyptian nationalists had gained their first victory. They now had administrative control over their own country and, in consequence, the influence as well as the numbers of British officials began to decline. But four so-called 'reserved points' – the security of imperial communications, defence against external aggression, the protection of the foreign community and minorities, and the Sudan – were left entirely within British discretion pending the negotiation of a treaty. These were then used to deny Egyptian claims to League of Nations membership. British officials harboured doubts about the political practicality of using force should this again become necessary, but as Allenby had recognised, the threat remained a prospect Egyptians had to reckon with.[17]

Britain was still more than capable of protecting its interests in Egypt. It controlled the Egyptian army, which was kept short of arms and ammunition, along with the police, with Britons in senior command in the big cities and a British Chief of Police. The European Security Agency in the Ministry of the Interior, set up in 1921, enabled Britain to protect the foreign communities. Britain retained ample sources of intelligence. The remaining British advisers – Judiciary, Interior, Finance and the Inspector General of the Army, provided important listening posts in the Egyptian ministries. The Oriental Secretary, who knew Arabic and Turkish, kept in close touch with Egyptian opinion. At least one High Commissioner's wife, Lady Lampson, also picked up a good deal of information from the wives of the Egyptian politicians she met.[18]

The Residency continued to be a key player on the Egyptian political scene, courted by politicians of all parties, both government and opposition seeking support or favour, as well as complaining about one another.[19] All were well aware of its ability to make and break governments, as well as to blackball politicians. According to Lord Lloyd, who was High Commissioner in the late 1920s,

> It was not necessary for the High Commissioner to step out into the arena: he could sit at home in the Residency, secure in the knowledge that his advice would be spontaneously sought, and his intervention behind the scenes invited. Provided that he kept clearly in his mind the declaration of 1922, and took no step which did not, upon a strict interpretation, accord with those terms, he would inevitably be invited to exercise a considerable influence upon the affairs of Egypt.[20]

The British practised a policy of divide and rule, playing the Palace and the Wafd off against each other. The Wafd presented the British with a real problem. It was by far the most popular political party in the country, winning the 1924 and all subsequent elections. It rejected a gradualist approach to independence, and was suspected of involvement in a number of assassination attempts against British officials. Fortunately for the British, it was strongly opposed by the Palace. King Fu'ad was an ambitious, determined and intelligent man, with a shrewd judgement of other people's weaknesses. He was also an autocrat, who never accepted his role as a constitutional monarch and was constantly anxious to extend his power at the expense of the political parties. His lack of popular support increased dependence on the British, to whom he owed his throne, and who, as he well knew, could depose him if he threatened their vital interests. They in turn depended on him to contain the Wafd.[21] One Foreign Office memo described Fu'ad as unreliable and untruthful, but noted that he had 'this in his favour compared with the Wafd, namely that his schemes [...] [did] not involve the elimination but rather the retention of British influence'.[22]

At the same time officials often disagreed as to how far Britain should go to oppose specific Egyptian proposals deemed directly or potentially inimical to British interests, or governments backing them. The general opinion in London was that Britain should disentangle itself from Egyptian responsibilities and keep such interventions to a minimum. This view was not always shared by the man on the spot, and the personality of the High Commissioner (and later ambassador) was an important factor in determining the style of this new version of informal empire.

Lord Lloyd, who succeeded Allenby, had previously been Governor of Bengal. He was an avowed imperialist whose ideas harked back to the days of Cromer. His style was vice-regal, his instincts autocratic. He believed that the 1923 constitution was 'utterly unsuited to the nature of the people', and was determined, in his own words, 'to show these people who is master'.[23] He had no qualms about summoning battleships to Alexandria in support of his interventions in Egyptian politics. He kept Zaghlul, and his successor as leader of the Wafd, Nahas Pasha, whom he described as always standing for a policy of 'uncompromising hostility' to Britain and the British connection, out of office. He was commensurately unpopular with Egyptian politicians, who accused him of ignoring facts and being untruthful, something which shocked them in a British High Commissioner.[24]

Lloyd enjoyed Cabinet support, notably from Churchill who had a low opinion of the Egyptians, but others were sceptical about the effectiveness of his bruisingly robust approach. They included members of Lloyd's own

Figure 3. Egypt's last Proconsul. Sir Miles Lampson, later Lord Killearn

staff, as well as the Foreign Office. One official complained that the High Commissioner was 'on the lookout for an excuse for intervention. To him non-intervention or failure to insist on the maintenance of privileges which are difficult to justify and out of harmony with modern developments, spells concession and concession disaster.'[25] The Foreign Secretary, Austen Chamberlain, would have liked to sack Lloyd, but was deterred by the prospect of trouble both in the Cabinet and the country. Instead Lloyd was warned in 1929 that intervention 'should be strictly confined to matters of real importance'. When a Labour government came to office in 1929 Lloyd was quickly forced to resign.

He was replaced by a professional diplomat, Sir Percy Loraine, who, unlike Lloyd, did not see himself as a policy maker. Loraine's aim was 'to take the sting out of Anglo-Egyptian relations. There is no loss of prestige or dignity in treating human beings as such.'[26] Although his instructions were for non-interference, in fact Loraine was expected to exercise influence without appearing to do so.[27] Loraine stayed for four years. His successor, Sir Miles Lampson, stayed for 12, longer than any other British representative except Cromer. Chosen for his ability to both charm and threaten the Egyptians, he is described by one of the editors of his diaries as 'a good public servant: shrewd, patient, experienced, not easily cast down by his own misjudgements nor bound by doctrinaire ideas, but flexible, willing to listen to others and to change his mind if necessary'.[28] Lampson's approach to Egypt is summarised in comments he made at the end of his Egyptian tenure, when he described partnership as 'splendid but nature has ordered that there must be a senior partner. The Egyptians are essentially a docile and friendly people, but they are like children in many respects. They need a strong but essentially a fair and helpful hand to guide them: "firmness and justice" is the motto for Egypt.'[29]

Lampson's main problem was with the Palace. Fu'ad's death in 1936 removed what the Residency had long regarded as an important stabilising force from the Egyptian political scene. His successor, Farouk, was still a minor, and had it proved necessary, Lampson would have been willing to ensure that the Regents were pro-British. Lampson's diary entry of 2 May gives the flavour of the British intervention. While he had no intention of interfering in purely Egyptian affairs, he told the main political leaders, it was essential that the Regents were men

> who realised the vital need of working harmoniously with us and men who were qualified by nature to do that. All three took my representations in extremely good part. Mohammed Mahmoud at one point asked whether I *insisted* in having the names submitted to me in advance. I said that was not the way to put it. Insistence was too strong a term to use. But what I did feel I ought to insist upon was that I should be able to satisfy myself that unsuitable men were not appointed.[30]

Lampson had previously been anxious that Farouk should spend some time in Britain, to gain 'some background of knowledge of British temperament and of British ways'.[31] His education at Woolwich Military Academy having been cut short by Fu'ad's death, the new plan was to import a tutor, Edward Ford, a former master from Eton, to provide character-building on English lines and give the young King what Lampson described as 'the right outlook on life'.[32] Farouk proved an elusive student. Ford later remarked that his mission had been doomed from the start. 'We had controlled Egypt so long, it was difficult for us to understand they no longer did what we told them.'[33] Lampson, however, was soon lecturing the young King on his unsatisfactory behaviour. It was the beginning of a very bad relationship, reminiscent of that between Cromer and Abbas II. Farouk did not appreciate what one of his biographers describes as Lampson's 'blustering and hectoring arrogance'.[34] For his part Lampson developed a dangerous animosity towards the young monarch.

Lampson's main achievement before World War II was the Anglo-Egyptian treaty envisaged by Milner. Despite British military concessions, which had involved the Cabinet overruling the Chiefs of Staff, a series of earlier negotiations had failed. A major stumbling point had been the Sudan. The Egyptians argued that their sovereignty over Sudan had never lapsed, while the British regarded themselves as trustees for ultimate Sudanese independence. But there was also a more fundamental political problem in that the Wafd, whose *raison d'être* was Egyptian independence, could not afford to allow any other party to negotiate a treaty. Fu'ad, meanwhile, preferred British troops in Cairo to a Wafd majority.[35]

By 1936, however, the Wafd was finally ready to negotiate a deal. A new Egyptian self-confidence allowed the Wafd to tone down its strident anti-British nationalism. But the party had also realised that its hard-line approach to the treaty played into Fu'ad's hands. Tired of remaining in the political wilderness, it now wanted power, which meant *rapprochement* with Britain. It helped that Nahas Pasha got on well with Lampson. Their new pragmatism is suggested by Nahas's reported remark during the negotiations that he was prepared to give Britain 'the substance if [they] could give him the form'.[36]

The British in turn were anxious finally to put their position in Egypt on a firm legal, as well as a more friendly basis. The urgency was underlined both by fears of violence on the scale of 1919, if Britain refused to reopen negotiations (there had been serious student rioting in late 1935), and by the deteriorating international situation. In October 1935 Mussolini had attacked Abyssinia. Britain had responded by calling for League of Nations sanctions against Italy. The Mediterranean Fleet was moved from Malta to Alexandria, and reinforcements sent to Egypt. The Italian victory in Abyssinia in May 1936 undermined British prestige, raising the possibility of Egypt coming to terms with Italy. March 1936 had seen Hitler's invasion of the Rhineland. The following month a general strike had broken out in Palestine, which required British reinforcements. The prime minister, Stanley Baldwin, believed it would be worth a great deal to Britain in the Near East, 'if we made alliance with a country of Moslem population'.[37] To these crucial strategic factors must be added two more personal ones; the departure of a hard-line Chief of the Imperial General Staff, Montgomery-Massingberd, who had insisted on continued British occupation of Helwan, and the arrival of an ambitious young Foreign Secretary, Anthony Eden,

The only British Foreign Secretary with a degree in Arabic and Farsi, Eden saw the treaty as a way of making a name for himself.[38]

The treaty was signed in August 1936, 16 years after the first Anglo-Egyptian negotiations. It finally legitimised the British military presence in Egypt, replacing occupation with alliance. Britain was allowed to station in peacetime a maximum of 10,000 troops, 400 pilots plus ancillary personnel in a specified zone in the vicinity of the Suez Canal, until such a time that both parties agreed that the Egyptian army was capable of taking on the responsibility. The RAF was given complete freedom of Egyptian airspace for training purposes, with the necessary landing fields provided by the Egyptians. Egyptian *amour propre* was preserved by the statement in Article 8 that 'The presence of these forces shall not constitute in any manner an occupation and will in no way prejudice the sovereign rights of Egypt.'[39] Egypt was also obliged to provide Britain with ports, aerodromes and means of communication during war or international emergency. Both sides agreed not to conclude treaties or adopt foreign policies inconsistent with the alliance. A strong War Office mission would supervise the modernisation of the Egyptian army. Egypt would be allowed to join the League of Nations, the remaining British advisers be withdrawn and the High Commissioner now became an ambassador.

From the British perspective, there had been two main concessions. The first was the withdrawal of troops from Cairo and Alexandria to the canal zone, which would make it more difficult to intervene in Egyptian internal affairs, although Lampson insisted that this would not reduce British influence in the country. The withdrawal of the advisers was seen as more problematic, since they had provided an important source of intelligence to the Residency.[40] Second, the treaty was for a 20-year period, at the end of which either side could request negotiations for a revision. This, as Baldwin noted in Cabinet, was a risk, but it must be hoped that Britain's position would be 'very much stronger than it was today' when the treaty expired in 1956. With the knowledge of hindsight, these words have a very ironic ring.[41]

Both sides, however, were for the time being content with the treaty's constructive ambiguity, which has led historians to significantly differing verdicts. According to Mary Innes the occupation would continue 'out of sight of Cairo, under the name of an alliance. Britain had simply achieved a long-sought Egyptian endorsement of her familiar method of indirect control.'[42] In D.A. Farnie's view the treaty 'changed the whole basis of Anglo-Egyptian relations while seeming to change nothing'.[43] Peter Mansfield argues that the 1922 declaration had given Egypt half its independence, the treaty went half the rest of the way. Egypt gained control of its own security forces for the first time since 1882, and the Capitulations, whereby foreign nationals were exempt from Egyptian law, were to be ended.[44] Certainly it was well received in Egypt. Two days after its signature, British troops were cheered in Alexandria. The Egyptian parliament approved it by 202 votes to 11. Eden, who had taken the lead role in pressing the treaty through a sometimes hesitant Cabinet, was honoured by having his head on an Egyptian postage stamp. Nahas subsequently received a GCMG.[45]

While Britain exercised less power in Egypt in 1939 than it had done in 1918, the power it retained was quite sufficient for its strategic purposes. That Egyptian nationalism had, from a British perspective, proved manageable was due to a combination of British pragmatism, disunity within the nationalist movement, and the continued willingness of Egyptian politicians to collaborate with British power. There was little attempt after 1919 to exploit the deep-seated British reluctance to resort to coercion. Any residual temptations had disappeared by the time the spectre of Italian imperialism appeared on the scene.

The British impact on the evolution of Egyptian politics remained mixed. They had helped ensure a liberal constitution in 1923, thereby undoing some of the damage done by their intervention in 1882, and British influence helped contain Fu'ad's autocratic tendencies. In Egypt's chequered modern history, these were the years when party politics worked best. But the British only felt themselves obliged to support democratic outcomes when it suited their purpose to do so. They certainly did not feel bound by the wishes of the Egyptian electorate, which on seven occasions after 1924 returned the Wafd with overwhelming majorities. Similarly in 1937 Lampson did not intervene to prevent Farouk from dismissing Nahas, despite his awareness that the King's action would damage Egyptian democracy.[46] Strategic interests trumped democratic values. In Steven Morewood's blunt words, Britain's 'overriding imperative in Egypt was to manipulate its leadership through persuasion, cajolery, and bullying, to serve the interests of the military base'.[47]

9

Client Kings

Iraq and Transjordan, 1921–39

When choosing their kings at the 1921 Cairo Conference, Churchill and his officials had sought potentially amenable figures. What transpired was inevitably more complex. Tension was inherent in Britain's relationship with her new Iraqi and Transjordanian clients. The British were feeling their way as to how much influence they could exert. Feisal and Abdullah badly needed British support in meeting the challenges of state building, but dependence grated, and both men sought to loosen the constraints imposed on them. Of the two, Feisal, ruler of the larger, and the politically and socially most complex of Britain's creations, with a vocal nationalist opposition, was the more successful.

A rich lowland area, surrounded by desert nomads to the south and west and mountain people to the north and east, Mesopotamia had long experience of foreign invasion. What was unprecedented about the latest intruders was not simply the way they had established a new state of some 2,849,000 people, but that they had been charged by a League of Nations with preparing the new country for independence. The British thus had a moral responsibility for Iraq's political, if not necessarily economic or social development. The task was formidable. They were to introduce self-government into a country without any sense of national identity, and with no political institutions or traditions, education or wealth. There were few police and no proper revenue system. Communications were poor and the country was largely unmapped. Baghdad had not been a proper capital since the collapse of the Abbasid Empire in AD 1258. There were hardly any public utilities, lighting and sanitation were rudimentary, and water had to be carried from the river by donkey or by hand in leather skins. The explorer and diplomat, Gerald de Gaury, described Baghdad as 'an ancient oriental hive, well integrated in its own still largely medieval way, nearly oblivious of the western world or, indeed, of distant parts of its own new kingdom'.[1]

The 1920s were dominated by a prolonged tussle between the British and Iraqis over the degree of control Britain would exercise. Iraqi pressure for independence was constant, tempered only by the inherent pragmatism which had got Feisal the throne in the first place. British policy too showed flexibility. Domestic pressure for economy meant that the British could not afford to be heavy-handed. But as the mandate provided a more than adequate cushion of security for British interests, it was not too difficult to make concessions. Iraq was in any case not of cardinal importance to Britain; Churchill at one point admitted that 'in my heart I do not see what we are getting out of it'.[2] But there was the hope of oil, as well as of staging posts on the new air route from Cairo to Karachi, important in the days when aircraft had short ranges and were still unreliable. In the 1920s the Iraqi desert became studded with fuel dumps and landing grounds. Iraq also provided an excellent training ground for the RAF. Basra was a potential base for the defence of Abadan and the Iranian oil fields.[3]

British intentions had been outlined by Churchill at the Cairo conference. The aim was not to hold Mesopotamia by force but

> by the acquiescence of the people of Mesopotamia as a whole in a government and Ruler, whom they have freely accepted and who will be supported by the Air Force, and by British organised levies, and by four Imperial battalions. At a later stage I contemplate still further reductions, and look forward eventually to the country being in the condition of an Independent Native State, friendly to Great Britain, favourable to her commercial interests, and costing hardly any burden on the Exchequer.[4]

With the Baghdad Residency well aware of Iraqi resentment at foreign tutelage, it was quickly decided to put relations on a treaty basis, the formula which Lord Milner was advocating for Egypt, in the hope of disguising the real level of British control. The aim was a nominally independent Iraqi government 'bound by obligation and gratitude'.[5] Gratitude, however, was unlikely, particularly when the proposed independence was so heavily qualified. Negotiations proved protracted and difficult. As a foreign ruler Feisal needed to demonstrate that he was no British puppet propped up by British bayonets. In signing a treaty placing a Muslim country under a Christian state, he further risked undermining his spiritual influence in the Islamic world. But over and above these political calculations, Feisal passionately believed in Arab independence, and resented the restrictions Britain wished to impose on him.[6]

Figure 4. A British-appointed King. Feisal I of Iraq

    The King's attitude had been made clear in August 1921, when he had nearly declined the throne in response to Britain's tactless insistence that he declare his subordination to the High Commissioner at his coronation. Over the following year it was the British, while recognising the pressures on the King, who came close to losing their patience. Extreme nationalists, including the Shi'a Ulama and leading supporters of the King, were denouncing 'mandated slavery' and demanding complete British evacuation. More moderate nationalists, whose views Feisal shared, wanted the abrogation of the mandate, a friendly and equal treaty and continued British support.[7] 'Six months ago', Churchill complained in November 1921, 'we were paying his hotel bill in London, and now I am forced to read day after day 800-word messages on questions of his status and relations with foreign powers.'[8] Cox became even more bitter, claiming that Feisal had displayed 'the cloven hoof. I have endeavoured to be absolutely straightforwards and frank with him, and to treat him like a brother, but there you are, when he is scratched deep enough the racial weakness displays itself.'[9]

When in August 1922 Feisal was struck by appendicitis, Cox seized the opportunity of taking control of the government, closing down hostile papers and banishing opposition leaders. The treaty was signed in October. But despite a subsequent concession limiting its term to four years, it was only ratified in 1924. Even then it had required a threat by the new High Commissioner, Sir Henry Dobbs, that he would otherwise prorogue the Constituent Assembly and institute direct rule.[10]

The terms of the treaty, and its associated agreements, were seen in Iraq as iniquitous. The British military were allowed maximum freedom of movement, facilities such as fuel storage, and the use of roads, railways, waterways and ports. Iraq's new armed forces were controlled through a network of British officers, and supervised by a British Inspector-General. Although the High Commissioner would no longer exercise executive authority, the King agreed to be bound by the former's advice on all matters affecting British interests. As in Egypt, the appointment of British officials as 'advisers' and inspectors in key departments, including the police, irrigation and land registry, provided the High Commission with a network of intelligence and influence. To add insult to injury an associated financial agreement required the Iraqis to pay various costs including half that of the Residency, thereby placing Iraq in a state of economic dependence on Britain – as well as retarding her development.[11]

Britain's position was further entrenched by the constitution, negotiated simultaneously with the treaty. Here British and Feisal's interests coincided. By ensuring substantial powers to the King at the expense of parliament, the constitution indirectly strengthened the High Commissioner's hand.[12] British economic interests were secured by a 75-year concession to the Turkish Petroleum Company, subsequently renamed the Iraq Petroleum Company. The British had managed to camouflage the oil issue during their campaign in the League of Nations for Mosul to be attached to Iraq – a claim hotly contested by the Turks – by making their case on ethnic grounds. Having been awarded Mosul, the Iraqis were pressured into making the oil concession by holding it as a precondition for the election of Iraq's first parliament. But with the Americans determined to prevent Britain from establishing a monopoly, London failed to obtain a majority shareholding in the company for British national groups. 'We shall probably have to let in the Americans somehow', one official had written in 1921. 'But we should prefer to do it as an act of grace rather than by compulsion.'[13] Britain nevertheless exerted a considerable influence over the company by virtue of the fact that it was registered in Britain and had a British chairman.[14]

Iraqi willingness to accede to so many demands reflected the government's heavy dependence on British assistance, most notably for security. The 'sheet anchor' of British power lay not in the threat to intervene militarily, but rather, as Dobbs noted, to withhold military intervention.[15] There was constant trouble in the southern provinces and in Kurdistan. Until the final settlement of the Mosul dispute in 1925, the northern province was threatened by Turkish irregular units. In the south-west, Ikhwan raiding from Ibn Sa'ud's kingdom of Najd continued on and off for seven years. This desert war, which had begun in 1924, reflected one of the difficulties of translating European notions of sovereign states with fixed frontiers into a region of nomadic tribes, whose very existence depended on their ability to migrate and graze freely. But the early raids also reflected the deep-seated hostility between Ibn Sa'ud and the Hashemites.[16]

The key to controlling these various conflicts was airpower. Lawrence had believed that aircraft 'could rule the desert'. Despite early technical problems, a political coalition between the RAF, anxious for a peacetime role to justify its continued existence as an independent service, and the politicians, led by Churchill, desperate to reduce costs in Iraq, ensured that air power became a covert means of pursuing empire in an increasingly anti-imperial age.[17] The Colonial Secretary was perhaps the only minister willing to gamble on turning such a large state over to a new, and still largely untried, method of imperial control. First deployed in the early 1920s, it became the main British instrument for ensuring order until Iraqi independence in 1932. Its value to the insecure, fledgling Iraqi government is attested by the fact that between August 1921 and 1932, the RAF came to the government's aid on 130 occasions.

Its long-term value to the British was also substantial. Iraq provided the RAF with operational training and a distinctive role. In his study of air power and colonial control, David Omissi credits Iraq with facilitating the independent survival of the Service, which had only been formed in 1918 and still faced opposition from the navy, army and Treasury, thereby helping ensure British victory in the Battle of Britain in 1940.[18] The Iraqi experience also lies behind the strategic bombing campaign of World War II, affording the RAF, including the future head of Bomber Command, Air Chief Marshall Sir Arthur Harris, with their only significant experience of bombing prior to 1939.[19]

Airpower was cheap, quick, flexible, and ideally suited to a large country with poor communications. It was particularly effective against tribal dissidence and border encroachments, while allowing control of remoter regions without the expense of occupation. Warnings were normally given and, according to at least one officer, aircraft did not generally inflict very heavy casualties, but achieved a moral effect by engendering a feeling of helplessness among tribesmen unable to reply effectively to attack. Squadron-Leader Harris, as he then was, wrote however that both Arabs and Kurds knew that 'within 45 minutes a full scale village can be practically wiped out and a third of its inhabitants killed or injured'. Despite official instructions, air control was also used to enforce revenue collection, sometimes becoming a substitute for good administration. It was quicker and easier to send aircraft than to investigate disputes and grievances on the ground. Similarly it was easier to bomb the Kurds than make political concessions to them. Either way air control did not encourage the Iraqi government to develop more peaceful means of extending control over its territory. But Leo Amery's verdict of 1925, that were the aeroplane 'removed tomorrow, the whole [Iraqi] structure would inevitably fall to pieces', appears to have been close to the mark.[20]

Iraq, however, needed forces of its own; according to the 1922 treaty, it was to take over responsibility for internal security and national defence within four years. Feisal wanted to introduce conscription, but the British objected, preferring the creation of a small, professional mobile army. Conscription promised poorly trained troops and threatened to divert funds from roads and railways essential to Iraqi development and British military mobility in the country. But there were two other reasons for the British opposition. A large army could become the instrument of a government with despotic aspirations. The other touched on one of the basic weaknesses of the new country. Whereas Feisal looked to conscription as a means of nation building, the British realised that it would be highly unpopular with the majority Shi'a community; they had no wish to become involved in any consequent enforcement activities for which they would then be blamed. The Iraqis suspected the real reason for British objection was that they did not want a strong Iraqi army.[21]

In addition to security, mandatory Iraq also needed British financial help and, at least in the early years, administrative expertise. According to de Gaury, ministers depended on the advisers for unbiased opinions and hard and quick work.[22] While the numbers of British advisers more than halved between 1923 and 1931, they nevertheless proved a potent source of Anglo-Iraqi friction. Stephen Longrigg, who was Inspector-General of Revenue, later wrote of 'an adolescent society and government impatient to be rid of foreign control, condescension, and wiseacre advice, which its politicians never wholly trusted and frequently misunderstood'.[23]

Every order and measure within a ministry had to pass through the Adviser before gaining ministerial signature. If the Adviser objected on the grounds that it was contrary to the treaty or good administration, the matter was raised with the High Commissioner, who in extreme cases 'advised' the King against it. A special Iraqi term, *al-Wadha al-Shadh*, translated as 'perplexing predicament', was invented to describe this much-resented system of dual responsibility.

As in Egypt, the High Commissioner would at times intervene over the appointment of ministers. Cabinets therefore tended to be dominated either by conservative elements or by young Iraqis willing to work with Britain. Iraqis coined the sarcastic epithet *Mukhtar dhak al-Saub* for the High Commissioner, loosely translated as boss on the other side of the River Tigris from the prime minister's residence.[24] Iraqi frustration with the mandate was captured by the poet, Ma'ruf al-Rasafi:

He who reads the Constitution will learn
that it is composed according to the Mandate
He who looks at the flapping banner will find
that it is billowing in the glory of aliens
He who sees our National Assembly will know
that it is constituted by and for the interests of any but the electors
He who enters the Ministries will find
that they are shackled by the chains of foreign advisers.[25]

Much to Dobbs's annoyance, Feisal was constantly trying to chip away at British privileges, to the point that by 1928 the two men could barely tolerate being together. Feisal's aim, however, was not complete British disengagement, something he knew he could not afford, but an end to the High Commissioner's interventions in Iraqi internal affairs.[26] The British were partially responsive. They could not afford a discontented Iraq, and recognised the growing risk that the continuation of the mandate would undermine Feisal's credibility on which they ultimately depended, so were therefore willing at least to loosen their control. But a new treaty in 1927 failed to provide the concessions Feisal wanted.[27] Two years of haggling and one tragedy followed. In 1929 the Iraqi prime minister, 'Abd al-Muhsin al-Sa'adoun, committed suicide. In the note he left for his son, he wrote that the Iraqis 'are weak, powerless and far from independence. They are incapable of accepting the advice of honourable people such as I. They think I am a traitor to the country and a slave of the English.'[28]

The treaty, which was eventually signed in 1930, provided for *de jure* if not de facto Iraqi independence. Britain retained two rent-free air bases, which were relocated away from Baghdad and Mosul to reduce friction with nationalist circles. There would be mutual help in time of war, including the right to transport troops across Iraq. Iraq would continue to buy military equipment from Britain, employ at its own expense the services of the British military mission, and send its officers exclusively to British military academies. There was to be 'full and frank' consultation on all foreign policy questions concerning their common interests. Iraq should normally employ Britons in posts held by non-Iraqis, thus continuing to give Britain considerable latitude in defence and administration.[29] Britain, however, ceased to have any responsibility in internal affairs, which meant that the RAF would no longer help with internal security. The High Commissioner became an ambassador, though with a higher status than that of other foreign envoys. Close contacts with the government continued. As of September 1932, the ambassador paid at least one weekly visit to the King, while the Prime Minister normally paid a weekly visit to the embassy.[30]

Iraq had agreed to these terms because it wanted admission to the League of Nations, as well as the assurance of continued British military support against external attack.[31] The treaty, nevertheless, met with widespread opposition. Many Shi'a feared that independence was a prologue to mass conscription; Kurds feared subordination in a predominantly Arab state. The League of Nations had for some time been uneasy about Iraq's intolerant policy towards its minorities. When the League had awarded Mosul to Iraq in 1925, it had demanded a 25-year Anglo-Iraqi treaty, as a means of guaranteeing Kurdish rights. Dobbs had once described the Kurds as 'the sheet-anchor' of British influence in Iraq.[32] There was also concern about the positions of the Assyrians, a Christian group who had come from Turkey after World War I. Many served in the Levies, an imperial rather than an Iraqi force, which the British regarded as more efficient and reliable than the Iraqi army, and which were used to guard the RAF bases. British attempts to intervene with the Iraqi government on behalf of both minorities were consistently rebuffed, a fact which the British were anxious to conceal from the League of Nations Permanent Mandate Commission. This cover-up allowed Iraq to become the first mandatory territory to be admitted to the League of Nations. For the Iraqis it was an important symbol of equality. To French displeasure, it also provided a potential precedent for Syria and Lebanon.[33]

The mandatory period of Anglo-Iraqi relations had lasted barely more than a decade. The British had provided a ruler, parliament and a Western-style constitution. They had provided the government and country with vital security and helped with the establishment of an administration. They had also helped ensure that Mosul, where oil was found in 1928, remained Iraqi. But they had not provided significant resources for economic development. In Iraq, as elsewhere in the Middle East, the Treasury was ungenerous. There had been minimal investment in education on the grounds that it would be dangerous to educate young people who would have no prospects for employment. In 1932 there were fewer than two thousand secondary school places in Iraq.[34]

Nor had the British helped to provide their awkward creation with something even more important, namely a political culture which might allow it to transcend its multiple divisions; indeed to some extent the British had actually hindered this development. Since Iraqis were never given real responsibility in government and regarded the constitution as an instrument of foreign control and manipulation, the constitution never took root.[35] Parliament was not representative of the country as a whole, but rather of those groups, notably the tribal sheikhs, whom the British had sought to bolster, while government was conducted for the benefit of the Sunni urban elite. In 1937 the British ambassador described elections as a 'dumbshow'. This undemocratic distribution of power could only serve to deepen the ethnic and religious divisions which Iraq had inherited.[36]

Sir Henry Dobbs had few illusions. 'My hope', he had written in retirement in 1929,

> is that, even without our advice, Iraq may now be so well established, that she may be able to rub along in a corrupt, inefficient, oriental sort of way, something better than she was under Turkish rule [...] If this is the result, even though it may not be a very splendid one, we shall have built better than we knew.[37]

He was over-optimistic. The end of the mandate was followed by a period of instability, with religious and ethnic groups asserting their claims to greater autonomy, renewed tribal unrest in the south and a distinct sense of disillusion with the constitutional system. Between 1936 and 1941 there were no less than seven military coups.[38]

The 1930s saw a notable decline in British influence, and one senior British official complained, the treaty failed to 'bring us the credit of friendship we might have acquired by leaving Iraq altogether – but at the same time – did not bring us power and control which we set out to secure'.[39] Feisal died in 1933. Despite being educated at Harrow, and having a taste for Savile Row suits, the young King Ghazi, who, like Farouk in Egypt, was very much the playboy prince, strongly resented British influence. In July 1936 the Foreign Office was considering forcing his abdication. The following year he opened a radio station, a gift from Hitler, in his palace. It attacked Zionism and British influence in the Gulf. His death in a drunken road accident in 1939 was widely attributed to the British, a theme played up by German radio.[40] Ghazi's views were representative of a younger nationalist generation, who resented the lack of full independence, and were influenced by the Arab revolt in Palestine. They saw the British as an obstacle to Arab unity and looked to European fascism as a successful new social model. Fascist ideas had a particular appeal among young army officers, who disliked continued British control and saw Germany as an example of how the army could become a 'school for the nation' and a vanguard of liberation from colonialism. Alignment with the Axis offered a means of liberating Iraq from dependence on Britain.[41]

Arms supplies were a particular bone of contention. Under the 1930 treaty Britain was obliged to sell the modern arms the Iraqis needed. But the requests made in the 1930s were not all met. In 1936 the Foreign Office was chary of a proposal to double the Iraqi air force, making it superior in numbers and quality to the RAF. The main problem, however, was the slow pace of the British rearmament. The Iraqis could not believe that a Great Power would be unable to supply their needs, and suspected that they were being deliberately kept short of arms. The delivery of German and Italian weapons in 1937, in clear breach of the 1930 treaty, facilitated Axis penetration of the armed forces. Senior Iraqi military figures visited Germany, establishing ties with German firms. Indeed by the mid-1930s, the German minister, Fritz Grobba, who had a good command of Arabic and Turkish and a deep knowledge of the region, was beginning to take on the social and political role once played by the British embassy. A British embassy report of April 1939 spoke of the Germans 'pouring money' into Iraq. The ambassador, Sir Maurice Peterson, found himself powerless to do much more than issue warnings to the Iraqis.[42]

The 1930s also witnessed the emergence of another problem which was to cause considerable trouble in future years. Following independence, Iraq laid claim to neighbouring Kuwait. It did so on the basis that it was a successor state to the Ottoman Empire and of the Anglo-Ottoman convention of 1913, which had stipulated that Kuwait was an autonomous district of the Empire and the sheikh an Ottoman official. This was despite the fact that the convention had remained unratified, that Turkey had renounced all claims under the 1923 Treaty of Lausanne, and that Iraq had in 1932 accepted the Iraqi-Kuwaiti border. The Iraqis pursued their case by a propaganda campaign, support for dissident elements in Kuwait and border incursions. All this was successfully opposed by Britain, which was responsible for the defence of Kuwait, and was already eyeing the sheikhdom as an alternative should they lose their Iraqi bases. But opposition came at the cost of further undermining Britain's position in Iraq.[43]

★★★

If the trajectory of Anglo-Iraqi relations was downwards, the British had little difficulty in maintaining their position in neighbouring Transjordan. Abdullah was weaker and thus more malleable than his brother, and Britain made a larger contribution to the process of state building. Described as the most artificial of the postwar Middle East creations, Transjordan was certainly the poorest. In 1922 its population numbered only 230,000, rising to 300,000 in 1938. It had no natural resources and four-fifths of the country was desert.[44] But it had the advantage of a largely homogeneous population, and its pragmatic new Amir, while often dismissed by British officials as an unreliable lightweight, was skilled in the arts of tribal politics, and in gaining popular affection.[45] Filling one of the interstices of empire, Transjordan's value to Britain lay in its geographical position as a land and air bridge between Palestine and Iraq, as well as a buffer against Saudi expansionism.

Over time Abdullah and the British would develop a successful partnership, but particularly in the early years, this grossly unequal relationship was far from easy. Abdullah's position was unenviable. He feared absorption into Palestine, an idea favoured by the High Commissioner, Sir Herbert Samuel, in Jerusalem. It was only in 1922 that the League of Nations agreed that the Palestine mandate should not be applied to the 'territory known as Transjordan', which was totally dependent on Britain for finance and security. What little room for manoeuvre Abdullah had, depended on his ability to exploit the fact that the British had no alternative ruler up their sleeve, and that in the final analysis they needed him as much as he needed them. A political realist, he would often seek to pre-empt formal prescriptions on issues vital to British interests, but on questions which were not vital, he would go his own way. When 'advice' on such matters was pressed on him, he would procrastinate until his advisers gave up out of sheer frustration. Abdullah hankered after Arab unity and the kingship of a Greater Syria. A contemporary described him as a falcon trapped in a canary's cage.[46]

Abdullah's early problems with his overlords derived from their disapproval of the way he set about running his new territory. There was a sharp difference over the style and nature of his rule. The British envisaged a modern administration along Western lines. Abdullah's approach to this largely tribal society was by contrast patrimonial, and he saw himself in a role analogous to other chieftains in Arabia, ruling over a tribal alliance. Efficient administration, which the British prized, was not his strong suit. British officials began to complain that he was lazy and feckless, that he failed to impose order in the country, and that his management of finances, involving what was after all British money, left much to be desired. A further cause of British complaint was the prominent role played by the nationalist *Istiqlalists*, who had been part of the Hashemite entourage in Damascus. From Abdullah's perspective these had the advantage of not being beholden to the British, who in turn, however, saw them as a source of instability and potential source of complications in Anglo-French relations. An *Istiqlalist's* attempt in April 1921 to assassinate General Henri Gouraud, the French High Commissioner for the Levant, was precisely the kind of incident the British wanted to avoid.[47]

Convinced of the virtues of good administration and anxious to keep the Middle East quiet at minimum expense, the British showed little understanding for Abdullah's difficulties. Since the sixteenth century, the area had been an unruly domain of warring tribes, and the Ottomans had had great difficulty in establishing their authority. Abdullah's problems were compounded by pressure from Syrian and Palestinian politicians to adopt policies he knew would be disastrous. At the same time the British were offering advice, much of which, in Kirkbride's later words, 'was ill-conceived and unsuitable for application in a primitive Arab country'.[48]

Matters came to a head following the appointment of Lt-Colonel Henry Cox as Adviser in Amman. Cox was an Englishman of a recognisable stamp. He has variously been described as 'a dedicated and unsentimental colonial official'[49] and 'a man of little imagination' who 'did not care for foreigners, or indeed outsiders of any description, though he tried conscientiously to be fair in any situation. He had no feel for the tangle of ambitions, hopes and frustrations which then constituted Arab nationalism.'[50] He viewed Abdullah as a minor ruler, whom he was not inclined to respect. 'Sound advice', Cox wrote in 1924, 'may be expected to be of little use with a man of the Amir's improvident habits and the only alternative is the unhesitating exercise of our powers as Mandatory accompanied by the removal of the Amir if necessary from his present position.'[51]

Cox, whose approach reversed the instructions to one of his predecessors 'to leave the Arab administration to function as freely as possible and intervene as rarely as possible', replaced the head of the government, Hasan Khalid, an old friend of Abdullah's, with Rida Rikabi, a former Ottoman administrator, who enjoyed full British confidence and was thus amenable to their will. He was a man the Amir disliked. Abdullah came to hate Cox, to the point of shuddering with repugnance at the sight of him, while nevertheless managing to remain polite and courteous.[52]

In August 1924, Abdullah was faced with an ultimatum, backed up by the arrival of British troops. He must allow the senior British officer in Transjordan to inspect and virtually direct the Arab Legion. A number of nationalists must be expelled from the country and the Amir was to accept 'immediately and without reservation such measures of financial control as HMG considers necessary'.[53] Abdullah had little option but to accept, and in Cox's satisfied words, he surrendered unconditionally. The Amir was now firmly under British supervision, at times being reduced to little more than the executor of British policy. As in Iraq and Egypt, there were British 'advisers' in key ministries including finance and justice. At the same time, the ending of financial mismanagement, along with the waning of the power of the *Istiqlalists*, paved the way for an improvement in relations between Cox and Abdullah. Long term, the tightening of British supervision eventually worked to Abdullah's advantage, enhancing nation building and in the process the position of the Hashemites.[54]

Not all Britons were yet convinced. In 1926 the Foreign Secretary, Austen Chamberlain, described Transjordan as 'an ill-controlled country ruled by an inefficient and untrustworthy prince, and a source of nothing but trouble to us'.[55] Two years later, however, a formal agreement codifying the relationship with Transjordan was signed. In contrast to the succession of contemporary treaty negotiations with Iraq, this remained in force until Jordanian independence was recognised in 1946. The agreement firmly emphasised British authority, with Abdullah repeatedly agreeing to be guided by British 'advice'. Britain retained control of all crucial government activities, including foreign affairs, finance, communications and the armed forces, which Abdullah was forbidden to raise without British consent. *The Times* described Transjordan's status as being 'equal, in fact, though not in law, to that of a protectorate'.[56] Nevertheless the agreement bolstered the standing of both Amir and country. A further advantage of the agreement for Transjordan was that Britain would meet the excess expenses of the administration.[57]

Abdullah and Transjordan were no less dependent on Britain for their security, which as in Iraq depended on a combination of aircraft and armoured cars. During the first of two tribal revolts, at Kura in 1921, the appearance of the RAF 'concentrated the villagers' minds on conciliation'.[58] The RAF was also used to counter tribal raiding – aircraft could outpace camels – as well as dispersing two Ikhwan raids which had penetrated close to Amman. As in Iraq, the border with Najd, which following the collapse of the Hejaz in 1924 was now contiguous with Transjordan, was highly sensitive. Concern that Ibn Sa'ud might claim the Aqaba-Ma'an region led the Cabinet to decide to annex it to Transjordan. The same year the British negotiated the Hodda border agreement with Najd, for which Transjordan was forced to make territorial concessions. Border raiding, however, remained a problem. The bias in the Foreign Office was in favour of Ibn Sa'ud, but this was a battle for the loyalty of the tribes which Abdullah could not afford to lose.[59]

The British solution in 1930 was to bring in Captain John Glubb from Iraq, where he had proved his skill in the use of irregular forces, ending cross-border raids from Najd. By 1932 he had also brought peace to the Transjordanian border. Glubb, who would stay until 1956, played a key role in Transjordan. One of the last of the colonial proconsuls, he was part administrator, part soldier, a man who was wholly devoted to the people and country he served, to the point indeed where he was sometimes accused of 'going native'.[60] He sought not simply to pacify the border, but to get the tribes to pay taxes and settle their differences through recourse to law, thereby easing Transjordan into the modern world under British tutelage.[61]

Glubb's *modus operandi* was to co-opt and cooperate with the tribes, respecting their customs and overcoming their suspicion of government. He was helped by a combination of good Arabic, an exceptional knowledge of nomadic life, and the distribution of money to sheikhs and ordinary tribesmen at a time of great hardship. He was probably the first man to turn the Bedouin, for whom he felt a strong affinity, into disciplined soldiers. The commander of the Arab Legion, Colonel Frederick Peake, had deliberately excluded the Bedouin. Glubb's Desert Patrol was recruited among the tribes.[62]

One of the most romantic of the irregular forces raised in the last phase of the British imperial era, the Desert Patrol quickly gained a reputation as an elite corps. It had considerable appeal to the tribesmen, especially the sons of the sheikhs, who having previously been groomed to lead raids, needed alternative employment. But the importance of the Desert Patrol, which Glubb himself described as not so much a police force as a patriarchy, went beyond security. It became a means of inculcating loyalty to a larger unit among the tribes and integrating them into the state. In Philip Robins' words, Glubb thus became one of the heroes of the state-building project in Transjordan.[63]

The social dimension of Glubb's work was based on the 'humane imperialism' pioneered on the North West Frontier of India. As applied to Transjordan this meant a sympathetic approach to tribal complaints, and the application wherever possible of tribal law, of which Glubb became chief arbiter. Glubb successfully encouraged the tribes to undertake settled cultivation. This helped diversify their economy, while providing another means of making up for the loss of traditional sources of income such as raiding. It also acted as a form of social anchorage. By 1938 'every section of every tribe in Transjordan' was officially described as being in possession of a certain 'amount of cultivation'.[64] In addition, Glubb initiated health and education systems in the desert, in the latter case financing it from his own pocket until government funds were forthcoming.[65]

Britain's other major contribution to state building came in the form of a campaign to settle land titles. This failed in its original intention of boosting agricultural production and tax revenues. But by allowing cultivators to secure their legal rights to their lands, which thus increased in value and were taxed lightly and fairly, the land programme went a long way towards securing their loyalty to the government. A few strategically placed British advisers also helped establish seed distribution schemes, experimental farms and small-scale irrigation facilities.[66]

By the end of the 1930s Abdullah, aided by the British, had gone a considerable way towards consolidating the paper state which had been established less than two decades previously. The borders had been secured, the tribes had been integrated into the state, and administration had been made efficient. The Arab Legion, which Glubb had taken over, had proved itself to be a highly professional military force, which in marked contrast to Iraq made no attempt to intervene in political affairs. The Legislative Council, whose composition had been designed to give both Abdullah and the British little trouble, proved duly malleable. The absence of a substantial urban educated class ensured that there was little nationalist agitation. Abdullah had gone up in British estimation as the country had remained quiet during a series of disturbances in neighbouring Syria and Palestine, while the 1936 Arab Revolt had encouraged greater British investment in the amirate. But the fact that he had won concessions by good behaviour rather than strikes and demonstrations meant that he was seen in the region as a British puppet.[67]

Figure 5. Friendly Game. General Sir John Glubb and Abdullah I

Transjordan was of course a smaller, much more homogeneous and less important state than Iraq, but the greater success of British policy, as seen from both the British and Transjordanian perspectives, was at least partially also a result of British sensitivity. With the exception of 1924, the British approach had been non-confrontational, a matter of subtle, behind the scenes interventions which made for what Yaov Alon describes as a 'more agreeable colonial rule'.[68] It helped that British officials, including Cox, Peake, Kirkbride and Glubb, remained in post for extended periods, thereby accumulating a reservoir of knowledge. So too did the unobtrusiveness of the British presence. The total British personnel in the 1920s and 30s numbered fewer than twenty. In 1936 the Arab Legion had only seven British officers. The absence of much direct British contact with the local population eased relations.[69]

In both Transjordan and Iraq, the process of consolidating the new client states required the cooperation of the Hashemites and the British. It was up to the former to try to gain legitimacy and establish a sense of national identity. The British ensured the conditions in which this could happen. They provided the necessary security, particularly vital during the early years, resolved border disputes and made available technical expertise and small amounts of money. What they could not do was overcome the tensions latent in the original design faults of the Iraqi state, namely its ethnic and sectarian divisions.

10

'Riding Two Horses at Once'

Palestine, 1921–39

'The problem is intolerably difficult. It would have been less difficult if the Balfour Declarations had been worded more clearly, if they had not tried to ride two horses at once.'

Ernest Bevin[1]

The British had done reasonably well in their choice of Hashemite proxies in Iraq and Transjordan. Their choice of the Zionists in Palestine by contrast would cause them nothing but grief. In following the story of the mandate, we need to bear in mind three very different perspectives – those of the British, the Zionists to whom they had made a commitment, and the Palestinian Arabs for whom they assumed they had a responsibility.

A small territory which had variously been conquered by the Assyrians, Babylonians, Persians, Greeks and Romans, in the 1920s Palestine was a sandy, marshy and derelict land. An impoverished peasantry was dominated by a small, often absentee landowning aristocracy. Yet within the strategic geography of the post-Ottoman Middle East, this was a territory of some importance, which the British wanted to exploit, as well as to deny to potential rivals, notably the French and the Italians. Palestine looked both south and east. It provided a buffer against naval and air attack against the Suez Canal, and a transit route via Iraq to India in the event of the canal's closure. It was also part of the new imperial air link to the east. The opening of a port and refinery at Haifa in the early 1930s created facilities for the Royal Navy, as well as a Mediterranean outlet for the pipeline from the oil fields in northern Iraq. The Chiefs of Staff had objected to the use of Syrian or Lebanese ports on the grounds that this would place Britain 'at the mercy of the French'.[2] (For their part the French Ministry of War had wanted a French outlet on the grounds that 'if England declared war on us, we could, for a while at least, block their supply of Iraqi petroleum'.[3]) And as international tensions increased in the late 1930s, the Chiefs of Staff considered establishing a strategic reserve in Palestine.

What made Palestine unique was the fact that instead of creating a new state with an approved pro-British government, Britain had committed itself to a political project, whose ultimate purpose was at once uncertain and bitterly contested. The Balfour Declaration had been written into the mandate, even though an important part of its wartime rationale was by now obsolete and much of the idealistic momentum which had also inspired the project had disappeared with the fall of the Lloyd George government in 1922. The British found themselves hoist by their own petard. They had no other excuse for remaining in Palestine. In addition, to quote the report of a Cabinet committee set up in the summer of 1923 to review the mandate, whether the policy was 'wise or unwise, it is well-nigh impossible for any government to extricate itself without a substantial sacrifice of consistency and self-respect, if not honour'.[4] Yet as the same report also noted, it was difficult to blame those who argued that 'the whole mandate is built on the fallacy of attempting to reconcile the irreconcilable'. The Zionist leader and future Israeli prime minister, David Ben Gurion, agreed. 'We and they [the Palestinians] both want the same thing. We both want Palestine.'[5] This could only mean that conflict, if not inevitable, was highly likely. Unless immigration was kept low, fear of creeping Jewish conquest and dispossession by an alien and visibly more modern and dynamic community, representing a threat to their culture and religion, seemed bound to produce a hostile reaction.[6]

Although Balfour and Lloyd George were on record as saying their understanding of the term 'national home' was in fact an eventual state, this was not the interpretation of subsequent governments.[7] According to the 1922 White Paper,

> The Jewish National Home in Palestine is not the imposition of a Jewish nationality upon the inhabitants of Palestine as a whole, but the further development of the existing Jewish community, with the association of Jews in other parts of the world, in order that it may become a centre in which the Jewish people as a whole may take, on grounds of religion and race, an interest and a pride.[8]

A subsequent draft definition for a speech by the Colonial Secretary in 1936, by which time anti-Semitism in Europe was on the rise, was somewhat more explicit. This referred to 'a safe home for refugees to which oppressed Jews may hope to escape provided the economic conditions of Palestine permit. Second, a cultural centre on a permanent physical basis where the Hebrew language and free Jewish life can flourish and to which Jews from all over the world can look for inspiration.'[9] But whether this meant that the Jews would eventually become the majority community, how long a national home would take to establish, or what was meant by the government using its 'best endeavours' to bring it about, remained unclear. Nor, although British governments came to stress the existence of a dual obligation to Arabs as well as Jews, was the meaning of the 'civil and religious rights' of the existing population which they were bound to protect, spelled out further.

In theory all these ambiguities gave future British governments a measure of wriggle room; in practice, however, British options were seriously limited. The ideal solution of trying to build up a bicommunal Palestinian citizenship, whereby Arab acquiescence would be acquired through the prosperity which Jewish immigration and capital would bring, with time working to sink differences between them, was never realistic. The flaw in this argument was outlined in the 1937 Peel Report, which noted that Arab feeling had been 'put in some such figurative language as this. "You say we are better off: you say my house has been enriched by the strangers who have entered it. But it is *my* house, and I did not invite the strangers in, or ask them to enrich it, and I do not care how poor or bare it is if only I am master in it."'[10]

None of the alternatives were attractive. The British could abandon their dual promise and impose a Jewish national home on the Arabs. But this implied the use of force, an expensive and undesirable option which would be unviable over the long term. There was no desire to have a second Irish insurgency.[11] They might restrict the size of the national home. The 1922 White Paper had referred to the need for immigration to take account of the country's economic absorptive capacity, although nobody in London or Jerusalem seemed aware of what it meant or how it was to be implemented. One of the great Zionist fears was that the British would seek to crystallise the national home before they achieved a majority. If they were kept in a permanent minority, the national home could become a death trap.[12] Or the British could try and muddle through. This, however would inevitably become more difficult as the Jewish population grew. It also assumed, which was not perhaps unreasonable in the 1920s, that Palestine could be managed without pressure from events elsewhere in the world.

Almost inevitably, this was the path chosen. Any more radical policy would have required sustained attention and the expenditure of political capital. There was little incentive to launch initiatives when it was impossible to gain the support of both communities, unless of course developments on the ground, which usually meant violence, made this imperative. The point is underscored by the sequence of events that began with the disturbances which broke out at the Western Wall in Jerusalem in August 1929. These were followed by attacks on Jews in various parts of the country, including old established Jewish communities which had no connection with the Zionists. A hundred and thirty-three Jews were reported to have been killed and 339 injured. Arab deaths were reported as 116 and 232 injured.[13] This led to a commission of enquiry and a White Paper which sought to restrict both immigration and land sales to Jews. The resultant storm of protest by the Zionists and their supporters in Britain led to retraction by the prime minister, Ramsay MacDonald. On this, as on other occasions, the continued influence in London of Chaim Weizmann, who had played a major role in persuading the government to issue the Balfour Declaration, served the Zionist cause well.[14]

Meanwhile facts were being created on the ground, as an embryonic Jewish state began to emerge in Palestine. The mandate had provided for the establishment of a Jewish Agency. A Jewish defence force, the Haganah, had been allowed to emerge in 1920. A form of Jewish government functioned continually from 1920, albeit without official recognition, meeting at least once a year. The Jews developed their own largely autonomous agricultural and industrial economy, as well as social and welfare institutions.[15] At the same time, however, the overall tendency in the interwar years, as the problems created by the Balfour Declaration came to be more clearly recognised, was to shift the emphasis in British policy from the promotion of the Jewish homeland to protection of the Arab community.[16] Local British officials had from the early days of the military occupation which preceded the mandate, tended to be pro-Arab. They felt that an injustice had been done to the Arab population and found the Jewish immigrants altogether too argumentative, self-righteous and discourteous. Nor did they overly care for the fact that these European settlers regarded the British as equals.[17]

The British officials' lot in Palestine was unenviable. They were constantly in crisis or under pressure. 'All this muddling and changing of policy has an effect upon everyone', wrote one young officer in 1930, '& nobody knows from one day to another which way they are facing.'[18] Six years later, at the time of the Arab general strike, the Commissioner for Migration noted that 'nearly nineteen years have passed since I first entered the country and I look back and see little that can give satisfaction for hard honest work in the best years of my life'.[19] There was a sense, as another official remarked, of 'ploughing sand when embarking on any constructive effort in Palestine', the image used by Naomi Shepherd as the title for her study of British rule in Palestine.[20] Friction was liable to arise from the smallest controversy between Jews and Arabs. This had consequences for the development of the country. With limited funds at its disposal, the Palestine administration used all its legislative and administrative ingenuity on what it hoped would defuse intercommunal tensions. Remaining disposable income went on police and prisons. Agricultural reform was one victim.[21] Education was similarly neglected. Between 1920 and 1940 the number of government schools rose from only 171 to 384, although the number of pupils, nearly all Arab, quadrupled from 10,600 to 43,000.[22] And improvements in health meant that by the end of the mandate the 'average' life expectancy of the *fellahin* increased from 35 to 50.[23]

Yet until at least 1929, if not the general strike of 1936, the prevailing British assumption remained that Palestine was a difficult but manageable problem. In 1923 Sydney Moody, a District Officer in Galilee, hoped that 'if we could go on long enough, with tact, patience and diplomacy, avoiding overt troubles, then time would bring a solution'.[24] Eleven years later, the Colonial Secretary Philip Cunliffe-Lister rejected the view that 'the lion will never lie down with the lamb and that the best you can hope for is a fairly divided and well-guarded zoo'.[25] Such optimism, whether forced or otherwise, drew encouragement from the absence of disturbances for most of the 1920s and the sporadic nature of Arab violence. There was also some evidence of Arab–Jewish cooperation, notably in the field of health and municipal self-government.[26] With outbreaks of violence brief, and levels of anti-Semitism in Europe relatively low, the mandate had been successfully insulated from both Arab politics and the wider affairs of the Jewish diaspora. Under these circumstances there was no pressure to think through the contradiction at the heart of the mandate, least of all in London where officials were at a safe distance from the problem. It after all was in British and Jewish interests to sustain optimism – the mandate depended on it.[27]

But there was dissent. In a private conversation at the Colonial Office in 1923, Sir John Shuckburgh, the senior official responsible for Palestine, admitted that he could see no solution to the problem. 'We had no idea of what we were doing and where we were going to.'[28] Sir John Chancellor, an experienced colonial administrator, who was High Commissioner at the time of the 1929 riots, believed the Balfour Declaration to have been a colossal blunder, and that British rule could only be perpetuated if the Arab

Figure 6. Law and Disorder. Jaffa riots, 1933

majority were favoured.[29] A 1934 proposal for cantonisation originated from an Arab official on the High Commissioner's staff who believed that the prevailing attitude among Palestinian Arabs in autumn 1932 was one of distrust and hatred towards Britain because of the way it was thwarting Arab national aspirations in favour of the Jewish national home.[30]

The early 1930s witnessed a gradual radicalisation of Arab opinion and a deterioration in law and order. There was rioting in Nablus in August 1930, while 1930 and 1931 saw a series of terrorist murders of Jews. More serious rioting took place in 1933, with another 27 deaths and 243 wounded. By the mid-1930s a subculture of violence was emerging, with rebel bands taking to the hills and gangs resorting to sabotage.[31] Legal immigration had increased from 4,075 in 1931 to 61,854 in 1935.[32] The immediate cause was increased Jewish immigration caused by the rise of anti-Semitism in Germany and Poland. Anti-Semitism had of course been a key motive behind the Zionist movement, but British policy makers had not previously taken on board the extent to which their control of policy might become hostage to this bacillus lurking in the European body politic. At the same time, however, the fact that so many Jews had been allowed into Palestine reflected Cunliffe-Lister's view that Palestine, like other colonies, was essentially an economic problem. He therefore welcomed the import of additional manpower, as well as capital, which would help generate growth and prosperity. In 1934 the Cabinet agreed that Palestine's absorptive capacity could be defined so as to take account of its potential rather than its immediate development.[33]

The economic results of this policy were gratifying. Between 1931 and 1935 imports and exports trebled. There was a building boom and overemployment, a situation from which Arabs as well as Jews benefited. But, as officials had failed to foresee, the political repercussions were disastrous. The dramatic increase in Jewish immigration between 1931 and 1935 raised the percentage of Jews from 17 to almost 30 per cent. The European dress of the new immigrants could be seen in every part of the country. Land and labour disputes increased.[34] The prospect of a Jewish majority within a decade created Palestinian fear and anger. There were warnings in the Palestine Arab press that the British were introducing Jews into Palestine 'to push the Arabs into the sea and finish them', and that Zionists were being incited to kill Arabs, attack and torture Arab women and to defile mosques.[35] Italian radio propaganda fanned the flames. The situation was then exacerbated by the end of the Palestinian economic boom, following the disruption of trade in the eastern Mediterranean caused by Mussolini's attack on Abyssinia, plus political developments elsewhere in the Arab world. The Egyptian disturbances of December 1935, which had resulted in negotiations for an Anglo-Egyptian treaty, had had a knock-on effect in Syria, where the French entered into negotiations for a treaty relationship. With Iraq independent, the Palestinians felt themselves to be losing out.

In April 1936 a newly formed Arab High Command called a general strike, which it declared would last until both immigration and Jewish land purchases were ended. It also demanded the establishment of representative government institutions. This was a turning point in the history of the mandate, an open rebellion which over the next three years would extend over the whole country and which for the first time was directed against the mandatory authorities. Perhaps more ominously from the British perspective, it attracted the attention of the gradually increasing number of independent Arab states. A Saudi offer to mediate with the Arab High Command was judged to be helpful. But a precedent had been set; the days when Palestine could be insulated from the wider politics of the Arab world were numbered.

London responded to the strike in classic fashion. A high-level Royal Commission, under a former Secretary of State for India, Lord Peel, was appointed. Unlike previous enquiries following the disturbances of 1921 and 1929, its brief was to examine not simply the immediate causes of the outbreak but the manner in which the mandate was being implemented. The results were damning. Here, Peel reported, was 'a conflict of right with right'. An irrepressible conflict had arisen between two national communities within the narrow bounds of one small country. Some one million Arabs were in strife with some 400,000 Jews, and there was no common ground between them. Their cultural and social life, their ways of thought and conduct, were as incompatible as their national aspirations. The conflict had grown increasingly bitter and would continue.[36]

Although the report had effectively shown the mandate to be unworkable, Peel rejected the idea that it should be abandoned. 'We are responsible for the welfare of the country. Its government is in our hands. We are bound to strive to the utmost to do justice and make peace.'[37] Peel's solution, drawing on the cantonisation proposal previously canvassed and rejected within the Colonial Office, was partition. A Jewish state would comprise the coastal plain and Galilee, with a much larger Arab state consisting of the rest of Palestine and Transjordan. There would also be a permanently mandated British enclave which would include the Jerusalem-Bethlehem area, and have a corridor to the sea. It was a measure of the complexity of the scheme that it would effectively cut the Jewish state in two. Britain would also have bases on Lake Galilee and in Aqaba. The mandate itself would be replaced by treaties based on the Iraqi model, which would in turn be accompanied by military conventions.

This was the first radical proposal for the resolution of what had become the Palestine conflict, presaging the eventual division in 1948 of Palestine between the new Israeli state and Jordan. But that was a solution produced by war. A diplomatic partition of the country posed as many questions as it sought to answer. The Colonial Office welcomed this 'means of escape [...] by which we can do substantial justice to both parties and clean our conscience of the odious imputation of breach of faith'.[38] Weizmann too showed interest. A small Jewish state would be preferable to the crystallisation of a minority Jewish National Home within a larger Arab entity and further restrictions on immigration. Others, however, were sceptical. The Liberal leader, Sir Archibald Sinclair, warned of the dangers of 'two racially totalitarian states side by side [...] with the Jews established along an indefensible coastal strip – congested, opulent, behind them the pressure of impoverished and persecuted world Jewry: in front of them Mount Zion'.[39] The former High Commissioner, Lord Samuel, feared that the proposed states, within their jigsawed frontiers, would be 'entwined in an inimical embrace like two fighting serpents'. The risk was clear. One or other state was likely to try to revise the settlement, whether by peaceful or other means. Partition, in other words, would change the nature of the conflict; it would not resolve it. What, however, finally turned the government against the proposal was the Foreign Office's concern over the opposition of the Arab states, and the prospect that partition might therefore play into Italian hands.[40]

With no solution thus in sight, the situation in Palestine deteriorated. A truce, which had been called in 1936, ended in October 1937, and the Arab Higher Command was declared an unlawful organisation. Its leader, Haj Amin Hussaini, the Grand Mufti of Jerusalem, escaped to Syria, where he remained until October 1939. From there he managed to direct some of the gangs operating in Palestine, though his influence waned later in the revolt. Despite the erection of an 18-foot barbed-wire fence the length of the Palestine–Syrian border, substantial arms supplies were reported to be going from Syria to Palestine. The French attitude to Palestine had long been equivocal. During the 1929 disturbances, they had, in Sir John Chancellor's words, been 'quite extraordinarily helpful and sympathetic'.[41] Ever suspicious of British motives in the Levant, however, the French now worried that partition was a plot to extend British influence in the Middle East. They feared that the establishment of a new Arab state comprising Transjordan and much of Palestine might make it impossible to maintain their hold over Syria. At the same time the measures the British authorities in Palestine were asking them to take would undermine the French position in negotiations for a Franco-Syrian treaty.[42]

This new stage of the revolt was an early example of what General Bernard Montgomery, commanding one of the British divisions in Palestine, described as 'rather a curious sort of war; you don't often see your enemy but all the time you are exposed to the risk of being murdered or blown up'.[43] The army, as Sir Gawain Bell, who was posted to Tiberias, later wrote,

> groped in the dark. Any innocent looking farmer driving his donkey along a village track might well be carrying arms or explosives and returning from or on his way to, a raid or an ambush. A shopkeeper could easily be a gang leader or an agent, watchful to report police or troop movements.[44]

It was also a peculiarly complicated affair involving racial, religious, familial and colonial elements, as well as a peasant struggle.[45] Almost as many Arabs as Jews were killed. Some of the Arab victims comprised the opponents of the Mufti; one element of the conflict was a struggle for the consolidation of Husseini hegemony in Arab Palestine.[46] The backbone of the longest revolt the British had so far experienced in the Middle East consisted of some thousand to one-and-a-half-thousand rebels, and by the middle of 1938 large areas of the country were under their control. Jewish settlements and buses were attacked and civilians murdered. The airport at Lydda was burnt, troop trains were derailed, the Haifa-Mosul oil pipeline was badly damaged, and roads were mined.[47] At the high point of the rising, rebels had taken virtual control of the Old City of Jerusalem. 'Sitting at home by the fire in England', one policeman wrote home to his family in June 1938,

> you cannot visualise a country only the size of Wales, where there is absolutely no law or order. Police & troops are powerless & our only object out here seems to be clearing up the mess after the crime had been committed, we are on the defensive all the time.[48]

As in 1929, the British authorities had allowed themselves to be taken by surprise. In the 1920s a combination of over-optimism and the pressing needs for economy had led the High Commissioner, Lord Plumer, a former Field Marshal, to approve the withdrawal of all British troops. When the 1929 revolt broke out, there were only 1,500 policemen in the country. The unsatisfactory state of this force had led to proposals for its reorganisation, including improvements to the CID and its vital intelligence-gathering functions. But despite the continued disturbances in the early 1930s, these had not been implemented, and in 1936 British intelligence remained weak, while the Arab section of the force proved unreliable.[49] British tactics, which had been amateurish at the outset, in 1938 became more aggressive, focused and concerted.[50] There was cooperation with the Haganah, which by now consisted of some 10,000 trained men with another 40,000 available for rapid mobilisation. It included the formation of Special Night Squads consisting of Haganah members with a stiffening of British officers and NCOs. The key figure here was Orde Wingate, a highly unconventional soldier who, thanks to his deeply rooted Protestant millenarianism, adopted the Zionist cause.

The turning point came in the autumn of 1938 with the decision to deploy an extra division, the imposition of martial law in the towns and the deployment of the army on the streets. But all this came at a real strategic cost. British rearmament had begun relatively late and the army was very much the Cinderella service. The revolt virtually eliminated the prospect of sending even a small expeditionary force to France at the time of the September 1938 Munich crisis. Both in the Foreign Office and the

Services, the rebellion was seen as the focus and emblem of a growing Arab nationalism that could undermine British supremacy across the region.[51]

As the revolt gradually wound down, a conference was convened in London, consisting of the Jews and Palestinian Arabs, as well as the Arab states. The prospects were not promising. In the words of the Foreign Secretary, Lord Halifax, 'Nothing short of the Archangel can bring order out of this chaos.'[52] But this was in fact a diplomatic exercise intended as much to show that Britain had tried to reach an agreement, as actually to attain one. War was approaching in Europe, and with the strategic importance of the Middle East now greater than ever, the region had to be stabilised. The Jews had little alternative but to support Britain against Hitler. If alienated by British policy in Palestine, the Arabs might easily turn to the Axis powers. The prime minister, Neville Chamberlain, starkly outlined the position in Cabinet committee: 'We are now compelled to consider the Palestine problem mainly from the point of view of its effect on the international situation [...] *if we must offend one side, let us offend the Jews rather than the Arabs*'[53] (emphasis in original). On 15 March 1939, the day that Hitler invaded Prague, the Colonial Secretary, Ramsay MacDonald, put Britain's final position to the conference, which broke up two days later.

Britain was now free to advance its own ideas, the first time the government had publicly outlined its long-term plans for the mandate. The White Paper published on 17 May marked the high-water mark of the shift in policy from Zionism towards the protection of Arab rights. Palestine was to gain independence within ten years, in treaty relationship with Britain. It was to do so as a bi-national state in which Arabs and Jews would share authority in such a manner that the interests of both communities would be protected. During an interim period self-government institutions were to be established, and 75,000 Jewish immigrants were to be allowed entry over the next five years. No Jewish immigration would subsequently be admitted without Arab acquiescence. This would lock the Jews into a permanent minority status of some 30 per cent of the population. An additional sting, from the Zionist perspective, was that the High Commissioner would be given the power to restrict the transfer of Arab lands in certain areas.[54]

For the Zionists this was a betrayal, made the more bitter by the worsening plight of the Jews of Central Europe. There was a furious exchange between the Colonial Secretary Malcolm Macdonald and Weizmann, during which the latter said that 'at least in Hitler one found the virtue of an absolute frank brutality, whereas Mr Macdonald was covering up his betrayal of the Jews under a semblance of legality. He added that Mr Macdonald was handing over the Jews to their assassins. Mr Macdonald showed great indignation and said that it was no use to talk to him like that.'[55] The White Paper was attacked in parliament by Churchill as a breach of faith, while Leo Amery declared that he would be ashamed to vote with the government. In the event, the government's majority, which was normally around 250, fell to 89.[56] But the White Paper succeeded in its immediate and most critical purpose. It split the Arab states off from the Palestinian Arabs, ensuring that there would be no major disorders in the Middle East. It was a policy of undisguised *realpolitik*. By 1939 there was no alternative.

11

Strong-men, Borders and Oil

The Gulf and Aden, 1918–39

The interwar years saw important changes in the Gulf region – the discovery of oil, the creation of Saudi Arabia under Ibn Sa'ud, and the strengthening of Persia under a new strong-man, Reza Khan. Five new states had come into being with the end of World War I – Yemen, Najd, Hijaz, the territory of the Asir and the principality of the Shammar, under Ibn Rashid. Britain, which controlled the four corners of the Arabian Peninsula at Aden Aqaba, Kuwait and Oman, would play a significant role in the subsequent power struggle. As this conflict was unfolding a mania for Arabia gripped British culture. Arabia supplanted Greece as the most romantic backdrop for the enactment of a certain kind of Englishness. The two-hour travelogue of American journalist, Thomas Lowell, on the Arab Revolt was seen by some four million people in Britain, the US and part of the Empire, turning Lawrence into the great celebrity of Britain's engagement with the Middle East. His account of the campaign, *Seven Pillars of Wisdom*, which first appeared in 1926, was a publishing success,[1] one of the few literary classics to emerge from empire.

Policy makers meanwhile were engaged with rather less romantic concerns. While Sherif Hussein had been the obvious horse to back in the struggle against the Turks, he quickly proved a loser in the inter-Arabian conflicts which followed the war. Hussein felt not so much aggrieved, as betrayed by the British failure to back Hashemite claims to Syria. He had, in his own words, 'become the victim of my trust and reliance on British honour'.[2] Against the advice of his sons and foreign secretary, Fu'ad al-Khatib, he flatly refused to sign a treaty with Britain which would have provided him with recognition and an element of protection, since this would have required him to recognise the realities of the postwar Middle East. Perhaps, as the military historian Basil Liddell Hart suggests, he was 'too honest to be a successful statesman'.[3] He was certainly too inflexible, and his

Figure 7. Coming Man, Ibn Sa'ud, December 1915

carping approach to the British, on whom he continued to rely, was unwise. Some officials showed understanding for his increasingly difficult behaviour. In September 1918 Sir Reginald Wingate described him as 'oppressed with affairs of state [...] at an advanced age and under conditions of exceptional difficulty'.[4] But this became very much a minority view. For Curzon he was 'that pampered and querulous nuisance'.[5] Officials complained of being 'linked arm-in-arm to a lunatic', and of his 'personal imbecility and continual obstruction and continual provocation'.[6] The fact that corruption and financial mismanagement were rife in the Hejaz, and that he alienated both the urban and tribal elites, did nothing to help his case.

His main rival, Ibn Sa'ud, was a man of very different calibre. 'Very shrewd and very difficult in negotiations', he was a man of commanding presence. Over six feet tall, he is described by a British diplomat as making little parade of royalty, preferring the dignified simplicity of a great Arab personage.[7] He had first made his mark in 1902 with the capture of Riyadh, and assumed the amirship of Najd the following year. Officials in London and India reacted very differently. The former saw him as a rebel against the Turks, whose empire they still supported. The latter viewed him as the strongest power in Arabia, and believed that Britain could not view Turkish attempts to crush him with indifference.[8] In December 1915 Britain and Sa'ud had concluded a treaty which marked a departure from Britain's traditional policy of avoiding engagements in central Arabia, but Ibn Sa'ud had proved too weak to be of much practical help in the war.[9] By 1920, however, he was being described by one official as 'by far the strongest man in Arabia at present'. He commanded a powerful military force in the form of the Ikhwan, Najdi tribesmen organised at oases in quasi-military settlements on strict fundamentalist ideas of Wahhabism. In contrast to Sherif Hussein, his ambitions were confined to Arabia. He also supported the mandates and was opposed to the concept of pan-Arabism. Well aware that he had to operate within the parameters of their power, the Saudi chieftain had been careful to cultivate the British. In Joseph Kostiner's words, he

> projected the image of a leader capable both of restraining his bellicose tribes to avoid harming British interests and of marshalling them to conquest when the opportunity arose. He also proved flexible enough to comply with British initiatives for local settlements and remain an ally despite British support for Hussein. He thus not only achieved a certain sympathy for his expansionist attempts but also managed to project the image of a thoughtful leader, one who was able to control his feelings and act pragmatically.[10]

Overt conflict between Ibn Sa'ud and the Sherif began in 1918, with a dispute over the oasis town of Khurma, strategically situated between the two rivals' territories. This caused considerable embarrassment for, as well as disagreement between, British officials who were anxious to avoid war between two of their protégés. In so far that they had a preference, it was still for Hussein. To abandon the Sherif, to whom they felt a sense of obligation, so soon after the war would damage Britain's reputation; besides, a Wahhabi invasion of the Hejaz and the subsequent growth of Wahhabi power and influence might, in Lord Curzon's view, lead to a repeat of

> the massacres such as those in 1801 at Kerbala and of 1802 at Taif; to repeated raids on Iraq; to the turning back from the Holy Places of all

Pilgrims who were unwilling to profess Wahhabi tenets; and possibly to costly and difficult military operations, or failing these to a loss of prestige for His Majesty's Government which His Lordship would regard as a capital disaster.[11]

As the crisis continued, policy swung back and forth for and against Hussein. Two ultimatums threatening to halt the subsidy Ibn Sa'ud had been receiving since 1917 were deliberately delayed by officials in Baghdad and Bahrain. In the event, war was postponed for two years, but the affair left a feeling among British officials that in supporting the Sherif they were backing the wrong horse.[12]

For the time being, however, Ibn Sa'ud was prevented from using his increasing power to move against British interests in Arabia by the continuation of his subsidy. This was his principal source of income, and the main means by which, as Churchill put it, Britain checked what Arabian chiefs did 'or rather what they are not doing'.[13] But when, in the summer of 1920, Ibn Rashid, who was regarded as anti-British, extended his territory so that it now bordered Palestine, the British looked to Ibn Sa'ud to rectify matters. Armed with an additional £10,000 a month in gold, along with rifles and four field guns and instructors, the Saudi leader took Hail, thereby consolidating his control over central north Arabia.[14]

Prior to his final assault on Hejaz in 1924, precipitated partly by the ending of his subsidy, Ibn Sa'ud had been careful to sound out British reaction. By now the latter were content to stand aside and let matters take their course.[15] The British declared a neutrality which could only work in the Sa'udi's favour. A Christian power could scarcely intervene in a battle for the Holy Places of Islam, but even without this consideration, the British were not disposed to rescue a man who had proved himself such an impossible ally.[16] Hussein abdicated in October and took refuge in Aqaba. When his presence threatened to incite a Wahhabi attack, he was removed by a British warship to exile in Ceylon. Britain had thus both facilitated and acquiesced in the creation of a dominant new Arabian superpower.

Following the Hejaz's surrender in December 1925, the Foreign Office was anxious to grant *de jure* recognition, leading the Colonial Office to complain that its 'alacrity to help Bin Saud is almost indecent. They consistently refused to help poor old Hussein for fear of [...] making it appear that HMG were trying to interfere. But as soon as the Hejaz falls into strong hands, the FO falls over them.'[17]

By the Treaty of Jeddah, concluded in 1927, Ibn Sa'ud became the first Arab ruler to have his complete and absolute independence recognised by Britain, which Feisal in Iraq took as a personal slight. Ibn Sa'ud in turn undertook to respect British treaties with the Trucial States, suppress slavery and facilitate the pilgrimage of British Muslim subjects.[18] During the 1928–9 Ikhwan revolt, Britain provided the King with arms, aircraft and pilots, while also helping ensure that the Ikhwan got no help from Iraq and Transjordan. They also carried out bombing raids against the Ikhwan in Najd at the King's request. This aid may have provided the narrow margin of victory which preserved Saudi dynastic rule.[19] The name of Saudi Arabia, adopted in 1932, was chosen in London. It was a reflection of confidence in the King's administrative ability in ruling his large, poor and thoroughly uninviting state of some 5–6 million people, and his benevolence towards Britain.[20]

The latter was a matter of necessity rather than conviction. Already in the 1920s Ibn Sa'ud was beginning to feel hemmed in by what he saw as puppet states created by his ally. According to Sir Alan Ryan, who was minister in Jeddah in the late 1920s, Ibn Sa'ud was fundamentally hostile to all Western influence, but realised that British friendship was a condition of his survival. He knew, Ryan goes on to claim, 'that we were trustworthy, if exacting'.[21] In his study of Anglo-Saudi relations, Clive Leatherdale summarises the King's attitude as 'The hand you cannot bite, kiss it.'[22]

Willing to accept Ibn Sa'ud's expansion at Ibn Rashid's and Sherif Hussein's expense, the British limited his incursions into Iraqi, Transjordanian and Kuwaiti territory. Ibn Sa'ud was chary about establishing frontiers, fearing they would not be recognised by his tribesmen, as well as being tantamount to acceptance of the new states ruled by his Hashemite enemies. But he was given little choice. At a conference in 1922, Sir Percy Cox laid down the law. Harold Dickson, who was translating, was astonished

> to see the Sultan of Najd being reprimanded like a naughty schoolboy by H.M. High Commissioner, and being told sharply that he, Sir Percy Cox, would himself decide on the type and the general line of the frontier [...] Ibn Sa'ud almost broke down, and pathetically remarked that Sir Percy was his father and mother, who had made him and raised him from nothing to the position he held, and he would surrender half his kingdom, nay the whole, if Sir Percy ordered.[23]

In fact the main loser was Kuwait, which had to surrender two-thirds of its territory to compensate Ibn Sa'ud for the loss of territory to Iraq. But Cox came up with an ingenious scheme to resolve another Sa'udi–Kuwaiti dispute in an area believed to contain oil, establishing a neutral zone, to be shared by both Ibn Sa'ud and Kuwait, immediately to the west of the sheikhdom. All of this was drawn by Sir Percy on the map with a large red pen, and then embodied in the Protocols of Al-'Uqayr, signed on 2 December 1922.

This did not prevent trouble continuing on the ground. Iraq had been given a strip of desert it did not want and was not equipped to rule, while the Bedouin found the new frontier, which was not actually demarcated, neither identifiable nor comprehensible. The raids into Iraq continued, and the 1925 Bahra agreement, which dealt with the extradition of refugee tribes and the conditions under which armed contingents could be raised, failed to pacify the border. Trouble again flared up in 1927, and in 1929 the RAF drove the Ikhwan 70 miles into Najd in order to prevent concentrations within the proximity of the Iraqi border.[24] Ibn Sa'ud and Feisal met aboard a Royal Naval ship in 1930 and an agreement was subsequently reached.

During the Najd–Hejaz war of 1924 and 1925 Britain had taken measures to detach Ma'an and Aqaba from the Hejaz, thereby securing Transjordan an outlet on the Red Sea and a right of way for any future railway from Aqaba to Baghdad. Ibn Sa'ud was thus prevented from obtaining a wedge of territory between Transjordan and Iraq, which would have separated the two Hashemite states and put the King astride the British imperial air route to the east. The frontier between Transjordan and Najd was established by the 1925 Hodda agreement.[25]

The 1930s saw a deterioration in Anglo-Saudi relations, beginning with British reluctance to provide Ibn Sa'ud greater support in his war against the Yemen in 1933. Attempts to resolve border disputes between Saudi Arabia and the sheikhdoms of the Gulf came to nothing, a failure which would cause serious problems in the 1950s.[26] The outbreak of the Arab revolt in Palestine created a new source of Anglo-Saudi discord. When the Peel Commission first recommended partition, the Saudi monarch warned that the creation of a Jewish state would be a perpetual irritant in the Middle East and a source of international danger. Should Britain persist with the plan, it would cause her downfall in the Middle East.[27] The idea was dropped, but this did not prevent a growing sense of mutual distrust.

Increasing Italian activity in the Red Sea area provided an additional source of Anglo-Saudi tension. The King might have referred to Mussolini as Miss O'Looney,[28] but he was not amused by a 1938 Anglo-Italian agreement whereby both countries agreed to respect each other's sphere of influence in the region, and pledged not to seek a privileged position in

Saudi Arabia or the Yemen. This suggested to the Saudis that Britain was no longer committed to cooperation with them in managing regional affairs. But while willing to make overtures to the Axis, Ibn Sa'ud, who preferred the devil he knew, was reluctant to commit himself to them.[29]

There was also a financial consideration. Oil was discovered in Saudi Arabia in 1938 by Standard Oil of California. During negotiations in 1933, the King had demanded a £100,000 down-payment in gold. The Iraq Petroleum Company was only prepared to offer £10,000, thereby allowing itself to be outbid. The British government had been unconcerned. They already had all the oil they seemed likely to need from Persia and Iraq, and were in any case dubious as to whether there was in fact oil in Saudi Arabia.[30] They would be proved spectacularly wrong. For the time being, however, the Kingdom remained poor and Ibn Sa'ud still hoped for a resumption of the subsidy Britain had discontinued in 1924. In 1939, the King enquired what Britain would do if Saudi Arabia was attacked by Italy. By now London was sufficiently anxious to prevent the Saudis siding with the Axis that they offered what was in effect a quasi-guarantee.[31]

Britain's relations with the other independent state on the Arabian Peninsula were more difficult. Since the Turkish withdrawal during World War I, the Yemen had been in the hands of the wily Imam Yahyah, who did not recognise the prewar Anglo-Ottoman border agreement. On the contrary, he claimed Aden and the whole of the Protectorates on whose territory he had begun to encroach. RAF action had not proved successful, and with an eye to preventing the Italians establishing a position on the east coast of the Red Sea, from where they could threaten Egypt and the Sudan, as well as communications through the Red Sea, Britain entered negotiations with Yahyah in 1926. When these failed, the army estimated that it would take a full infantry division, costing over a million pounds, to dislodge the Yemenis. The RAF offered to do the job at a fraction of the price. The effectiveness of this new air action was proved in February 1928 when, following the kidnapping of two Protectorate chiefs, Taiz and other Yemeni towns were bombed. Yemeni morale was sufficiently shaken that all occupied territory was evacuated.[32] There were no further encroachments. An Anglo-Yemeni agreement was signed in 1934. While it ensured that future relations would remain friendly, the Imam did not abandon his claims.[33]

The arrival of the RAF was quickly felt in the Protectorates, which ceased to be regarded as indefensible outworks maintained only for political reasons, becoming instead Aden's first line of defence. To be effective, aircraft needed intelligence of impending attack, and this meant establishing a network of forward intelligence operatives, pushing Political Officers into the most remote areas. The establishment of the Aden Protectorate Levies in 1928 to replace British troops opened up new links between British officers and sections of South Arabian society with which there had previously scarcely been any contact. Aden remained a thriving entreport, with coal and, by the 1930s, oil fuelling facilities. But while still referred to as an 'imperial outpost', its strategic value had diminished, along with some of the fortress mentality. Official policy increasingly became to re-orientate town and port to the hinterland, with Aden being treated more as an Arab town than an outwork of India.[34]

The construction of a chain of landing sites in the Hadhramaut, linking Aden with the Persian Gulf, strengthened contacts between Aden and Mukalla. This was another area whose importance had been increased by Italian activities. According to the writer and traveller, Freya Stark, 'The Hadramis were anxious for more active protection and restive under what we like to call non-interference and they are apt to think of as neglect. The British Empire decided, out of its immense resources, to grant one man.'[35]

An incident in 1937, when a sub-tribe interfered with road security and fired on the British flag, brought in the RAF. This provided the opportunity for the new Political Officer, Harold Ingrams, to end a local war which had been tearing Hadhrami society apart. Ingrams was another of those British figures who made a real local difference. What became known as Ingrams' or the English peace, involved the conclusion of more than a thousand local truces, and Ingrams was subsequently greeted as 'Friend of the Hadhramaut'. His aim was to extend the authority of the local sultans rather than that of the British government. Under a new 1937 treaty, Sultan Salih of Mukalla agreed to take British advice on matters other than religion. This facilitated reforms, including those of the Sultan's armed forces and finances.[36] Ingrams' diplomatic skills were subsequently tested by difficulties in reconciling the Sultans' view that advice meant support for his authority with the Colonial Office's opinion that it meant British control to introduce beneficial notions of British government. Ingrams believed that the system would only work if his advice were accepted as that of a friend, rather than as the agent of an alien authority. He dressed and lived as an Arab, which some of his colleagues and subordinates thought something of a charade.[37]

Concern in the late 1920s that Britain could no longer claim rights without the assent of local parties in the Persian Gulf led to the formation of a Cabinet subcommittee. This concluded that 'modern developments, such as air power, cross country traction, and the probability of the construction of a railway between northern Persia and Gulf, have increased the potential risks to which our interests are exposed'. Since the importance of the region to Indian security and imperial interests was deemed if anything greater than in the past, Britain should maintain the status quo along the whole Arab littoral.[38]

The most important of the new developments was aviation. Half a century after the opening of the Suez Canal, the 1921 Cairo conference had decided to establish an air route between Transjordan and Iraq, intended as a link in the chain of imperial communications, which would eventually run across India to Australia. The RAF began an air mail service from Cairo to Baghdad the same year, cutting the time which mail took from England to Iraq from four weeks to nine days or less. In 1928 Persia had allowed Imperial Airlines to use landing facilities along the north side of the Persian Gulf. But the permission only ran for three years, after which the airline had to use an interior route which was unsuitable because of mountains. This meant switching to the southern side of the Gulf. The ongoing war against Iraq led Ibn Sa'ud to refuse to allow refuelling rights at Hasa in 1927, but thanks to the availability of longer-range aircraft it became possible to use facilities in the tiny sheikhdom of Sharjah.[39]

Oil was described by the Cabinet's subcommittee as 'entirely a war question'. The development of motor transport, tanks and aircraft during World War I had underscored oil's strategic importance. As of 1938, the Middle East only supplied some 5 per cent of world production.[40] But the discovery in 1931 of oil in Bahrain by an American consortium nevertheless raised political as well as commercial questions. Under the terms of prewar agreements with Bahrain, Kuwait and other sheikhdoms, oil development was only to be entrusted to British companies. To US oil companies, this looked like a cunning ruse to exclude them from the Gulf. In fact, as Daniel Yergin notes, 'the British government felt harried, beleaguered and very much on the defensive before the greater American power, as it struggled to maintain positions it regarded as crucial to the empire'.[41]

In the event, the US Socal consortium was allowed to operate in Bahrain, though only under conditions guaranteeing continued British political primacy. Communications from Socal to the Ruler had to be made via the British Political Agent. The British were again resistant to American involvement in Kuwait, fearing in the words of one official, 'losing influence and position to another, richer nation, in an arena critical to its imperial interests'.[42] But nor did they want an oil war with the US. This time an Anglo-American consortium was established, operating on a

50-50 basis, in the form of the Kuwait Oil Company. Once again the British insisted on guarantees which would ensure their dominance over political developments in the country. In 1935 Qatar was given aerial protection against serious and unprovoked attack in return for an oil concession for the Anglo-Persian Oil Company.[43]

The sheikhdoms posed relatively few political problems for Britain. 'We achieve our object with astonishing economy', one Political Resident noted in the 1930s, ascribing this to goodwill accruing from 'non-interference, square deals and genuine protection'.[44] This did not mean that the British were entirely indifferent to their internal affairs. The appointment of Charles Belgrave, as Adviser in Bahrain, succeeded in imposing administrative disciplines unparalleled in the Arab world. Against the background of disaffection against the Ruler in 1938, the British had attempted to encourage Kuwaiti administrative liberalisation and democratisation, for fear the malcontents would otherwise look to Iraq. But there were limits as to how far the British were willing to get involved. As one official put it, 'We certainly do not want to administer their disgusting territories and people.'[45]

Referring to the Persian side of the Gulf, the Cabinet subcommittee's 1928 interim report had referred to the desirability of maintaining the status quo 'to the utmost limit that political considerations will admit'.[46] By then, however, British influence in Persia had substantially diminished, thanks not simply to Curzon's misjudged attempts to impose a treaty after the war, but also to one of the key developments in modern Persian history, the coming to power of an officer of the Cossack Brigade, Reza Khan. On hearing news of the coup in February 1921, General William Ironside, who until shortly before had been commander of British forces in Persia, noted in his diary, 'I fancy that all the people think I engineered the *coup d'état* [...] I suppose I did strictly speaking.'[47] Ironside had provided the conditions as well as the encouragement which made the coup possible. He had been worried about the impending British withdrawal from Persia, and feared that only a strong military dictatorship could preserve the country from Bolshevik revolution. But he had acted without knowledge of the Foreign Office, and without consulting the British Minister in Tehran.[48]

Britain was now saddled with Ironside's choice. Sir Percy Loraine, who became British Minister in 1920, believed that Reza Khan was a man with whom he could do business, and advocated a policy of non-interference to calm acutely anti-British feeling.[49] 'In the old days', he wrote, 'we could have taken him [Reza Khan] in hand and supported him: today that would rush him.'[50] Loraine, who was determined to intervene as little possible in Persian politics, believed Reza was the man Persia needed.

Reza Khan was a blunt, brutal soldier who in 1925 had himself crowned as Shah. Ashamed by Persia's backwardness, he set out to modernise the country. First, however, he had to establish central control, which was to create an embarrassment for Britain. One of Reza's targets was Sheikh Khazali of Mohammerah. Britain's dilemma derived once again from conflicting promises. According to the 1907 Anglo-Russian agreement, Britain was bound to protect Persia's integrity, meaning in effect to support the central government. But, as already noted in chapter 2, it had also repeatedly pledged to support Khazali's autonomy 'in the event of any encroachment by the Persian government', although the latter promises were qualified by the stipulations that Khazali must observe his obligations to the Persian government and be guided by British advice.[51]

These potentially conflicting assurances did not matter so long as the central government in Tehran was weak. But when in 1924 Reza Shah moved against Khazali, who had joined the opposition against Reza, the British were confronted with an awkward choice. Their position was further complicated by the belief that while Reza Shah represented the best bulwark against the Russians, abandoning Khazali would damage British prestige among Gulf rulers. In November 1924 Loraine asked for a battalion of troops to be sent to Basra. But Curzon had now left the Foreign Office, and there was no taste in Britain for military adventures overseas. Loraine was advised to resolve the crisis by other means. This he did, helping to negotiate an agreement which gave Reza control over the area. The Sheikh was subsequently removed to Tehran, where he was placed under house arrest. There was no British protest.[52]

A further and more ominous source of conflict with Reza Shah arose over the terms of the concession of the Anglo-Persian Oil Company. Big oil companies were more than simply commercial enterprises, being inescapably involved with the economic, political and social development of the countries in which they operated.[53] APOC was of vital economic importance to Persia, providing two-thirds of its export earnings and a considerable part of the government's revenue. Persian nationalists saw APOC as a remote and privileged foreign body. The company discriminated on lines of race, with staff and labour divided into three classes. The First Class, so named until the late 1930s, consisted of all British employees plus a few handpicked Persians who had been trained in Britain. Salaried office workers and technical men, whether Persian or Indian, constituted a second class. The third class consisted of skilled and unskilled Persian workers. The company saw itself as under no obligation to provide more than the minimum of amenities. 'If we gave a little', one manager later wrote, 'they would ask for more so it was best not to give at all where such giving was not made imperative by the operations of the company.' Other senior managers spoke of the Persians with contempt.[54]

All this was naturally resented by the Persians, whose sense of national pride was further offended by a feeling of being exploited. 'I see you people have provided a much better way of living for yourselves here in the desert', one minister complained, 'than exists for 99 per cent of the people in Tehran.'[55] Aware of a rising tide of nationalism, APOC had in the late 1920s entered into negotiations for a new agreement, but no deal had been reached, and in 1932 its concession was unilaterally cancelled. The news was greeted with rejoicing throughout the country. Two days of holidays were declared with illuminations throughout the provinces. The official British view was that the crisis had been brought about by Reza Shah's 'greedy violation of a legally valid contract'.[56]

The immediate reason for nationalisation was the dramatic fall in revenue from the company as a result of the world depression. But Reza Shah was also determined to curb an independent power centre in the country, and vent his anger at the British government, which remained the company's largest shareholder. He was also furious with Britain for its recognition of Iraq, which he regarded as an invention of British imperialism, as well as its protection of Bahrain, on which Iran had a claim. After an unsuccessful naval display in the Persian Gulf, the matter was referred to the League of Nations, and within four months a new agreement had been signed. This reduced the concession area by two-thirds and increased Persian revenues, which rose from £1.5 million to £4.3 million in 1939, although the concession was extended until 1993. Sir John Cadman, APOC's chairman, felt that 'we had been pretty well plucked', but its essential position had been preserved, and relations with the company during the rest of the decade were reasonably good.[57] APOC was renamed the Anglo-Iranian Oil Company when Reza Shah changed Persia's name in 1935.[58]

Reza Shah looked to Germany as a counterweight to Britain and Russia. The modernisation of Iranian industry was undertaken largely under German auspices, and the German percentage of Iranian trade increased from 8 per cent in 1932–3 to at least 45 per cent in 1940–1. The Germans provided teachers, founded cultural institutions and educated Iranian students in Germany. A special decree of 1936 even exempted Iranians as 'pure Aryans' from Nazi racial laws.[59] At the same time Reza Shah sought to diminish British influence in the Gulf. His irritability with foreign press criticism led to some official attempts to change the attitude of the British press to the Shah – a forerunner of similar British efforts in the 1970s. The embassy's private view, however, was unflattering. In 1934 the ambassador described the Persians as 'vainglorious, intriguing, witty, untruthful, cowardly, sensual, money-loving and corrupt'. Despite an occasional Occidental veneer, Iran was still, in the embassy's opinion, an oriental despotism rather than a modern state.[60]

Assessing British interests in Arabia in 1926, Sir John Shuckburgh commented that there appeared to be no case for framing an Arabian policy on a grand scale. Even were this desirable, the politics of the peninsula were altogether too fluid to make this possible.[61] If this reads as a classic statement of Foreign Office pragmatism, the fact remains that Arabia and the Gulf posed few major problems for Britain in the interwar years. Those which did arise were readily dealt with on a case by case basis. Nevertheless, the decline in Britain's positions in Saudi Arabia and Persia in the 1930s was a troubling symptom of the wider difficulties in British foreign and imperial policy as a new world war approached.

12

Egypt and World War II

World War I had resulted in British paramountcy in the Middle East. World War II, the first major conflict in which the Empire did not expand, marked the beginning of the end. Although Britain held the Middle East, with the exception of the last three years of the war, from here on British power was either on the defensive or in retreat. The alarm bell had begun ringing following Mussolini's Abyssinian campaign, which demonstrated that Italy had now to be considered a potential enemy. For the first time in its imperial history Britain was therefore faced with simultaneous threats on the European Continent, in the Mediterranean and in the Far East. As the Chiefs of Staff quickly warned, Britain lacked the strength to meet this triple threat. Italy might only be a second-class military power, with no economic staying power in war.[1] But in the mid- and late 1930s Britain lacked the men or resources to reinforce the Middle East.

'Of all the Great Powers in Europe', Mussolini declared in 1934, 'the nearest to Africa and to Asia is Italy.'[2] Italy, he believed, 'would only be great if we have Egypt'.[3] He described Britain to Hitler as 'our gaoler: it wants to hold us shackled in the Mediterranean'. Early signs of Italy's forward policy in the Middle East included attempts to get King Fu'ad of Egypt to copy fascism and suspend the constitution, the provision of arms to the Yemen and subsidising Jewish immigration into Palestine.[4] Mussolini also began to wage a war of words. Although the number of sets was still small, radio was a new and ideal propaganda medium in an area of high illiteracy such as the Middle East. Radio Bari, which began broadcasting in March 1934, was originally an exercise in cultural propaganda. With the Abyssinian crisis, it took on a markedly anti-British tone. Along with the supply of free films, magazines and papers, Radio Bari helped to make the Italians talked about in the region. It had some success in embarrassing the British, as well as in creating a British phobia of 'the Italians under the bed'. But its wider impact was limited. The Arabs were no fonder of the Italians than of the British, and their claims to sympathise with Muslims were inconsistent with Italian actions in Libya, where large-scale white settlement was being encouraged at the expense of the Arab population.[5]

The British response came with the creation of an Arabic Service, the first of the BBC's language services, which started broadcasting in January 1938. This became popular in Iraq, Saudi Arabia and the Red Sea area, but not in Egypt and Palestine.[6] Its target audience were the coffee shops as well as politicians, its news bulletins being designed to appeal to what its historian describes as 'the still small voice of reason, and also, on occasion, to the slightly louder voice of regional self-interest'.[7] To Foreign Office annoyance, its first news bulletin included a story about the execution of two Arab prisoners in Palestine. But this helps explain why, unlike Radio Bari, the BBC Arabic Service was still broadcasting three-quarters of a century later.

Mussolini's successful conquest of Abyssinia had undermined British prestige in the Middle East, while whetting the Italian's ambitions. He was now in control of the source of the Blue Nile, while flanking the Straits of Bab el Mandeb at the mouth of the Red Sea from Massawa to Assab. There was also a potential threat to Aden.[8] More ominous was the build-up of Italian forces in Libya. The troops were untrained, and acutely short of vehicles and wirelesses. No war plans were made to attack Egypt until the fall of France in June 1940. But the headline military figures looked alarming. By September 1939 there were some 215,000 troops in Tripolitania. This worried the Egyptians, who were acutely aware of the inadequacy of their air defences, while the British were concerned that Mussolini was capable of some kind of 'mad dog' irrational act.[9]

British reinforcements which arrived in Egypt in the late summer of 1935 were welcomed, the first time this had ever happened. At the time of the 1938 Munich crisis, the embassy in Cairo warned that Britain's ability and willingness to protect small states, including Egypt, was being seriously questioned. But the Chiefs of Staff turned a deaf ear to requests for additional forces, insisting that the German threat to the British homeland must have priority and calling instead for *rapprochement* with Italy.[10] 'Horrible' risks in Egypt were deemed unavoidable.[11]

The Chiefs of Staff got their Italian agreement at Easter 1938, providing, *inter alia*, for a reduction in the Italian garrison in Libya, as well as a cessation of propaganda broadcasts.[12] It proved a very temporary arrangement. In contravention of the agreement, Italian forces in Libya were reinforced during the Munich crisis, and again during the Italian occupation of Albania in April 1939. Britain responded by moving the Mediterranean Fleet to Alexandria.[13] But by the eve of World War II, when a Middle East command was established, Britain still had no coherent strategy for the region, and its forces there were woefully underequipped. There were a paltry 48 anti-tank and eight anti-aircraft guns.[14]

It was the collapse of France and expulsion of British forces from Continental Europe in June 1940 which brought the Middle East to the centre of British strategic thinking. Britain was suddenly and totally unexpectedly deprived of its main ally, on whom defence planning in the Mediterranean, as well as in North and East Africa, not to mention hopes of winning the war had all relied. Churchill was temperamentally loath to stay on the defensive, nor could he afford to do so. He needed a new theatre to show first the Americans, whom the Prime Minister was assiduously cultivating, then Stalin, who after the German attack on Russia in June 1941 was constantly calling for a second front in Europe, not to mention his own people that Britain was still actively fighting the war. He also needed victories, not least to restore British prestige in the colonial world.[15] The only place to look was, as in World War I, the Middle East and the Mediterranean, which effectively constituted a single combat theatre.

From the autumn of 1940 until the defeat of German forces in North Africa in May 1943, the Middle East thus became one of Britain's two pivotal theatres of the war, along with the battle of the Atlantic. It was regarded as second in importance only to the United Kingdom itself. In his War Memoirs, Churchill described the region as 'the hinge of fate on which our ultimate victory turned'.[16] With invasion looming in the summer of 1940, tanks were actually diverted from Britain to the Middle East. This was Britain's last independent military 'show', producing the victorious Eighth Army, and Britain's only hero-general of the war, Montgomery. It was the only Allied command which remained under exclusively British control until the end of the conflict. In contrast to World War I when the central British military effort had been on the Western Front, this time there was little to no talk of sideshows. Those military commanders unwise enough to question the scale of Britain's military effort in the Middle East were firmly put in their place.[17]

Conversely, the loss of the Middle East would, in the views of both Churchill and the Chiefs of Staff, have been a disaster of the first magnitude, entailing the loss of the Mediterranean, Suez and Middle East oil.[18] According to an American assessment, a British defeat in 1941 in the Middle East would have severed the most important link with the Soviet Union, doomed India, foreshadowed the confluence of German and Japanese armies, and paved the way for the occupation of North and Northwest Africa; the latter in turn would have endangered shipping in the south Atlantic and communications between the United States and Latin America.[19]

This was not an immediate threat in the summer of 1940, when the prospect of easy pickings led Mussolini to enter the war. On paper, at least, the Italians continued to enjoy a substantial numerical advantage – some half a million men compared to the 85,775 soldiers in Wavell's command. But the value of Italian numbers was undermined by myriad weaknesses. Italian senior commanders often lacked an even rudimentary grasp of modern warfare. There was little by way of initiative, teamwork or precision. The army was under-gunned, under-armoured, poorly trained and lacked anti-aircraft protection.[20]

The Italian invasion of Egypt in September 1940 was therefore quickly reversed when, at the end of the year, General Richard O'Connor's forces advanced into Libya to El Agheila on the Gulf of Sirte. Nineteen Italian generals and more than 130,000 troops were captured. A boost to British morale, the victory helped facilitate the passage through the US House of Representatives of vital Lend-Lease legislation, on which Britain's ability to continue the war depended.[21] But there was a sting in the tail, for the real danger posed by the Italians lay precisely in their weakness. As the Italian forces fell back, Hitler began to worry that an Italian collapse would allow the redeployment of British troops. He was particularly anxious to avoid them reaching the frontiers of French North Africa, where he correctly believed that the French commander, General Maxim Weygand, was in contact with the British.[22] Hence the despatch in February 1941 of one of Germany's most audacious commanders.

General Erwin Rommel's arrival on the North African scene marked the beginning of two extremely difficult years for the British in the Middle East. Churchill, who took a very close interest in the theatre, sacked two commanders-in-chief – Wavell, and his successor General Claude Auchinleck. Wavell's troubles had begun with the withdrawal of troops in early 1941 in a failed attempt to help Greece against first Italian, and then German invasion. This had allowed Rommel to reach the Egyptian frontier. In the year and a half following the German invasion of Russia in June 1941 and the early reverses suffered by the Red Army, British commanders therefore faced a potential pincer movement from Rommel in the west and a German army debouching through the Caucasus in the event of a Russian collapse. Were this to happen, then according to the German Foreign Minister, Joachim von Ribbentrop, speaking to the Japanese prime minister, the war would be over.[23]

His remark was made weeks after the fall of Tobruk in May 1942, news of which deeply distressed Churchill, who was then in Washington. By early July, Axis forces had penetrated 250 miles inside Egypt, and were within 70 miles of Alexandria. There was a major 'flap', a euphemism for panic. The Mediterranean Fleet left port, where demolition squads prepared to blow up the docks and bunkering stations. Alexandria gave the impression of a ghost town. In Cairo a thick mist arose over the British embassy, as huge quantities of documents were burnt; trains and roads towards Palestine were jammed. Arab bystanders watched with contempt at the rush for seats by Europeans at Cairo airport. The Germans tried to contact Farouk and the Egyptian 'Free Officers' movement to prepare an uprising, while a hopeful Mussolini arrived in Tripoli with the white charger on which he intended to make his triumphal entry into Cairo.[24]

It was a wasted journey. Rommel was held at the first battle of El Alamein, a nondescript little railway station on the Egyptian coast in early July, and defeated at the second battle in November. Church bells were rung in Britain. The Egyptian elite now warmed considerably to the British. Two months previously, notes Artemis Cooper, 'their chic princesses would have scorned to dance with a British officer; now they accepted with pleasure'.[25] The surrender of Axis forces on 13 May 1943, a few months after the Soviet victory at Stalingrad ended any danger of a German advance from the north, meant that the Middle East was finally secure.

As during World War I, Egypt was the hub of military operations, becoming, along with India, Britain's most important overseas base and power centre. Churchill visited Cairo five times, more often than he went to Washington. Freya Stark described the Egyptian capital as 'the artery of our oil and our communications, the keystone of our Middle Eastern arch. It had returned to the days of the Ptolemys when it was the gate to Parthia and India and all the spice trade. You could hear every European language (except German) in its streets', as also every English, Scottish, Welsh and Irish accent. She goes on to describes embassy parties

> round a swimming pool in the open with lights dimmed so that men late
> from their offices would peer among bare jewelled shoulders and mess
> uniforms [...] to find their parties at the little tables. These blue lights

bewitched Cairo into the *Pélleas* and *Mélisande* remoteness that seemed to belong to the precarious time.[26]

Yet for all the romance and glamour, which contrasted so strongly with austere London, Cairo provided the headquarters for a commander-in-chief whose remit covered an area of some 3.5 million square miles, stretching east as far as Iraq and south to British Somaliland.[27] Wavell was responsible not only for operations in the Western desert, but against Italian forces in Ethiopia and the Red Sea, successfully concluded in November 1941, as well as for the Balkans. With Malta under constant attack, Alexandria was the Mediterranean Fleet's main base. The Middle East command comprised what Churchill described as an extraordinary amalgam of military, political, diplomatic and administrative problems of extreme complexity.[28] In the summer of 1942 it had become so big that a separate Iraqi-Iranian command was created.

Between January and July 1941, 239,000 British and Commonwealth troops arrived in the region, along with more than one million tons of military supplies. Port loading facilities at Suez and Port Said, which had been stretched to the limit, were improved, and a large programme of road and rail building stretching north into Syria was embarked on. This was a major undertaking. With the closure of the Mediterranean, the Middle East became one of the most distant areas of the world to supply from Britain, with supplies taking some 8–12 weeks to arrive. India, which was the nearest significant source of supply, was three thousand miles away. By November 1941 Auchinleck, who had succeeded Wavell during the summer, had 750,000 British, Australian, Canadian, Indian, New Zealand, Greek, French and Polish troops under his command.[29] Irregular armies emerged, including the Long Range Desert Group, SOE, which used Cairo for operations in the Middle East and Balkans, and the SAS, formed in Egypt in 1941.

A hundred and forty thousand of Auchinleck's troops were stationed in and around Cairo, which was surrounded by some 30 airfields and landing strips. Headquarters proliferated, including intelligence, propaganda, subversion and the Middle East Supply Centre. There was a large Treasury delegation. The build-up was accompanied by intrigue and turf wars. By 1941 it was felt necessary to try to relieve the Commander-in-Chief of some of his political and administrative burdens, by appointing a Minister of State with Cabinet rank to reside in Cairo. His jobs included relations with the Free French and the emperor of Ethiopia, the conduct of propaganda and economic warfare, giving political guidance to the military, and trying to coordinate the policy of British representatives in the region. A 'coral reef' of theatre and regional organisations gradually formed around him.[30] The job required a high order of political and diplomatic skills.

Little of this helped Anglo-Egyptian relations. British lives touched those of the indigenous inhabitants only superficially, at the level of bartender, waiter, shopkeeper, nightclub hostess, and the workers in British military establishments. Egypt came as a profound cultural shock to many British troops, who were by no means always well behaved.[31] Many soldiers came away with a very low opinion of the Egyptians, although a smattering of Arabic – *bint, floozie, shufti* – found its way into the English language. Novelists took rather more interest. Evelyn Waugh used his experience in Egypt to comic effect in *Officers and Gentlemen*. Olivia Manning set three of her wartime novels in Egypt, while the last of Lawrence Durrell's *Alexandrian Quartet* is set in wartime Alexandria.

From the British military perspective, it was vital that their Middle Eastern base should remain secure, while only tying up a minimal number of troops for local security. But there was little sense of identification in the Arab world with the Allied war effort. On the contrary, while some Egyptians may have feared that Italian or German occupation could prove more disagreeable than the British, the prevailing sentiment was that they had once more become caught up in somebody else's war.[32] Italian and German propaganda was able to play on a combination of nationalism and the appeal of Nazism to elements of the Middle Eastern youth movements.[33] The string of British defeats between the Norwegian debacle of April 1940 to the fall of Tobruk inevitably encouraged a disposition to reinsure with the Axis.

Britain's legal position in Egypt was strong. The 1936 Anglo-Egyptian treaty had given Britain extensive military rights in the country, and at the outset of the war in September 1939 the Egyptian government broke off diplomatic and commercial relations with Germany, interned all German subjects unable to establish an anti-Nazi record, and sequestered German property. A state of siege was declared, ports were placed under British naval control, and strict censorship of post, telephones, telegraphs and press was introduced.[34]

Politically, however, the British were rather less secure. Despite British pressure, the Egyptian government had refused to declare war on Germany. Farouk was in a difficult position. He could neither afford to appear subservient to the British, nor to earn their hostility. But his sympathies were with the Axis, and he was in contact with both the Italians and the Germans. In communications via the Egyptian ambassador in Tehran, he expressed admiration for Hitler, offered to 'come to the aid of the Axis troops at the decisive moment', and provided intelligence on British military dispositions.[35] The Germans were also in contact with elements of the Egyptian army.[36] A secret anti-British association had been founded in both the army and air force by Ali Maher Aziz al-Masri, the Army's Inspector General, whom the British had removed. He subsequently tried to defect to the Axis with details of British troops' strengths. Among its members was a future Egyptian president, Anwar Sadat. Small wonder that the British regarded the army as unreliable and kept it in a defensive role.[37]

Small wonder also that they reverted to more active intervention in Egyptian affairs. The first of a series of incidents occurred in June 1940, the most dangerous moment in modern British history. Italy had just declared war and the French were suing for an armistice. Close links existed between Italy and Egypt, including Abdin Palace. Although Ali Maher's government was ready to break diplomatic relations, it was not willing to declare war. Italian suspects were not interned and Allied interests were obstructed. Lampson described Ali Maher as 'non-cooperative, unreliable and indeed double-faced'.[38]

With the Egyptians evidently seeking to reinsure against a potential Axis victory, the War Cabinet laid down the law. Farouk

> must either fall in line with our wishes or vacate the throne. The latter alternative would be welcome to us. If Nahas Pasha were unwilling to form a government on the conditions which we thought essential, the British authorities would have to govern Egypt under Martial Law.[39]

Lampson's instruction were that Farouk was not allowed to flee to Egypt, becoming Pretender to the Egyptian throne.[40] The Egyptian prime minister was duly forced from office.

In November, when Anthony Eden visited Cairo, he suggested that Farouk be kicked out. Lampson replied that he had come to this conclusion long ago, but that there had always been some reason against it. Britain would never get real cooperation from Farouk, and there would always be the feeling that if things went badly 'we shall be stabbed in the back'.[41] Lampson got his opportunity to get rid of Farouk in February 1942, but at the last moment he fluffed it. The British had deposed two previous Egyptian rulers in 1879 and 1914, and made frequent interventions in Egyptian internal affairs. But the Abdin Palace incident, when the British ambassador surrounded the palace with armoured cars, and demanded the appointment of a Wafd government on pain of the King's abdication, stands apart as a seminal moment in modern Egyptian history and a turning point in Anglo-Egyptian relations.

This was again a very difficult moment in the war. Benghazi had just fallen and the Japanese had invaded Malaya and Burma. The British needed a strong and freely elected Egyptian government they could trust, to replace Husayn Sirri, whom the King had forced to resign. The Wafd had signed the 1936 treaty and had no Axis sympathies. It enjoyed more popular support than any other political group and could be relied upon to oppose the King.[42] But the humiliating method which Lampson chose, and the pleasure which by his own admission he took from the incident, suggest a more personal agenda.

At the very last moment Farouk gave way and asked for another chance, which Lampson reluctantly allowed him, so that the warship standing by at Alexandria to carry him into exile in the Seychelles was not needed. Lampson had good reason for holding back. Farouk's removal would have been illegal. It would also have removed one leg from the Wafd-Palace-High Commission 'tripod'. Long term the British might still need the Palace against the Wafd, while public opinion in both Egypt and Britain would have been opposed once it was known that Farouk had been ready to give way. But the ambassador quickly regretted his decision, complaining in his diary the next day that 'we still have a rotter on the throne'.[43]

Lampson's handling of the affair was approved by Churchill, who retained his low opinion of the Egyptians and always warmed to firm action. Lampson was ennobled as Lord Killearn, an unusual honour for an ambassador still *en poste*, although there was a precedent in the case of Cromer. But his action appalled many in the British community in Cairo. General Stone, who commanded British troops in Egypt and had accompanied Lampson, sent Farouk a private letter of apology.[44] Those Egyptians who knew about the affair, which was officially hushed up under the censorship rules, regarded it as a humiliation and outrage. It tarnished Britain's reputation for fair play, and undermined the nationalist credentials and thus the very *raison d'être* of the Wafd. The army felt the slight to Egyptian national dignity deeply.

Something of this was recognised in the Foreign Office. A minute written in October 1942 warned that anything like a repetition of the February events would provoke an outcry, 'for even well-disposed Egyptians resent seeing their king manhandled'. Another official referred to the 'Lampsonian fallacy' that it was impossible to raise contentious issues in potentially hostile Egyptian quarters without having tanks behind you.[45] Nevertheless there were two other incidents – one in April 1943 and another in April

1944 – when Farouk wanted to rid himself of the Wafd, but was forced to back down. The former incident followed the publication of a 'Black Book' alleging corruption charges against the Wafd. Eden was unmoved, minuting to Churchill that it would be 'more damaging to us to have to face the charge of dropping our friends than one of condoning corruption'.[46] Churchill, his eye possibly caught by Lord Killearn's warning that 'weakness never pays in this semi-Oriental country', ordered a reluctant military to back the ambassador.[47]

The Prime Minister was again in action a year later, arguing that 'we must not be frightened about using tanks', though General Paget, the Middle East commander-in-chief, opposed the use of force against the King on the grounds of 'expediency and wisdom'.[48] Farouk backed down, but Lampson, who still referred to him as 'the boy', was beginning to have doubts about the wisdom of continuing to support the Wafd, whose unpopularity was rubbing off on their protectors. At the next crisis, which occurred when the ambassador was out of the country, Nahas was allowed to fall. It was clear by then that he was too corrupt and unpopular to survive.[49]

Egypt seemed to attract powerful British proconsuls, and the circumstances of war required one. That was certainly Churchill and Eden's view, and the hard-line policy which Killearn pursued against the King would have been impossible without their backing. But it was dangerously influenced by personal dislike, which militated against a more prudent, long-term view of Anglo-Egyptian relations. Paradoxically it was the diplomat who always seemed to be advocating tough measures, while the military commanders, who would have had their troops tied up by unrest resulting from an enforced abdication, urged caution. Some of them, including Air Marshall Sholto Douglas, got on well with the King.[50] There would have been other ways of handling Farouk which would have caused less long-term damage to British interests.

13

Holding the Middle East

World War II, 1939–45

In Egypt British tanks were used in a show of strength. In Iraq they were used in anger. The British military presence in Iraq was much smaller, while anti-British sentiment in a country remote from any immediate threat of Axis attack was much more pronounced, not least within the army. It was fanned both by the German embassy and by the Mufti, who had arrived from Syria in October 1940 and quickly established himself as a dominant figure in Iraqi political life.[1]

In this atmosphere, the influence of the pro-British prime minister, Nuri al-Said, waned. Iraqis had no interest in a conflict over Poland when Syria and Palestine were under foreign occupation, although in July 1940 the Iraqis had offered to declare war in return for British concessions over Palestine.[2] Under the subsequent premiership of Rashid Ali al-Gailani, a lawyer and nationalist politician who was also a co-founder of the Muslim Brotherhood, Iraq refused to break diplomatic relations with Italy. In discussion with the German minister, Franz von Papen, on 5 July, one Iraqi minister, Naji Shawkat, suggested that Iraq would fight with Germany when the proper time came.[3]

Concern over the Iraqi situation led to a decision in July 1940, in the event reversed because of opposition from the Viceroy and the commanders-in-chiefs of the Middle East and India, to send an Indian division to Iraq. In November there was an unsuccessful and counter-productive British attempt to oust Rashid Ali.[4] Matters came to a head in the spring of 1941, with an attempt by the Prime Minister, General Taha al-Hashimi, to post one of four leading pan-Arab nationalist and anti-British officers, nicknamed by the British 'the Golden Square', out of Baghdad. The Golden Square then forced the resignation of the Prime Minister, who was succeeded by Rashid Ali, at which the Regent fled to the British base at Habbaniya, some 50 miles west of Baghdad. Rashid Ali insisted he would

East oil industry dropped from 49 to 14 per cent, while Britain's share of oil production fell from 53 to 24 per cent, with the Americans the main winners. But BP had been forced to diversify the sources of its supplies so successfully that the 40 per cent of Iranian production now met its needs.[67]

Lord Strang, who had been Permanent Under-Secretary at the FO, wrote later that 'in the end we saved a great deal out of the wreck, suffering much loss and humiliation in the process'. The British government had originally wanted 50 per cent of the consortium, and it got only a small fraction of the compensation it demanded.[68] But this was outweighed in the medium term by the fact that the coup served to entrench the Shah's rule for another 25 years. In his valedictory despatch from Tehran in 1979, written immediately after the Iranian revolution, the ambassador, Sir Anthony Parsons, wrote that the Shah's regime 'stood us in good stead through a generation of turmoil and change in the region. Britain reaped great benefits from his conduct of Iranian affairs in terms of foreign and strategic policy, as well in the 1970s in economic, commercial and industrial terms.'[69]

The Iranian perspective was rather different. According to Mossadegh's most recent British biographer, the coup was a catastrophe from which Iran never fully recovered. The Shah's reign became increasingly autocratic and the revolution which began in 1978 turned the country into an even more oppressive theocracy. The economic outcome, while better than the terms before nationalisation, was probably less favourable than what Iran could have achieved earlier in the crisis.[70]

The events of the early post-war years boded ill for the British in the Middle East. They had failed to reach agreement with Egypt over the future of their most important base in the Middle East, or to modernise their informal empire by shifting from pashas to peasants as Bevin had wanted. They had been run out of Palestine by militant Zionism and lost their monopoly of Iranian oil. In both crises they had found themselves up against the Americans, who were increasingly critical of their approach to nationalist politics of the region, and whose effective veto over British military action Attlee's government had accepted. These pressures were containable so long as what some officials referred to as the 'virus of nationalism' manifested itself on a national rather than a regional basis.[71] That, however, was about to change with Nasser's advent to power in Egypt, and the inauguration of Cairo radio's Voice of the Arabs. These in turn would spark the British backlash which had already threatened over the Iranian oil crisis and the proposed withdrawal from the Suez Canal zone base.

16

The Road to Suez

Egypt, Jordan and Iraq, 1954–6

On 23 July 1952 King Farouk was overthrown by a group of army officers, initiating what would become a period of acute instability in the Middle East. The coup also proved the harbinger of a new and turbulent phase of Anglo-Egyptian relations. Long the lynchpin of Britain's position in the Middle East, Egypt would now play a key role in the British retreat from the region. According to Lord Trevelyan, who became ambassador in Egypt in 1955,

> To the average Englishman Egypt had become the symbol of the decline of the British Empire, although it was never a part of the Empire, and the feeling of impotence and frustration natural in this period of transition, found expression in attacks on any Minister who could be represented as weak in dealing with Nasser.[1]

By 1956 the Egyptian leader, who had quickly emerged as the real leader of the Free Officers, had come to succeed Mossadegh as Britain's Public Enemy Number One, a man seen as posing a more immediate threat to British interests than the Soviet Union. As late as 1967 a senior official likened Egypt to Ireland as 'one of those countries with whom we have never for long got our relations quite right'.[2]

Hostility to the British occupation had helped motivate the coup. According to one of his biographers, whenever as a child he saw an aeroplane passing overhead, Nasser shouted, 'Oh God almighty, may a calamity overtake the English.'[3] Along with other Free Officers, including General Mohammad Neguib and Anwar Sadat, Nasser viewed Lampson's treatment of Farouk in February 1942 as an insult to Egypt. Military indignation was further fuelled by the Egyptian defeat in the 1948 Palestine war. Discussion of a coup, however, only began in early

1952 in the wake of Black Saturday, the murderous rioting in Cairo which followed a battle with the British army in which 46 Egyptian police were killed.[4]

Although the Cairo embassy was aware that a revolutionary situation existed in the country, the coup took MI6, whose contacts were with the old guard, by surprise.[5] Crucially, there was no British intervention, and while Churchill deplored the end of the monarchy, the initial diplomatic assessments of Nasser were generally favourable; he was seen as a man with whom Britain could do business.[6]

The problem of the Sudan, which had plagued earlier Anglo-Egyptian negotiations, was resolved in principle in 1953, with an Anglo-Egyptian agreement to grant the territory independence. This left the base. For the Free Officers, withdrawal and an end to occupation were absolute priorities. In Nasser's words, it was a matter of Egyptian dignity. 'We cannot feel free and sovereign until they [the British troops] go.'[7] Withdrawal, however, stuck in Churchill's craw. He had opposed Egyptian independence back in 1921 and now foresaw 'a prolonged humiliating scuttle before all the world, without advantage, goodwill or fidelity from those Egyptian usurpers to whom triumph is being accorded'.[8] It was equally objectionable to members of the so-called 'Suez Group' of 41 MPs in the Conservative Party who raged against the dying of the imperial light. It articulated a groundswell of popular sentiment and had strong support among constituency associations, party organisations and Commons committees, as well as being encouraged behind the scenes by senior ministers and helped by MI6. Its leader, Captain Charles Waterhouse, cherished an almost religious belief in empire and was determined to call a halt to the growing succession of retreats.[9] Like the later controversy over British EEC/EU membership, withdrawal was a gut issue.

Yet by the early 1950s the case for leaving had become overwhelming. A guerrilla campaign launched shortly after Egypt's abrogation of the 1936 treaty was tying up some 80,000 troops at a time when there were strong financial pressures to make military economies. Moreover, as Eden – the man who had negotiated the 1936 Anglo-Egyptian treaty and who was still very much the diplomatic pragmatist – pointed out, like it or not, Britain had to adjust to the changing facts of Middle East life. British policy must be designed to harness the force of nationalism, not struggle against it. Britain could not in the second half of the twentieth century 'hope to maintain our position in the Middle East by the methods of the last century'. A continued British presence risked a clash with the Egyptians and reoccupation of the country, with serious international repercussions.[10]

In the end common sense prevailed, helped by the explosion of the first H bomb in 1954, which put the whole rationale of big bases, let alone another major war in the Middle East, into doubt. In 1954, only two years before the expiry of the 1936 treaty, and with the important help of American mediation, agreement was finally reached.[11] All British troops would be withdrawn within eighteen months. Britain would have the right to reactivate the base for a period of seven years in the event of war, including attack on Turkey, a NATO member. Meanwhile the facilities would be maintained by civilian contractors. The Egyptians had refused British demands for British soldiers to remain for the purpose, the uniforms being regarded as a symbol of the hated occupation. For Britain, and even more for Egypt, it was a historic agreement.

The hope on both sides was that a new chapter in Anglo-Egyptian relations could now be opened. It was wishful thinking.[12] Although Nasser respected the British for their historical achievements and industrial and commercial skills, the legacy of the occupation was debilitating. The point was graphically illustrated by the meeting between Eden and Nasser in Cairo, in February 1955. According to his confidant, Mohammed Heikal, Nasser felt the 'humiliation of Egypt's colonial subservience' when he entered the British embassy. 'Heritage, upbringing, appearance, dress, experience, outlook, ambitions, everything conflicted.'[13] Nor did it help that Nasser was of a highly suspicious disposition, tending to see Britain's hand everywhere in the Middle East. He was pathologically sensitive about the foreign, and especially the British press and radio, notably the BBC Arabic Service.[14]

Such factors mattered disproportionately in the acutely unstable dynamics of the new politics of the Middle East. What both the British and Egyptians had failed to appreciate was the sheer complexity of the emerging Middle Eastern tangle of oil, the Cold War, inter-Arab rivalries, the Arab–Israeli conflict and the ongoing conflict between Arab nationalism and a retreating and angry European imperialism. As Egypt immediately sought to exploit its new independence with a bid for leadership of the Arab world, its interests were bound to clash with Britain's determination to maintain its influence in the region.

Nasser was the political phenomenon of the Middle East of the 1950s, embodying the ideal of Arab unity and the regeneration of the Arab world after five centuries of Ottoman and Anglo-French rule. The leader of the most populous country in the Arab world, he was determined to avoid entanglement in Cold War alliance systems which Britain and the United States had been promoting, in favour of the Third World neutralist movement which took shape at the 1955 Bandung conference in Indonesia.

Here, however, he found himself challenged by Iraq. Unlike Nasser, the Anglophile Nuri genuinely feared a Soviet threat, and to counter it sought alliances with other members of the so-called northern tier of states bordering, or close to, the Soviet Union – Turkey, Iran and Pakistan. British membership of what in 1955 became the Baghdad Pact promised to kill several birds with one stone. It provided an organisational framework for British defence arrangements in the Middle East, and an umbrella for the renewal of the 1930 Anglo-Iraqi treaty. Britain could thus keep its bases in Iraq under the guise of a regional agreement, while Nuri could retain the British defence link. If other Arab states joined, British influence in the Middle East would be maintained.[15]

From Nasser's point of view, it was precisely these advantages which made the arrangement so objectionable. Far from leaving the Middle East, the British were simply rebranding their informal empire in new Cold War form. The Baghdad Pact – the very name was offensive to Cairo – threatened to shift the centre of political gravity in the Middle East from Egypt to the Iraqi capital, while splitting the Arab world. Egypt risked finding itself isolated, without access to arms, which would go to Baghdad Pact members, and left to face Israel on its own.[16]

Britain's impending withdrawal from the Suez Canal base removed a key buffer between Israel and the Egyptian army, thus increasing Egyptian–Israeli tensions. So worried was Israeli military intelligence that it attempted to stage a series of incidents in Cairo and Alexandria, designed to try to dissuade Britain from withdrawal.[17] More seriously, in February 1955 the Israelis had launched a major raid into Gaza, in which 37 Egyptian soldiers were killed and another 31 wounded. Nasser now badly needed weapons. Unable to get them from the United States or Britain, he turned to the Soviet Union.

News of the arms deal, ostensibly with Czechoslovakia, shocked London. The Soviet threat, a matter of concern since the late 1940s, was at last materialising, with Moscow beginning to displace British influence. This was dangerous in its own right, but it also created a major dilemma in terms of how to handle the Israelis. Hitherto Britain, the US and France had operated what was in effect a cartel to control the supply of arms to the Arabs and the Israelis, under the so-called Tripartite agreement of 1950. Now they faced a completely new situation. If they provided Israel with arms equivalent to the quantities Egypt would receive from the Eastern bloc, Britain would lose all influence with the Arab world. If they refused, the Israelis might become desperate and launch a preventive war. Then, as the Foreign Secretary, Harold Macmillan, noted, 'Jordan may come in and we are in great trouble.'[18]

By mid-1956 the British estimated that the Egyptians had taken delivery of some £150 million pounds' worth of arms, nearly five times the value of all British supplies to Egypt, Iraq, Jordan and Lebanon between 1948 and 1956. In addition the Egyptians were buying industrial equipment from the Soviet bloc, which in turn was taking a large part of the Egyptian cotton crop. In London ministers became convinced that Nasser had gone over to the Soviet bloc.[19]

The growing hostility to Nasser was further fuelled by his success in preventing Syria and Saudi Arabia from joining the Baghdad Pact, along with the highly effective propaganda campaign which he had launched against it. The Voice of the Arabs projected Nasser's ideas on Arab nationalism and pan-Arab unity across the region, bypassing governments to appeal directly to their citizens. It changed the ordinary Arab's self-image and attitude to foreign tutelage. The Arab world was electrified. Cairo radio also broadcast in Swahili, supporting the Mau Mau insurgency in Kenya, while Egyptian material support was provided to the Eoka terrorist movement in Cyprus, demanding union with Greece.[20]

The effectiveness of Egyptian propaganda served to highlight the fact that Britain was still allied with the pashas, and it got under British ministerial skins. In his memoirs Selwyn Lloyd, who had succeeded Macmillan as Foreign Secretary in December 1955, complained of an Egyptian propaganda machine 'which even Dr. Goebbels would have envied', pouring out 'a cascade of abuse of Britain and anything British in the Middle East'.[21] It contributed to an atmosphere of crisis in London in which Nasser's strengths were easily overestimated. Nasser was a tactician rather than a strategist. As Lord Trevelyan wrote after Nasser's death, the Egyptian leader saw 'the tactical situation of the moment, but not where his policy was leading him'. A conspirator at heart, he earned no one's trust.[22] The fact that Cairo radio could stir up trouble for Britain's allies did not, however, mean that Nasser could then control it. 'Don't exaggerate my importance,' he had told Selwyn Lloyd in Cairo, in March 1956.[23]

The occasion was the news in March 1956 of the dismissal of General Glubb as commander of the Arab Legion. This was the climax of a crisis which had begun the previous December, when, against American advice and contrary to assurances Nasser believed he had been given, Britain tried to get Jordan to join the Baghdad Pact.[24] Iraq was feeling isolated as the only Arab member, and Macmillan was anxious to make a new attempt to draw the Arab world away from both Nasser's and Soviet influence. Since the British paid Jordan's critical subsidy, they felt entitled to ask something in return.[25] It was a serious miscalculation. Cairo radio now orchestrated a campaign which sparked some of the most serious rioting in Jordanian history, demonstrating popular hostility not only to Jordan's links with the West, but also to the local establishment. When the British bid was turned down, Britain suffered what Eisenhower regarded as its worst diplomatic defeat in recent years.[26]

If Glubb's unceremonious dismissal had at least been encouraged by Cairo radio, its roots lay deeper. The General was widely regarded in Jordan as a survivor of a former epoch, who had stayed on too long and become too powerful. The dramatic action by the young King Hussein, who had come to the throne in 1952, boosted his own popularity and gave Jordanians a new sense of national pride; they had taken on the British Empire and won.[27] In London, where the news coincided with the breakdown of talks over Cyprus, it induced a sense of panic. 'We have reached a state', Evelyn Shuckburgh, the senior Foreign Office official responsible for Britain's relations with the Middle East, recorded in his diary on 15 March, 'where each telegram that comes in causes Ministers to meet, telephone one another, draft replies and curse everybody. Not only does each of our telegrams contradict the one before, but each paragraph in each telegram contradicts the paragraph before.'[28]

The trigger to the crisis which had been building up came in July, when the Americans, with British agreement, withdrew an offer to finance construction of the Aswan dam. It is perhaps surprising, and certainly unfortunate, that neither London nor Washington anticipated Nasser's response. With the last British troops having just left the Canal zone base, Nasser felt able to take over the remaining potent symbol of imperial prowess, and thus of Egyptian humiliation, the Suez Canal. This was the second nationalisation of an important British Middle Eastern economic asset in five years. In Iran in 1951, the idea of using force had been rejected. This time a military operation was launched in the face of even stronger American opposition and in a particularly ill-judged fashion.

The result was the great crisis of end of empire and one of the dramas of twentieth-century British politics. Within the space of seven months, a British government had ended the occupation of Egypt, tried to reinvade the country, and then again evacuated, outdoing the Grand Old Duke of York, who had only marched his troops to the top of the hill and then marched them down again. This, however, was no laughing matter. Suez led to bitter domestic political controversy, dividing families and friends.

This attempt to put the imperial clock back was an action completely out of character. It went against some of the key norms of British foreign policy – the primacy of the Anglo-American alliance, respect for international law and concern for Britain's good name. It was also at total variance with Eden's long career as a diplomat. The Prime Minister rationalised the Anglo-French-Israeli collusion which preceded the attacks on Egypt as 'the highest form of statesmanship',[29] a phrase suggesting a policy which had lost its traditional moorings.

Like the AIOC nationalisation, Suez was a crisis fuelled by emotion, but without the firm restraining hand which Attlee had exercised in 1951. Eden was under pressure from his own party – his gamble in negotiating the Suez Canal zone base had evidently failed and his reputation was on the line. He was tense and ill, and, unlike Macmillan, now Chancellor of the Exchequer, who was if anything more anxious for military action, he did not know how to relax. Eden was, in addition, unusual among postwar British prime ministers in having at best an equivocal view of the US.[30]

Personalities and domestic political context, however, explain only part of the very different outcomes of the Suez and the AIOC crises. More important is the way the two Middle Eastern protagonists were perceived in London. Mossadegh was seen as posing a threat to vital British interests. Nasser was regarded as posing an existential threat to Britain. Like the Iranian nationalisation, Nasser's action was regarded as endangering sterling, with fears that Britain might be forced to devalue.[31] Unlike the AIOC crisis, the nationalisation of the canal, which carried some two-thirds of Europe's oil, also seemed a threat to British oil supplies.

Britain's energy insecurity was a new, and unnerving condition. 'No Cyprus,' Eden had declared in 1955, 'no certain facilities to protect our supply of oil. No oil, unemployment and hunger in Britain. It is as simple as that.'[32] When the Soviet leaders, Nikita Khrushchev and Nikolai Bulganin, had visited Britain in April 1956, they had been warned that Britain would fight for its oil. According to Khrushchev's account of the exchange, Eden had told the Soviet leaders that without oil Britain would choke, holding his hand up to his throat to demonstrate the point. In July 1956 Eden spoke of Nasser's hand 'on our windpipe'.[33]

These fears were intensified by the sense that imperial retreat was turning into rout, with Britain in danger of turning into a second-class power, 'another Netherlands' as Macmillan put it. His diary records a meeting of the Egypt Committee, the key decision-making body during the crisis, on 24 August, where Eden 'strongly supported by me and [Lord] Salisbury – and [Lord] Home – took the view that we had no alternative.

We must secure the defeat of Nasser by one means or another. If not, we shd [sic] rot away.'[34] It was a view shared by the American Secretary of State, John Foster Dulles, as well as by parts of the press and Conservative Party. The Permanent Under-Secretary at the Foreign Office, Sir Ivone Kirkpatrick, spelled out an even more apocalyptic vision.

> If we sit back while Nasser consolidates his position and gradually acquires control of the oil-bearing countries, he can, and is according to our information, resolved to wreck us. If Middle East oil is denied us for a year or two, our gold reserves will disappear. If our gold reserves disappear, the sterling area disintegrates. If the sterling area disintegrates and we have no reserves, we shall not be able to maintain our force in Germany, or, indeed, anywhere else. I doubt whether we shall be able to pay for the bare minimum necessary for our defence. And a country which cannot provide for its defence is finished.[35]

Nasser had thus succeeded in doing something which Hitler had failed to do. He caused a government composed of experienced ministers, the most senior of whom had held office during World War II, to panic. Nobody on the Egypt Committee appears to have recalled the lines from Kipling's *If*:

> If you can keep your head when all about you
> Are losing theirs and blaming it on you

Reasoning from fear, frustration and anger, ministers were determined, come what may, to regain control over the canal, while using the opportunity to get rid of Nasser. This became the imperative, analogous to Tony Blair's preoccupation with the risk of rogue states providing weapons of mass destruction to terrorists in 2003, which overrode all consideration of the risks and impracticalities of military intervention. It led to a catalogue of mistakes and misjudgements which graphically illustrate the way in which a misconceived premise, here the nature of the Nasserist threat, served to distort judgement and compound difficulties.

Key decisions were not properly thought through. The most important of these was the cooperation – collusion as it quickly became known – with Israel. Despite Churchill's occasional enthusiasm, and the early establishment of intelligence links, Britain had been careful since 1948 to steer clear of any suggestion of an alliance with Israel. Successive British governments had been all too aware that Israel was regarded by the Arabs as a British creation and instrument of British policy, and that appearing to let British policy coincide with the Jewish state's was dangerous.[36] But with time running out before bad weather made military operations impossible in the autumn of 1956, the Eden administration badly needed an excuse for intervention. The transparency of the charade, whereby Britain and France would intervene to separate the combatants following an Israeli attack on Egypt, was thus not subject to adequate scrutiny. As Macmillan later admitted, 'I can't honestly say I liked it [the final plan] but I agreed to it – as I was all for going in.'[37]

Nor was adequate consideration given to the all-important question of an exit strategy. The problem would not have been in defeating the Egyptian armed forces, but the guerrilla operation which would probably follow. A government set up by the occupying forces would not have survived. If some kind of international canal management were to be established, it would require the continued presence of foreign troops for its protection. Eventually, however, they would have to leave, and as Lord Trevelyan later wrote, 'the British would again figure in the Egyptian school-books, this time not only as the aggressors, but as the aggressors defeated by the Egyptian heroes'.[38]

Inadequate financial contingency plans were made. As Macmillan was well aware, because of sterling's role as a reserve currency, the Suez operation meant that Britain was much more vulnerable to financial pressure than France. There was an obvious risk of a run on the pound. Yet no plans were made to prevent this, nor was money drawn from the IMF, the International Monetary Fund, in advance of the military action.[39]

Ministers committed other cardinal errors. Expert advice was either excluded – none of Britain's ambassadors in the Middle East were consulted about the military operation – or selectively chosen. Ministers either discounted evidence which did not suit their purposes or overlooked obvious difficulties. Like Israel, France, which had stood aside when Britain had first invaded Egypt in 1882, was not an obvious partner. With the exception of the 1950 Tripartite declaration, Britain had been careful to avoid association with France, and growing French military cooperation with Israel had provoked British criticism, to the point that in spring 1956 Eden referred to the French as 'our enemies in the Middle East'.[40] But if France might provide a military substitute for the US, it could not shield Britain from active American hostility towards the operation.

Like all American presidents of the period, Eisenhower's preoccupation was with the Cold War. He saw all the dangers of the way in which the operation would rebound to Soviet advantage across the Third World,

Figure 8. Less impressive than they look. British
aircraft carriers during the Suez operation

which the Eden government ignored. But he also had a strong personal
interest in avoiding any action which might endanger Republican chances
in the presidential and congressional elections due on 7 November. That
the significance of this date, along with American objections, repeatedly
expressed, did not register more strongly in London is in the first place due
to the strength of the overriding imperative to overthrow Nasser. But there
was also a difficulty inherent in the very idea of a 'special relationship'. As
Selwyn Lloyd later wrote:

> Perhaps we were all personally on too good terms, influenced too much by
> our previous close and friendly relations with Eisenhower. We felt that we
> might argue away like members of a family but at the end of the day would
> never seriously fall out. Not having the Americans on the same side, or at
> least benevolently neutral, was unthinkable.[41]

Had the occupation of the canal been swift, the British might have presented
Washington with a *fait accompli* which Eisenhower would reluctantly have

accepted.[42] But British forces were unable to sail from Malta, some six days away, until the Anglo-French ultimatum on 30 October had been issued, to avoid the impression that Britain had foreknowledge of the attack. An angry President, who felt he had been both double-crossed and damaged just before the presidential election, thus moved to rein in his errant allies with uncharacteristic brutality. The American Sixth Fleet in the Mediterranean sought to harass the British task force, while in the face of a run on sterling, the American Treasury blocked British belated attempts to gain IMF support. Once again the government panicked – this time calling off the operation on 6 November before it had achieved its military objectives. (The threat of Soviet intervention in the Middle East also weighed with some ministers.[43]) This, however, was not the end of the British humiliation. American economic pressure was maintained until the British and French agreed to withdraw their forces. There was acute bitterness on both sides of the Atlantic; family feuds are often the worst.

Britain had stood to lose from the Suez affair whatever course it had taken. The Cabinet's assessment the day after nationalisation that failure to hold the canal 'would lead inevitably to the loss one by one of all our interests and assets in the Middle East' may have been overstated, but it was not groundless.[44] A negotiated settlement would have entailed its own costs in terms of lost prestige and the confidence of allies, though these would have been smaller than those of the botched military operation and enforced withdrawal. At first sight the impact seemed surprisingly slight. Although Eden was forced to resign, he was replaced by a man who had been equally culpable in the operation, Harold Macmillan, who went on to win the 1959 election with a handsome majority. For all the apocalyptic fears expressed in the summer of 1956, the heavens had not fallen in. The loss of residual access to the Canal zone base did not greatly disturb the British military, while the economic costs of the crisis, including the temporary closure of the Suez Canal, proved to be serious but not critical.[45] Britain's remaining position in the Middle East, in Jordan, South Arabia and the Gulf, did not collapse.

Nevertheless, Suez left a deep mark. This was the point at which the realisation that Britain was no longer a Great Power finally sunk in. A CIA visitor to London immediately after the affair was struck by 'the deep cynicism and world weariness of the British, shorn of Empire and humiliated by Suez'.[46] The damage to self-confidence and Britain's international reputation, two of the intangible assets critical to a successful foreign policy, lingered.[47] There was some subsequent reluctance to engage in solo military operations, evident in the unwillingness to force an end to Rhodesia's unilateral declaration of independence in 1964, and again following the Turkish invasion of Cyprus in 1974. In her memoirs, Margaret Thatcher referred to the 'Suez syndrome', whereby having previously exaggerated their importance, the British now underestimated it.[48]

Suez divided Britain from the French, who had been infuriated by the unilateral British decision to halt the operation, about which they had been informed rather than consulted. The West German Chancellor, Konrad Adenauer, who happened to be in Paris at the time, is said to have remarked that Europe will be your revenge. While the primary lesson of Suez learned in Whitehall was never again to be divided from the Americans, the conclusion drawn in Paris was the need to create an alternative European power base in the form of the EEC. This policy was vigorously followed by General de Gaulle, whose advent to power in 1958 owed something to the way in which Suez had weakened the Fourth Republic. The subsequent intensification of Anglo-French rivalry culminated in the General's two damaging vetoes in the 1960s of Britain's EEC membership bids. In all it proved a high price for what was in the final analysis a self-inflicted wound.[49]

17

Still Fighting Nasser

Eastern Mediterranean, Iraq and Yemen, 1957–70

In the Middle East the repercussions of the Suez crisis reverberated for the next two years. Nasser's prestige was greatly enhanced, that of Nuri al-Said mortally damaged. Suez deepened the split between Nasser's supporters and opponents, which now became a factor in the internal affairs of other Arab states.[1] Yet while Cairo radio continued to inveigh against imperialism, Nasser was no more in control of events in other Arab countries after the crisis than he had been before. Moreover, thanks to Suez, he now faced a new and more formidable adversary, as the Americans moved to fill the vacuum left by the debacle, unilaterally when necessary, but in cooperation with Britain if possible.

Eisenhower and Macmillan were old wartime friends and collaborators, who rapidly moved to repair the Anglo-American breach. London and Washington still had their differences over Nasser, with the British determined to 'cut him down to size'.[2] But with the Americans now determined to prevent the spread of Soviet influence in the region, the two allies could again sing from the same hymn sheet, if not always quite in tune. The Americans reluctantly took over the British subsidy to Jordan which ended with the abrogation of the Anglo-Jordanian treaty in early 1957. With access to Jordanian bases in doubt and the Arab Legion now effectively beyond British control, Jordan's value as an ally had become marginal. When in April 1957, in the first major set-back for Nasser in the Arab world, King Hussein dismissed his pro-Egyptian prime minister, Suleiman Nabulsi, it was the Americans who moved to shore up the Jordanian monarchy. The British kept their heads down.[3]

Nevertheless, the ending of the treaty led to a distinct improvement in Anglo-Jordanian relations. These were now based on equality and plain-speaking on both sides, partnership rather than alliance, with advice only being offered when requested.[4] Here was a successful example of the transformation of informal empire into a constructive post-imperial relationship.

The next crisis, which allowed Britain to move closer to the centre of the action, involved Syria, the first Arab country to experience a military coup in 1949, and the first to turn towards the Soviet Union in 1955. The following year SIS and the CIA had coordinated a plan for the overthrow of the government, but Operation Straggle had been aborted thanks to Suez.[5] The struggle between radical and pro-Western forces, however, remained more violent than elsewhere in the region, and by the late summer of 1957, the country seemed to be on the point of disintegration. The fear in Washington and London was of growing Soviet influence. The British response, however, was ambivalent. On the one hand Foreign Office reporting suggested that there was in fact little by way of communist penetration, while Macmillan worried over any threat to the IPC oil pipeline running through Syria, which carried some 37 million tons of oil per year from Iraq and Saudi Arabia. Serious disruption could affect both British and West European oil supplies, and stability in Iraq. At the same time the crisis offered a golden opportunity to improve cooperation with Washington over the Middle East. The Prime Minister rather savoured the fact that this time it was the Americans who were pressing for action, while the British were urging restraint.[6]

Nevertheless, Macmillan was still in apocalyptic mood. According to his diary entry of 6 September:

> Unless Russian influence in the Middle East could be stopped, Britain and Europe 'have had it' (as they say). Only the Americans can bring the power to bear (a) to stop the Arabs, etc., from falling, (b) to risk the consequences – i.e. Russian threat to Turkey, Iraq etc., (c) to stop this degenerating into global war.[7]

An Anglo-US plot was hatched in Washington, based on the aborted Operation Straggle, which would have involved MI6 and the CIA helping to promote unrest in Syria and incidents on the Iraqi and Jordanian border, thus providing an excuse for intervention by both countries.[8] In late September Macmillan enquired what military measures Britain could take if Iraq were at war with Syria and attacked by Egypt and then called upon British support. A highly classified Foreign Office assessment of likely Soviet reaction to a US-engineered coup, warned that while Syria was not a first class or vital Soviet interest, the Soviet response both in and beyond the Middle East would probably be 'strong and determined'.[9] In the event, the crisis fizzled out, but not before Dulles had privately expressed pleasure at the new level of Anglo-American cooperation over the Middle East, reflected in the establishment of an Anglo-American Syrian Working Group in Washington to share intelligence and coordinate policy.[10] The same group was subsequently charged with contingency planning for possible interventions in Lebanon and Jordan.

Ironically it was Nasser who moved to stabilise the Syrian situation, first with the despatch of troops, then with the creation in February 1958 of the United Arab Republic, effectively a Syrian–Egyptian union controlled by Egypt. To the Iraqis, who had long angled for a union of the countries of the Fertile Crescent, this was a threat, and their riposte came in the form of a much less popular Iraqi–Jordanian union. Macmillan was worried. A diary entry for 15 March, following a lunch with Eden during which Suez had loomed large, noted that

> however tactically wrong we were, strategically we were right. If the Americans had helped us, the history of the Middle East would have changed. Now, I fear, Nasser (like Mussolini) will advance his Arab empire, and it may take war to dislodge him. Yet (in these nuclear days) limited war is difficult and dangerous.[11]

The creation of the UAR also put pressure on one of the most fragile states in the region, pro-Western Lebanon, where the 1943 National Pact laying down the division of power between Muslims and Christians was beginning to unravel. Lebanon became the battlefield between the Americans, anxious to promote pro-Western regimes against communism, and the Nasserists, equally anxious to unite the Arabs against foreign intervention.[12] With the threat of civil war following a political assassination in May, President Camille Chamoun enquired whether Britain, France and the United States would be prepared to provide military assistance within 24 hours of a formal request.

Despite the view of the British ambassador, Sir George Middleton, that the conflict was essentially domestic, London was anxious to accede. If Lebanon fell, or so the Cabinet believed, it was doubtful whether Iraq and Jordan would be able to maintain their independence. But less than a year after Suez, Macmillan was anxious to keep the British military contribution as small as possible.[13]

Over the next weeks preparations were made in Britain for a state visit on 16 July by the 21-year-old King Feisal II of Iraq. According to one of the briefs prepared for the occasion:

It remains to be seen whether he has the toughness to bring the Iraqi monarchy through the stresses through which it is bound to be subjected over the next few years, or the resilience and imagination to bring it more into line with modern conditions, but he has grown up a good deal in the last three years.[14]

The young King never got the chance. Two days before he was due in London, he, along with his uncle, the former Regent and Nuri, whose political career stretched back to 1922, were murdered. In a particularly macabre twist, one of Nuri's fingers was sent to Nasser.[15]

The British should not have been taken by surprise. Rumours were rife and on 8 July the Oriental Counsellor, Sam Falle, had written a minute in which he predicted an imminent revolution. It had been dismissed by the ambassador, Sir Michael Wright, a somewhat proconsular figure who did not speak Arabic, as not according with the facts.[16] But as Falle knew from his travels in Iraq, a revolutionary situation had existed for some time. Its roots, as Peter Sluglett notes,

> were essentially socio-economic and political: the overwhelming inequalities caused by the formation of large landed estates in the late nineteenth and twentieth centuries; the extraordinary concentration of wealth in a very few hands; the nature and extent of the influence of Britain and its supporters; the limitations which this imposed on political discussion and debate; and, in general, widely-held aspirations, however vaguely and loosely conceived, for political independence and economic development.[17]

A Free Officers movement in the army, about which MI6 had failed to gather any intelligence, drew impetus from Iraq's isolation in the Arab world over the Baghdad Pact, Cairo radio's attacks on the Iraqis as stooges of British imperialism, and of course, Suez.[18] When in July Nuri ordered General Abdel Karim Qasem, an outstanding officer with a reputation for bravery in the 1948 Palestine war, to move into Jordan to foil a coup against King Hussein, the General had instead mounted a coup of his own. Symbolically the British embassy was burnt.

The coup was greeted with public jubilation. In the words of a popular Iraqi poet:

> The sun shines in my city
> The bells ring out for the heroes
> Awake, my beloved, we are free.[19]

Yet the results for Iraq were disastrous. This was the beginning of a period of military dictatorship and instability which would continue until the overthrow of Saddam Hussein in 2003 and beyond. In London the coup came as devastating news.[20] This was the development the British had long tried to pre-empt with their repeated but unsuccessful advocacy of reforms. But it was a revolution their misjudgements had also helped precipitate.

The immediate effect was to throw the Middle East into a major crisis. Once more, Nasser's malign hand was seen – wrongly – to be behind events. Speaking in parliament on 17 July, Lord Home, the Commonwealth Secretary and a strong proponent of Suez, warned that unless somebody put a stop to the process which 'the UAR is fomenting in this part of the world, then not only shall we see the whole of the Middle East go, but the rot will spread to Africa, and far beyond'.[21] In a telephone conversation with Eisenhower, Macmillan was at his most emotional, arguing for a major operation in the Middle East: 'you cannot confine it to one place. It is likely that the trouble will destroy the oilfields and the pipeline and all the rest of it [...] But I am all for it if we are determined to see it through.'[22]

Eisenhower, however, was not playing. His primary objective was not to shore up the whole region, but to prevent a loss of confidence among the countries of the northern tier.[23] The Americans would confine themselves to support for Lebanon, where on 15 July US marines landed on the Beirut beaches, to be greeted by nothing more formidable than a small army of purveyors of chewing gum and coca cola. The Americans had declined an offer of a symbolic British contingent, apparently fearing that British participation would tarnish the operation locally.[24] Both countries were determined to exclude the French. This went down badly in Paris, where de Gaulle had just returned to power. The General, who had a long memory when it came to insults, had not forgotten his wartime conflicts with Britain over Lebanon and Syria.[25]

Excluded from Lebanon, and denied a larger regional operation, the British government was determined not to be left out of the action. Eighteen months after the abrogation of the Anglo-Jordanian treaty, British paratroopers returned to Jordan. The primary aim was to bolster King Hussein in the face of a possible coup, which according to intelligence reports was planned for the 16th, and reassure British friends in the Gulf, although there was also briefly hope that the British presence might secure Hussein's rear, allowing him to restore the situation in Iraq.[26]

It is testimony to the degree of British concern about the Middle East situation that ministers agreed on a risky intervention in full knowledge that if it went wrong, it could bring down the government. Only two battalions of lightly armed paratroopers were available, there was uncertainty over the loyalty of some units of the Jordanian army, and there was no exit strategy. Israel created difficulties over British overflights. Ben Gurion's position was equivocal. On the one hand he was, as ever, suspicious of Britain and its motives in Jordan; on the other he thought overflights could be used as a bargaining chip to get a close working partnership with Britain. The Americans, who did not believe Hussein could survive, and suspected Britain of trying to get them to pull their chestnuts out of the fire, confined their support to finance and logistics.[27]

Yet this proved a case of all's well that ends well. 'Fortitude' turned out to be a model politico-military operation, which achieved all its objectives.[28] The small British presence – its size was kept a tightly guarded secret – in Hussein's later words 'gave us a chance to breathe. The famous Red berets on the streets made people realise we were not alone.'[29] According to one of his biographers, Avi Shlaim, British moral and material support helped Hussein 'more than any other factor to recover his confidence in himself and his customary resilience'.[30] This was the last crisis in Jordan until the Six Day War in 1967, and the new-found stability allowed the King to turn his attention to development. A UN resolution put forward by the Arab states and backed by Britain and the US pledged Arab non-interference in each other's affairs and paved the way for British and American withdrawals. By the end of November British troops had left.

July 1958 marks the turning point in the Middle Eastern crisis of the mid-1950s. The British were strikingly quick to appreciate that the new Iraqi government, far from being in Nasser's pocket, had come into conflict with him. They thus seemed almost indecently anxious to come to terms with their former allies' killers.[31] The loss of the bases, which were by now only used as staging posts, was not serious, nor was Iraq's departure from the sterling area. The Baghdad Pact, minus Iraq, rebranded itself as CENTO, the Central Treaty Organisation. With tensions in the region declining, London saw the advantage of disengaging from inter-Arab politics, and taking a more pragmatic approach to Arab nationalism. An Anglo-Egyptian economic agreement in 1959 was greeted by Egyptians with a sigh of relief. Macmillan shook Nasser's hand when the two met at the United Nations in 1960. According to Heikal, Nasser was delighted. He had hankered after some kind of gesture. Ambassadors were finally exchanged in early 1961.[32]

The *rapprochement* proved short-lived. The two sides remained suspicious and wary of each other.[33] In September 1962 there was another coup in the Middle East, this time in Yemen. Seeking to compensate for his loss of prestige following the break-up of the UAR in 1961, Nasser sent the Egyptian army to support the new government against the Royalist opposition. This brought Egyptian forces into the proximity of Britain's main Middle Eastern base. Macmillan feared a threat to Aden and the Gulf. Nasser claimed to have no designs on the colony, and offered a deal whereby the new Yemeni regime would drop its territorial claims against its neighbour in return for British recognition. The Foreign Office supported recognition, while the Colonial Office and Ministry of Defence were against. At one meeting Macmillan is quoted as remarking he was 'reminded of Scotland in 1745; the Highlanders were more attractive but one knew that the Lowlanders would win in the end'.[34] Nevertheless, in a fierce Whitehall battle in which arguments about the security of the base were heavily tinged with anti-Nasserist sentiment, the opponents of recognition won the argument.[35] Britain and Egypt embarked on a cycle of mutual intervention against their respective enemies, from which the British came out the worst. London might have done better if it had followed the new prime minister, Sir Alec Douglas-Home's prescription in April 1964 – by which time Egyptian forces were already bogged down in Yemen – of leaving Nasser alone and letting him 'stew in his own juice'.[36]

It is difficult, if not impossible, to work out the sequence of intervention and counter-intervention. Egyptian intelligence began to arm Aden nationalists soon after the Egyptian intervention. But it was only in 1964 that Nasser declared full-scale war on the British presence in Aden, the eviction of which, as he became increasingly frustrated with his Yemeni adventure, now became an obsession.[37] British intervention, for which there were precedents in the 1950s, took two forms. The first were very limited covert operations in 1964, aimed at countering the activities of Egyptian intelligence officers along the Yemeni border. The constraints imposed by London meant that these were never more than an irritant for the Egyptians.[38]

Second, there were the activities of the so-called Aden Group. This was a powerful, quasi-parliamentary body, including former members of the old Suez Group. It was motivated by animus against Nasser, allied to a moral certitude that clandestine warfare represented a legitimate means to secure what was seen as Britain's rightful position in the Middle East. With good access in Whitehall – one of its more prominent members, Julian Amery, sometimes known as the 'Minister for Yemen', was Macmillan's son-in-law and a junior minister – the Aden Group helped undermine the Foreign Office's case for recognition in late 1962. To the considerable discomfort of the Egyptians, it also promoted the activities of some 50 mercenaries, financed by the Saudis, who helped train and advise the Royalist forces. According to Jesse Ferris, the mercenaries brought 'coordination, determination and imagination to an otherwise feckless resistance'. The authorities in Aden turned a very blind eye.[39]

The consensus of ministerial opinion in the summer of 1964 was that a crisis with Nasser would assist the Conservatives' electoral prospects; Amery described Nasser as 'probably the most hated man in Britain'.[40] Although Labour won the 1964 election, its attempts to improve relations with Nasser got nowhere. At a farewell interview with the departing British ambassador, Sir Harold Beeley, the previous June, Nasser had remarked he sometimes felt the West 'hates us'.[41] The feelings seemed mutual. According to a 1965 Cabinet memorandum, Nasser sought the elimination of Western influence in the Middle East, including Britain's expulsion from South Arabia, thereby rendering 'untenable our position in the Persian Gulf'.[42] Egypt broke diplomatic relations over Rhodesia's unilateral declaration of independence in December 1965. Two months later, following the announcement that Britain would leave Aden in 1968, Nasser reversed an earlier decision to withdraw his own forces from the Yemen. The Egyptian leader saw his British adversaries as the more dangerous because they were now on the defensive, and feared that they might try to rearrange the Arabian Peninsula on the way out, thereby permanently shifting the balance of power in the Arab world.[43]

Nasser was by now in an unenviable position. He had miscalculated badly over the Yemen. 'I sent a company to Yemen and had to reinforce it with 70,000 soldiers', he later complained.[44] Some Egyptian officers began reading British counter-insurgency manuals. The war had pushed him closer into the arms of the Soviet Union, which had provided transport aircraft, pilots and equipment, but undermined his position in the Arab world.[45] It was partly to restore Egyptian prestige that Nasser made his next big miscalculation. Following a major escalation of tensions on the Israeli–Syrian border in early 1967, on 23 May Nasser closed the Straits of Tiran at the mouth of the Red Sea to Israeli shipping, and demanded the withdrawal of the United Nations Emergency Force in Sinai, which had been established after Suez. The Secretary General, U Thant, complied. The result was a war which led to the collapse of Nasser's pan-Arabism across the Middle East, Israeli occupation of Sinai, the Golan Heights and the West Bank, and an enhanced Soviet position, including military bases, in Egypt.

Britain was the one country to make a serious effort to try to defuse the impending crisis. Acutely conscious of its economic interests in the Arab world, during the past decade Britain had maintained a low profile over the Arab–Israeli conflict and abstained from any peace initiatives.[46] But with the prospect of an Israeli preventive war, the prime minister, Harold Wilson, and his Foreign Secretary, George Brown, proposed the establishment of an international naval force to ensure freedom of navigation through the Straits of Tiran.

This proved to be one of the relatively rare occasions when a prime ministerial initiative for military action in the Middle East was successfully blocked. The ghost of Suez stalked the Cabinet discussions. The majority of ministers, including the Defence Secretary, Denis Healey, regarded the proposal as 'reckless and foolhardy'. Opposition centred on the likely economic consequences for Britain of an action which would be seen in the Arab world as pro-Israeli, and its military practicalities, or rather impracticalities. None of the basic questions – What would happen if Egypt resisted? Would force be used? Would it be necessary to bomb Egyptian airfields? – had been thought through. With the Americans preoccupied with Vietnam, and the French and the Soviet Union refusing to support the British initiative, the proposal was dropped.[47]

The dramatic success of the Israeli attack on 5 June led Nasser to accuse the British and Americans of connivance. Much of the Arab world then broke diplomatic relations, there were anti-British demonstrations across the Middle East and Britain was denied oil supplies. More damaging economically was the closure of the Suez Canal, with the additional cost to the British trade account in 1967 estimated by the Treasury at some £90 million. In addition, significant movement out of sterling by Arab states cost the reserves some £80 million. Coming on top of the effects of a dock strike, these developments helped precipitate the devaluation of the pound in November 1967.[48]

Yet while Britain suffered economically from a conflict it felt unable to prevent, Nasser was by far the greater loser. By September the Egyptians were willing to admit publicly that Britain had legitimate interests in the Middle East and to call for the resumption of an Anglo-Egyptian dialogue. 'As has often been said,' Heikal wrote in the *Sunday Times*, 'we Arabs cannot drink our oil, so we must sell it.'[49] Ironically Egyptian forces left Yemen at the same time that the British withdrew from Aden. British standing in the Arab world rose following a speech by George Brown, stressing the inadmissibility under the UN charter of the acquisition of territory by force, and the British role in drafting Security Council Resolution 242, which became a key document in the Arab–Israeli peace process.[50] When Nasser died in 1970, the Foreign Secretary, Sir Alec Douglas-Home, attended the funeral. Nasser and his British protagonists were quits. Nasser had suffered a string of disasters – the break-up of the UAR, Yemen and the Six Day War. Not since Muhammad 'Ali's defeat in 1840, notes Jesse Ferris, had a rising power suffered such imperial contraction.[51] Britain's imperial contraction, to which Nasser had contributed, was even more dramatic. But the feud was over.

Conflict between Britain and Nasser's Egypt had been inevitable. The belief that the withdrawal from the Suez Canal zone base offered the prospect of a new start in Anglo-Egyptian relations was a delusion. A *modus vivendi* would only have been possible on Egyptian terms, which meant at the expense of Britain's allies. Both sides became fixated on the machinations of the other. As one British diplomat later noted, while Nasser looked everywhere for British influence operating against him, 'so we on our side were inclined for a time to find Nasser under every bed'.[52] While the Egyptian leader was unique in the postwar Afro-Asian world in posing a regional threat to Britain's declining imperial position, London was far too ready to equate the rhetoric of Cairo radio with actual Egyptian power. Nasser had provided a useful scapegoat. It was easier to blame external forces for local instability, rather than admit its essentially indigenous causes.[53] At one level the analogy between Nasser and Mussolini did have something to be said for it; both proved ineffective when it came to the battlefield. At another, it was a reflection of a loss of British nerve and sense of proportion.

18

Oil, Force and Bases

The Gulf and Aden, 1945–71

In one respect the British were fortunate. While informal empire in Egypt, Palestine and Iraq was in terminal decline, their power still held good in the one part of the Middle East which was of vital interest. The last pocket of imperial power, by the early 1950s the Persian Gulf was ceasing to be a backwater. Qatar had begun producing oil in 1949, Abu Dhabi in 1964 and Oman in 1967. By far the most important of the new producers, however, was Kuwait, where production had started in 1946, increasing substantially in the wake of the AIOC nationalisation. By 1957 Kuwait was providing half of British oil requirements, though the figure had fallen to 40 per cent by 1961.[1] Kuwaiti oil was exceptionally cheap to produce and half of the Kuwait Oil Company was owned by BP. As production increased so did the country's sterling reserves. In 1958 Kuwait's sterling balances stood at £260 million. An official estimate in 1959 put Gulf balances, which largely meant Kuwaiti, as equivalent to a quarter of Britain's gold and foreign exchange holdings. Any significant Kuwaiti diversification out of sterling threatened to undermine confidence in sterling as an international currency.[2]

Britain played an important role in this early period of oil modernisation in the Gulf. It ensured the security of the sheikhdoms against attack or subversion by their larger neighbours, provided a secure environment for oil prospecting, including helping resolve a number of border disputes in the Lower Gulf, and in a couple of cases removed rulers who refused to spend their oil wealth. In the process Britain also helped exclude the spread of communist influence.

Britain's success was in part due to good relations with the ruling families, whose 'free and aristocratic tribal background', to quote one former official, meant that unlike nationalists in Egypt and Iraq, they had no chip on their shoulders *vis-à-vis* their protectors. The Gulf rulers appreciated the fact that, unless things got seriously out of hand, British protection generally came without the kind of interference in internal affairs which Egypt had experienced. Only in cases of gross maladministration was there serious interference as opposed to advice and cajoling. But from the rulers' perspective this was still preferable to absorption by a powerful Arab nationalism. The British were in fact often able to exceed their treaty rights with the tacit consent of the rulers, and sometimes at the latter's request.[3]

Given their small size, and their sometimes tiny populations – a mere two to three thousand in the case of three of the smallest Trucial States – the occasional military deployments could be relatively easily managed. A British-officered force, the Trucial Oman Levies, later renamed Scouts, had been formed in 1950 under the command of the Political Resident. He was said to be the only example of a British diplomat commanding a private army. Cooperating closely with the local police, the Scouts established basic law and order in the Lower Gulf, still riven by tribal feuds, piracy and gun running.[4] Until the 1960s, there was no significant British military presence to enflame nationalist sentiments.

Following Indian independence, responsibility for the Gulf shifted to the Foreign Office, although much of the Raj ethos survived. In a despatch written in 1964, James Craig, the Political Agent in Dubai, described the atmosphere as that of imperial India.

> The guard at the compound gate hoist the flag at sunrise [...] The Agent sits in court below the Royal Coat of Arms and sees the old procession of clerks and petition writers. His servants wear turbans and puggarrees and long *shirwani* coats. He inspects gaols and pursues smugglers, runs hospitals and builds roads [...] He makes State tours with reception tents and dining tents and sleeping tents, trestle tables, carpets and military escort.[5]

The senior official in the region remained the Political Resident, who had moved from Bushire to Bahrain and whose status now lay somewhere between that of a proconsul and ambassador. He was still addressed by the Gulf rulers as *Ra'is al Khahj*, Chief of the Gulf, while local people habitually talked of Britain as *Ad-Daula* – the Power.[6] Under the Resident came five Political Agents in Qatar, Bahrain, Abu Dhabi, Dubai and Kuwait, although the latter also communicated directly with the Foreign Office, while there was a Consul-General in Muscat. These officials had judicial and administrative functions in respect of non-Muslim foreigners, analogous to the Capitulations which had once prevailed in China (as well as supervising the import of alcoholic drinks for non-Muslims). Among their more modern duties were persuading the rulers of the oil-producing states to dispose of their large incomes in a manner which would not be detrimental to sterling, and watching oil negotiations for new or amended agreements liable to be damaging to the position of either the British or the rulers.[7] There were still no non-British diplomatic representatives.

The artificial status quo in the Gulf, with three large states – Iran, Iraq and Saudi Arabia – and ten small and potentially vulnerable sheikhdoms, plus Oman, suited the British well. The larger the number of independent producers, or so it was believed in Whitehall, the greater the prospects that the price of oil would remain low, and the greater the security of British supply.[8]

Two regional threats preoccupied Britain. The first was the Saudi claim to the Buraimi oasis, which controlled important caravan routes in south-west Arabia. It consisted of nine villages, six of which in Britain's view belonged to Abu Dhabi, the other three to Oman. The Saudis, who had maintained an intermittent occupation of the Muscat territory between 1800 and 1869, thought otherwise, and in 1949 advanced a series of claims to Abu Dhabi and Omani territory. The smell of oil was in the air, and despite an agreement in 1951 that neither side should put forces into the area, a small Saudi expedition occupied the village of Hamasah the following year.[9]

The need to preserve their credibility in the Gulf meant that Britain could not allow the occupation to stand. Nevertheless, anxious to avoid a war in Arabia, and mindful of American support for the Saudis, Eden prevented Sultan Said bin Taimur of Oman from retaking the area. The Sultan was furious. It was probably also a mistake. Quick action might well have carried the day and saved a great deal of later trouble.[10] Instead the tiny Saudi force was blockaded by the Trucial Oman Scouts. Diplomacy followed in the form first of a standstill agreement, and then an arbitration tribunal. When in 1955 it appeared that the Saudis had been bribing members of the tribunal, the British expelled the Saudi force. 'We cannot', Eden subsequently told the Americans, 'allow this primitive, irresponsible and expansionist power to seize control of sources, from which we draw an essential part of our fuel.'[11]

The result was a fuss quite out of proportion to the forces involved – a mere 15 policemen on the Saudi side. But the Saudi loss of face meant that it took seven years until Anglo-Saudi relations, broken off at Suez, were restored. British action also rankled in Washington, which had been given no prior warning of it. The Americans believed, wrongly, that Saudi expansion into the coastal region was inevitable. They also worried, in the event unnecessarily, about how the British action might affect Aramco and the future of America's base at Dharan. Sir Bernard Burrows, who was

Political Resident in the Gulf in the 1950s, suggests that at some levels in Washington it was a question of backing 'their' Arabs against 'our' Arabs. Buraimi provides one element in the background to the Anglo-American split over Suez.[12]

The defence of Kuwait was an altogether more complex affair. Unease about Kuwaiti security had first arisen in early 1958, when the Iraqis had put considerable pressure on the emirate to join the proposed Iraq–Jordanian Federation. Kuwaiti money was needed to offset the costs of subsidising Jordan, which would otherwise have fallen on Iraq, and the issue became something of an obsession with Nuri. This was embarrassing to the British, who, to the Emir's distress – he worried about Nasser's popularity in Kuwait and suspected Iraqi intentions – nevertheless put some pressure on the Kuwaitis to accede.[13] The Iraqi coup led to fears of something similar happening in Kuwait. There was talk of sending in troops without the Ruler's consent, even of running Kuwait as a Crown Colony. In his diary Macmillan noted, 'the usual dilemma. Shall we go in now? If so, it is aggression. Shall we wait? If so, we may be too late.'[14]

Once the crisis subsided, military planning began for the defence of the sheikhdom. It took place against the background of a gradual loosening of British controls of Kuwaiti foreign policy. The Ruler, as the Political Agent, Aubrey Halford-Macleod, noted in February 1959, wanted it 'both ways – our support and also freedom to appear independent of it'. In August Halford advised that since independence was inevitable, Britain should 'accept this necessity and be prepared to meet it before it becomes too urgent and a source of dissension between us'.[15]

Two years later this advice was accepted. The Ruler, Sheikh Abdullah Al-Salim Al-Sabah, was experienced and well regarded and there was no undue concern in London that independence would undermine Britain's substantial interests in the sheikhdom, which would continue to look to Britain for its defence. What had not been anticipated was that Qasem would respond to Kuwaiti independence by renewing the Iraqi claim, and back this with troop movements. Whether he intended an invasion was unclear, and there were differences of opinion as to how to respond. The Political Agent, Sir John Richmond, doubted Iraq's capacity or will to invade, while in London some ministers and officials worried about Arab reaction to any British military deployment. On the other hand Qasem was unpredictable – the Political Resident, Sir William Luce, described him as unbalanced, and as the Joint Intelligence Committee (JIC) in London pointed out, an invasion could occur with virtually no warning[16] (a point underscored by the Iraqi occupation of August 1990). This was a view shared by the military, along with other ministers who were reflecting opinion in the City of London that no risks should be taken with Kuwait.[17] Richmond was instructed to get the Ruler to ask for British aid, and some 5,700 British troops plus two squadrons of Hunter fighter-bombers began to arrive at the beginning of July. Their reception was mixed. 'Your troops are occupying our hospitals and schools,' one minister complained. 'Is this independence?'[18]

Anxious to minimise hostile reaction in the Arab world, Britain was more than willing to withdraw in favour of an Arab League force. Arrangements were made for forward British deployment in Bahrain to allow speedy reaction in case of future attack, although Macmillan had privately said that the operation could never be repeated.[19] The lesson for the Kuwaitis, however, was the need to demonstrate that, in Richmond's words, it was 'more than a collection of oil wells sheltering under a new form of British imperialism'.[20] A Kuwait Fund for Arab Economic Development was established, and, to some British irritation, Kuwait began hosting political groups from Bahrain, Aden and Oman opposed to the British-supported order in the Gulf.[21]

When it came to internal security, political structures in the sheikhdoms were mostly reasonably well geared to cope with change. The sheikhdoms were not immune to nationalist pressure. Cairo radio kept up a steady stream of attacks on the rulers and their British patrons right up to the Six Day War. (The broadcasts then stopped; Egypt needed Gulf money.) In the 1950s Nasser's portrait could be seen on communal town walls, side by side, however, with that of the local ruler. Conservatism and paternalism were tempered by the provisions of Islamic law and customs of tribal consultation, including ready access to the rulers so that grievances could be aired, which some British officials described as a form of indigenous democracy.[22] With two exceptions discussed below, oil wealth was distributed. Comparing Kuwait in 1969 with Libya, where King Idris had just been overthrown, one official described Kuwait as

a compact little state with a royal family so numerous that they and their protégés can occupy all the nodal points of power including those in the army: indeed the Sabah form almost a political party of their own. They marry widely among all the leading merchant families, and are part of the social fabric, not a superimposed clique. Idris was old and distant and the first Arab to unite the country. The Sabah have been here for two hundred years and many of them are young and accessible.[23]

Nevertheless, British officials did worry about being held responsible for some of the failings of ruling families, particularly in relation to maladministration of oil revenues or development programmes. The dilemma, as the Political Resident, Sir George Middleton, lamented in 1960, was that 'if we seek to interfere directly, we are decried as old-fashioned imperialists. If we seek to acquiesce in the existing state of affairs we are decried as the prop of outmoded reaction.'[24] Options were limited by the resistance of rulers to any British attempts to impinge on their domestic prerogatives, as well as their nervousness over liberalisation. 'If you let the dog bark too loudly,' one Gulf minister was quoted as saying, 'he will end up biting you.'[25] Ultimately the British had no alternative but to work with the emirs. Advice to the Ruler of Kuwait, Eden had instructed in 1953, 'must not be pressed beyond the point at which it defeats its own ends and arouses feelings which might weaken the position of the Agency'.[26]

The country which caused most problems was Oman. In 1955 the British had backed the Sultan's operation to extend his authority over central Oman. This led in 1957 to what Macmillan described as a 'very dangerous' Saudi- and Egyptian-backed revolt by the deposed Imam's brother. With the Sultan's forces unable to cope, the British had to come to his aid. This was embarrassing. They would be intervening in an internal power struggle, and any British military action, particularly air attacks – it was initially considered too hot to use ground troops – would be criticised at the UN, as well as, potentially, by the United States. It was less than a year since Suez, and some ministers had serious doubts about getting involved. But Oman was Britain's oldest ally in the Middle East and the RAF used airfields at Masirah and Salalah. If the revolt succeeded, the Saudis might again move against Buraimi. Small wonder perhaps that, as Macmillan complained in his diary, 'we spend as much time on its details as if it were a real war'.[27]

In the event, the RAF and a few British troops managed to deal with the situation. But the Americans were unhelpful, only abstaining in a Security Council debate called by the Arab League to discuss British 'aggression', while the leaders of the revolt escaped to the inhospitable Jebel Akhbar plateau. Here they were heavily attacked by the RAF, operations which this time were conducted without publicity. The rebels were eventually winkled out by the SAS in 1959.[28]

In 1965 a new insurgency broke out, this time in Dhofar province in the south-west of the country, where the terrain was particularly suited to guerrilla warfare. By 1970, only the capital Salalah was tolerably safe. The key problem was the Sultan, who resolutely refused to spend his revenues. Said had ruled since 1932. His worldview has been described

Figure 9. Sultan Qabus of Oman, shortly after coming to
power in a British-engineered coup in 1970

as 'exemplifying the values of colonial conservatism, coupled with a streak
of anti-modernism'. He deplored the effects of oil money on local culture
and the observance of Islam. He himself is quoted as telling a British
development officer who argued the need to establish primary schools,
'That is why you lost India, because you educated the people.'[29] Such
obstructionism might have been possible in Cromer's day. In 1970 it was
making unwinnable an insurgency in the state controlling the southern
shores of the Strait of Hormuz at the mouth of the Gulf, and which some
feared threatened a domino effect in the Lower Gulf.

The British moved against Said with some reluctance. His son, Qabus,
was an unknown quantity, and a coup would place British officers in the
Sultan's service in an awkward position. By July 1970, however, the situation
had deteriorated to the point where Said was removed in a British-designed
and -implemented operation. He was flown out by the RAF, dying two
years later in the Dorchester hotel in London. The change proved popular
in Oman, and the British quickly moved to help consolidate Qabus in
power.[30] It was an example of what might be described as constructive
regime change, the beginning of what would prove to be a very long reign.

Said's deposition was the third instance of British-instigated regime
change in the Gulf in six years. The removal of Sheikh Shakhbut of Abu

Dhabi in 1966 was analogous to that of Said. Shakhbut, who had ruled for 38 years, was a tiny, most intelligent but eccentric man who had once enquired of a visiting diplomat about the possibility of engaging a place for himself and a small number of bodyguards in a future spaceship. (The possibility of a moon landing had been in the news.) But after a lifetime of poverty he found it almost impossible to adapt to sudden wealth, and feared the changes which development would bring to his own sheikhdom.[31] Sir William Luce had been arguing the case for regime change as early as 1962. Two previous attempts to depose Shakhbut failed because his brother, Zayed, was unable to rally the rest of the family, and because the British were reluctant to be seen to be interfering in Abu Dhabi's internal affairs. The plan eventually approved in 1966 was for Zayed to seize power with secret British guarantees of recognition and short-term military assistance, so as to make it appear as though Britain was responding to Zayed's request. With the Trucial Oman Scouts on hand, a furious Shakhbut was removed (though he was later allowed to return). Zayed immediately implemented British proposals for the reform of administration in Abu Dhabi.[32]

A year earlier Sheikh Saqr of Sharjah had been deposed, albeit for different reasons. In 1965 Egyptian influence made serious headway in the Gulf, when attempts by the Arab League to gain a foothold found favour among some of the smaller Trucial States, notably Sharjah. 'It is inconceivable to me', Sir William Luce thundered, that Britain could abandon its peace-keeping role 'at the first flick of the whip by Nasser and a couple of insignificant self-serving sheikhs'. Since the British had no constitutional power to depose a ruler, they had to obtain a written request from family members. Fortunately for them, the ruler was unpopular, partly it is alleged because of the amount he spent on whisky. Once again the Trucial Oman Scouts were on hand.[33]

Bahrain differed from the other emirates, not least as the scene of the formation of the first political party in the Gulf, the Higher Executive Committee, in the early 1950s. Although it looked to Egypt for support, its demands were regarded as reasonable by the Political Residency. With the autocratic al-Khalifa family unwilling to negotiate directly, the British reluctantly found themselves mediating between them and the Committee. Continued support for the ruling family was effectively being made conditional on reforms, a position deeply resented by the al-Khalifas.[34] The Adviser, Sir Charles Belgrave, who was regarded by British officials as having stayed too long, was eased out.

The British authorities were never complacent about their position in the Gulf, which since Suez had been a subject of debate within the Foreign

Office. The relationship with the sheikhdoms was held by some officials to be an anachronism, which seemed liable to cause Britain difficulties in its relations elsewhere in the Arab world.[35] This later proposition was debatable. Although a number of states, including of course Egypt, objected to the British presence, they much preferred the status quo to one of their rivals annexing a sheikhdom. Hence Nasser's willingness to facilitate the orderly withdrawal of British troops from Kuwait in 1961. Hence also an improvement in Anglo-Saudi relations in the wake of the operation. Having previously been obstructive, the Saudis now made no objection to the basing of additional forces in Bahrain after 1961.[36]

The need to safeguard British oil interests by military means came under scrutiny after the Kuwait operation. This was an important if tricky argument, since in the absence of disaster, neither side could prove their case. Did Kuwait retain its money in sterling because of British protection, or because of the City of London's reputation and high interest rates?[37] Britain, Luce argued, filled a power vacuum in the Gulf, which would otherwise become 'a jungle of smash and grab'. The resultant chaos would affect oil supplies and deter investment in the oil industry. Maintaining the independence of conservative Gulf sheikhs ensured that oil would not be concentrated in a small number of hands, with the greater risk of consumers being held to ransom. Conservative producers were also less likely to nationalise oil companies than revolutionary ones.[38] Besides, assuming the cost was not too high, why undertake the 'high risk experiment' of dispensing with military power?

The cost, however, estimated by one official in 1964 at £190 million a year, was precisely what the Treasury worried about. The oil industry, one Treasury official had remarked when Kuwaiti independence was under consideration, had 'astonishing powers of recuperation and improvisation, and reacts very quickly and effectively to any emergency'. The bargaining power of the newly established Organisation of Petroleum Exporting Countries (OPEC) was liable to increase regardless of the British military presence. Oil producers could not drink their oil, and only British and American companies could explore for and produce it.[39]

These latter arguments gained ground over the 1960s in the face of Britain's growing economic difficulties. In 1966, George Brown told the Cabinet that Labour had inherited a position 'which we could not afford to maintain indefinitely. We must therefore complete a gradual and orderly withdrawal from the Middle East.'[40] 'By the mid-1970s', an official report of July 1967 noted, 'we must expect a world where almost all colonial and quasi colonial traces have disappeared and the overseas deployment of British power has contracted further than at present. If we have not gone from the Gulf, the pressures on us to go are likely to be very severe indeed.'[41]

Matters came to a head following the devaluation of sterling in November 1967. Major cuts in government expenditure were required. Withdrawing from the Gulf saved relatively little money – some £25 million in budgetary costs and £12 million in foreign exchange. But for a Labour government, cuts in defence, including a final withdrawal from the Far East, were the essential *quid pro quo* for highly unpopular cuts in social spending. Britain's failure to prevent either the Six Day War or subsequent economic reprisals against her had in any case inevitably weakened the case for staying on.[42] And with Britain still intent on joining the EEC despite de Gaulle's latest veto, it was felt that Britain should prioritise European defence rather than support neo-colonial conflicts in the East.[43]

What is perhaps most striking about the decision is that the Cabinet ignored not only strong American displeasure – deeply involved in Vietnam, the US was anxious not to be left alone as the world's sole policeman – but also the risks of leaving now. A joint memorandum by the Foreign and Commonwealth Secretaries, George Brown and Lord George Thompson, pulled no punches, warning that 'An immediate withdrawal would carry with it the certainty of friction and the probability of hostilities, particularly between Iran and Saudi Arabia. Repercussions over this could put at risk not only our own, but all Western oil interests in the region.'[44]

Their Cabinet colleagues were unimpressed. Nor were they moved by the distress the decision would cause among Gulf rulers, who had for so long relied on British protection, and who were especially nervous because of the Dhofar war. But there was little sympathy within the Labour Party for 'feudal sheikhs'. This was a decision which a Conservative government would not have made, and which the Heath government, which came to power in the 1970s, hoped to reverse.

Yet in contrast to Palestine and Aden (discussed below), this withdrawal was well managed by a very strong diplomatic team. The diplomats enjoyed two advantages. They were not under local pressure to leave, and the successor powers, Saudi Arabia and Iran, had a strong interest in ensuring continued regional stability. The most dangerous territorial disputes involved Iran, which had a long-standing claim to Bahrain, as well as to two tiny islands at the mouth of the Gulf, Abu Musa and the Tunbs. The Bahraini problem was resolved relatively easily. Realising that it was wiser to settle before rather than after Britain left, and viewing the Bahraini claim as something of a millstone around his neck, the Shah accepted a face-saving British proposal that the UN should be asked to ascertain Bahraini wishes.[45] Agreement was also reached with Sharjah over Abu Musa. But Iranian troops occupied the Tunbs on the eve of the British departure, thereby successfully deflecting anger against the departing imperial power. Iraq broke diplomatic relations with Britain, while Libya nationalised British oil interests.

The other key problem was the future of the Trucial States, none of which had viable futures as independent states, indeed five of the seven were penniless.[46] The idea of a Gulf federation had been around since the 1950s, but so long as the *Pax Britannica* continued, the rulers had no incentive to overcome their various jealousies and differences. British diplomats now sought to act as midwife to what became the United Arab Emirates. Sir William Luce was brought out of retirement. He cajoled, persuaded and advised, giving

> the impression to Arabs and others, including the Americans, that he was taking them entirely into his confidence, while giving nothing away [...] What Luce did was to reason patiently with each of the rulers, suggesting [...] that it was in their own interests to hang together, because otherwise they would all hang separately.[47]

Nobody was sure that the United Arab Emirates would survive,[48] and British power was no longer sufficient successfully to mediate a dispute over offshore drilling rights between three of the states.[49] Yet the overall result was probably the most successful of the British attempts at state making in the Middle East. In his final despatch, the last Political Resident, Sir Geoffrey Arthur, wrote of 'the smoothest and most friendly parting that anyone could have wished for: the political and military "presence" faded together and nobody had anything but good to say of the way our soldiers, sailors and airmen conducted themselves during their stay in the Gulf'.[50]

★★★

The withdrawal from Aden four years earlier had occurred under very different circumstances, indeed success in the Gulf had in part only been achieved at the price of failure in South Arabia. Aden had also grown in importance in the 1950s. The population had increased rapidly from 140,000 in 1955 to 220,000 in 1960, and now included a very large Yemeni community. Many of these had been attracted by the construction of a refinery to replace Abadan; Aden as sovereign British territory was regarded as a safe site. The activities of one of the world's busiest bunkering ports added to the colony's prosperity.[51]

So too did the creation of Britain's last big base in the Middle East. Although this had begun with the transfer of responsibilities for the Gulf from Iraq to Aden in 1956, it was after Suez that the centre of gravity of British military policy shifted to Aden from the Mediterranean with the establishment of a new command, British Forces Arabian Peninsula. By 1962 Aden was one of the largest RAF stations in the world, handling some 5,000 aircraft movements per month, and large numbers of passengers and freight. Along with Singapore, Aden was becoming a cornerstone of what in the 1960s was coming to be known as the 'East of Suez' policy, the first attempt to deal with disorder in the newly independent states of the Third World. This was part of Britain's attempted answer to Dean Acheson's much-quoted and much-resented jibe, made in late 1962, that Britain had lost an empire but failed to find a role.[52]

Aden's main military attraction was its geographical location – there was at the time nowhere else to put the necessary command and logistic units, plus the fact that it was a colony.[53] But the climate was terrible and in the era of Cairo radio, nationalism could no longer be ignored even in the remoter areas of the Arabian Peninsula. If the base was to be secured into the 1970s, new political arrangements would have to be made. This in turn raised questions about its long-term relationship with the tribal hinterland.

By contrast to Aden, the Protectorates remained wild, desperately poor and desperately insecure country. According to Sir Kennedy Trevasksis, who in 1951 was appointed Deputy Agent in the Western Protectorate,

> almost every clan seemed to be both hunter and hunted: seeking some victim to kill and, at the same time, knowing that for some neighbour they themselves were the prey. Conflict was endemic and one generation after another had been locked in a fierce competitive struggle for survival.[54]

This was despite the fact that after the Colonial Office took over Aden from the Indian government in 1937, local officials had begun an active policy of pacification. For the first time huge areas of the interior were brought under British control, albeit of a loose and indirect character, accompanied by a limited amount of development. Remarkably late in the history of empire, advisory treaties were concluded with 14 of the 20 Western and Eastern Protectorates between 1944 and 1954.[55]

This forward policy was by no means invariably welcome. Traditional patterns of life were disrupted, which in some cases had the unintended side-effect of helping stimulate nationalism.[56] The Yemeni government regarded it as a breach of the 1934 treaty, and resumed support for tribal dissidence and border raiding. In the political climate of the 1950s, these caused the British authorities a good deal of trouble. So-called 'hot pursuit' across the border risked international accusations of aggression. But with the Yemen viewed in the wake of Suez as the front-line in the battle against Arab nationalism, the authorities in Aden were given wide licence to pursue the battle into Yemeni territory.[57]

Tension was particularly acute in 1958, when in a defensive move against the British border attacks, Yemen affiliated itself with the newly established UAR. Sir William Luce, then Governor of Aden, regarded this as 'a major advance for Nasser's campaign for Arab unity under Egyptian leadership'.[58] There was little doubt as to what to do when the Sultan of Lahej showed signs of following suit. The Sultan 'has gone over to Nasser (as we know from secret [i.e. intelligence] sources)', Macmillan noted in his diary on 6 July. 'He will have to be deposed.'[59] British concern was accentuated by Soviet arms sales to Yemen, reportedly followed by rapid economic and political penetration of the country. Luce advocated a ruthless response. (One of his predecessors, Sir Tom Hickinbotham, had remarked that 'like small boys and other primitive animals the Yemenis react favourably to strength and nothing else'.[60]) Although proposals for a coup and invasion were discarded, Britain and the United States appear to have assisted in, if not actually instigated, disturbances in the Yemen that year.[61] In the event, Britain won this border war.

A second consequence of the forward policy was to focus British minds in Aden on the idea of a local federation of Protectorate states, in part to rationalise their administration and to provide for their long-term viability, in part to protect the territories against Yemen and Arab nationalism. But the idea found favour neither with the local rulers, who feared that their power would be diminished, nor in London, where the preference was to continue a policy of divide and rule. It was only in response to the formation of the UAR that some of the rulers became interested in federation, and in 1959 the Federal Arab Amirates of the South was formed, initially of six local states.[62]

This in turn raised a further prospect – a merger between Aden and the new Federation. Port and hinterland were naturally complementary, and neither had much prospect of successful independence on their own.[63] There was an obvious advantage in getting the colony to finance the hinterland. As, if not more, important from London's perspective, federation, a fashionable concept of the 1950s, seemed to offer a means of securing the base. Ministerial instincts had been to try to hang on to sovereignty, which appeared the best guarantee of security of strategic tenure. Proposals put forward by Luce in 1958 for an early merger between colony and Protectorate, with the new state in treaty relationship with Britain to acquire independence within less than ten years, but with provision for the continuation of the base, had been rejected as too risky.[64]

But in an era of decolonisation some other formula had to be found. The great attraction of federation was that it would be dominated by the friendly rulers of the hinterland, thereby it was hoped, containing the much more radical politics of Aden, with its large Yemeni population and active trade-union organisation. But it would be a shot-gun marriage. There was a long-standing antipathy between Aden and its hinterland, accentuated by radical social and developmental differences in terms of respect for law and order, level of education, administrative experience and system of government. Johnston referred to the difficulties 'of bringing together not only of urban and rural but of different centuries as well; modern Glasgow say and the 18th century highlands'.[65] Lack of knowledge of the area among British politicians and public meant that the federation's flaws were not properly appreciated in London.[66]

In the event, federation, one of the last acts of imperial will, was forced through the Legislative Council by a single vote against a background of some violence.[67] Sir Reginald Turnbull, who was High Commissioner between 1964 and 1967, later wrote of the colony having been 'shanghaied' into the Federation.[68] The new Federation, consisting of eight sultans from the protectorates, four members from Aden and no nationalists, was inaugurated in January 1963. (The Eastern Protectorates were excluded, remaining in special treaty relationship with Britain.)

If this high-risk venture was to come off, it would require good management, determination and resources. It says something about the policy-making process that while large amounts were spent on the base, the Treasury remained niggardly when it came to economic development. It was a classic failure to view policy in the round.[69] The success of the South Arabian venture also required luck. News of a coup in Yemen, which had long been predicted, arrived the day after the Legislative Council vote. It was warmly welcomed in Aden. The idea of merger with a revolutionary Yemen suddenly became much more attractive than it had been under the theocracy of the old Imam, while the potential for subversion within both Aden and the Protectorates was enhanced by the arrival of the Egyptian army. Trevaskis, Johnston's successor, found himself with the unenviable task of trying 'to safeguard a military base with Nasser on the doorstep and at a time when there is an international witch hunt in full cry against Colonialism'.[70]

Whitehall was no less perplexed. Outlining four options in April 1964 – a deal with Nasser, hitting back at him in Yemen, withdrawal from Aden and granting the Federation independence, one official commented that 'it would take the wisdom of Solomon to know what is the better course to take'.[71] In the event, the independence option was chosen at a constitutional conference held in the summer, after which Britain would enter into a defence agreement with the new state. But the proposed constitution was not acceptable to the political parties in Aden.[72]

Three months later, a Labour government was elected in Britain. Unusually in British Middle East policy, this change of government led to changes in policy. Whereas Conservative ministers were happy to work with the tribal leaders of the Federation, the sympathies of their Labour successors lay with the Adeni trade unionists. Trevaskis, who was seen as too close to the Federal leaders, and possibly also to Conservative ministers, was dismissed. But attempts to devise an alternative policy in which the balance of power would be shifted from the tribal leaders to the Adenis got nowhere. In September 1965, Turnbull was forced to suspend the constitution.

This constitutional impasse provided the backdrop to a deteriorating security situation. Egyptian and Yemeni subversion had originally made itself felt in the inhospitable terrain of the Radfan area of the hinterland, where two military operations had been mounted in 1964. The first was successful militarily, but as soon as the Federal and British forces were withdrawn, the dissidents returned. The second, involving some 3,000 British troops, lasted three months, and presented political as much as military challenges. Using British troops to support 'feudal sultans' against 'the forces of nationalism', along with aircraft and heavy weaponry against 'defenceless tribesmen and civilians', did not present a good public image.[73] British forces nevertheless were forced to remain until June 1967.

The most vulnerable point of the Federal project, however, was Aden. Insurgencies require no more than the passive support of the population, and thanks to dislike both of the Federation and the methods used to impose it, this was not difficult to achieve. The first terrorist incident in Aden occurred in December 1963, with an assassination attempt on Trevaskis. There were 36 incidents in 1964; the following year there were 286, involving 239 casualties. The main insurgent organisation was the NLF (the National Liberation Front). Formed in Sana in the Yemen in 1963, this developed into a sophisticated, well-organised, and increasingly Marxist force, which managed to infiltrate the police, the civil service and schools. In early 1966, the NLF joined with the Organisation for the

Liberation of Southern Yemen, OLOS, which hitherto favoured political rather than military action, to form FLOSY, the Front for Liberation of Southern Yemen (from whom they subsequently split). Unlike the NLF, FLOSY was very much under Egyptian influence.[74]

The insurgency, as much as the pressure for defence cuts, explains the decision, announced in early 1966, to withdraw from Aden, even though additional construction work on the base had been authorised as late as February 1965.[75] Some of the British forces would then be relocated to the Gulf. Having now no long-term strategic interest in Aden, the Labour government decided, against the advice of Turnbull, the Foreign Office Arabian Department and Luce in the Gulf, to announce that it would not provide South Arabia with a defence treaty after independence in 1968. The Federation's prospects were already dubious. Turnbull later described it as 'a ramshackle contrivance, crippled by internal dissensions and commanding no confidence anywhere'.[76] The February 1966 announcement sealed its fate. With its patrons having effectively announced that they were to cut their losses and wash their hands of what had become an acute embarrassment, the Federation lost all prospect of commanding support.[77]

From here it was all downhill. As Lord Trevelyan, the former ambassador in Cairo and Baghdad who replaced Turnbull in May 1967, pithily observed, 'when a colonial power turns its back, it presents its bottom to be kicked'.[78] The level of insurgency increased further; 510 terrorist incidents in 1966, and around 2,900 in the ten months of 1967 before the final British withdrawal.[79] In a sign of the way the wind might be blowing, Trevelyan had insisted at his appointment that he would not want to be associated with 'a scuttle on Palestine lines'.[80] In fact there was no scuttle, but it was a close thing. Writing on 21 August, two months after a mutiny in the Aden police and South Arabian army, Trevelyan reported that 'the situation changes continuously and rapidly. No assessment can be guaranteed to remain valid.'[81] By then the NLF was rolling up the Federal states.

Trevelyan preferred to negotiate with the NLF rather than FLOSY, because they were independent of Egypt and seemed to offer the prospect of a more pragmatic relationship with Britain after independence.[82] Once the NLF had defeated FLOSY in a battle in Aden in September, in which the British had conspicuously absented themselves, last-minute negotiations opened in Geneva. Britain offered £12 million in aid in the first six months after independence, with the possibility of more to follow.[83] The British withdrawal was successfully completed on 29 November. Somebody had a sense of humour. Instead of 'Auld Lang Syne', the military band played

'Fings Ain't Wot They Used T'be'. 'We left without glory but without disaster', wrote Trevelyan.[84]

The NLF saw things differently. 'At that moment', one member later recalled, 'I had the feeling that Captain Haines had been defeated and that he had been thrown out of our country in the same manner as he had forced his way into it.'[85] But South Arabia had been given no preparations for independence, and the departure of the base coming on top of the interruption of the bunkerage trade as a result of the closure of the Suez Canal meant that it was deprived of its main sources of revenue. The war between the NLF and FLOSY led to the establishment of the only Marxist state in the Middle East, Soviet naval access to Aden, and active support by the new People's Democratic Republic of Yemen, as the territory now became known, for the Dhofar insurgency in Oman. Some Adenis would later refer to the British era prior to the insurgency as the good old days. Along with Palestine, this was one of the worst shambles of the end of empire.[86]

The story of Britain's last two decades in Arabia juxtaposes success and failure. In the Gulf Britain had succeeded in protecting her own interests, while at the same time easing the transition to an oil-based modernity. This reflected a combination of propitious circumstances, the absence of a serious challenge, and a combination of determination, skill and pragmatism. According to Glen Balfour-Paul, there was also an element of bluff.[87] The price, however, was paid in South Arabia, which paradoxically became of crucial importance to Britain at the very end of the imperial era, when it was least able to protect its interests there. The base became the overriding imperative driving British policy. Sir Sam Falle was a diplomat in Aden in 1967. His verdict is damning:

> Like most political tragedies and wars, this one could and should have been avoided. It all sounds obvious in hindsight, but the British could have done a deal with moderate South Arabians up until the early 1960s. It was the insistence on keeping the base which snarled things up initially and it was just plain crazy to set up the federal government.[88]

If there was a chance of securing the facility deemed necessary for the defence of Kuwait, it lay, as Luce had argued in 1958, in getting ahead of the nationalist curve and offering independence.[89] To ministers in London, however, this represented too much of a risk. What they failed to appreciate was that by the late 1950s sovereignty provided only the illusion of security, and a dangerous illusion at that. It encouraged them to hang on too long, thereby provoking the very nationalist reaction which would make the base untenable.

Part Four

Post-Imperial, 1971–2016

19

Just a Trading Nation

Eastern Mediterranean and the Gulf, 1971–9

The 1970s mark a watershed in British engagement with the Middle East. Informal empire had finally all gone, and with it the framework within which Britain had pursued its interests in the region for well over a century. No longer able to prioritise those interests over the will of local states, or to claim special privileges, Britain now accepted that its relations with Middle Eastern countries were on a new moral and political basis, more appropriate to a post-imperial age. The guiding principle was that of equality. Speaking in Cairo in 1971, the Foreign Secretary, Sir Alec Douglas-Home, defined British interest in the Middle East as 'that of a trading nation which has no interest in power politics or military bases and no wish to interfere in independent countries'.[1]

At the same time Britain's connections with the Middle East were expanding. Following the dramatic oil price rises of the 1970s, large numbers of expatriate Britons went to work in the Gulf. Gulf Arabs meanwhile increasingly came to London for business, education, medical treatment, tourism, to live, and, to the irritation of some Arab governments, as political refugees.[2] Arab newspapers began to publish in London, while Arab shops and restaurants opened on the Edgware Road.

As North Sea oil production came onstream during the 1970s, Britain became much less dependent on Middle East oil. By 1981 it was nearly self-sufficient in terms of the volume of its oil needs, though it continued to import heavy crude from the Middle East to meet the requirements of its refineries. The link between oil and sterling had been broken with the winding up of the sterling area following British entry into the EEC in 1973. On the other hand, the British economy was sensitive to the dramatic increases in oil price during the decade. The 1973 Arab–Israeli war led prices to rise by 470 per cent to 11 dollars a barrel. They again almost doubled, to 20 dollars, as a result of the 1979 Iranian revolution, although a production glut in the 1980s underscored the fact that prices could fall as well as rise.[3] The great beneficiaries of the price rises were the Gulf producers, who quickly emerged as an important market for Britain as it sought to increase exports to pay for more expensive oil imports.

The threats to British interests were also changing. Moscow's lack of political leverage over Israel counted against it once the Arab–Israeli conflict entered a diplomatic phase after the October war. But the decline also owed much to the insensitivities of Soviet diplomacy. Soviet arrogance and condescension, not to mention their unwelcome pursuit of treaties and bases, suggested that they had learned nothing from Britain's mistakes in the Middle East.[4] While Soviet influence, along with the risk of superpower confrontation in the region, had peaked in the early 1970s, the Middle East remained what one former senior British official described as 'the most dangerous area in a dangerous world'.[5] Although the era of large-scale Arab–Israeli war ended in October 1973, the Palestinian dimension to the conflict was far from resolved. The outbreak of civil war in Lebanon in 1975 was a pointer towards longer-term trouble in the states created out of the Ottoman Empire.

Terrorism was again emerging as a significant threat. There were a number of assassinations in London of Arab diplomats, along with the serious wounding of the Israeli ambassador in 1982.[6] In the early 1970s Libya provided arms to the Provisional IRA. According to the latter's Chief of Staff, Joe Cahill, Colonel Qadaffi possessed 'an awful hatred of England'.[7] More substantial arms shipments were made in the mid-1980s. Libya was responsible for the bombing of a Pan Am flight over Lockerbie in Scotland in December 1988.[8]

The British frequently found themselves on the sidelines of the major events of the 1970s and 80s, part of the supporting cast rather than lead players. They still enjoyed a degree of residual influence in some areas, notably the Gulf and Jordan under King Hussein. But the protection and furtherance of British interests now depended heavily on ad hoc coalitions and existing alliances. The most important of these remained the United States, which by the 1970s was the dominant power in the region. British diplomats were adept at working the agencies of government in Washington, as well as Capitol Hill, to try and influence decisions before they were taken. A reputation for expertise on the Middle East helped.[9] There was also the new forum provided by the EEC, which Britain finally joined in January 1973. The Middle East was one of the first areas in which the EEC sought to develop a common foreign policy. For very different reasons, however, both Washington and Brussels were to prove the cause of much British frustration.

The limits of British influence were most evident in the eastern Mediterranean. September 1970 witnessed a major Jordanian crisis following the hijacking of four airliners by the Popular Front for the Liberation of Palestine. As in 1958, King Hussein's throne was in danger. But concern over oil and potential damage to British interests in the Arab world, the risk to the British hostages held by the PFLP, plus a lack of confidence in Hussein's future, meant that this time Britain was anxious to avoid involvement.[10] The King sometimes passed messages during the crisis via the British embassy. According to Henry Kissinger, then White House National Security Adviser, this caused delays, as London added its own appreciation, influenced by concern that the US might act precipitately. The impression, which Kissinger says was erroneous, nevertheless suited American purposes, as 'a deterrent to rash action if London informed other capitals that things threatened to get out of hand. London delicately suppressed its misgivings with us, without however failing to suggest that it favoured a more measured pace.'[11] In addition to close cooperation with the US, the Heath government, anxious to gain French approval for its third EEC membership bid, was careful to coordinate its position with France.[12]

Hussein survived, and after 1970 was seen as an important force for regional moderation whom the British were anxious to support. They found the kingdom congenial. Douglas Hurd, Foreign Secretary from 1989–96, writes of being 'attracted by the strong British flavour which Jordan's rulers gave to their version of Arab life. The streets of Amman were as clean as those of Guildford [...] Jordanian politicians admitted me to their jokes and gossip in a way which would have been inconceivable in any other Arab capital.'[13]

The King was an Anglophile, who understood the British.[14] Sir John Coles, who was ambassador in Amman in the 1980s, saw him regularly, and had the impression that in outlining his thinking, the King seemed almost to be dictating the ambassador's telegram back to London paragraph by paragraph.[15] The King's standing in Britain was reflected in the memorial service for him at St Paul's after his death in 1999. It was a unique occasion, a descendant of the Prophet and a Muslim head of state honoured in an Anglican cathedral. Paradoxically perhaps, British influence declined under his successor, Abdullah II, whose mother was British.

Britain's one direct foray into the Lebanese civil war was brief. Following a request by the Lebanese government, Britain agreed to contribute a token contingent to the American-led Multinational Force established after the 1982 Israeli invasion. The prime minister, Mrs Thatcher, however, had done so reluctantly. The MNF was much too small to fulfil its mandate of assisting the Lebanese authorities to restore control over the Beirut area, and the Prime Minister worried over the American disposition to take what she saw as too tough a line with Syria. To her relief, the MNF was withdrawn in 1984. Among the lessons she drew from the affair, but which failed to imprint themselves into long-term governmental thinking, was the dangers of intervening 'unless you have a clear, agreed objective and are prepared and able to commit the means to secure it'.[16]

Of much greater concern to British policy makers was the Arab–Israeli conflict. During the 1973 October war, the prime minister, Ted Heath, declared that the superpowers 'did not control what happened in the world. There would always be a role of the middle powers, particularly perhaps for countries like Britain, which had a long experience of adventure and diplomacy.'[17] Events belied this claim. London sought to leverage an apparent neutrality to negotiate an end to the conflict, thereby gaining both Arab gratitude and ensuring that there would be no Arab oil embargo against Britain.[18] In contrast to the 1967 war, an arms embargo was imposed on both sides. Since their main battle tank was British, the refusal to supply ammunition fell particularly heavily on the Israelis. It revived old Israeli suspicions of British policy dating from 1948, and impaired intelligence contacts for much of the 1970s.[19] It also meant that Britain had no immediate leverage over the Israelis, although even had supplies been forthcoming, it is most unlikely that Britain would have been able to negotiate a cease-fire.

The hard reality, as a senior official, Sir Anthony Parsons, minuted on 12 October, was that the British had very little leverage over either the belligerents or the Americans.[20] Indeed, London and Washington were once more at cross purposes in the Middle East. The problem began with an American request on 12 October for Britain to table a cease-fire resolution in the UN Security Council. The British embassy in Washington reported that Kissinger was looking to America's 'traditionally most intimate ally' to take this first step towards a settlement of the Middle East problem 'with the adroitness which he expects of us and admires in us'.[21] Having discovered from Sadat that there was no prospect of a cease-fire, London demurred. Kissinger, who appears to have been told by the Soviet Union that Egypt would agree, believed that Britain was playing its own game.

This was a misunderstanding on the part of Kissinger, the master manipulator. But British restrictions on the use of bases in the UK and Cyprus for reconnaissance over the battlefield, along with diplomatic signals that a request to use British bases to resupply Israel might not be granted, made the absence of a common position between London and Washington all too clear. Then, at the very end of the war, after the Americans had picked up indications of possible Soviet intervention, US forces were briefly put on a heightened state of nuclear alert. The British were informed rather than consulted. This infuriated Heath, who, like Eden, had a temperamental dislike of the 'special relationship', and saw the alert as typifying America's 'irrational obsession' with Cold War brinkmanship.[22]

The underlying problem was familiar. Kissinger saw the crisis through the lens of the Cold War, and spied an opportunity to try to squeeze the Soviet Union out of the Middle East. London was preoccupied with energy security at a time when Arab countries were beginning to use oil as a diplomatic weapon. Implicit in this difference in perspective were the widening power disparities between the two allies. Kissinger complained to Nixon that the British were 'behaving badly'; by 'just passively sitting there picking up the pieces, they are not shaping anything'. They didn't try to change Sadat's mind or 'want to run any risks'.[23] Unlike the US, however, Britain was in no position to run the risks necessary to manage the outcome of the war so as to facilitate a successful peace process.

But there was also another problem. The war came at a time when Anglo-American relations were already strained over British reluctance to support an American initiative for a 'Year of Europe', to the point at which the Americans had in July suspended some intelligence contacts.[24] The war marked the second time in one year that the Heath government seemed to prefer coordinating with its new European partners, rather than acting in its traditional role as America's loyal lieutenant. For Kissinger this suggested a worrying trend, made worse by the fact that he believed that the West Europeans had acted disgracefully – jackals was the word he used in private – by distancing themselves from the US to protect themselves against Arab oil sanctions.[25] In one testy exchange with his British counterpart, the US Secretary of Defense, James Schlesinger, complained about British policy taking on a character of 'decayed Gaullism'.[26] This had not, however, prevented Britain from making what the ambassador in Washington, Lord Cromer, described as a 'very considerable contribution' to the raw intelligence available to the US during the war.[27]

For the rest of the decade Washington drove a peace process which culminated in an Egyptian–Israeli peace settlement, and disengagement on the Israeli–Syrian border. In London, officials sometimes had to cajole ministers into taking an interest in the Arab–Israeli peace process. In Sir James Craig's words:

> They had never heard of the McMahon correspondence. They were exasperated by the Arabs' exigency, obsession and incompetence. Sir Alec Douglas-Home saw the Arabs as unruly children; Mrs. Thatcher saw them as losers. Ministers were exposed to the Zionist lobby and the idea of Israel as the magical revival of a dream once lost for ever.[28]

When they did take an interest, they found British influence marginal. Occasionally circumstances favoured a British initiative. In 1978 the British sponsored Egyptian–Israeli peace talks at Leeds Castle; in 1987 the Israeli Foreign Minister requested Britain to facilitate contacts with Jordan.[29] Several British prime ministers, notably Wilson, Thatcher and Tony Blair, were notably pro-Israeli, but this did not afford them significant leverage. The British could never force the Israelis to do anything they did not want to do, though neither, unless they really put their mind to it, could the Americans.

As the conflict narrowed down to its intractable Israeli–Palestinian core, London and Washington's positions often seemed to be reversed, with the British trying to cajole the reluctant Americans to take a more active role to try and defuse the conflict. The result, particularly evident in 2002–3, when Tony Blair tried hard to get a serious American commitment to the peace process in order to neutralise Arab accusations of double standards in the run-up to the invasion of Iraq, tended to be frustration. According to his Foreign Secretary, Jack Straw, Blair's 'profound emotional support for Israel' got in the way of his ability to deliver hard messages to Bush and the Israeli premier, Ariel Sharon.[30]

Britain's other forum of indirect influence was the EEC/EU. The British and French took the lead in the 1980 Venice declaration which referred to the Palestinian right of self-determination, and for the first time associated the PLO with the peace negotiations. But this was a period when European policy was of a largely declaratory nature, tending to annoy rather than influence both Israel and the US.[31] It did, however, keep Jerusalem and the 1967 borders on the agenda and, over time, the Europeans made themselves more relevant to the peace process. The EU became directly associated with the establishment in 2002 of the so-called Quartet, consisting of the US, Russia, the EU, and the Secretary General of the UN. Tony Blair became its representative, but achieved little. Probably more important was the technical know-how and money which the EU provided to the Palestinian Authority established in the wake of the 1993 Oslo peace accords, and to which Britain made a significant contribution. Between 2011 and 2015 Britain provided £129.5 million to the Palestinian Authority.[32]

The key area of the Middle East for Britain, however, remained the Gulf, by now a centre of burgeoning wealth, and it was here that residual British influence remained strongest. Despite the 1971 withdrawal, Britain had unfinished business in Dhofar, where the insurgency had taken on a Cold War dimension, with the Popular Front for the Liberation of the Occupied Arab Gulf receiving support from Russia, China, Cuba and Vietnam, as well as the PDRY, Libya and Iraq. The Sultan was supported militarily by Jordan and Iran and financially by Saudi Arabia and Abu Dhabi. The British contribution came in the form of SAS units, plus seconded and contract British military personnel, including the commander of the Sultan's forces. Despite anxiety in the early 1970s lest Britain be sucked into a 'mini Vietnam', the war was won by a combination of overwhelming superiority of forces, and an effective 'hearts and minds' campaign based on Britain's experience of the successful Malayan campaign against a communist insurgency of the 1950s. The aim in Oman was 'to secure Dhofar for civil development'.[33] The diplomat and colonial administrator, Sir Gawain Bell, described it as 'a successful and satisfactory chapter in the history of Britain's imperial twilight'.[34]

Oman would remain the most overtly pro-British of the Gulf states. Sultan Qabus, who had been trained at Sandhurst and spent six months with a British regiment, had a predilection for the British, which even the Foreign Office admitted could sometimes verge on the embarrassing, and to many people Oman had the appearance and aura of a British colony. British ministers found Oman much more congenial to visit than Saudi Arabia.[35] There was some concern at the time that if the Sultan fell, the British position could collapse overnight, and he had been advised to broaden the decision-making process.[36] Douglas Hurd wrote that 'this proud and sensitive man had to be handled with great care'.[37] Like his father, he had an impressive track record in getting British ministers to change their minds.[38]

Although no other Gulf sheikdom faced similar problems to Oman, they were rich, small states which were for the first time learning to cope on their own. An increasingly rapid process of modernisation created social and political pressures, while heavy dependence on large immigrant populations, often Palestinian, was a source of unease. Nation building had to begin from scratch in the UAE, whose seven member states had little in common other than language, religion and their old treaties with Britain. The new Federation was encumbered by a top-heavy administration, and divided by tribal strife, local rivalries and border disputes.[39]

Britain played a significant role in the resolution of a 1978 constitutional crisis in the UAE.[40] But the fact that British forces were now almost entirely committed to NATO, and that Labour ministers were 'intellectually and emotionally sceptical' about the durability of Gulf rulers, limited British engagement.[41] British advisers continued to work in the UAE, Bahrain and Oman at the side of the emirs and sultans, as well as in the local armed forces. In 1973 there were some 1,500 loan service personnel in the Gulf, including 635 in Oman, where the Dhofar insurgency was still in progress, though by 1981 the numbers were down to 336, with the largest contingents in Oman and Kuwait.[42] In addition there were advisory and assistance British military visits to the Gulf states, while military personnel from Gulf countries, including members of Gulf royal families, attended training courses in Britain. Personal contacts made at Sandhurst provided invaluable subsequent political access to Gulf decision makers.[43] It was only in 1979, following the Iranian revolution and the advent of the Thatcher government, that Britain began to engage more closely in defence and political dialogues with Saudi Arabia and the sheikhdoms. But the emphasis remained on developing local defence capabilities, with the British role confined to training and an over-the-horizon presence.[44]

Britain's primary interest in the Gulf, as back in the eighteenth century, was now commercial. By 1978 the Gulf was taking some 7.5 per cent of British exports, making it the third-largest British market after the United States and EEC.[45] The two biggest customers were Iran until the 1979 revolution and Saudi Arabia, which became the senior British diplomatic post in the Middle East. Britain remained a big player in Saudi Arabia, and the Kingdom's closest Western partner after the US. There were three diplomatic missions, three military missions and 'vast' commercial and defence interests.[46] The British expatriate community in the 1980s numbered some 30,000. This was a country in which almost any conceivable change to the status quo was regarded as being to the West's disadvantage.[47]

Anglo-Saudi relations, however, were often far from easy to manage. This was dramatically underscored in 1980 by the Saudi response to the British television film *Death of a Princess*, about the execution of a Saudi princess and her lover. The British ambassador, Sir James Craig, was 'rusticated', and British commercial interests appeared at risk.[48] This Saudi reaction drew on a combination of the film's offence to family honour, divisions within the royal family, and religious sensibilities. The Foreign Secretary, Lord Carrington, publicly warned that, 'We must understand that though in this country we have grown a crust which affects our sensitivities in a wide range of affairs, political, personal, religious and so on, other countries are not so insulated.'[49] It was a warning which would resonate over the next decades in the face of growing sensitivity in the Muslim world to what were seen as Western slights. But in 1980 there was also bitterness at what Saudi officials saw as the barely concealed contempt for Arabs in Britain.[50]

Although the affair was relatively quickly resolved, the memory of the affair lingered, and management of Anglo-Saudi relations remained tricky.[51] As the retiring ambassador, Sir Andrew Green, noted in 2000:

> The gap between our cultures is more like a chasm, and Western ability to comprehend foreign cultures is in sharp decline. It is not easy to explain Sharia criminal procedures to a Western press fixated on the possible execution of British nurses. Nor is it easy to explain to Saudi princes the apparently unlimited freedom permitted to Arab dissidents in London.[52]

Thanks to the legacy of British intervention, Britain's relations with Iran were also sensitive. Following the Mossadegh coup, Britain had told the Shah that it would not again intervene in internal affairs, and the embassy was very chary of either having contact with opposition groups, or offering any kind of advice which would risk 'a whole colony of fleas in our ear'.[53] The Shah had an underlying neurosis about the British, and seemed obsessed with the idea that the BBC was being used against him, as it had been against his father in 1941. He also had a vindictive streak, which further deterred official British criticism.[54] The result in the early 1970s, by which time the Foreign Office had concluded that Britain needed the Shah more than he needed Britain, was something suspiciously approaching a policy of appeasement. In the damning words of the Foreign Office's internal report on the events leading to the Iranian revolution, 'Since the Shah could have a crucial influence on which foreign trading partners were favoured with big contracts, it was thought wise to pander to his wishes wherever possible. How the Shah ran his country was his own affair. Britain should make hay while the sun shone.'[55]

The embassy relayed the Shah's complaints about the BBC Persian Service, prompting the Head of the FCO's Information and Guidance Department to point out that the rationale behind BBC language service broadcasts was 'to operate in the medium to long term, influencing those who may one day form an alternative government'.[56] Attempts were even made to stop the London Underground being besmirched with anti-Shah graffiti. It was only in 1978 that a Foreign Office minister wrote that it would be wrong to conduct relations with the Shah on the basis of 'bootlicking'.[57]

There was a further complication in British relations with the Gulf which came to the fore in the 1970s. Historically Britain had seen arms sales to the Middle East primarily in political terms – a means of gaining and maintaining influence. Economic interests, however, now predominated. This, despite the dangers outlined following a visit to the region in 1968, by the Director of Army Sales, who noted that

> knowledge and judgement in defence matters is vestiginal and even those who are poor seem little concerned with costs. They all want to run too far too fast [...] The British aim is to restrain their ambitions as far as possible to reduce costs, to avoid buying a lot of equipment which cannot be operated or maintained, and to avoid the build-up of a number of local forces which will then battle, however ineffectively, for local supremacy.[58]

The reality was that arms sales were a cut-throat business; if Britain, which as officials later put it, was no longer in the business of 'nannying' Gulf states, didn't sell, its competitors would.[59] And Britain badly needed the business. Arms were one of the most successful sectors of Britain's remaining manufacturing industry, involving in 1991 some 80,000 jobs. Exports not only contributed to the balance of payments. They helped sustain an industry which might not otherwise have been able to operate on the basis of domestic orders alone, which would mean buying more of Britain's own arms abroad. Arms sales also helped maintain a high technical base and provided an impetus for commercial and other bilateral relations. Of the ten largest customers for British arms between 1964 and 1997, five were in the Gulf.[60]

By far the most important was Saudi Arabia. Under the Al-Yamamah programme first signed in 1985, Saudi Arabia bought 122 Tornado combat and Hawk trainer military aircraft, helicopters and naval vessels, as well as contracting for Britain to build two air bases. The largest foreign trade deal ever concluded by Britain, it prevented the Tornado production from closing.[61] In 2012 Saudi Arabia was still providing some 14 per cent of British Aerospace's profits. When negotiations to buy 72 Typhoon fighters were finally concluded in 2014, it was reported that, without the order, fighter production might eventually have been lost in the UK.[62]

The Shah had also been a very large customer, reflecting his ambition to become the new policeman of the Gulf in succession to Britain. Iran, however, dramatically demonstrated the downside of unrestricted arms sales. Britain's own tank production lines became dependent on a country whose stability was being undermined by the diversion of expenditure from civil to military programmes.[63] Like the Iraqi revolution of 1958, the Iranian revolution came as a major shock. The weakness of the Shah's position had not been appreciated by the Foreign Office, or indeed by most other international observers.[64] The British, however, had got too close to the Shah, to the point not simply that they tended to downplay some of the more unsavoury aspects of his regime, including torture, but that it became impossible to believe that he could be overthrown. Sir Anthony Parsons, who was ambassador at the time, later wrote of a failure of imagination. The British assessments of the political situation had been further handicapped by the self-imposed restrictions on contacts with the political and religious opposition. Resources had also been too heavily invested in commercial work at the expense of political reporting.[65]

Britain, like the US, had made a one-way bet. They had banked their whole policy on the Shah, because he seemed strong and brooked no opposition. When in 1978 opposition nevertheless mounted to the point that his throne was in danger, they had no alternative but, in the words of one policy paper, to support him 'warts and all, while occasionally offering treatment for the warts'.[66] The BBC Persian Service, which had increased its audience between 1977 and 1979, remained a particular source of tension between Britain and the Shah, to the point that, according to Parsons, the whole country was glued to the BBC every evening. With local television censored, the BBC was the only means by which the opposition, including Ayatollah Khomeini, could get their views heard. The Shah considered the BBC Public Enemy No. 1 and in November 1978 its broadcasts were jammed.[67] Parsons believed that an attack on the British embassy on 5 November had been carried out by agents of the security organisation, SAVAK, and soldiers in plain clothes, 'to teach the British that it was futile to continue to press the Shah to look for political solutions'.[68]

According to a note for the Cabinet of 14 December 1978, Britain could do little to influence the situation. 'The Iranians must work out their own salvation.'[69] Once the Shah fell, Iran ceased to be a friendly state. Large orders were lost, as was some advanced military technology which had been sold to the Iranians.[70] The British embassy was closed, reopening only in 1988. Suspicion of Britain, however, remained intense and Anglo-

Iranian relations were plagued by a succession of crises and diplomatic incidents. The most serious of these involved a *fatwa* issued in 1989 by Ayatollah Khomeini for the death of the British-born writer, Salman Rushdie, for alleged blasphemy in his novel, *The Satanic Verses*. The affair was a disconcerting pointer to the future – the first major example of the globalisation of outrage and what has been described as 'the assassin's veto'.[71]

20

A Return to the Gulf

Iraq, the 'Arab Spring' and ISIS

The impact of the Iranian Islamic revolution in the Middle East was even more far-reaching than that of the Egyptian nationalist revolution of 1952. The first in a succession of interlinked crises which wracked the Middle East into the twenty-first century, it led to the creation of a Shi'a Islamist state ready to export its revolution across the region and determined to pursue a nuclear programme with serious potential repercussions for the international non-proliferation regime. Within a year, the long peace in the Gulf secured by the *Pax Britannica* was over. In 1980 Iraq attacked Iran, and though it won the eight-year war, the huge debts it accumulated precipitated the seizure of Kuwait in 1990. From here on, Iraq and the US were on a collision course, culminating in the 2003 American-led invasion of Iraq. The botched aftermath left Iraq vulnerable to the rise of ISIS in 2014, as civil war in Syria unleashed by the 'Arab Spring' spilled across the border, threatening the break-up of the country. As of 2014 a regional war across much of the Fertile Crescent was in progress, evoking the imagery of W.B. Yeats's *The Second Coming*,

> Things fall apart; the centre cannot hold;
> Mere anarchy is loosed upon the world.

As Roula Khalaf wrote, 'Today's Middle East is decomposing as if by chemical reaction, a region overwhelmed by a collective mayhem in which the rot of decades of authoritarianism and bottled up sectarianism are taking over.'[1]

These events brought a return of British forces to the Gulf. Historically, Britain had perceived threats to its interests *in* the Middle East. Now, it worried about threats *from* the Middle East, as violence in the region threatened to spill onto British streets and threaten British holidaymakers abroad. But the return also reflected Britain's continued role as an activist global player, still one of the world's richest states and largest defence spenders, closely allied to the United States. These were coalition interventions in increasingly difficult political conditions with decidedly mixed results.

The outbreak of the Iran–Iraq war led to the establishment of the Royal Navy's Armilla patrol to help ensure the safety of shipping in the Gulf, followed later by a small minesweeping operation. Iran's defeat did not, however, mean the return of stability. In early 1990 the JIC in London had flagged up the possibility that Iraq might at some point move against Syria or Kuwait, but like most if not all of its allies, Britain was taken by surprise when on 2 August 1990, Saddam Hussein invaded Kuwait.[2] This flagrant breach of international law, coming immediately after the end of the Cold War raising hopes for the establishment of a 'new world order', generated an unusually strong international response. The seizure of Kuwait made Iraq the dominant power in the Middle East, controlling some 20 per cent of the world's oil reserves. This represented a political threat to Egypt and Syria, and a direct military threat to Saudi Arabia.[3] Speaking to President George Bush, Mrs Thatcher warned that the Iraqis 'won't stop here. They see a chance to take a major share of oil [...] Losing Saudi oil is a blow we couldn't take.'[4] Here was a test of an unwritten British and American commitment to the security of the Gulf states. The Prime Minister knew the Gulf and its rulers, and General Pinochet apart, she loathed dictators.[5] She had fought a successful war in the Falklands in 1982, at the end of which she had declared that Britain had 'ceased to be a nation in retreat'.[6] This crisis, as the American Secretary of State, James Baker, later put it, provided Britain, as also France, with 'an opportunity to emphasise their heritage as global players'.[7]

The first aircraft to arrive in Saudi Arabia were American, with RAF Tornadoes following shortly after. The Saudis badly needed external help. Their ground forces were small, and unlike the Iraqis', lacked combat experience. If the bulk of that support would inevitably come from the US, the British contribution was nevertheless welcome, not least for political reasons. The Saudis did not want to be left alone with the Americans, nor according to Prince Khaled bin Sultan, the Sandhurst-trained commander of the coalition, 'did the Americans want to be left alone with us'.[8] But the success of this unprecedented Anglo-Saudi alliance depended on British responsiveness to Saudi sensitivities, not least the presence of Western forces in proximity to the Holy Places. Osama bin Laden's alienation from the Saudi monarchy and the United States dates from the events of August

1990. British forces in the Kingdom were therefore subject to some unusual deprivations, including alcohol, live entertainment, and pork (although there was some bacon in the British rations).[9] Suspicious of Western intentions in the Gulf, the Saudis were additionally nervous about the prospect of a war launched from their soil by mainly American troops. As the Foreign Secretary, Douglas Hurd, put it, they needed 'constant encouragement and reassurance'.[10]

At the Anglo-American level, the first joint military operation in the Middle East since World War II worked well. The British provided the third-largest contribution to the coalition after the US and Saudi Arabia, some 46,000 troops. The British commander, General Sir Peter de la Billière, quickly established good relations with his American counterpart, General Norman Schwarzkopf, and was able to secure a British voice in US military planning.[11] De la Billière also managed to persuade a reluctant Schwarzkopf to allow the British armoured brigade to operate independently, rather than coming under the command of the US marines, which the army regarded as beneath them.[12] In Washington the process of Anglo-American military and intelligence consultation 'moved smoothly up several gears'. It was, as Sir Percy Cradock, the foreign policy adviser at No. 10, later wrote, 'a situation we were both familiar with and for which our arrangements were tailor made'.[13] Surveying his allies in mid-October, Bush noted that 'the Brits are strong and the French are French [...] The rest of the Europeans do not want to use force.'[14] John Major, who, somewhat to the consternation of the Saudis, had succeeded Mrs Thatcher in December, was the first foreign leader told the details of American military planning. But he was informed rather than consulted.[15]

Back in 1961, Britain had sent a mere 5,700 troops to pre-empt an Iraqi attack on Kuwait. Thirty years later, with some half a million Iraqi men in and around Kuwait, the international coalition assembled to expel the Iraqis was more than a hundred times larger than the original British force. To deter the use of Iraqi chemical and biological weapons, Saddam was warned of 'altogether unacceptable consequences' should these be used. This nuclear threat was a bluff, but it may have served its purpose.[16] As a further precaution against the use of biological weapons against British cities, a number of Iraqis in Britain were detained or deported.[17] The British homeland was no longer immune from war in the Middle East. In the event, no chemical or biological weapons were used in the war, which began on 16 January 1991. It proved to be a very one-sided affair. Iraqi numbers were no match for US technological superiority. A sustained air campaign was followed on 24 February by a brief land operation which liberated Kuwait at the cost of remarkably few allied casualties. Church bells were rung in Britain.[18] It seemed, and indeed was, too good to be true.

The question of how the war should end, and how far Saddam should be pursued, had been raised on more than one occasion in Washington, but with the answers left far from clear.[19] The allies had no mandate to pursue Saddam Hussein into Iraq. As Major later wrote, 'If the nations who had gone to war on the basis of international law were themselves to break that law, what chance would there have been in future of order rather than chaos?'[20] The international coalition, most notably its Arab component, would rapidly have fallen apart. Nor was there any appetite in either Washington or London for taking on the burden of occupying Iraq.[21] In the event, the timing of the decision to halt the fighting was made in Washington, without consultation with London. Bush liked the idea of pressing for peace before peace was pressed on him. There was concern at the high casualty rate among Iraqi troops, as well as over the need to ensure that Iraq remained strong enough to contain Iranian ambitions for regional primacy. The Americans believed, wrongly, that several elite Republican Guard divisions were trapped in Kuwait, and that Saddam had been sufficiently humiliated for the Iraqi army to ensure his overthrow.[22] But the Iraqi military did not revolt. Those who did, the Shi'a in the south and the Kurds in the north, were brutally repressed.

It was at this point that the law of unintended consequences began to kick in. Neither the British nor Americans had any desire to get involved in these revolts. But the impact of television images of Kurdish refugees was nevertheless such as to lead Major to take a politico-humanitarian initiative for the creation of a so-called Kurdish safe haven. Some creative and innovative thinking in London made it possible to find a middle way between Article 2 of the UN charter, forbidding interference in internal affairs of member states, and the immediate humanitarian imperative. Sir Percy Cradock, who was closely involved, described it as 'patchwork stuff' constantly opposed and evaded by the Iraqis, but better than nothing.[23] Although they were initially chary of the idea, the Americans, along with the British, French, Dutch and Italians, provided the necessary troops. In addition, two Iraqi 'no-fly zones' policed by American, British and, for a time, French aircraft were created in northern and southern Iraq, covering one-third of the country's airspace. The southern zone provided ample early warning of any troop build-up against Kuwait, and was thus also of value to Saudi Arabia.[24] Combined with the safe haven, the northern no-fly zone raised the prospect, by no means welcome in Saudi Arabia or Turkey with its own large Kurdish minority, of the emergence of an independent

Kurdish state. Regional assembly elections were held in 1992, leading to the creation of the Kurdish Regional Government.[25]

The most important consequence of the war, however, was the way in which it put Iraq's WMD capability on the international strategic agenda. A highly intrusive UN inspection regime was instituted, based on a British proposal for a Special Commission to investigate and destroy what turned out to be an alarmingly extensive programme. There was also an arms sales ban, plus economic sanctions, the toughest in UN history, which had the effect of undermining the regime's capacity to deliver services, and began the decline of the Iraqi state which would be accelerated by the 2003 Iraq war.[26] Saddam played cat and mouse with the inspectors. Not long after their departure in 1998, the RAF joined the Americans in a brief air campaign, known as Desert Fox, against Iraqi WMD capabilities. Coincidentally or otherwise, it began the same day that the US House of Representatives began a debate on the impeachment of President Clinton over the Monica Lewinsky affair. With another war under way in the Balkans, Tony Blair was 'determined to keep the US alliance intact and functioning at what was a crucial moment'.[27] But, as at least one British ambassador had predicted, the air strikes achieved little; Saddam Hussein was not significantly weakened, the UN weapons inspectors did not return, the UN Security Council remained split and Britain and the US were left with a war of attrition in the air.[28] By 2001 the containment regime was in serious disrepair. There was growing concern that the Iraqis might shoot down a British aircraft, and that sanctions were not only hurting the Iraqi people, but, like the no-fly zones, were losing Arab and international support. The idea of more targeted 'smart' sanctions was blocked by the Russians.[29]

Then came 9/11. Previously, terrorist incidents had been limited in scale and effect – a matter of bombings and hijackings which hit the headlines, but did relatively limited damage and did not therefore seriously affect policy. In their choice of targets, methods and the scale of casualties – this was the largest civilian loss of life in homeland America since the Civil War – bin Laden's televised attacks took terrorism into new and deeply disconcerting territory. Al-Qaeda had shaken the American psyche, disorientating the George W. Bush administration and seriously impairing its judgement. The first military response was in Afghanistan, where al-Qaeda had its safe havens.

Iraq had had nothing to do with the attacks. Nevertheless Saddam Hussein was also quickly in Washington's sights. Here was an ideal target for the US to demonstrate to potential proliferators its determination to eliminate all potential WMD threats, 'and that mere suspicion of association with terrorists could cost them dearly'.[30] But there may also have been another factor. Perhaps, as one American commentator wrote, 'victories against small bands of terrorists in the mountains could not expiate the pain or trauma of 9/11. Perhaps we needed to enlarge the enemy to be commensurate with the damage to our national psyche.'[31] This, moreover, was America's hyperpower moment, when its military power reigned supreme, but Washington was inhabited by an inexperienced president and an unusually ideologically driven administration. The Neo-Cons saw a moral imperative, as well as advantage, in spreading democracy and recasting the Middle East. A US-led overthrow of Saddam Hussein would 'put America more wholly in charge of the region than any power since the Ottomans, or perhaps the Romans'.[32] Or as a Bush aide put it, 'We're an empire now, and when we act, we create our own reality.'[33] When Tony Blair visited Bush at his ranch at Crawford, Texas, in April 2002, he was told that military planning against Iraq was already under way.

The scene was now set for a major foreign policy blunder. Seen from the British perspective, the similarities with Suez are striking. Here was another attempt to overthrow a Middle East leader by military means, driven by an overriding imperative – the perceived need to end Iraq's WMD programme, which served to distort proper assessment of the costs and risks of the operation. Far more than in the case of Suez, which was strongly backed by the most senior members of the government, this was a prime ministerial war. It would have been difficult though not impossible – Harold Wilson had resisted strong US pressure to send a contingent to Vietnam – for any prime minister to have refused to participate in the US operation. For Tony Blair, however, the 'special relationship' was an article of faith. He had managed to establish the closest friendship that George W. Bush enjoyed with any foreign leader, and had no difficulty with the idea that supporting America in her wars was the price Britain paid for influence in Washington.[34] Well aware of Neo-Con influences in Washington, not least their disdain for the UN, Blair was anxious to prevent the US from playing the Lone Ranger or becoming disengaged from global affairs.[35]

US thinking on Iraq was badly in need of some sceptical probing. Blair was not the man to provide it. Having pursued the most activist British foreign policy of any prime minister since Macmillan, seemingly defying the gravity of relative decline, and having conducted a series of successful military interventions in Sierra Leone, Bosnia, Kosovo and Afghanistan, the Prime Minister was becoming overconfident. He was later quoted as saying that he had taken the view that 'we had to remake the Middle East'.[36]

To some observers, including the former Foreign Secretary, Dr David Owen, this seemed to border on hubris.[37] Blair was a firm believer in the moral rightness of intervention against dictators. One of his ministers was quoted as accusing him of 'moral imperialism'.[38]

At the same time he had a fear, amounting to an obsession, that extreme religious terrorists could in future get access to some form of WMD, which they would have no compunction about using in Britain. He had seen 9/11 as an attack not on the US but on the West, and believed that the whole calculus of risk had changed.[39] The proliferation of WMDs, ranging from poison gas to anthrax and nuclear weapons, could no longer simply be contained or 'managed'. The Iraqi programme might be less of a concern than those of Iran, Libya and North Korea, but Saddam Hussein was, in Blair's words, an 'almost psychopathic man'.[40] He was conveniently in breach of UN resolutions, and the Americans now wanted to 'get' him. Once Iraq was disarmed, the other proliferators would, Blair believed, be easier to deal with.[41] All this was allied to a lack of attention to detail, an impatience with sceptics and a tendency not to think policies through at great length. The Prime Minister's preference was for an informal style of government, militating against collective political judgement.[42]

This was unfortunate since the Prime Minister's thinking was based on a series of shaky premises. As a highly centralised, secretive police state, Iraq was a very difficult intelligence target.[43] On the critical question of Iraq's WMD programme, MI6 had, in the words of one intelligence analyst, 'accepted dubious human intelligence uncritically, failed to check it out with the DIS [Defence Intelligence Staff] experts and fed unreliable and indeed wholly untrue' raw intelligence to the Prime Minister.[44] For its part the JIC had for years unconsciously exaggerated the Iraqi WMD programme. Nobody realised that Saddam's campaign against the inspectors had been designed to hide not WMDs but the *absence* of WMDs. As to the potential link between proliferators and terrorists, the former head of MI5, Dame Eliza Manningham-Buller, later termed this 'a hypothetical theory' which 'wasn't of concern in either the short or the medium concern to my colleagues and myself'.[45] Brian Jones, who was head of the DIS's nuclear, biological and chemical sections, wrote that he was unaware that there had ever been a detailed discussion involving Whitehall experts of the risk, and described the link, at least as far as chemical and biological weapons were concerned, as 'rather simplistic'.[46] This seems an instance of the threat assessment being a greater danger than the actual threat.[47]

Yet the strategic case for trying to remove Saddam and disarm Iraq would have had to have been very strong to justify the high political risk such an operation would entail. The Iraqi brief should have come with red warning stickers marked, 'Fragile State; Handle with Care'. It required only a cursory knowledge of Iraqi history to realise that this was a country with a violent past and considerable potential for anarchy.[48] The expertise was available both in Whitehall and the academic community. But although the possibility of Sunni–Shi'a violence, as of the country splitting into Shi'a, Sunni and Kurdish parts, was indeed raised by officials, these possibilities never appear to have been considered serious enough to bring the proposed operation into question. Like Eden, Blair preferred to cherry-pick his advice to suit his purposes. When a group of academic experts tried to explain the complexities of the country to Blair in late 2002, they discovered that the Prime Minister 'only seemed to want them to confirm to him that "Saddam Hussein is uniquely evil"'. As one of the group later wrote, they found themselves 'up against a vision that was both moralising and simplistic'.[49] In focusing so exclusively on the personality of Saddam, as Eden had done on Nasser, the Prime Minister overlooked the much more complex Iraqi dimension to the operation.

The war which finally broke out on 20 March 2003 played once more to America's overwhelming technological superiority. This time, however, it was not simply a military question of forcing the Iraqi army out of a small neighbouring sheikhdom, but of occupying Iraq, deposing its leader and seeking to manage a transition from dictatorship to democratic rule, which had a poor track record in Iraq. The invaders were immediately out of their depth. They had failed to anticipate that, as one Iraqi exile had warned on the eve of the invasion, in getting rid of Saddam they would end up with 'a thousand little Saddams'.[50] The Americans lacked the troops to contain the violence which immediately broke out in Baghdad, or to seal the Iraqi borders and guard the huge arms dumps in the country, from which weapons quickly leaked. They then compounded their difficulties by further mistakes, including the disbanding of the army and removal of too many layers of Ba'ath party members from the Iraqi machinery of government.[51] Britain had lacked the leverage in Washington to counter the insouciance which the Neo-Cons, with what one British official later described as their 'deep faith in the natural democratic nature of man', brought to post-invasion planning, which even Secretary of Defence Donald Rumsfeld later acknowledged to have lacked 'interagency coordination, clear lines of responsibility, and the deadlines and accountability associated with a rigorous process'.[52]

Yet Britain's own 'Phase Four' planning, as the military called it, was also deficient. Although a good deal of work had in fact been done in Whitehall, it failed to anticipate the problems which were actually encountered. The focus was on humanitarian and ecological disasters – in 1991 Saddam Hussein had set Kuwaiti oil wells ablaze – rather than looting and violence in the power vacuum which Saddam Hussein's removal created. The planners were hampered by the fact that there had been no British embassy in Baghdad since 1991. Nobody realised just how broken Iraqi society was after 45 years of dictatorships, two wars and UN sanctions.[53] A more immediate problem was uncertainty over which part of Iraq British forces would occupy – it was only in January 2003 that it became clear that British forces would not be allowed to enter from Turkey – or indeed, whether public opinion would allow Britain to fight at all. Parliament had only voted to approve the war on 18 March, when 139 Labour MPs had defied the party whip. Distracted by the attempts to get a second UN resolution authorising force, ministers had no time to worry about what would happen next in Iraq. The Foreign Office, where the Iraq Planning Unit was only set up in February 2003, found it difficult simultaneously trying to prevent and prepare for the same war.[54]

Formally the British had chosen to become the joint occupying power by virtue of being America's key ally, and because, as Blair later said, 'we believed in it'.[55] This was the second British occupation of Iraq (the third if the 1941 invasion is taken into account) so the British inevitably carried a weight of historical baggage. If some Iraqis looked back nostalgically to earlier British influence, others took a more jaundiced view. 'You are not particularly welcome here,' one British general was told in 2003. 'Remember what happened when you were here last time.'[56] There was suspicion that the invaders had come 'to steal the oil, crush a potential rival, or stamp on Islam and Arabia'.[57] British efforts were concentrated on a semi-independent operation in the four southern provinces, where Blair hoped to conduct an 'exemplary' occupation. Basra was the second city in Iraq and the area was important not least because it held 90 per cent of the country's oil reserves, and produced 70 per cent of the government's revenues.[58] Predominantly Shi'a, who had suffered most under Saddam Hussein, the south initially presented far less of a security problem than the Americans experienced elsewhere in Iraq. But here too the lack of planning told. According to Frank Ledwidge, author of *Losing Small Wars*, a study of British performance in Iraq and Afghanistan, it was during this early period that the British effectively lost the war in the south. They failed to build a government in Basra which might have been able to forestall the rise of the radical Shi'a militias, and which could take gradual control of the city.[59]

Ultimately, however, everything depended on what the Americans decided in Baghdad, where the 'special relationship' was conspicuous by its absence. Paul Bremer, the head of the Coalition Provisional Authority, had no previous experience of the Middle East, nor any obvious affinity for working with Brits. He had not wanted a British deputy, and set no store by British advice, particularly when it involved reversing decisions or went contrary to a seven-point plan for the establishment of democratic government in Iraq which took scant account of the actual situation on the ground.[60] Sir Jeremy Greenstock, Britain's UN representative, who was sent out to try to exert British influence, found himself working with a superpower that liked to do things its own way, with top decisions taken by 'a closed circuit of Americans'. It says something of the dysfunctionality of the American operation, that Colin Powell, the US Secretary of State, was reading British telegrams from Baghdad in order to find out what was actually happening there. But there was also another problem. As in 1991, the British had made what, in terms of the size of their armed forces, was a substantial military contribution, including one-third of the RAF's front-line aircraft, but it was still not enough to play more than a strategically auxiliary role. Their contribution to the occupation in manpower and resources was much smaller. Quantity meant influence with the Americans as much as argument or position as America's main ally, and the Brits were 'low quantity' partners.[61]

Resources – economic and military – were also in short supply in Basra. The draw-down in troops had been rapid. Having had some 46,000 in the country in April 2003, the numbers were down to 9,000 in July and 4,000 in 2007. These were quite insufficient to deal with a deteriorating security situation. But a combination of the small size of the British army and the domestic unpopularity of the war meant that reinforcements were unavailable. The problem was compounded by the decision to launch a second, and similarly ill-prepared operation in Afghanistan in 2006.[62] Continued muddle and disjointed thinking further hampered the British effort. There was no strategic plan, and as the situation deteriorated, there was an absence of ministerial leadership and political guidance.[63] To make matters worse, the army had very little understanding of Iraq and, as in Palestine from 1945 to 1948, had difficulty in getting to grips with the nature of the threat. It was neither equipped, nor trained, for counter-insurgency operations.[64] Ledwidge writes of

> a failure to adapt, antediluvian structures and intelligence systems, deployment schedules that ensured a lack of continuity, a cavalier attitude to post-entry planning, a mentality geared to an excessive readiness to use extreme violence, an attachment to archaic traditions and imagined histories.[65]

The final withdrawal in 2009 marked the first British military defeat since the withdrawal from Aden 42 years earlier. It was an episode the armed forces preferred to forget.[66]

The Iraqi war had two positive outcomes. Although it turned out that Iraq had no WMDs, the war helped convince Colonel Qadaffi, who feared he might be next, to abandon his nuclear programme. In Iraq itself, Saddam Hussein was removed, and democracy of a sort was re-established. But the civil war which regime change had unleashed brought al-Qaeda onto the scene, ushering in a new era of horror to rival that of Saddam. Ahmed Saadawi's novel, *Frankenstein in Baghdad*, tells the story of a rag picker. Angered by the lack of respect paid to the growing number of corpses from suicide bombings and massacres, he begins to collect body parts and sew them together. This creature comes to life, wreaks vengeance on behalf of its component parts, and then finds it needs further flesh for its own survival.[67] Estimates of violent civilian deaths as a result of invasion and civil war in Iraq range between 125,000 and 400,000.[68] Some 4 million Iraqis were displaced.[69] Regionally the invasion played into Iranian hands by shifting power to the Shi'a in a heartland Arab nation for the first time since the fall of the Fatimid Caliphate in 1171.[70] All of this might have happened in any case had the so-called 'Arab Spring' spread to Iraq, but the coalition invasion should at least have provided an opportunity for the tensions on Saddam Hussein's displacement to be managed. The Iraq campaign had the further disadvantage that the US and Britain took their eye off Afghanistan, where the Taliban was able to make a come-back.

In Britain the Iraq war raised a new domestic problem. Until 1947, the impact of British policy on its Muslim population had been a matter of constant concern to the government of India. Following independence, immigration from the subcontinent meant that Britain acquired a significant Muslim minority, some 2.7 million in England and Wales, equivalent to 5 per cent of the population in 2011.[71] The Iraq and later Syrian civil war served to radicalise elements of domestic Muslim opinion. In an unprecedented move, MI5's budget was doubled in 2003, and according to its director the agency was 'pretty well swamped'.[72] There were terrorist attacks in London in July 2005, when 52 people were killed and 966 injured, a substantially higher toll than in the IRA attacks between the 1970s and 1990s. Between July 2005 and November 2014, 40 planned terrorist attacks were foiled. David Cameron described the battle against Islamic extremism as 'the struggle of our generation' and described ISIS as a 'death cult'. The Chancellor, George Osborne, expressed concern about the possibility of ISIS cyber-attacks on air-traffic control centres and hospital systems. Aviation was regarded as under threat, while ISIS an al-Qaeda were expected to try to acquire chemical, biological and radiological weapons.[73]

As after Suez, Britain's international reputation was damaged, as was self-confidence.[74] The combined failures in Iraq and Afghanistan made it much more difficult for governments to make the case for future military intervention, which on the precedent set by Tony Blair in 2003 was now deemed to require parliamentary approval and scrutiny. As Peter Hain, who had been a minister in the Blair government, declared during the debate on British air action against ISIS in Iraq in September 2014, 'We went to war on a lie, and the aftermath was disastrous. That has made me deeply allergic to anything similar in the region and certainly anything remotely hinting at cowboy western intervention.'[75] The implications of this became clear as the 2011 revolts across the Arab world exposed the fragility of key Middle East states. This raised a series of very difficult decisions about whether to intervene in highly fluid situations, in support of rebel groups of whom not much was known. Dictators rarely go quietly. Colonel Qadaffi had no compunction about using force against his opponents. The immediate case for British intervention was a determination not to stand aside in the face of a potential humanitarian disaster. But there was also concern to be seen on the side of rebels in what appeared at the time to be a major pro-democratic upheaval across the Middle East, and a fear that, if they were defeated or Libya divided, Qadaffi might revert to support of international terrorism.[76] What made intervention politically possible only two years after the withdrawal from Basra was an authorising UN resolution and the fact that it could be confined to airpower. The 'boots on the ground' were provided, with British encouragement, by Qatar and the UAE, although British special forces helped the rebels to become more organised and tactically astute, while also acting as forward controllers for air strikes.[77]

Mission creep soon emerged, however, as the Anglo-French-led operation, with critical American logistic support, morphed into a campaign against Qadaffi. Once he was overthrown, the political follow-up dimension of the operation, vital given the power vacuum left by the removal of a dictator of over forty years' standing, was again neglected. At the time of writing in early 2015, one commentator described Libya as looking like intervention 'on the cheap, without responsibility'.[78] By then the country was on the edge of chaos, with an ISIS presence. Weapons had leaked to Islamist groups in neighbouring African countries, notably Mali, where the French were forced to intervene in 2013.[79]

Compared with the situation created by the Syrian civil war, the Libyan problem, however, had seemed relatively simple. This time the humanitarian case for intervention in a particularly brutal conflict was reinforced by concern to prevent a highly complex and increasingly sectarian conflict from spreading, becoming a proxy conflict between Shi'a Iran and Hezbollah on the one hand and Sunni Saudi Arabia and Qatar on the other. Of more immediate concern to West European security agencies, the war attracted young Muslim *jihadis*, who might pose a potential terrorist threat on their return to the UK. In 2014 over half of MI5's case work involved Britons travelling to Syria. [80]

Against this was the risk that arms supplies to the disunited opposition forces would fall into the hands of more extreme Islamist groups, which increasingly came to dominate the conflict, and that intervention would only make things worse. Options were circumscribed by the Russians, who felt cheated by the way in which a Security Council resolution in Libya had been used to bring about regime change, and blocked any UN-supported action aimed against their long-term ally, President Bashir Assad. More important, President Obama was extremely chary of repeating his predecessor's mistakes in Iraq and Afghanistan. Plans drawn up by the Chief of the Defence Staff, Sir David Richards, to train a rebel army outside Syria were judged too risky.[81] When in August 2013, following the Syrian government's use of chemical weapons, the Cameron government proposed joining the US in punitive air strikes, it was defeated in a parliamentary vote, the first time a British government had been prevented by parliament from going to war in 150 years.[82] With the experience of Iraq still very fresh in the mind and the Afghan war not going well, MPs and their constituents were in no mood for another potentially ill-conceived military operation, whose outcome was at best uncertain. The subsequent exodus of Syrian refugees to Europe, was not foreseen.

Yet almost exactly a year later parliament approved British air action in Iraq by a majority of 481. By now the Syrian civil war had become a multi-dimensional power struggle, spreading into Iraq. ISIS's self-proclaimed Sunni Caliphate straddled both sides of the Syrian and Iraqi borders, ostentatiously proclaiming the end of the post-Ottoman settlement.[83] In Iraq ISIS capitalised on Sunni anger over their displacement by the Shi'a majority following the 2003 invasion and fear of government forces. Rampant government corruption, and the weakening over the previous two decades of the fabric of the Iraqi state, meant that the latter was unable to meet this new threat. Few Iraqi politicians seemed able to put country above religious sect or ethnicity, minority rights were disrespected and intolerance prevailed.[84]

Although the immediate danger was to British allies in the Middle East, Cameron argued the case for air action in terms of British national security, declaring that 'This is about psychopathic terrorists who are trying to kill us and we have to realise that […] they have already declared war on us.'[85] MPs were in measure reassured by the fact that this time Britain would be responding to a request from the Iraqi government and would, as in 1991, be acting as part of a broad international coalition including Arab states. But their unease was nevertheless palpable.[86] Almost exactly a hundred years since British forces had first landed there, the RAF was once again in action over Iraq, this time also using drones operated from Lincolnshire. Their military impact was questionable, however, with the small size of the British deployment suggesting to one critic that it had more to do with transatlantic relations than with effective counterterrorism.[87] That said, bombing was at best a temporary palliative for what were ultimately political problems deeply rooted in the dysfunctionality of parts of the post-Ottoman settlement.

The cascade of events following the Iranian revolution strained the fragile post-Imperial order in the Middle East which Britain had played such a prominent role in drawing up, far more seriously than the Arab Cold War of the 1950s and 1960s had done. These were conditions in which successful intervention was peculiarly difficult, with the law of unintended consequences a particular hazard. If Britain was more than just another coalition player, it was nevertheless doubly vulnerable – to its own mistakes, as to those of the Americans. The most serious misjudgements – the timing of the end of the first Gulf war and the catastrophic failure to plan for the political aftermath of the 2003 Iraq invasion – were made in Washington. But this was of little consolation to London. True, the US in 2003 had been an unusually dangerous ally, though it was also argued that Blair failed to capitalise on the political value of British support for Washington.[88] Yet the underlying problem, which could only accentuate following the 2010 defence cuts, was that the British military was simply not large enough to provide the influence which might have prevented these mistakes. Britain was punching not so much above as beyond its weight. But that did not mean the end of the story. According to the 2015 Strategic Defence Review a new British defence staff would be established in the Middle East, while Britain would build a more permanent and substantial military presence in the Gulf 'to reflect our historical relationships, the long-term nature of both challenges and opportunities, and to reassure our Gulf allies'.[99] And in December 2015, in the wake of ISIS bombings in Paris, and following a fraught public and parliamentary debate, parliament voted to extend military action against ISIS to Syria.

Part Five

Perspectives

21

Matters of Scruple

The story so far has been a classic tale of the exercise of imperial power, skilled and often ruthless at advancing its interests over those of others. But Britain was also a global power with an interest in the stability provided by a rules-based international system, as well as a Christian, liberal state, based on the rule of law, whose politicians and citizens believed in probity, justice, decency and fair play. The potential for conflict between national interest, enlightened self-interest and ethics was considerable, most starkly illustrated by the controversies over Suez and the 2003 Iraq war. Officials had various ways of resolving this dilemma, including keeping doubtful acts out of the limelight and rationalisation. They did not subscribe to the view of one member of the UN Special Committee on Palestine in 1947 that 'One might say that the British are really cursed by their possession of the world's largest empire; in their desire to keep it intact they apply methods which their ethical principles certainly would prohibit them from using in private dealings.'[1]

In its imperial heyday Britain was both supremely self-confident and high-minded. The world's leading power had a sense of being in harmony with the progressive forces of the universe. Having reached the top of the ladder of Progress, men like Palmerston and Cromer saw their task as being to lead the way and direct the march of other nations, in particular less favoured or less civilised ones.[2] Rule over non-Europeans was regarded well into the twentieth century as part of the natural order of things. In the case of the Middle East, this approach was tinged by the view of Islam as a danger to be opposed, as by an assumption that the region was somehow exempt from normal European moral codes.[3] In 1843 *Blackwood's Magazine* ascribed the occupation of Aden to the habit of 'taking the previous owner's consent for granted, whenever it suited our views to possess ourselves of a fortress, island or tract of territory belonging to any nation not sufficiently civilised to have representatives at the Congress of Vienna'.[4]

Justifying air control in Iraq to parliament, a minister claimed that many of the tribesmen loved fighting for fighting's sake and had no objection to being killed. According to Priya Satia, Britons in the 1920s regarded the moral world of Arabia to be distinct from their own, where the use of bombing, at the time a new feature of warfare, would have been regarded very differently.[5]

At the same time, empire was also considered to confer obligations. Its governance was seen as a sacred trust. The men who went out to Egypt after 1882 went not just to exercise British control of the country, but to serve it. In a draft note of advice for young officials in Egypt, the Oriental Secretary, Harry Boyle, wrote that

> the one and only subject which we should keep in view approaches pure altruism [...] to confer upon a people whose past is one of the most deplorable ever recorded in history, those benefits and privileges which they have never enjoyed at the hands of the numerous alien races who have hitherto held sway over them; and to endeavour to the utmost of our power to train up, by precept, generations of Egyptians who in the future may take our place and carry on the tradition of our administration.[6]

The Englishman was in Egypt 'as a guide and friend, not as a master'.[7] Curzon went so far as to argue that Britain should be judged not by its domestic achievements, but on the marks it left on the people, religions and morals of the world.[8]

Foreigners might raise a sceptical eye at such talk. An Italian remarked to a British diplomat on 'a strange dogma in your religion: that the British empire was conceived without original sin'.[9] But if policy was at best a mixture of self-interest and obligations, the high-minded sentiments dating from the Victorian era was not simply hypocritical. In Egypt, as in the Aden Protectorates or Palestine and Iraq under the mandates, there was a genuine belief that Britain had a responsibility for the promotion of good government and welfare, and that officials were doing good, rather than simply selfishly promoting British national interests. As Stephen Longrigg, who helped set up the Iraq mandate, wrote in 1953, 'local British officials, children of their own country and centuries-old standards, did what they could, with a real devotion in scores of cases, to guide and help and strengthen'.[10] The British could take credit for ending the slave trade in the Persian Gulf and the *corvée* system of forced labour in Egypt, along with the creation of security in hitherto insecure tribal regions.[11]

Where practice failed to live up to precept, as was frequently the case regarding money for development, individual consciences were pricked. Sir Bernard Reilly, who had a long career in the Aden Protectorates, spoke of his shame at their neglect.[12] The manner in which the Palestine mandate ended caused genuine distress. The Colonial Secretary's report on Palestine of June 1948 deplored the fact that Britain's 'task has concluded in circumstances of tragedy, disintegration and loss'.[13] This sense of responsibility for the welfare of people in the Middle East extended beyond the narrow confines of British sovereign territory, to include the mandates and Egypt under the 'veiled protectorate'. It also extended to Persia, where the British took an interest in the fate of various minorities, including the Zoroastrians, Jews, Assyrians and the large Armenian population of Azerbaijan.[14]

The exercise of power in informal empire was tempered by a series of unwritten rules and constraints, deriving from a mixture of values, the codes of conduct which officials had been brought up with, and notions of enlightened national self-interest. They were certainly not always observed, but disregard made policy makers uneasy and exposed them to criticism. Perhaps most important was the belief that commitments should be honoured. Diplomacy would be undermined, and prestige would suffer, if Britain was believed not to keep its word. In the tribal societies of Arabia breaking one's word was an especially heinous sin.[15] But it was also a matter of honour. Officials regarded imputations of bad faith as odious.[16]

Their view was not necessarily shared by ministers. At the coronation in 1953, the Ruler of Bahrain buttonholed Churchill to lobby for support in a dispute with neighbouring Qatar. 'Tell him', said a very tired Prime Minister, 'that we try never to desert our friends.' He then paused. 'Unless we have to.'[17] (The translator diplomatically omitted the qualification.) The list of those who felt themselves let down by the British is quite extensive. Commitments came into question where circumstances changed, promises had been given to rulers who had little hold over their territories or lost their influence, and where promises proved in conflict with each other. Turning down a request for protection by Ibn Sa'ud, the Political Agent in Kuwait declared that 'the Great [British] Government does not accord protection rashly or without much forethought'.[18] That, however – as the conflicting wartime promises to the Arabs, Zionists and French, which left officials with a deeply uneasy conscience, underscored – was not always true. In the early 1920s the British found themselves caught between conflicting promises to the Persian government and the sheikh of Mohammerah. Having failed to mediate between the two, and being unwilling to use force, the British opted to support the more powerful side. Official consciences, however, were far from easy – one official spoke of 'throwing our friends to the wolves' – and questions were asked in parliament.[19] A later Political Resident in the Gulf, Sir Bernard Burrows, describes the Sheikh's treatment as 'one of the most disreputable episodes in British imperial history'.[20]

A second cluster of dishonoured commitments arose at the end of empire when British power was in terminal decline. Back in the late 1930s, the Peel Report had insisted that 'the spirit of good faith' forbade abandonment of the mandate. Britain could not 'stand aside and let the Jews and Arabs fight their quarrels out'.[21] A decade later, when this task seemed impossible, it was abandoned. Aware that they had exposed themselves politically by allying with the British, the leaders of the South Arabian Federation were uneasy as to how far they could rely on their ally, despite a succession of assurances from both Conservative and Labour ministers.[22] Yet in February 1966 the Labour government, which found the Federal rulers ideologically distasteful, announced that following the withdrawal of the Aden base there would be no British defence guarantee. The reaction among Federal ministers was a mixture of anger and dismay. 'We cannot', the chairman of the Federal Council told the junior minister sent out to inform them of the decision, 'believe that it is your wish that we shall be sacrificed just because after many years of repeated promises to the contrary, the British government finds that it suits its own self-interest, to desert its friends and leave them in the lurch.'[23]

There was a similar response from former Conservative ministers as well as British officials, some of whom took the unusual step of forming an action committee to try to change the government's mind.[24] The former Colonial Secretary, Ian Macleod, denounced the breaking of pledges to Gulf rulers in 1967 as 'shameful and criminal',[25] while several senior diplomats in the Gulf wrestled with their consciences over whether they could 'decently continue to represent HMG after this double-dealing'.[26]

Closely related to the belief that commitments should be honoured was concern to act honestly and honourably. Britain should not deceive, lie and deliberately mislead, or otherwise act in a manner to impair its good name. Again, this was a precept often honoured in the breach. The most famous instance is the discomfort of British officers involved in the Arab Revolt, on learning of the provisions of the Sykes–Picot agreement. The Arab Revolt, Lawrence wrote in *Seven Pillars of Wisdom*,

> had begun on false pretences [...] In the East persons were more
> trusted than institutions. So the Arabs, having tested my friendliness and
> sincerity under fire, asked me, as a free agent, to endorse the promises

of the British government. I had no previous or inner knowledge of the McMahon pledges and the Sykes–Picot treaty [...] But, not being a perfect fool, I could see that if we won the war the promises to the Arabs were dead paper. Had I been an honourable adviser I would have sent my men home, and not let them risk their lives for such stuff. Yet the Arab inspiration was our main tool in winning the Eastern war. So I assured them that England kept her word in letter and spirit. In this comfort they performed their fine things: but, of course, instead of being proud of what we did together, I was continually and bitterly ashamed.[27]

Similar unease was expressed by other senior British officers with the Arab Revolt, as well as later by officials in Palestine. One High Commissioner, Sir John Chancellor, wrote privately that the Arabs had been treated 'infamously [...] That destroys the moral basis on which the Government must stand if one is to do one's duty with confidence and conviction.'[28] At the Colonial Office Sir John Shuckburgh spoke of 'a sense of personal degradation' at the way Zionists and Arabs were being told two different things.[29]

Much of the controversy over Suez focused on the belief that in 'colluding' with Israel the government had acted deceitfully and dishonourably. Sir Frank Cooper, then head of the Air Ministry's Air Secretariat, later described 'the shame of Suez' being in the way it was handled by Eden and Selwyn Lloyd, who did it 'in such a hole-in-the corner way'.[30] The air commander of the operation, Air Chief Marshall Sir Denis Barnett, accidentally found out about the plot. 'I couldn't believe that it could be so. I didn't think that we would behave like that.'[31] This aspect of the affair caused much less concern in the French military.[32]

Disposing of other people's territory was frowned upon. The 1907 division of Persia into spheres of British and Russian influence was greeted by a chorus of disapproval from radicals and Labour MPs.[33] Harold Dickson, who was Political Agent in Kuwait, considered that the 1922 Uqair settlement in which Kuwait lost two-thirds of its territory to compensate Ibn Sa'ud for concessions to Iraq 'savoured of surrender pure and simple of a strong state to a weak state'. Sir Percy Cox 'grievously harmed a great reputation for fair dealing'.[34]

Other issues which raised ethical objections include the sequestration of Jewish property as part of the Palestine counter-terrorism campaign in the 1940s, and a proposed response to an Israeli demand for a 'partnership' as the price of British overflights to Jordan in 1958.[35] A senior Foreign Office official objected:

I confess I do not much like the idea of sucking up to the Israelis now when we need them and dropping them as soon as this need is over. It seems to me highly dishonest, and also liable to destroy any lingering trace of respect or confidence in us that the Israelis may retain.[36]

Several years earlier, when Kuwaiti sterling reserves were under discussion, another official had warned that using 'our influence in Kuwait towards a solution of this problem which is intended to help the UK rather than Kuwait would be dubious ethics'.[37]

Arms sales became ethically sensitive with the dramatic growth of Middle East defence markets in the 1970s. Sales to the most unsavoury regimes were ruled out, but the restrictions were insufficient to prevent controversy. According to Sir Anthony Parsons, by then in retirement, the Middle East arms race encouraged conflict, aggravated already grisly human rights behaviour and multiplied the human cost of war. The Liberal leader, David Steel, described the sight of the developed nations pouring weapons into the Middle East and then collectively wringing their hands when they were used as 'appallingly hypocritical'.[38] There was strong criticism when in 2006 Tony Blair halted a Serious Fraud Office investigation into bribery allegations concerning the vast al-Yamamah arms contract with Saudi Arabia, unconvincingly citing reasons of national security.[39]

A third unwritten precept of informal empire was the need to observe international law, along with other international norms. Yet ministers were not above rewriting the rules to meet the perceived exigencies of particular situations. The occupation of the Buraimi oasis in 1955 took place despite the fact that the legal position was, in Macmillan's words, 'rather tricky'. He went on to complain that the Attorney General 'was rather wet about this'.[40]

In the view of its critics, Gladstone's government had broken international law in Egypt in 1882. The Radical, John Bright, denounced the British 1882 bombardment of Alexandria and occupation of Egypt as 'a manifest violation of international and moral law', while Lord Randolph Churchill accused Gladstone of an act of criminal aggression.[41] Eden's position over Suez was that 'we should not allow ourselves to be involved in legal quibbles'.[42] A few lawyers, notably the Lord Chancellor, Lord Kilmuir, argued that a legal basis existed for taking the canal by force. But this view was not supported by the top international lawyers at the Foreign Office or the government's two law officers, the Attorney General and the Solicitor General.[43] The latter formally dissociated themselves from a telegram sent to British diplomatic posts in the Middle East following Israel's attack on Egypt.[44] In July 1958, when the

Cabinet discussed sending British forces to Jordan, Macmillan was careful to ensure that the Attorney General was in on all of the discussions.[45]

If, as the historian Peter Hennessy writes, the legal question 'lurked from the outset' of Suez, by the time of the 2003 Iraq war, it was centre stage.[46] With the establishment of the International Criminal Court, the Chief of the Defence Staff required a formal statement by the Attorney General to the effect that the war was lawful.[47] Legal sanction was also vital to Blair to prevent a significant number of ministerial resignations and a mass revolt by MPs.[48] The key question was whether, in the absence of a second UN resolution explicitly authorising the use of force, Security Council Resolution 1441, passed in autumn 2002, would provide an adequate legal justification. Until early February 2003 the Attorney General, Sir Peter Goldsmith, had argued the need for a new resolution. On 7 March, with the prospects for this looking increasingly unlikely, Sir Peter stated that while a second resolution would still be the safest legal course, a reasonable case could be made for going ahead without it, adding, however, that were the matter ever to come to court, that court might disagree.

Once it was clear that there would be no second UN resolution, Sir Peter was asked for a straight yes or no ruling. He then determined that military action would be legal provided the government certified that Iraq was in 'further material breach' of UN resolutions. His view was not shared by the senior Foreign Office Legal Advisers, the former Lord Chief Justice, Lord Bingham, or the UN Secretary General, Kofi Annan.[49] Under the 2007 Ministerial Code, ministers were obliged 'to comply with the law including international law and treaty obligations'. The Conservative government was keen to stress the legality of operations against Libya in 2011 and ISIS in 2014.[50]

There was a fourth set of ethical constraints on informal empire. While the British could indeed be ruthless, there were limits as to how far it was regarded as acceptable to go. A character in Naguib Mahfouz's novel, *Sugar Street*, describes British imperialism as 'tempered perhaps by some humane principles'.[51] The brutality which marked French policy in Algeria, particularly in its early and final stages, is largely absent. Nor is there any British equivalent of either the French shelling of Damascus in 1926 and 1945 or the extensive use of torture in the Algerian civil war.

But there were a series of instances involving what could euphemistically be described as excesses. Some of these were spontaneous, a matter of bored, frightened or angry troops or police running amok. But in Palestine in the late 1930s, the smashing up of property, looting and violence appear to have had tacit support from the military authorities, who saw them as a means of frightening the rebellious population into submission. There certainly appear to have been hardly any successful prosecutions of servicemen on such charges.[52] In other cases the brutality was deliberate. In Palestine, as later in Aden in the 1960s, torture was used to gain information. According to the High Commissioner, Sir Reginald Turnbull, without so-called 'effective interrogation' the authorities would have no forewarning of terrorism.[53] Some soldiers were sufficiently uneasy about these practices to refuse to hand over prisoners to the Intelligence Corps.[54] There was frequent recourse in Palestine to collective punishment. In the largest such instance, which occurred in Jaffa in 1936, troops blew up between 220 and 240 houses, leaving some 6,000 Palestinians destitute.[55] Such actions, which served to fracture and impoverish the Palestinian population, were, however, within the letter of the law and emergency regulations in force in Palestine.[56] The same was not true of the final phase of the Aden insurgency when the Argyll and Sutherland Highlanders acted with considerable brutality. One soldier reported that instead of shouting *Waqaf* (halt) three times as prescribed under the stop and search procedures, British troops shouted 'Corned Beef' and then instantly gunned civilians down.[57] The 2003 invasion led to a significant number of Iraqi claims for mistreatment and unlawful detention.

Where such actions became public, there was protest. The excesses of the battle of Omdurman in 1898, when Ansar wounded were killed, the Mahdi's tomb destroyed and his body thrown into the Nile, led to parliamentary questions and the publication of a White Paper to try to quieten public opinion.[58] The military's behaviour in Palestine in the 1930s drew protests from within the Palestine administration, and also from the Anglican clergy. Bishop George Graham-Brown was particularly vocal, at one point describing military and police action as 'terrorism for which the Government is morally responsible'.[59] The 1906 Dinshawi incident (see page 64) generated strong criticism in Britain.

On other occasions ministers and officials prevented what they regarded as excesses. When Allenby demanded an indemnity following the assassination of the Sirdar and Governor-General of Egypt, Sir Lee Stack, in 1924, London objected that 'the appearance of a vindictive penalty' was not in the British tradition.[60] In 1940 Wavell rejected contingency plans which had been drawn up for a scorched-earth policy in Egypt, saying he refused to be responsible for a famine in the country.[61] Both the First Sea Lord, Lord Mountbatten, and the First Lord of the Admiralty, Lord Hailsham, expressed deep unease over early plans for the Suez operation which would have involved naval bombardments liable to cause civilian casualties.[62]

Air policing in Iraq was subjected to parliamentary criticism, primarily on the grounds that it was indiscriminate, and that women and children were attacked.[63] In 1924 the Labour Colonial Secretary felt it necessary to present a defence to parliament which stressed that destruction was neither the aim nor normal result of air action. But since no independent observers were present, most of the destructive impact of air policing could be concealed by editing out details and the use of euphemisms.[64]

Assassination seems generally to have been ruled out. The Foreign Office was horrified when Sir Percy Cox suggested the assassination of Wilhelm Wassmuss, a highly successful German agent operating in Persia during World War I. The idea was described as repugnant and reference to the subject was ordered to be deleted from despatches.[65] The rejection of proposals to assassinate the Mufti during World War II and Egyptian intelligence officers in Yemen in the 1960s, however, reflected the view that these were liable to be counter-productive, rather than ethical considerations.[66] Nasser's assassination was considered in 1956, but ruled out as much for practical as ethical reasons.[67] The 1957 Anglo-American plan for overthrowing the Syrian government included the 'elimination' of three Syrian figures.[68] According to press reports, active consideration was on several occasions give to the deposition or assassination of Colonel Qadaffi, while British, along with American, French and Israeli officials, discussed the assassination of Saddam Hussein in the run-up to the 1991 Gulf war.[69]

If there was broad agreement as to what, ideally at least, Britain should not do, what, over and above the promotion of good government, did the British feel themselves morally obliged to try and do? There were two schools of thought as to how far Britain was obliged to try to promote its values in the Middle East. On the one hand was the view that representative institutions did not represent a panacea for all the troubles of Eastern countries,[70] and that, in Curzon's words, 'the ways of Orientals are not our ways, nor their thoughts our thoughts. Often when we think them backward and stupid, they think us meddlesome and absurd.'[71] In the summer of 1957, the ambassador to Jordan, Sir Charles Johnston, commented that while it was disappointing that a country built up under British traditions should have resorted to a 'special brand of paternal authoritarianism', nevertheless 'taking facts, and Arabs as we find them', British interests were better served by maintenance of stability and the Western connection than 'an untrammelled democracy rushing downhill towards communism and chaos'.[72]

To an Arab critic like Rashid Khalidi, such attitudes smacked of 'the casual, borderline racist cynicism of Westerners who saw Arab politics as inevitably authoritarian and corrupt'.[73] In a speech in Kuwait in 2011 during the 'Arab Spring', David Cameron expressed regret for Britain's role in sustaining Middle East strong-men in the mistaken belief that they maintained stability.[74] This was in line with an alternative body of opinion, going back to the nineteenth century, that Britain had a responsibility to support liberal democracy. Hence criticism of the way Britain had throttled democracy in Egypt in 1882 and pressure on the government to support the Persian constitutional movement in the early 1900s.[75] Overall, however, short-term political objectives tended to outweigh concern for the promotion of values.

The promotion of human rights first came to the fore during David Owen's period as Foreign Secretary in the late 1970s, and again in 1997, when the new Labour Foreign Secretary, Robin Cook, stressed the need for an ethical dimension to British foreign policy. The Middle East presented Britain with a particular dilemma. Authoritarianism was prevalent across the region, including the Gulf, where, as the case of the Shah had first shown, there was an inevitable reluctance to press friends and customers too hard on what they regarded as purely domestic affairs. A 2006 House of Commons Foreign Affairs Committee report described the human rights situation in Saudi Arabia as being the cause of grave concern, while also noting that Britain's relationship with the Kingdom was of 'critical and strategic importance'.[76] Britain promoted a quiet dialogue between Human Rights Watch and the Saudi authorities, and worked to improve the human rights situation in Bahrain following the 'Arab Spring'.[77] In the later Mubarak years, British government agencies supported projects in Egypt intended to promote a credible electoral process, human rights and a free media, but with very limited results.[78]

The humanitarian case for military intervention was an early twenty-first-century phenomenon, invoked with regard to Iraq in 2003, Libya in 2011 and, unsuccessfully, with Syria in 2012.[79] Here seemed a benevolent elision of interests and values. In the words of one commentator,

Civilised nations cannot stand idly by while innocents are murdered by despots; Britain has a national interest in the spread of democracy; Europe cannot escape the consequence of failed and pariah states on its doorstep; the rules of international order must be upheld; interests and values can coincide; inaction as well as action has consequences.[80]

Certainly, after Iraq, humanitarian arguments on their own were unlikely to be decisive.

For the most part the liberal conscience was manifest outside government. Sometimes it was articulated by individuals such as Wilfrid Scawen Blunt, a staunch critic of British policy in Egypt during and after 1882. The case for the Persian constitutionalist movement was championed by a Cambridge professor, E.G. Browne.[81] By contrast, around a million people demonstrated in London in February 2003 against the Iraq war.[82] Like Suez, this was an event which evoked real anger. The human rights lawyer, Dame Helena Kennedy, described the 2003 Iraq war as 'one of the most wretched events of my adult life'.[83] The composer Sir Peter Maxwell Davies referred to it as 'a betrayal, totally scandalous and illegal'.[84]

Parliament and press were the main forums in which the imperial conscience was articulated, usually, though by no means exclusively, by those with radical or left-wing views. Churchmen also spoke up. Archbishop Cosmo Lang supported the cause of the Assyrians in Iraq, along with Leo Amery, Lord Lloyd and Robert Cecil.[85] In the post-imperial era there were pressure groups such as Amnesty International and the Campaign Against the Arms Trade.

Critics and government sometimes seemed to be speaking a different language. Compare one Labour leader's description of Grey, apropos of his Persian policy, as a man 'who would coolly enter into an alliance with the Prince of Darkness provided that he deemed that British interests were furthered thereby',[86] with the complaint of a former head of the Foreign Office about 'the enthusiastic philanthropy which insists on messing about in other people's affairs which it does not understand'.[87] Nevertheless, democratic governments had to take public opinion into account. They had either to conceal, defend or rationalise breaches of the four main ethical constraints on policy, and they were not always very good at doing so. The transparency of the Anglo-French claim that they were intervening to separate the two sides at Suez, Eden's subsequent determination to deny collusion in the face of all the evidence, and the contrast between British indecisiveness and French resolution, all underscore the historian A.J.P. Taylor's verdict that, like most respectable people, British government 'make poor criminals, and had better stick to respectability. They will not be much good at anything else.'[88]

Ethical issues weighed more heavily with officials than ministers. Probity was important to the ethic of public service. The men on the spot dealt with the consequences of policy at firsthand. Those who had given assurances to local rulers felt, in a way that ministers far away in London did not, that their honour was personally engaged if these were broken. Yet it was precisely because they did not bear ultimate political responsibility that officials, like opposition MPs and leader writers, could afford to allow greater latitude to notions derived from private morality than could ministers. It was the latter who had to weigh the need to protect Britain's good name against other considerations of the national interest. They might deplore the choices this entailed. In his memoirs, David Owen described his recommendation as Foreign Secretary that the Shah should not be allowed asylum in Britain as a 'despicable' act.[89] But he had no doubt that the recommendation should be made.

Occasionally there were resignations. Along with several junior ministers and a Foreign Office legal adviser, Robin Cook, by then Leader of the House, resigned over the Iraq war. The Minister of State at the Foreign Office, Anthony Nutting, resigned over Suez. But few officials felt sufficiently strongly to override their sense of professional obligation to serve the government of the day. They might deplore what had happened, but as good civil servants, once decisions had been made, they saw it as their responsibility to support them as best they could. Of course, career interests were also a factor. 'If you have three small children', Sir Sam Falle wrote apropos of Suez, 'and no private means you do not throw your job away just because the boss has gone barmy.'[90]

Ultimately the impact of ethical constraints depended on the importance of the interests against which they were pitted. It was no coincidence that questions of international law were overridden or finessed in questionable fashion over Suez and Iraq, two instances where governments perceived an overriding imperative for military action to the point where ends were regarded as justifying means. As Sir Stephen Wall, a senior foreign policy adviser at No. 10 remarked of the Iraq war, 'We allowed our judgement of the dire consequences of inaction to override our judgement of the even more dire consequences of parting from the rule of law.'[91]

Yet conscience or scruple could temper the exercise of British power in the Middle East. They may have nagged more than they constrained, and they were less of a constraint than considerations of economic and political costs, but they established lines which, however blurred and indistinct, governments were cautious about crossing, if only because they knew there would be trouble if they were caught out. And they help explain why, though they may not have been very human, the British were, insurgencies apart, generally humane.[92]

22

How Did the British Do?

Since the Napoleonic wars Britain has faced three broad categories of threats to its interests in the Middle East. The first, and most demanding, came from Great Power rivals, all of whom were effectively seen off. This, particularly in the two world wars, was a matter of sheer determination and superior local military power, But some of the threats were exaggerated, while Britain was also lucky in its rivals. Neither the Russians nor the French were ever a serious military menace. Mussolini was at his most dangerous when his military weakness brought Rommel to North Africa. But Hitler's interest always lay in the Soviet Union. The Middle East was for him a diversion and sideshow. By the time the Soviet ambitions began to emerge in the 1950s, the Americans were on hand to contain the danger. Whatever the political tensions, and the Middle East often shows the vaunted 'special relationship' with Washington in a very ordinary light, Britain was able to hand over power in the Middle East to a friendly successor, a rare luxury for a declining imperial power.

The second threat was a reaction to the political infrastructure of informal empire. Generally, this stood Britain in good stead. It made empire affordable, and where it took consensual form, as in the Persian Gulf, it provided Britain with a secure political framework from which to protect its interests. But it had its downsides. In Egypt, by its very ambiguity, it became a source of tension, since nobody was quite sure where they stood.[1] It could be as intrusive as formal empire, while leaving power in the hands of local rulers and governments who were often less efficient and honest than British administrators would have been. Where it was imposed, therefore, informal empire did not protect Britain against nationalist anger. At the same time it could be more difficult to withdraw from informal than formal empire. And it was easier to reinvade. Would a British government have gone back into Egypt in 1956 if it had just gone through the ceremony of sending a member of the royal family and hauling down the flag at midnight?

Until World War II, the British responded pragmatically to nationalist pressure, adapting to change in an orderly and timely fashion. By the 1950s, however, informal empire outside the Gulf had become untenable. This meant the loss of bases and a weakening of Britain's residual claims to Great Power status, but, in part again thanks to the Americans, in part due to mutual commercial interest, it did not critically affect Britain's increased economic interests. The end of empire, by contrast, brought potentially more unmanageable threats in consequence of the new regional disorder which has afflicted the Middle East. The spill-over from the crises unleashed by the Arab–Israeli conflict, the Arab Cold War, the Iranian revolution and the 'Arab Spring' variously meant insecurity of oil supplies, dramatic fluctuations in price and the prospect of terrorism on European, including British, streets.

While, overall, British interests fared remarkably well in the Middle East, there is often a sense of this having occurred despite, as much as because of policy. For much of the nineteenth century, policy was sure-footed. British power was more than sufficient to secure those British interests which were not already protected by the Ottoman Empire. The main problem, of which both London and Calcutta were well aware, was to avoid being sucked too far into the region. Yet even then there were instances of key decisions – the 'anti-piracy' campaigns in the Gulf at the beginning of the nineteenth century, the 1882 intervention in Egypt – being taken without proper appreciation of their potential long-term consequences.

This failure became much more marked with the outbreak of World War I. Nobody in India realised where the despatch of Force D to the Gulf in 1914 would lead to, nor, apart from Curzon, did Cabinet members have any inkling of the repercussions of the Balfour Declaration. In taking on the role of overseeing the redistribution of the Ottoman Empire, the British had saddled themselves with a virtually impossible task. These difficulties were compounded by the political, military and emotional pressures of a world war, the rushed and uncoordinated expansion of British power which it generated, and the unwieldiness of the relevant machinery of government. Hence the contradictions and inconsistencies of policy over Syria and Palestine, the delays in making decisions on Iraq, and the failure to take adequate account of newly assertive nationalism in Egypt, Iraq or Persia.

The next cluster of failures and mistakes – the abandonment of the Palestine mandate in 1948, the Baghdad Pact, the South Arabian debacle of the 1960s, and above all Suez – occurred during the difficult quarter-century following World War II. End of empire is inherently messy. The Middle East was too important to be let go in the orderly fashion which marked the end of the colonial empire, leading policy makers, who had not fully grasped the scale of British decline, to substitute wishful thinking for hard-headed judgement.

The final cluster of mistakes centres on the interventions in the increasingly volatile politics of the early twenty-first centuries. The problems here lay in failure to understand the conditions under which such operations could and could not succeed, misjudgement of situations on the ground, and a failure to appreciate the importance of dovetailing the political and military phases. The same criticisms could of course be made of the 1882 Egyptian intervention.

Failures and mistakes are not of course the same thing. The abandonment of Palestine was a failure, reflecting the impossibility of the British position in the late 1940s. The mistake had been, first, the Balfour Declaration, and then its subsequent confirmation after the potential difficulties had become clear. Impelled by a combination of religious sentiment and oversensitivity to an imagined French threat to Suez, the British had been too clever. They would have been much better advised to stick by the Sykes–Picot agreement, which would have internationalised Palestine. Nor are mistakes equal in degree. The ones linked to World War I, when Britain had so much more power, tended to have more serious long-term consequences than those at the end of empire. The latter made the process more difficult and expensive than it need perhaps have been, but did not significantly shorten informal empire's tenure. Even without Suez or Aden, its days would in any case have been numbered.[2]

The point is underscored by what happened once informal empire was over. The Middle East remained vulnerable to external intervention, just as it remained heavily dependent on outsiders for arms, security and diplomatic mediation. But there was no British or French succession for the taking. Nasser's bid for Arab hegemony failed, as did the Soviet attempt to gain long-term influence and bases. Soviet forces were unceremoniously bundled out of Egypt in 1972, while a Soviet ambassador in Syria is said to have complained that the Syrians took everything from Moscow except advice.[3] American influence has shown the staying power that its Cold War rival lacked, but the US made no attempt to reproduce the British political infrastructure of informal empire, and its diplomacy was frequently frustrated. It has been the insufficient as much as the indispensable superpower.[4]

Blunders tended to occur in periods of distraction and disorientation. The pressures generated by World War I, the sense of being in retreat in the Middle East in the 1950s, the shock of 9/11, all militated against forethought. Decisions were not properly thought through. Jonathan Powell, Blair's Chief of Staff, later admitted that 'we probably hadn't thought through the magnitude of what we were taking on in Iraq'.[5] The same could be said of both the Balfour Declaration and Suez. The failure was both intellectual and in the due process of government. Eden and Blair used prime ministerial power to press through policies on the basis of assumptions that were never properly scrutinised or challenged in Whitehall.

Most mistakes were made at ministerial level in London. There are obvious exceptions – the 1906 Dinshawi incident in Egypt, the 1920 revolt in Iraq and Lampson's 1942 ultimatum to Farouk, all of which reflected a local arrogance or carelessness. Experts got things wrong, notably Curzon with the 1919 Anglo-Iranian treaty. But most of the big failures or blunders involved the exclusion of the regional experts. Poor coordination between departments and power centres, notably during and immediately after World War I and the critical last years in Aden, were contributory, rather than primary causes of mistakes. They resulted in decisions being fudged or delayed, rather than fundamentally misconceived.

Although lack of documentation makes the overall record difficult to assess, the post-1945 period was marked by a series of intelligence failures. Policy makers were taken by surprise by Nasser's response to the withdrawal of the offer to finance the Aswan dam, the Egyptian, Iraqi, Libyan and Iranian revolutions, Sadat's assassination, the 1961 Iraqi threats to Kuwait, the 1973 Arab–Israeli war, the 1990 Iraqi seizure of Kuwait and the absence of weapons of mass destruction in Iraq in 2003. Intelligence was also critically lacking during the Palestine insurgency of the late 1940s and the Aden insurgency of the 1960s. The repercussions of some of these failures were serious. The course of recent Middle Eastern history might have been different had there been the foreknowledge which might have made it possible to pre-empt the 1958 Iraqi coup or the occupation of Kuwait in 1990.[6] And had it been known that Saddam Hussein no longer had a WMD programme in 2003, much of the rationale for the war would have been undercut.

The Middle East in the second half of the twentieth century was of course highly volatile, and most of the intelligence failures were shared by Britain's allies. Britain's problem was often a lack of human sources, most notably in Palestine and Aden, where insurgents enjoyed popular support, and with highly authoritarian regimes, such as Iraq, where agents were difficult to recruit. MI6 had a particular problem in penetrating conspiratorial nationalist movements, which were of their very nature anti-British. On the other hand it had the advantage of signals intelligence – Britain had broken Egyptian codes and ciphers[7] – while judgements about the political situation in Iraq in 1958 and Iran in the run-up to the fall of the Shah were simply wrong.

Lessons were not normally learned. There were public enquiries after the military disaster at Kut in 1916, the various disturbances in Palestine in the 1920s and 30s, and the 2003 Iraq war, though not after Suez. The lessons of the latter, particularly about the need to keep close to the Americans, were perhaps too obvious, besides which Macmillan had no intention of embarrassing himself by an enquiry. While the in-house Foreign Office post-mortem enquiry into the Iranian revolution commissioned by David Owen was widely read by officials,[8] ministers were usually unaware of their predecessors' errors. They neither knew the history, unless very recent, nor were they normally briefed. (And when they were, they did not always listen.)

Had Whitehall established a brief list of dos and don'ts in the Middle East, to be handed to all senior figures responsible for key decisions in the region, they would have included:

- Always think policy through properly.
- Ensure that means and ends are properly aligned.
- Remember that military interventions are inherently tricky. Only intervene if you are clear about the risks and objectives and understand the local situation.
- Be sure you have clear and attainable objectives and some notion of an exit strategy.
- Pay at least as much attention to the political as to the military phase of the operation.
- Never cherry-pick advice or intelligence to suit predetermined policy.
- Be sure to consult and listen to the experts.
- Ensure that policy is properly coordinated.
- Distrust colleagues with obsessions or bees in their bonnet.
- Remember the law of unintended consequences.
- Remember Kipling's *If*, the poem the Eden Cabinet forgot.

The other part of the balance sheet for British policy covers its impact on the Middle East. The British presented multiple faces to the countries of the Middle East. They helped and they meddled. They were arrogant, condescending and sympathetic. They were ruthless, manipulative and sought to do good. At times they pursued a common good, at others a narrowly British interest. It is sometimes argued that the British legacy in the Middle East was essentially intangible. At a conference in 2000 on the withdrawal from the Gulf, the list included a respect for law and order, a love of football, walking on the pavement and ironing trousers (the latter two attributed to an Aden taxi driver).[9] Britain helped bring about significant material improvements in Egypt under Lord Cromer and in Palestine under the mandate. But due to the informal nature of empire, the British impact on the people of the Middle East, as opposed to the political elites, was mostly both limited and indirect. Britain's impact on the political geography of the region, by contrast, was far-reaching. The British were the main political cartographers of the modern Middle East, drawing borders and making states. Iraq, Jordan and the ill-fated South Arabian Federation were British creations. Britain had a hand in the emergence of Israel, the United Arab Emirates and even Saudi Arabia. The survival of Kuwait, Bahrain and Qatar as independent states owes much to Britain.

On the credit side of the ledger, Britain's major contribution to the region during the imperial era was security and the creation of order. The British protected the Middle East against more ruthless invaders and helped reduce regional insecurity. The British era, like that of its Ottoman predecessors, was relatively peaceful. The British performed the role of policemen and adjudicators. They established a *Pax Britannica* in the Gulf, ended tribal raiding and provided some help in the process of state building. For many rulers and tribal leaders in Arabia and the Gulf, the British were not intruders, as they appeared to twentieth-century nationalists, but protectors and subsidisers. Britain's most successful relationships were with the smaller states – Jordan, Oman and the Gulf sheikhdoms – which relied most on her for security. Capable indigenous leadership enjoying broad local legitimacy, and the lack of obtrusive intervention in domestic affairs (Transjordan apart) also helped smooth relations.

The main complaints about informal empire were four-fold. Where informal empire could not be achieved by acquiescence, the British exercised the privilege of the strong *vis-à-vis* the weak, prioritising their interests, intervening in domestic affairs and viewing local populations as moral and social inferiors. Relations were most difficult with Egypt and Iran, the two countries where the British not only interfered most, but where their attitudes betrayed contempt. Sir Anthony Parsons quotes an

Egyptian friend as telling him in the 1950s, 'You despised the Egyptians, and it showed.'[10]

Reviewing the history of British intervention in Iranian domestic affairs, Jack Straw, who as Foreign Secretary at the beginning of the twenty-first century tried hard to improve Anglo-Iranian relations, remarks that 'it is not an impressive story [...] We would not have appreciated it if the roles had been reversed.'[11] The Iranian belief that a British hand lay behind almost everything in the country, satirised in Iraj Pezeshkzad's 1973 novel, *My Uncle Napoleon*, became obsessive. The fact that, unlike with Iran, Anglo-Egyptian relations returned to an even keel after 1970 owes something to the fact that the Egyptians decisively won their independence from Britain and that Nasser's revolution ran out of steam much earlier than the 1979 Islamic revolution. That said, British interventions in Egypt are not forgotten. As Mostafa El-Feki notes, today's Egyptian image of Britain is formed

> of a strange mixture of love and hate. Egyptians admire the British style of life. They sometimes say 'He's as sharp as the British.' The British are known for their firmness and objectivity. But there are certain events in our history which remain very much alive in the history of our two nations.[12]

Economic resources were not ransacked in the Middle East as they had been earlier elsewhere in empire. But the balance of power in the first half of the twentieth century between local oil producers and the oil companies, American as well as British, lay very much in the latter's favour. In Steven Galpern's view, 'the British government exploited Iranian oil as it exploited the Indian economy: as a vehicle to benefit British financial welfare, often at the expense of what Iranians and Indians wanted for themselves'.[13]

The second charge, originally levelled against Britain after World War I, was the creation of artificial divisions in the Arab world. At issue here are not the facts but the degree of damage thus caused.[14] However seductive, a unified Arab world may well have been a dream. But it was also, as British officials during World War I were well aware, not in their interest. The states they established soon evolved interests and identities inimical to close cooperation, let alone unity.[15] To some, albeit limited, extent Britain compensated for this by subsequently indirectly encouraging a sense of unity by dealing administratively with the region through a single Colonial Office department and the promotion of the Arab League. All parts of the region were linked by a network of air, sea, oil and motor routes.[16] A single

BBC Arabic Service was heard from the Maghreb to the Iraqi–Iranian border. The Middle East Supply Centre was a regional organisation established during World War II.

Third, and more topically, there is the question of how much responsibility Britain bears for the post-imperial violence and disorder which have wracked the region. Middle Eastern countries have paid a high price for their independence. Empire, both Ottoman and British, had been a successful exercise in managing the ethnic and religious diversity of the Middle East. The Middle East of the early twenty-first century, which is in deep crisis, boasts remarkably few prosperous, stable and successful states.

Writing on the eve of Sudanese independence in 1955, one official noted that while Britain was not solely responsible for the past, it was an inescapable fact that 'for 50 years or two generations, we were in charge and the policy that inspired our stewardship during that period cannot be left out of account'.[17] Nowhere was this more true than of Palestine, a conflict which, unlike Cyprus and the Kashmir dispute, which also festered after independence, Britain had created. Having tried and failed for the next 30 years to resolve it, Britain then abandoned the mandate, leaving the protagonists to fight it out. The local and regional consequences, both human and political, were devastating. If Israelis and Palestinians bear their own responsibility for the failure to resolve the conflict, its continuation into the twenty-first century despite the immense international diplomatic effort invested in peace making attests to the intractability of this British legacy. Palestine can only be read as a stain on the British record.[18]

The other troubled British creation of the post-Ottoman settlement was Iraq, a state which, like another troubled British colonial creation, Nigeria, its citizens neither desired nor designed.[19] Iraq was a state born out of British mission creep during World War I and Britain bears direct responsibility for the country's original design faults; the prospective difficulties of turning such a heterogeneous society into a cohesive state were never adequately addressed by British officials. It also bears a measure of indirect responsibility for the failure of the Iraqi government under the mandate to do more to reconcile domestic tensions. Peter Sluglett argues that it is profitless to blame Britain, since this is to misunderstand the nature of imperialism. But he goes on to note that many of the failings of the Iraqi state during and after the monarchy

> can be traced to the mechanisms and institutions founded at the time of the British occupation and continued under the mandate: tribal policy,

land policy, a political system which could not function independently of British backing, inadequate safeguards for the minority groups, even the policy of working through a network of police informers.[20]

Just how much more Britain could have done is debatable. The mandate was very brief and continuous Iraqi pressure to end it stood in the way of sustained British attempts at advocating reform. But at the end of the day the impact of imperialism was felt in terms of what it did not do, as well of what it did, and these acts of omission contributed to what by 1958 had become a revolutionary situation.

Iraq raises a larger question, namely the more general failure of the British, as also French, to devise a post-imperial order capable of preventing ethnic, religious and tribal divisions degenerating into the kind of conflict also witnessed in Syria and Lebanon. The problem here was as much conceptual as political, namely the extent to which the nation state has monopolised modern thinking on international order. The Middle East did not lend itself to the creation of homogeneous nation states of the kind which had emerged in Western Europe, a point only partially grasped in the British debate in 1920 about whether to include the Mosul *vilayet* in the proposed new Iraqi state. Greater stability might have resulted from the creation of forms of federation or confederation, an idea which received surprisingly little attention at the time. (Given the shot-gun nature of the South Arabian Federation marriage, too much should not be read into its failure. The UAE, by contrast, has survived and prospered.) Had Britain and France allowed the newly liberated territories of the Ottoman Empire the self-determination they promised in November 1918, this might have produced political entities better capable of commanding local loyalties, although the problem of minorities would almost certainly have remained. What is certain is that some 60 years after the countries of the Middle East gained de facto independence, practical ideas for reproducing the order of the imperial Ottoman or British eras, without a regional hegemon, are conspicuous by their absence.

The final question mark over the British record in the Middle East concerns the failure to do more to establish democratic government beyond the introduction of liberal constitutions in Egypt and Iraq in the 1920s. Had the region been part of the formal empire, more efforts would have been made, at least in the run-up to independence. As it was, the protection of British strategic and economic interests did not obviously require political capital to be expended on what often seemed a thankless quest. According to Francis Fukuyama, states that democratise before they acquire the capacity to rule effectively are bound to fail, a particular problem in the case of Iraq.[21] But Britain aborted the 'Urabi experiment in constitutional government in Egypt in 1882, and had little compunction in keeping the Wafd out of office until the mid-1930s, despite their repeated electoral successes. In Iran, Britain's limited support for the constitutional movement of the early 1900s was more than outweighed by its role in overthrowing Mossadegh, the first man to try to build a modern Middle Eastern state on the basis of collective and individual liberties.[22] The Islamic revolution, with its bloody and repressive aftermath, can be seen as an indirect result.

Britain's record in the Middle East defies simple summary. It is perhaps best seen as shaping the transition from the imperial order to a flawed modern state system which is unlikely to prove permanent. As empires go, it was relatively benevolent. But the British did harm as well as good, often because of muddle and short-sightedness. Verdicts inevitably vary, depending on whether states, rulers and politicians benefited or suffered from British policy, and on whether informal empire was consensual or imposed. And perspectives shift with the passage of time. The long view is probably more favourable than the difficult 40 years which comprised Monroe's British 'moment' in the Middle East. But the verdict on the post-1971 period remains open. The Middle East has an extraordinary capacity to surprise and confound observers.

Notes

Introduction: 'The Pedigree of a White Stallion'

1 David Breeze and Brian Dobson, *Hadrian's Wall* (London, 1978 edn), pp. 152, 255.

2 Sari Nasir, *The Arabs and the English* (London, 1976), p. 22.

3 John Marlowe, *Anglo-Egyptian Relations* (London, 1965), p. 15.

4 D.A. Farnie, *East and West of Suez* (Oxford, 1969), p. 564.

5 Elizabeth Monroe, *Britain's Moment in the Middle East* (London, 1963), p. 11.

6 William Roger Louis, *Ends of British Imperialism* (London, 2006), p. 9.

7 BBC News, 6 December 2014; 'We're Back', *The Economist*, 13 December 2014.

8 D.R. Thorpe, *Eden* (London, 2003), pp. 545–6.

9 Edward Ingram, 'A Preview of the Great Game in Asia: I – The British Occupation of Perim and Aden', *MES*, January 1973, p. 5.

10 Ronald Hyam, *Britain's Imperial Century* (London, 1976), p. 24.

11 Aaron Klieman, *Foundations of British Policy in the Arab World* (Baltimore, 1970), p. 28.

12 Anthony King and Ivor Crewe, *The Blunders of Government* (London, 2013), p. 4.

13 Sir James Craig, *Shemlan* (Basingstoke, 1998), p. 113. Sir John Glubb, *The Story of the Arab Legion* (London, 1948), p. 113.

14 Peter Hinchcliffe et al. (eds), *Without Glory in Arabia* (London, 2006), p. 76.

15 Gary Troeller, *The Birth of Saudi Arabia* (London, 1976), p. xviii.

16 Andrew Rawnsley, *The End of the Party* (London, 2010), p. 185.

17 John Darwin, *Unfinished Empire* (London, 2012), pp. 86–7. James Onley, *The Arabian Frontiers of the British Raj* (Oxford, 2007), pp. 30–2.

18 Afaf Lutfi al-Sayyid-Marsot, *Egypt and Cromer* (London, 1968), p. 68.

19 Glen Balfour-Paul, *The End of Empire in the Middle East* (Cambridge, 1991), p. 103.

20 Paul Kennedy, *The Rise and Fall of the Great Powers* (London, 1988), pp. 128, 255.

21 Tancred Bradshaw, *Britain and Jordan* (London, 2012), p. 40.

22 Sir Lawrence Grafftey-Smith, *Bright Levant* (London, 1970), pp. 91–3. William Roger Louis, *The British Empire in the Middle East* (Oxford, 1984), p. 316. Sir James Craig, 'The British and the Arabs', in Paul Tempest (ed.), *Envoys to the Arab World*, Vol. ii (London, 2009), p. 10. See also Craig, *Shemlan* and Leslie Mcloughlin, *In a Sea of Knowledge* (Reading, 2002).

23 Sir Anthony Parsons, *They Say the Lion* (London, 1986), p. 19.

24 Louis, *British Empire*, p. 315.

25 Ronald Blythe, *Akenfield* (London, 1969), p. 202.

26 Kathryn Tidrick, *Heart-Beguiling Araby* (Cambridge, 1981). David Cannadine, *Ornamentalism* (London, 2001), p. 72.

27 Gerald Butt, *The Lion in the Sand* (London, 1995), p. 69.

28 Parsons, *They Say the Lion*, p. 24.

29 Hyam, *Britain's Imperial Century*, p. 39.

30 Muhammad al-Qasimi, *The Myth of Arab Piracy in the Gulf* (London, 1986), p. xiv.

31 Naguib Mahfouz, *Palace Walk* (London, 1994 edn) p. 347. David Landes, *Bankers and Pashas* (Cambridge, MA, 1973 edn), p. 323.

32 Monroe, *Britain's Moment*, p. 11.

33 Ali Allawi, *Feisal I of Iraq* (New Haven, 2014), p. 201.

34 Roger Adelson, *London and the Invention of the Middle East* (New Haven, 1995), pp. 22–6.

Chapter One: Persia's Doubtful Friend

1 *Financial Times*, 6/7 July 2013.

2 Patrick French, *Younghusband* (London, 1995), pp. 302–3.

3 John Darwin, *Unfinished Empire* (London, 2012), pp. 175, 187.

4 Ronald Robinson, John Gallagher and Alice Denny, *Africa and the Victorians* (London, 1967), p. 13.

5 Hyam, *Britain's Imperial Century*, p. 206.

6 Niall Ferguson, *Empire* (London, 2002), pp. 173–4.

7 John Darwin, *The Empire Project* (Cambridge, 2009), p. 10.

8 J.B. Kelly, *Britain and the Persian Gulf* (Oxford, 1968), p. 263.

9 Denis Wright, *The English Amongst the Persians* (London, 2001), p. 128. William Roger Louis, 'Introduction', in William Roger Louis and Judith Brown (eds), *The Oxford History of the British Empire: The Twentieth Century* (Oxford, 1999), p. 6.

10 Francis Robinson, 'The British Empire and the Muslim World', in Louis and Brown (eds), *The Oxford History of the British Empire*, p. 405. David Fromkin, *A Peace to End all Peace* (London, 1991 edn), p. 97.

11 Karl Meyer and Shareen Brysac, *Tournament of Shadows* (London, 2001). Firuz Kazemzadeh, *Russian and Britain in Persia* (New Haven, 1968), p. 322.

12 M.E. Yapp, *Strategies of British India* (Oxford, 1980), p. 15. Edward Ingram, *In Defence of British India* (Oxford, 1984), p. 128.

13 Wright, *The English*, p. 1.

14 Rose Greaves, *Persia and the Defence of India* (London, 1959), p. 42. Kazemzadeh, *Russia and Britain*, p. 286. Rose Greaves, 'Iran's Relations with Great Britain and India', in Peter Avery et al., *The Cambridge History of Iran*, Vol. vi (Cambridge, 1986), p. 424.

15 Wright, *The English*, p. 4.

16 Ingram, *In Defence of British India*, pp. 78, 95, 99.

17 Wright, *The English*, pp. 4–5. Yapp, *Strategies of British India*, pp. 25–9.

18 Robert Tombs, *The English and their History* (London, 2014), p. 396.

19 Wright, *The English*, p. 7.

20 Kelly, *Britain and the Persian Gulf*, p. 91. Robert Gleave, 'The Clergy and the British', in Vanessa Martin (ed.), *Anglo-Iranian Relations since 1800* (London, 2005), pp. 42–4.

21 Wright, *The English*, p. 53.

22 Ibid., p. 15. Yapp, *Strategies of British India*, p. 89.

23 Kelly, *Britain and the Persian Gulf*, p. 261.

24 Wright, *The English*, p. 19.

25 Kelly, *Britain and the Persian Gulf*, pp. 297–8.

26 Ibid., pp. 471, 479–80.

27 Greaves, 'Iran's Relations with Great Britain and India', p. 395.

28 Kelly, *Britain and the Persian Gulf*, pp. 466–98. Wright, *The English*, pp. 60–1.

29 *Cousins at War*, BBC 2, February 2014.

30 Greaves, *Persia and the Defence of India*, pp. 23–4.

31 Kelly, *Britain and the Persian Gulf*, p. 261. A.P. Thornton, 'British Policy in Persia', Part 1, *English Historical Review*, October 1954, pp. 567–8.

32 Kazemzadeh, *Russia and Britain*, pp. 331, 485.

33 Greaves, *Persia and the Defence of India*, pp. 36, 54, 60. Hyam, *Britain's Imperial Century*, pp. 210–11.

34 Ibid., pp. 20, 40–7, 67, 88.

35 Thornton, 'British Policy in Persia', Part 2, p. 57. *English Historical Review*, January 1955, p. 55.

36 Ibid., p. 57. Greaves, 'Iran's Relations with Great Britain and India', p. 423. Greaves, *Persia and the Defence of India*, p. 90.

37 Wright, *The English*, chapter 6.

38 Kazemzadeh, *Russia and Britain*, p. 461.

39 Wright, *The English*, p. 40.

40 Ibid., p. 130.

41 Ibid., pp. 102–3.

42 Thornton, 'British Policy in Persia', January 1955, pp. 55–6. Kazemzadeh, *Russia and Britain*, p. 461.

43 Greaves, *Persia and the Defence of India*, pp. 142, 175–7, 225. David Gilmour, *Curzon* (London, 1994), p. 76.

44 Greaves, 'Iran's Relations with Great Britain and India', pp. 406, 410. Ishtiaq Ahmad, *Anglo-Iranian Relations* (London, 1974), p. 34.

45 Kazemzadeh, *Russia and Britain*, p. 386. Gilmour, *Curzon*, p. 202. Greaves, *Persia and the Defence of India*, pp. 18–19. David McLean, *Britain and her Buffer State* (London, 1979), p. 33.

46 Ibid., p. 42.

47 Ibid., pp. 59, 68. Greaves, 'Iran's Relations with Great Britain and India', p. 414.

48 Pankaj Mishra, *From the Ruins of Empire* (London, 2012), pp. 1–2.

49 McLean, *Britain and her Buffer State*, pp. 73, 75. Zara Steiner, *Britain and the Origins of the First World War* (London, 1977), pp. 80–2.

50 Kazemzadeh, *Russia and Britain*, p. 508.

51 Ibid., p. 44. Mclean, *Britain and her Buffer State*, p. 140.

52 Mansour Bonakdarian, *Britain and the Iranian Constitutional Revolution of 1906–14* (Syracuse, NY, 2006), pp. 50, 121. Wright, *The English*, pp. 47–8. Mataza Nouraei, 'Ordinary People and the Reception of British Culture in Iran, 1906–41', in Martin (ed.), *Anglo-Iranian Relations*, pp. 72, 75–6. Nikki Keddie, 'British Policy and the Iranian Opposition', *Journal of Modern History*, no. 3, 1967, pp. 281–2. Mclean, *Britain and her Buffer State*, p. 89.

53 Ibid., pp. 88–9.

54 Bonakdarian, *Britain and the Iranian Constitutional Revolution*, pp. 63, 67. Christopher Clark, *The Sleepwalkers* (London, 2013), p. 322.

55 Ahmad, *Anglo-Iranian Relations*, pp. 76, 78. Peter Avery, *Modern Iran* (London, 1965), p. 135. Kazemzadeh, *Russia and Britain*, pp. 635, 668. Mclean, *Britain and her Buffer State*, p. 89.

56 Wright, *The English*, p. 87.

57 Daniel Yergin, *The Prize* (New York, 2003 edn), pp. 154–6.

58 Marian Kent, *Moguls and Mandarins* (London, 1993), p. 55.

59 Greaves, 'Iran's Relations with Great Britain and India', p. 419.

60 Wright, *The English*, pp. 71–2.

Chapter Two: Toeholds in Arabia

1 Briton Busch, *Britain and the Persian Gulf* (Berkley, 1967), p. 108.

2 Arnold Wilson, *The Persian Gulf* (Oxford, 1928), p. ix

3 James Onley, 'The Politics of Protection in the Gulf', *New Arabian Studies*, no. 6, p. 42.

4 Wilson, *The Persian Gulf*, p. 210. Penelope Tuson, *Playing the Game* (London, 2003), p. 19.

5 Sarah Searight, *The British in the Middle East* (London, 1979), pp. 145–6.

6 Onley, *The Arabian Frontier of the British Raj*, p. 45. J.F. Standish, 'British Maritime Policy in the Persian Gulf', *MES*, July 1967, pp. 341–2.

7 Kelly, *Britain and the Persian Gulf*, p. 809.

8 Ibid., p. 722.

9 Onley, *The Arabian Frontier of the British Raj*, pp. 4, 70.

10 Kelly, *Britain and the Persian Gulf*, p. 365. Uzi Rabi, 'Britain's Special Position in the Gulf', *MES*, May 2001, p. 355. Wright, *The English*, chapter 5.

11 Ibid., p. 73. Troeller, *The Birth of Saudi Arabia*, p. 3. Onley, *The Arabian Frontier of the British Raj*, p. 53. Rabi, 'Britain's Special Position in the Gulf', p. 355. Kelly,

Britain and the Persian Gulf, p. 554.

12 Justin Marozzi, *Baghdad* (London, 2014), p. 256.

13 Kelly, *Britain and the Persian Gulf*, pp. 1–2.

14 Ivor Lucas, Collected Papers, p. 275. Wilson, *The Persian Gulf*, pp. 232–3.

15 Onley, *The Arabian Frontier of the British Raj*, p. 44. Al-Qasimi, *The Myth of Piracy in the Persian Gulf*, pp. xv–xvi. Kelly, *Britain and the Persian Gulf*, p. 156.

16 Ibid., p. 205.

17 Onley, *The Arabian Frontier of the British Raj*, p. 71.

18 Ibid., pp. 75–6. Kelly, *Britain and the Persian Gulf*, pp. 358, 368–9, 380, 525–6.

19 Ibid., pp. 635–7. Standish, 'British Maritime Policy', pp. 337–8.

20 Wright, *The English*, pp. 70–1. Busch, *Britain and the Persian Gulf*, chapter 9.

21 Kelly, *Britain and the Persian Gulf*, p. 500.

22 Ibid., p. 553. Lucas, Papers, pp. 296–8. Ravinder Kumar, *India and the Persian Gulf Region* (London, 1965), pp. 67–70.

23 Farnie, *East and West of Suez*, p. 13. Kelly, *Britain and the Persian Gulf*, p. 302.

24 Ibid., pp. 741–2, 826, 834–5. Kumar, *India*, p. 125. Troeller, *The Birth of Saudi Arabia*, pp. 7–8.

25 Onley, *The Arabian Frontier of the British Raj*, p. 207.

26 George Kirk, *A Short History of the Middle East* (London, 1948), p. 89.

27 Busch, *Britain and the Persian Gulf*, p. 74.

28 Ibid., pp. 88–9.

29 Troeller, *The Birth of Saudi Arabia*, pp. 5–6.

30 Kazemzadeh, *Russia and Britain*, pp. 433–9, 470. Greaves, 'Iran's Relations with Great Britain and India', p. 416. Busch, *Britain and the Persian Gulf*, p. 356.

31 Ibid., p. 307. Kirk, *Short History*, pp. 89–93. Kumar, *India and the Persian Gulf*, pp. 151–86. H.V.W. Winstone, *The Illicit Adventure* (London, 1982), pp. 78–9.

32 Ibid., pp. 13, 86. Troeller, *The Birth of Saudi Arabia*, pp. 8–9. Busch, *Britain and the Persian Gulf*, p. 346.

33 Gilmour, *Curzon*, p. 200.

34 Ibid., pp. 268–70. Busch, *Britain and the Persian Gulf*, p. 259. Tuson, *Playing the Game*, p. 26.

35 Ibid., p. 43. John Gordon Lorimer, *Gazetteer of the Persian Gulf, Oman and Central Arabia* (Calcutta, 1908–15).

36 Balfour-Paul, *The End of Empire in the Middle East*, p. 102.

37 Ingram, 'The British Occupation of Perim and Aden in 1799', pp. 12–13.

38 Asher Orkaby, 'The Final British–Egyptian Imperial Battlefield', *MES*, no. 2, 2015, p. 197. Thomas Marston, *Britain's Imperial Role in the Red Sea Area* (Hamden, CT, 1961), p. 60.

39 R.J. Gavin, *Aden under British Rule* (London, 1965), p. 27.

40 Ibid., pp. 102–3. Farnie, *East and West of Suez*, p. 272.

41 Gavin, *Aden*, pp. 174, 176. Marston, *Britain's Imperial Role*, pp. 372–3.

42 Ibid., p. 367. Gavin, *Aden*, p. 172.

43 Ibid., pp. 112–17. Marston, *Britain's Imperial Role*, pp. 82, 95, 136, 205.

44 Gavin, *Aden*, pp. 129, 412.

45 Marston, *Britain's Imperial Role*, p. 416.

46 Ibid., p. 418. Gavin, *Aden*, pp. 210–11, 225.

47 Ibid., pp. 142–4, 150.

48 Ibid., pp. 217–24, 240.

49 Sir David Roberts, 'The Consequences of the Exclusive Treaties: A British View', in Brian Pridham, *The Arab Gulf and the West* (London, 1985), pp. 5–9.

Chapter Three: Mediterranean Approaches

1 Robert Holland, *Blue Water Empire* (London, 2011), p. 101.

2 Clark, *Sleepwalkers*, chapter 5.

3 Mishra, *From the Ruins of Empire*, p. 64. Stuart Cohen, *British Policy in Mesopotamia, 1903–14* (London, 1976), p. 236.

4 Robert and Isabelle Tombs, *That Sweet Enemy* (London, 2006), p. 229.

5 Ibid. Halford Hoskins, *Britain's Routes to India* (London, 1966 edn), p. 55. Kelly, *Britain and the Persian Gulf*, p. 62. Lawrence James, *The Rise and Fall of the British Empire* (London, 1998 edn), pp. 156–7. Jean-Joel Brégeon, *L'egypte de Bonaparte* (Paris, 1991), pp. 87, 97.

6 N.A.M. Rodgers, *The Command of the Oceans* (London, 2004), pp. 459–60.

7 Barbara Tuchman, *Bible and Sword* (London, 1956), p. 106.

8 William Hague, *William Pitt the Younger* (London, 2004), p. 432.

9 M.S. Anderson, *The Eastern Question* (London, 1966), pp. 39–40. John Marlowe, *Perfidious Albion* (London, 1971), p. 121.

10 Ibid., p. 135. Marlowe, *Anglo-Egyptian Relations*, p. 50.

11 Ibid., p. 159. Eugene Rogan, *The Arabs* (London, 2009), p. 75.

12 Marlowe, *Perfidious*, pp. 175–6, 186. Jasper Ridley, *Lord Palmerston* (London, 1970), pp. 209–11.

13 Norman Rose (ed.), *From Palmerston to Balfour: Collected Essays of Mayir Vereté* (London, 1992), p. 167. Holland, *Blue Water*, p. 61.

14 Ridley, *Palmerston*, p. 222.

15 Marlowe, *Perfidious*, p. 226.

16 Ibid., p. 290.

17 Brendan Simms, *Europe: The Struggle for Supremacy, 1453 to the Present* (London, 2013), p. 203.

18 Marlowe, *Perfidious*, p. 274.

19 Ibid., p. 240.

20 Kirk, *Short History*, p. 81.

21 David Rodogno, 'The "Principles of Humanity" and the European Powers' Intervention in the Ottoman Lebanon and Syria, 1860–1', in Brendan Simms and D.J.B. Trims (eds), *Humanitarian Intervention* (Cambridge, 2011), pp. 173–6.

22 Ibid., pp. 85–6. Ridley, *Palmerston*, pp. 535–6.

23 Fromkin, *A Peace to End all Peace*, p. 268.

24 Ibid., pp. 268–9. Tuchman, *Bible and Sword*, pp. 113, 127–8.

25 Simon Sebag Montefiore, *Jerusalem* (London, 2011), p. 355.

26 John Moscrop, *Measuring Jerusalem* (Leicester, 2000), pp. 218–29.

27 George Eliot, *Daniel Deronda* (Oxford World Classics, 1998 edn), p. 688.

28 Tuchman, *Bible and Sword*, p. 152.

29 Mishra, *From the Ruins*, p. 88. Kirk, *Short History*, p. 76.

30 Hyam, *Britain's Imperial Century*, p. 54.

31 Philip Mansel, *Levant* (London, 2011), pp. 108–9.

32 Robert Tignor, *Modernisation and British Colonial Rule in Egypt* (Princeton, 1966), p. 13. A.G. Hopkins, 'The Victorians and Africa', *Journal of African Studies*, no. 27, 1986, p. 379.

33 Farnie, *East and West*, pp. 30–1.

34 Kirk, *Short History*, p. 82.

35 Farnie, *East and West*, p. 88. Hoskins, *Britain's Routes*, p. 346.

36 Kirk, *Short History*, p. 83. Farnie, *East and West*, p. 171.

37 Ibid., p. 171. Tignor, *Modernisation*, pp. 136–7, 457–8. Robert Harrison, *Gladstone's Imperialism in Egypt* (Westport, CT, 1995), p. 25. Damian O'Connor, 'The Suez Crisis, 1871–82', *RUSIJ*, June 2001, p. 75. Keith Kyle, *Suez* (London, 1991), p. 14.

38 Landes, *Bankers and Pashas*, p. 128.

39 Ibid., p. 315. Mishra, *From the Ruins*, p. 74.

40 Mansel, *Levant*, pp. 107, 127.

41 Mishra, *From the Ruins*, p. 82.

42 Mansel, *Levant*, p. 102. Landes, *Bankers and Pashas*, pp. 323–4.

43 Ibid., p. 317. O'Connor, 'The Suez Crisis', p. 74.

44 Jonathan Parry, *The Politics of Patriotism* (Cambridge, 2006), pp. 246–7.

45 A.J.P. Taylor, *The Struggle for Mastery in Europe* (Oxford, 1954), p. 287.

46 Colin Newbury, 'Great Britain and the Partition of Africa', in Andrew Porter (ed.), *The Oxford History of the British Empire*, Vol. iii (Oxford, 1999), p. 633.

47 Andrew Roberts, *Salisbury* (London, 1999), pp. 228–9. Al-Sayyid-Marsot, *Egypt and Cromer*, p. 4.

48 Ibid., p. 14. Roberts, *Salisbury*, p. 265. Agatha Ramm, 'Great Britain in Egypt', in Prosser Gifford and William Roger Louis (eds), *France and Britain in Africa* (New Haven, 1971), p. 94. John Galbraith and al-Sayyid-Marsot, 'The British Occupation of Egypt: Another View', *BJMES*, no. 4, 1973, p. 475. Tignor, *Modernisation*, p. 12. Donald Reid, 'The Urabi Revolt and the British Conquest', in M.W. Daly, *The Cambridge History of Modern Egypt*, Vol. ii (Cambridge, 1998), p. 228.

49 Mansel, *Levant*, p. 117. Farnie, *East and West*, pp. 262–3.

50 Harrison, *Gladstone*, pp. 77, 89. Roy Jenkins, *Gladstone* (London, 1995), pp. 506–8. Although Jenkins refutes any suggestion this influenced his policy.

51 Harrison, *Gladstone's Imperialism in Egypt*, p. 93.

52 Mansel, *Levant*, p. 122.

53 Galbraith and al-Sayyid-Marsot, 'The British Occupation of Egypt', p. 474.

54 Robinson, Gallagher and Denny, *Africa*, p. 113. Farnie, *East and West*, pp. 291–2. Hopkins, 'The Victorians and Africa', pp. 373–4.
55 Ibid., p. 387. Galbraith and al-Sayyid-Marsot, 'The British Occupation of Egypt', p. 481.
56 Ibid., p. 482.
57 Roberts, *Salisbury*, p. 266. Peter Mansfield, *The British in Egypt* (London, 1971), p. 47. Robinson, Gallagher and Denny, *Africa*, p. 118, Mansel, *Levant*, p. 117.
58 Hourani, *A History of the Arab Peoples* (London, 1991), p. 283. Hyam, *Britain's Imperial Century*, p. 194.
59 Galbraith and al-Sayyid-Marsot, 'The British Occupation of Egypt', p. 474. Alexander Schoelch, 'The "Men on the Spot" and the English Occupation of Egypt in 1882', *Historical Journal*, no. 3, 1976, p. 781. Hopkins, 'The Victorians and Africa', p. 375.
60 Farnie, *East and West*, pp. 285, 295.
61 Robinson, Gallagher and Denny, *Africa*, p. 115.
62 Ibid., p. 120.
63 Darwin, *Unfinished Empire*, p. 145. Mansfield, *Britain in Egypt*, p. 49.
64 Ibid., p. 53. Harrison, *Gladstone's Imperialism*, p. 152. Mansel, *Levant*, p. 126.
65 Ibid., p. 127.

Chapter Four: Unintended Consequences

1 Robert Hunter, 'Tourism and Empire', *MES*, September 2004, p. 46.
2 David Gange, 'Unholy Water', in Astrid Swenson and Peter Mandler (eds), *Britain and the Heritage of Empire* (Oxford, 2013), p. 103.
3 Farnie, *East and West*, pp. 389–91.
4 Robinson, Gallagher and Denny, *Africa*, pp. 129, 159.
5 Roberts, *Salisbury*, p. 436. David Steel, 'Britain and Egypt in 1882', in Keith Wilson (ed.), *Imperialism and Nationalism in the Middle East* (London, 1982), p. 13.
6 Robinson, Gallagher and Denny, *Africa*, pp. 139–40. Alfred Milner, *England in Egypt* (London, 1893), pp. 103, 123.
7 Donald Reid, 'The Urabi Revolt and the British Conquest', p. 233.
8 Roberts, *Salisbury*, p. 436. Robinson, Gallagher and Denny, *Africa*, p. 144.
9 A.J.P. Taylor, *The Struggle for Mastery in Europe*, p. 290. Paul Kennedy, *The Rise of Anglo-German Antagonism 1860–1914* (London, 1980), p. 184.
10 Ibid., p. 200. Roberts, *Salisbury*, pp. 436–7. Tignor, *Modernisation and British Colonial Rule in Egypt*, pp. 83–4.
11 Al-Sayyid-Marsot, *Egypt and Cromer*, p. 51.
12 Hyam, *Britain's Imperial Century*, p. 125. G.N. Sanderson, 'The Origins and Significance of the Anglo-French Confrontation at Fashoda', in Gifford and Louis (eds), *France and Britain in Africa*, pp. 290–2.
13 Derek Hopwood, 'Earth's Proud Empires Pass Away', *BJMES*, November 2002, p. 115.

14 Sanderson, 'The Origins and Significance of the Anglo-French Confrontation at Fashoda', pp. 285, 321–3. Hyam, *Britain's Imperial Century*, p. 124. Philip Bell, *France and Britain*, Vol. i (Harlow, 1996), pp. 23–9.

15 Jenkins, *Gladstone*, pp. 510–14. Darwin, *Unfinished Empire*, p. 296. Roger Owen, *Lord Cromer* (Oxford, 2004), p. 189.

16 Ibid., p. 287.

17 Gabriel Warburg, *Egypt and the Sudan* (London, 1985), p. 14. Hyam, *Britain's Imperial Century*, pp. 108–9. Meyer and Brysac, *Kingmakers*, p. 49.

18 Sanderson, 'Origins and Significance', p. 325. Mansfield, *Britain in Egypt*, pp. 79–80. Owen, *Cromer*, p. 300. Tignor, *Modernisation*, pp. 217–19. Al-Sayyid-Marsot, *Egypt and Cromer*, p. 134.

19 Hyam, *Britain's Imperial Century*, pp. 95–9.

20 Al-Sayyid-Marsot, *Egypt and Cromer*, pp. 63–4.

21 Robinson, Gallagher and Denny, *Africa*, p. 274.

22 Christopher Long, 'An Experience of Egypt, 1964–2007', in Tempest (ed.), *Envoys to the Arab World*, Vol. ii, p. 237.

23 Owen, *Cromer*, p. 281.

24 Boyle Papers, File 2, 14 January 1904. MECA.

25 Boyle Papers, File 3, 26 July 1906.

26 Milner, *England in Egypt*, p. 34.

27 Ibid., p. 357. Owen, *Cromer*, p. 241.

28 Milner, *England in Egypt*, p. 106. Lord Lloyd, *Egypt since Cromer*, Vol. i (London, 1933), p. 281. Tignor, *Modernisation*, p. 394.

29 Meyer and Brysac, *Kingmakers*, p. 50. Milner, *England in Egypt*, p. 34. Farnie, *East and West of Suez*, p. 300.

30 Owen, *Cromer*, pp. 185–241. Milner, *England in Egypt*, pp. 35–6.

31 Valentine Chirol, *Fifty Years in a Changing World* (London, 1927), p. 34.

32 Hopkins, 'The Victorians and Africa', p. 389. Marlowe, *Anglo-Egyptian Relations*, p. 173.

33 Tignor, *Modernisation*, pp. 111, 115, 382.

34 Al-Sayyid-Marsot, 'The British Occupation of Egypt from 1882', in Porter (ed.), *The Oxford History of the British Empire*, Vol. iii, p. 659.

35 M.W. Daly, 'The British Occupation', in Daly (ed.), *Cambridge History of Egypt*, Vol. ii, p. 244.

36 Hyam, *Britain's Imperial Century*, p. 257. Tignor, *Modernisation*, pp. 89–92, 357.

37 Ibid., p. 320.

38 Ibid., p. 346. Owen, *Cromer*, pp. 313–16.

39 Clara Boyle, *Boyle of Cairo* (Kendal, 1965), p. 49. Al-Sayyid-Marsot, *Egypt and Cromer*, pp. 201–2. Tignor, *Modernisation*, p. 256. Hyam, *Britain's Imperial Century*, p. 263.

40 Tignor, *Modernisation*, pp. 327–8.

41 Hyam, *Britain's Imperial Century*, pp. 157–8.

42 Tignor, *Modernisation*, pp. 193–5.

43 Amira El-Azhary Sonbol, *The Last Khedive of Egypt* (Reading, 1998), p. 250.

44 Lord Cromer, *Abbas II* (London, 1915), p. 10.

45 Owen, *Cromer*, p. 264.

46 Cromer, *Abbas II*, pp. 22, 25.

47 Ibid., p. 39. Al-Sayyid-Marsot, *Egypt and Cromer*, pp. 109–11, 115, 118.

48 Cromer, *Abbas II*, pp. 50–6. Owen, *Cromer*, pp. 271–3.

49 Sonbol, *Last Khedive*, p. 253. Tignor, *Modernisation*, pp. 159, 177. Al-Sayyid-Marsot, *Egypt and Cromer*, pp. 133, 136.

50 Ibid., pp. 56–7. Marlowe, *Anglo-Egyptian Relations*, p. 183.

51 Major E.W. Polson Newman, *Great Britain in Egypt* (London, 1928), p. 153.

52 Chirol, *Fifty Years*, pp. 49–50. Owen, *Cromer*, pp. 231–3.

53 Al-Sayyid-Marsot, *Egypt and Cromer*, p. 78.

54 Ibid., pp. 65, 201–2. Mansfield, *Britain in Egypt*, p. xii. Chirol, *Fifty Years*, p. 34. Owen, *Cromer*, pp. 395–6.

55 Lord Edward Cecil, *The Leisure of an Egyptian Official* (London, 1941 edn), p. 187. Boyle, *Boyle of Cairo*, pp. 176–7. Tignor, *Modernisation*, p. 2. Al-Sayyid-Marsot, *Egypt and Cromer*, pp. 65, 145, 159–60.

56 Ibid., pp. 140–1. Tignor, *Modernisation*, pp. 270–1.

57 Ibid., pp. 272–3.

58 Marlowe, *Anglo-Egyptian Relations*, p. 169.

59 Ronald Storrs, *Orientations* (London, 1937), pp. 92–3. Owen, *Cromer*, p. 345.

60 Tignor, *Modernisation*, pp. 286–7. Archie Hunter, *Power and Passion in Egypt* (London, 2007), p. 169.

61 Ibid., p. 165. Tignor, *Modernisation*, p. 289. Boyle Papers, File 5. Letter, 24 April 1907. Middle East Archive, St Antony's College, Oxford.

62 Ibid., p. 294. Marlowe, *Anglo-Egyptian Relations*, pp. 198–200. Hunter, *Gorst*, pp. 176, 187.

63 Ibid., pp. 226, 293–302. Tignor, *Modernisation*, p. 307.

64 Ibid., pp. 315–16. Derek Hopwood, *Tales of Empire* (London, 1989), pp. 80–1.

65 Sonbol, *The Last Khedive*, p. 230.

Chapter Five: The Battle for the Middle East: On the Defensive, 1914–16

1 Clark, *Sleepwalkers*, p. xxi.

2 Meyer and Brysac, *Kingmakers*, p. 134. Monroe, *Britain's Moment*, pp. 37–8.

3 Timothy Paris, *Britain, the Hashemites and Arab Rule* (London, 2003), pp. 109–12.

4 Hew Strachan, *The First World War* (Oxford, 2001), p. 814.

5 Monroe, *Britain's Moment*, p. 23. David Fromkin, *Peace to End*, p. 74.

6 D.K. Fieldhouse, *Western Imperialism in the Middle East* (Oxford, 2008), p. 46.

7 Fromkin, *Peace to End*, p. 73. Sean McMeekin, *The Berlin–Baghdad Express* (London, 2010), p. 117.

8 Anderson, *The Eastern Question*, p. 314. Joseph Heller, 'Sir Louis Mallet and the Ottoman Empire', *MES*, January 1976, p. 6.

9 Fieldhouse, *Western Imperialism in the Middle East*, p. 40.

10 McMeekin, *Express*, pp. 13–16.

11 Ibid., pp. 27, 65–6. Fritz Fischer, *Germany's Aims in the First World War* (London, 1967), pp. 120–1.

12 McMeekin, *Express*, pp. 86–9.

13 Steve Coll, 'Hitler and the Muslims', *New York Review of Books*, 2 April 2015.

14 Donald McKale, *War by Revolution* (Kent, OH, 1998), pp. 5, 25.

15 John Buchan, *Greenmantle* (London, 1916), p. 115.

16 Eugene Rogan, *The Fall of the Ottomans* (London, 2015), p. 47.

17 McKale, *War by Revolution*, pp. 25–6, 86.

18 Ibid., pp. 67–8. Bruce Westrate, *The Arab Bureau* (University Park, PA, 1992), p. 106. McMeekin, *Express*, pp. 209, 235. Sean McMeekin, *The Russian Origins of the First World War* (Cambridge, MA, 2011), p. 193.

19 Howard Sachar, *The Emergence of the Middle East* (London, 1969), p. 40. Fischer, *Germany's Aims*, p. 128.

20 Ibid., p. 128. Strachan, *The First World War*, p. 734. Farnie, *East and West*, pp. 535–48.

21 Marlowe, *Anglo-Egyptian Relations*, p. 221. Matthew Hughes, *Allenby and British Strategy in the Middle East* (London, 1999), p. 30.

22 Fischer, *Germany's Aims*, pp. 128–30. Rogan, *Fall of the Ottomans*, pp. 239–41, 250–2.

23 William Olson, *Anglo-Iranian Relations during World War One* (London, 1984), pp. 50–1. Wright, *The English*, pp. 171–2.

24 Fischer, *Germany's Aims*, pp. 126–7. McMeekin, *Express*, p. 282.

25 Olson, *Anglo-Iranian Relations*, p. 54.

26 Briton Busch, *Britain, India and the Arabs* (Berkley, 1971), p. 4. Kristian Coates Ulrichsen, *The First World War in the Middle East* (London, 2014), p. 39.

27 Ibid., pp. 12, 17. Charles Townshend, *When God Made Hell* (London, 2010), p. 35.

28 Busch, *Britain, India*, p. 24. Elie Kedourie, *England and the Middle East* (London, 1987), p. 176. John Fisher, *Curzon and British Imperialism in the Middle East* (London, 1999), pp. 14, 43.

29 Philip Ireland, *Iraq* (London, 1937), p. 65.

30 Townshend, *When God Made Hell*, p. 133.

31 Ibid., p. 142. Adelson, *London and the Invention*, p. 122. Marian Kent, 'The Great Powers and the End of the Ottoman Empire', in Marian Kent (ed.), *The Great Powers and the End of the Ottoman Empire* (London, 1984), p. 186. Ulrichsen, *The First World War*, p. 126.

32 Ireland, *Iraq*, p. 64.

33 Polly Mohs, *Military Intelligence and the Arab Revolt* (London, 2008), p. 22. Rogan, *Fall of the Ottomans*, pp. 256, 267, 273.

34 Rudyard Kipling, *Mesopotamia*, 1917.

35 Ulrichsen, *The First World War*, p. 138.

36 James Barr, *A Line in the Sand* (London, 2011), pp. 13–15. Fromkin, *Peace to End*, p. 142. Jonathan Schneer, *The Balfour Declaration* (London, 2011), pp. 42–3.

37 Ibid., p. 43.

38 John Le Carré, *Tinker, Tailor, Soldier, Spy* (London, 1974), p. 138. Mohs, *Military Intelligence*, p. 147.

39 Fromkin, *Peace to End*, pp. 86, 148. Barr, *Line*, p. 89.

40 George Antonius, *The Arab Awakening* (London, 1938), p. 140. Westrate, *The Arab Bureau*, pp. 115–16.

41 Elie Kedourie, *In the Anglo-Arab Labyrinth* (London, 1976), pp. 66, 109. McKale, *War by Revolution*, pp. 154, 159. Jeremy Wilson, *Lawrence of Arabia* (London, 1989), pp. 204–5. Fieldhouse, *Western Imperialism*, p. 57. Barr, *Line*, p. 23.

42 Kedourie, *In the Anglo-Arab Labyrinth*, pp. 89–90. Wilson, *Lawrence*, p. 207. Schneer, *Balfour Declaration*, p. 76.

43 Fieldhouse, *Western Imperialism*, p. 56.

44 Ibid., p. 101.

45 Ibid., p. 55.

46 Monroe, *Britain's Moment*, p. 33. Allawi, *Feisal*, p. 103. Wilson, *Lawrence*, p. 215.

47 Ibid., p. 214.

48 Ibid., p. 229.

49 Sachar, *Emergence*, p. 161. Monroe, *Britain's Moment*, p. 33.

50 Allawi, *Feisal*, p. 100.

51 Barr, *Line*, pp. 27, 30–1.

52 Wilson, *Lawrence*, pp. 237–8, 282. Monroe, *Britain's Moment*, pp. 32, 35.

53 Barr, *Line*, p. 32.

Chapter Six: The Battle for the Middle East: Onto the Offensive, 1916–18

1   Margaret Macmillan, *Peacemakers* (London, 2002), p. 401. Sachar, *Emergence*, p. 135. Andrew Roberts, 'Wisdom's Source', *Times Literary Supplement*, 21/28 December 2007. Priya Satia, *Spies in Arabia* (Oxford, 2008), p. 143.

2   Ibid., p. 49.

3   Wilson, *Lawrence*, p. 357.

4   Ibid., p. 521. Fromkin, *Peace to End*, p. 196. Westrate, *Arab Bureau*, p. 80.

5   Wilson, *Lawrence*, p. 391.

6   Barr, *Line*, pp. 39–40.

7   Wilson, *Lawrence*, pp. 502, 511–12.

8   Sachar, *Emergence*, p. 182. McKale, *War by Revolution*, p. 174.

9   Farnie, *East and West*, p. 544. Allawi, *Feisal*, pp. 98, 122.

10 Schneer, *Balfour Declaration*, pp. 358–9. Matthew Hughes, *Allenby and British Strategy* (London, 1999), p. 91.

11 Ibid., p. 26. Monroe, *Britain's Moment*, p. 37.

12 Townshend, *When God Made Hell*, pp. 368–9.

13 Ibid., pp. 340–1, 387. Sachar, *Emergence*, pp. 224–6. Rogan, *Fall of the Ottomans*, pp. 322–3.

14 Fromkin, *Peace to End*, p. 307.

15 Ibid., p. 308.

16 James Barr, *Setting the Desert on Fire* (London, 2007), p. 160.

17 Hughes, *Allenby*, p. 13. Satia, *Spies in Arabia*, pp. 80, 84. Eitan Bar-Yosef, 'The Last Crusade?', *Journal of Contemporary History*, January 2001, p. 106.

18 Ibid., pp. 94–6. John Grigg, *Lloyd George*, Vol. iv (London, 2002), pp. 342–3. Rogan, *Fall of the Ottomans*, pp. 350–1.

19 T.E. Lawrence, *Seven Pillars of Wisdom* (London, 1962 edn), p. 464.

20 Grigg, *Lloyd George*, pp. 343–4.

21 The Zionists were the only settler colony in the Middle East, though in north Africa there was the case of Algeria.

22 Ibid., p. 357. Schneer, *The Balfour Declaration*, p. xxviii.

23 Gilmour, *Curzon*, pp. 480–1.

24 Ibid., p. 481, Grigg, *Lloyd George*, p. 350. Tuchman, *Bible and Sword*, pp. 199, 202.

25 Hughes, *Allenby*, pp. 27–8. Schneer, *Balfour Declaration*, p. 168. William Roger Louis, *In the Name of God, Go!* (New York, 1992), p. 70. Sachar, *Emergence*, p. 202. D.Z. Gillon, 'The Antecedents of the Balfour Declaration', *MES*, May 1969, p. 144.

26 Farnie, *East and West*, p. 539.

27 Grigg, *Lloyd George*, p. 350. Fisher, *Curzon*, p. 83. Louis, *In the Name of God*, pp. 71–2.

28 Fromkin, *Peace to End*, pp. 281–2.

29 McMeekin, *Express*, p. 354. 'Britain in Palestine: An Exhibition of British Rule in Palestine', SOAS, 2012.

30 CAB24/30/6, 'The Future of Palestine', 26 October 1917.

31 CAB23/4/35, 31 October 1917.

32 Barr, *Setting the Desert*, p. 244.

33 Eryatar Friesel, 'British Officials and the Situation in Palestine' *MES*, April 1987, p. 207.

34 Busch, *Britain, India*, p. 349.

35 Fieldhouse, *Western Imperialism*, p. 129. John Marlowe, *The Seat of Pilate* (London, 1959), pp. 28, 40. Storrs, *Orientations*, pp. 410–11.

36 Adelson, *London*, p. 159.

37 Ibid., p. 161.

38 Andrew Syk, 'The 1917 Mesopotamia Commission', *RUSIJ*, August 2009, p. 99. Wright, *The English*, pp. 177–8.

39 Hughes, *Allenby*, p. 60.

40 Ibid., pp. 99–102. Fromkin, *Peace to End*, pp. 334–9, 343–4, 370–3. Helmut Mejcher, 'Oil and British Policy towards Mesopotamia', *MES*, October 1972, pp. 387–8.

41 Adelson, *London*, p. 171. Rogan, *Fall of the Ottomans*, p. 71.

42 Grigg, *Lloyd George*, p. 344.

43 Westrate, *Arab Bureau*, p. 207.

44 Busch, *Britain, India*, p. 162. Adelson, *London*, p. 171.

45 Ulrichsen, *The First World War*, pp. 113–15, 176. Rashid Khalidi, 'The Arab Experience of the War', in Hugh Cecil and Peter Liddle (eds), *Facing Armageddon* (London, 1996), pp. 644–7.

46 Ibid., p. 646.

47 Ibid., p. 642.

Chapter Seven: 'Present at the Creation'

1   Janet Wallach, *Desert Queen* (London, 1996), pp. 215–16.

2   Meyer and Brysac, *Kingmakers*, p. 224.

3   Jukka Nevakivi, *Britain, France and the Arab Middle East* (London, 1969), p. 106. Erik Goldstein, 'British Peace Aims and the Eastern Question', *MES*, October 1987, p. 433.

4   Christopher Catherwood, *Churchill's Folly* (New York, 2004), p. 119.

5   Macmillan, *Peacemakers*, p. 392.

6   Henry Foster, *The Making of Modern Iraq* (London, 1936), p. 87.

7   Ephraim and Inari Karsh, *Empires of the Sand* (Harvard, 1999), p. 261. Helmut Mejcher, *Imperial Quest for Oil: Iraq, 1910–1928* (London, 1976), p. 177.

8   John Marlowe, *Late Victorian: The Life of Sir A. Talbot Wilson* (London, 1967), p. 134.

9   Macmillan, *Peacemakers*, p. 297.

10 Meyer and Brysac, *Kingmakers*, p. 144. Ireland, *Iraq*, p. 262.

11 Fieldhouse, *Western Imperialism*, p. 69.

12 Peter Sluglett, 'An Improvement on Colonialism? The "A" Mandates and their Legacy in the Middle East', *International Affairs*, March 2014, p. 414.

13 *British Documents on Foreign Policy*, Vol. xiii (London, 1963), p. 264.

14 Goldstein, 'British Peace Aims and the Eastern Question', p. 424.

15 John Darwin, *Britain, Egypt and the Middle East* (London, 1981), p. 134. *British Documents on Foreign Policy*, Vol. iv, p. 343.

16 Fromkin, *Peace to End*, p. 385.

17 Ibid., p. 470. Catherwood, *Churchill's Folly*, p. 72. John Townsend, *Proconsul to the Middle East* (London, 2010), p. 182.

18 Busch, *Britain, India*, pp. 272–3.

19 Macmillan, *Peacemakers*, p. 416. Ireland, *Iraq*, p. 263.

20 Allawi, *Feisal*, p. 249.

21 Ibid., p. 253. Sachar, *Emergence*, pp. 259–60.

22 Nevakivi, *Britain, France*, p. 154. Busch, *Britain, India*, p. 313. Bell, *France and Britain*, Vol. i, pp. 126–7. Paris, *Britain, the Hashemites*, p. 62.

23 Ibid., p. 55. Barr, *Setting the Desert*, pp. 165, 302.

24 Nevakivi, *Britain, France*, p. 208. Kedourie, *England and the Middle East*, p. 148.

25 Allawi, *Feisal*, p. 276.

26 Fromkin, *Peace to End*, pp. 436–9.

27 Nevakivi, *Britain, France*, p. 256. William Jackson, *Britain's Triumph and Decline in the Middle East* (London, 1996), p. 15.

28 Sachar, *Emergence*, p. 376.

29 Townshend, *When God Made Hell*, pp. 454, 514–16. Marlowe, *Late Victorian*, pp. 162–4. Townsend, *Proconsul*, p. 183.

30 Kwasi Kwarteng, *Ghosts of Empire* (London, 2011), p. 25.

31 Nevakivi, *Britain, France*, p. 91. Mejcher, 'Oil and British Policy towards Mesopotamia', pp. 384–5. Catherwood, *Churchill's Folly*, pp. 75, 205.

32 Peter Sluglett, *Britain and Iraq* (London, 2007 edn), p. 4. Fieldhouse, *Western Imperialism*, p. 70.

33 Busch, *Britain, India*, p. 356. Marlowe, *Late Victorian*, pp. 136–7, 170, 255–6.

34 Marozzi, *Baghdad*, pp. 290–1, 304.

35 Ibid., pp. 165–6. Charles Tripp, *A History of Iraq* (Cambridge, 2000), p. 39.

36 Ibid. Marlowe, *Late Victorian*, p. 125. Stephen Longrigg, *Iraq* (London, 1953), p. 118.

37 Ibid., p. 122. Townshend, *When God Made Hell*, p. 463. Tripp, *History*, p. 44. Nevakivi, *Britain, France*, pp. 257–8.

38 Kwarteng, *Ghosts of Empire*, p. 23.

39 Darwin, *Britain, Egypt*, p. 200. Sachar, *Emergence*, p. 373. Rogan, *The Arabs*, p. 173. 'Top Shi'a Cleric Piles Pressure on Maliki', *Financial Times*, 21 February 2014.

40 Marozzi, *Baghdad*, p. 299.

41 Allawi, *Feisal*, p. 384. Marlowe, *Late Victorian*, p. 256.

42 Ibid., p. 183, Busch, *Britain, India*, p. 423, Darwin, *Britain, Egypt*, pp. 215–16.

43 Cannadine, *Ornamentalism*, p. 75.

44 Townshend, *When God Made Hell*, pp. 480, 522.

45 *Documents on British Foreign Policy*, Vol. xiii, p. 324.

46 Darwin, *Britain and Egypt*, p. 221. Paris, *Britain, the Hashemites*, pp. 140–1. Townsend, *Proconsul*, p. 162.

47 Catherwood, *Churchill's Folly*, p. 132.

48 Marozzi, *Baghdad*, p. 301.

49 Fromkin, *Peace to End*, p. 450.

50 Meyer and Brysac, *Kingmakers*, p. 143. Busch, *Britain, India*, p. 469. Townshend, *When God Made Hell*, pp. 505, 507–9. Allawi, *Feisal*, pp. 385–6. Kerim Yildiz, *The Kurds in Iraq* (London, 2004), pp. 11–12.

51 Wallach, *Desert Queen*, p. 237 (emphasis added).

52 Fromkin, *Peace to End*, pp. 323, 325, 520. Fisher, *Curzon*, p. 220. Klieman, *Foundations*, p. 171. Michael Cohen, 'Churchill and the Balfour Declaration', in Uriel Dann, *The Great Powers in the Middle East* (New York, 1988), p. 103.

53 Howard Sachar, *A History of Israel* (Oxford, 1976), p. 129.

54 Sachar, *Emergence*, p. 284.

55 Nigel Ashton, 'A "Special Relationship" in Spite of Ourselves', *JICH*, no. 2, 2005, p. 240.

56 Paris, *Britain, the Hashemites*, p. 174. Fromkin, *Peace to End*, pp. 442–3. Mary Wilson, *King Abdullah, Britain and the Making of Jordan* (Cambridge, 1987), p. 44.

57 Christopher Sykes, *Crossroads to Israel* (London, 1965), pp. 61–2. *British Documents on Foreign Policy*, Vol. xiii, pp. 337–8. Sir Alec Kirkbride, *A Crackle of Thorns* (London, 1956), pp. 20–8.

58 Allawi, *Feisal*, p. 330. Fromkin, *Peace to End*, pp. 505–6. Karsh and Karsh, *Empire*, p. 319. Klieman, *Foundations*, p. 116.

59 Ibid., p. 131. Catherwood, *Churchill's Folly*, p. 158.

60 Christopher de Bellaigue, *Patriot of Persia* (London, 2012), p. 53.

61 Fromkin, *Peace to End*, pp. 456–7.

62 Homa Katouzian, 'The Campaign against the Anglo-Iranian Treaty of 1919', *BJMES*, May 1998, p. 10.

63 Wright, *The English*, p. 178.

64 Gilmour, *Curzon*, p. 516.

65 Wright, *The English*, p. 31.

66 Katouzian, 'The Campaign against the Anglo-Persian Treaty', p. 5. De Bellaigue, *Patriot of Persia*, p. 54.

67 Ulrichsen, *The First World War*, p. 142.

68 Allawi, *Feisal*, pp. 347–9.

69 Antonius, *Arab Awakening*, pp. 274, 277–8.

70 Allawi, *Feisal*, p. 280.

71 Mohammed Heikal, *Cutting the Lion's Tale* (London, 1986), p. 2.

Chapter Eight: 'An Inferior Independence'

1 Christine Riding, 'Travellers and Sitters: The Orientalist Portait', in Nicholas Tromans and Rana Kabbani (eds), *The Lure of the East* (London, 2008), p. 61.

2 Monroe, *Britain's Moment*, p. 71.

3 Rogan, *The Arabs*, p. 207.

4 Fromkin, *Peace to End*, pp. 418–19.

5 John Richmond, *Egypt* (London, 1977), p. 173. Elie Kedourie, *The Chatham House Version* (London, 1970), p. 103. Ulrichsen, *The First World War*, p. 184.

6 Janice Terry, *The Wafd* (London, 1982), pp. 91, 202–3.

7 Mary Innes, 'In Egyptian Service' (D.Phil, Oxford, 1981), p. 130.

8 Adel Sabit, *A King Betrayed* (London, 1989), p. 12. P.G. Elgood, *Egypt and the Army* (Oxford, 1924), pp. 368–9. Darwin, *Britain, Egypt and the Middle East*, p. 75. Richmond, *Egypt*, p. 176.

9 Chirol, *Fifty Years in a Changing World*, p. 68. Grafftey-Smith, *Bright Levant*, p. 72.

10 Mansfield, *The British in Egypt*, pp. 233–4.

11 Innes, 'In Egyptian Service', pp. 182–4.

12 Lady Richmond (ed.), *Selected Letters of Gertrude Bell* (London, 1953), p. 253.

13 Mansfield, *British in Egypt*, p. 235. Lord Lloyd, *Egypt since Cromer*, Vol. ii (London, 1934), p. 4. Kedourie, *The Chatham House Version*, pp. 121, 123–4.

14 Innes, 'In Egyptian Service', pp. 228–9. Grafftey-Smith, *Bright Levant*, p. 84, Terry, *Wafd*, pp. 144–6, 206.

15 John Darwin, *End of the British Empire* (Oxford, 1991), pp. 132–6.

16 Hopwood, *Tales of Empire*, p. 23.

17 Innes, 'In Egyptian Service', p. 237. Afaf Lutfi al-Sayyid-Marsot, *Egypt's Liberal Experiment* (Berkley, 1977), p. 69. Hassan Ibrahim, *The 1936 Anglo-Egyptian Treaty* (Khartoum, 1976), pp. 44–5.

18 Ibid., p. 90. Malcolm Yapp, *Politics and Diplomacy in Egypt* (Oxford, 1987), p. 11. Terry, *Wafd*, p. 242. Grafftey-Smith, *Bright Levant*, pp. 91–3.

19 Ibid., pp. 158–9. Sabit, *King Betrayed*, p. 71.

20 Lloyd, *Egypt*, Vol. ii, p. 156.

21 Ibrahim, *1936 Treaty*, pp. 25–6. Martin Kolinsky, *Britain's War in the Middle East* (Basingstoke, 1999), p. 34. Grafftey-Smith, *Bright Levant*, p. 46. Al-Sayyid-Marsot, *Egypt's Liberal Experiment*, p. 60. Marius Deeb, *Party Politics in Egypt* (London, 1979), pp. 125, 331.

22 Ibid., p. 239.

23 Lloyd, *Egypt*, Vol. ii, p. 142. Ibrahim, *1936 Treaty*, p. 149.

24 Terry, *Wafd*, pp. 186–7, 190–1. Al-Sayyid-Marsot, *Egypt's Liberal Experiment*, p. 102.

25 John Charmley, *Lord Lloyd and the Decline of the British Empire* (London, 1987), pp. 147, 159.

26 Al-Sayyid-Marsot, *Egypt's Liberal Experiment*, p. 136. Gordon Waterfield, *Professional Diplomat* (London, 1973), p. 160.

27 Ibid., p. 187.

28 Yapp (ed.), *Politics and Diplomacy*, pp. 5–6. Terry, *Wafd*, p. 227.

29 Hoda Gamal Abdel Nasser, *Britain and the Egyptian Nationalist Movement* (Reading, 1994), p. 296.

30 Yapp, *Politics and Diplomacy*, p. 526 (emphasis in original).

31 Ibid., p. 50. Sabit, *King Betrayed*, p. 35.

32 Yapp, *Politics and Diplomacy*, pp. 689, 691.

33 William Stadiem, *Too Rich: The High Life and Tragic Death of King Farouk* (London, 1992), p. 145.

34 Sabit, *King Betrayed*, p. 68.

35 Yapp, *Politics and Diplomacy*, pp. 20–3. Waterfield, *Professional Diplomat*, pp. 147, 181. Al-Sayyid-Marsot, *Egypt's Liberal Experiment*, pp. 156–7. Marlowe, *Anglo-Egyptian Relations*, p. 291.

36 Ibid., p. 308. Mansfield, *Britain in Egypt*, p. 308. Ibrahim, *1936 Treaty*, p. 25.

37 Oded Eran, 'Negotiating the Anglo-Egyptian Relationship between the World Wars', in Wilson (ed.), *Imperialism and Nationalism*, pp. 69, 71. Yapp, *Politics and Diplomacy*, pp. 562–3, 70.

38 Steven Morewood, *The British Defence of Egypt* (London, 2005), p. 90.

39 Ibrahim, *1936 Treaty*, pp. 137–51.

40 Yapp, *Politics and Diplomacy*, p. 672.

41 John Darwin, 'Undeclared Empire', *JICH*, May 1999, pp. 170–1.

42 Innes, 'In Egyptian Service', p. 323.

43 Farnie, *East and West*, p. 605.

44 Mansfield, *Britain in Egypt*, p. 265.

45 Marlowe, *Anglo-Egyptian Relations*, p. 302. Yapp, *Politics and Diplomacy*, p. 9, Monroe, *Britain's Moment*, p. 84.

46 Kolinsky, *Britain's War in the Middle East*, p. 39. Deeb, *Party Politics*, p. 1. Terry, *Wafd*, p. 153.

47 Morewood, *The British Defence of Egypt*, p. 153.

Chapter Nine: Client Kings

1 Sluglett, *Britain and Iraq*, p. 204. Gerald de Gaury, *Three Kings in Baghdad* (London, 2008 edn), p. 29. Allawi, *Feisal*, p. 367.

2 David Omissi, *Air Power and Colonial Control* (Manchester, 1990), p. 31.

3 Ibid., p. 254. Daniel Silverfarb, *Britain's Informal Empire in the Middle East* (Oxford, 1986), pp. 23–5. Clive Leatherdale, *Britain and Saudi Arabia* (London, 1983), p. 95. Jafna Cox, 'A Splendid Training Ground', *JICH*, January 1985, pp. 175–6.

4 Toby Dodge, *Inventing Iraq* (London, 2003), p. 217.

5 Ibid., p. 26.

6 Ireland, *Iraq*, pp. 314, 338–9. Antonius, *Arab Awakening*, p. 360. Allawi, *Feisal*, p. 433. Townsend, *Proconsul*, p. 178.

7 Sluglett, *Britain and Iraq*, p. 45. Longrigg, *Iraq*, p. 140.

8 Dodge, *Inventing Iraq*, p. 184.

9 Ibid., p. 65.

10 Fieldhouse, *Western Imperialism*, p. 94. Mejcher, *Imperial Quest for Oil*, pp. 81–4.

11 Allawi, *Feisal*, pp. 443–4. Liora Lukitz, *Iraq* (London, 1995), p. 15. Phoebe Marr, *The Modern History of Iraq* (Boulder, CO, 1985), p. 38.

12 Ibid., p. 39. Ireland, *Iraq*, pp. 472–3, 484.

13 Mejcher, *Imperial Quest for Oil*, p. 162.

14 Silverfarb, *Informal Empire*, p. 94.

15 Dodge, *Inventing Iraq*, p. 140.

16 Omissi, *Air Power*, pp. 25, 32. Sluglett, *Britain and Iraq*, pp. 82–3. Sir John Glubb, *The War in the Desert* (London, 1960), pp. 62–3, 193–7.

17 Priya Satia, 'The Defence of Inhumanity', *American Historical Review*, no. 1, 2006, pp. 42, 51–2.

18 Philip Towle, *Pilots and Rebels* (London, 1989), pp. 9, 13. Dodge, *Inventing Iraq*, p. 149. Mohammed Tarbush, *The Role of the Military in Politics* (London, 1982), p. 18. Lukitz, *Iraq*, p. 18. Omissi, *Air Power*, p. 211. Jackson, *Britain's Triumph and Decline in the Middle East*, p. 24.

19 Satia, *Spies in Arabia*, p. 253.

20 Ibid., pp. 191–2. Dodge, *Inventing Iraq*, p. 145. Cox, 'A Splendid Training Ground',

pp. 172, 174. Omissi, *Air Power*, p. 35. Towle, *Pilots and Rebels*, p. 21.

21 Lukitz, *Iraq*, p. 16. Dodge, *Inventing Iraq*, pp. 137, 142. Paul Hempshill, 'The Formation of the Iraqi Army, 1921–33', in Abbas Kelidar (ed.), *The Integration of Modern Iraq* (London, 1979), p. 96.

22 De Gaury, *Three Kings*, p. 31.

23 Longrigg, *Iraq*, p. 180. Foster, *Modern Iraq*, pp. 272–4.

24 Ireland, *Iraq*, pp. 364–9. Sluglett, *Britain and Iraq*, p. 58. Marr, *Modern History*, p. 39. Hugh Arbuthnott, Terence Clark and Richard Muir, *British Missions Around the Gulf* (London, 2008), p. 137.

25 Tarbush, *Role of the Military*, p. 40.

26 Allawi, *Feisal*, pp. 482, 487, 510, 517.

27 Dodge, *Inventing Iraq*, p. 335. Sluglett, *Britain and Iraq*, pp. 118–20. Silverfarb, *Informal Empire*, pp. 16–21.

28 Allawi, *Feisal*, pp. 512–13.

29 Fieldhouse, *Western Imperialism*, pp. 95–6. Foster, *Modern Iraq*, pp. 288–9. Sluglett, *Britain and Iraq*, p. 156.

30 Ibid., p. 159.

31 Silverfarb, *Informal Empire*, p. 22. Longrigg, *Iraq*, p. 189.

32 Allawi, *Feisal*, pp. 520, 534. David McDowell, *A Modern History of the Kurds* (London, 1996), pp. 170–1.

33 Hourani, *History of the Arab Peoples*, p. 329. Sluglett, *Britain and Iraq*, pp. 129–42, 154.

34 Ibid., pp. 193–5.

35 Marr, *Modern History*, p. 40.

36 Sluglett, *Britain and Iraq*, p. 211. Tarbush, *Military in Politics*, pp. 71–2, 151. Paul Kingston, *Britain and the Politics of Modernisation in the Middle East* (Cambridge, 1986), pp. 94–5. Fieldhouse, *Western Imperialism*, pp. 74–6, 100.

37 Dodge, *Inventing Iraq*, p. 38.

38 Matthew Elliott, *Independent Iraq* (London, 1996), p. 12. Liora Lukitz, 'Axioms Reconsidered: The Rethinking of British Strategy in Iraq during the 1930s', in Michael Cohen and Martin Kolinsky, *Britain and the Middle East in the 1930s* (Basingstoke, 1992), p. 122.

39 Marr, *Modern History*, pp. 77–8.

40 Kwarteng, *Ghosts of Empire*, pp. 51–2. Tarbush, *Military in Politics*, pp. 133–4. Marr, *Modern History*, pp. 77–8.

41 Ibid., pp. 69–70, 77–8. Lukitz, *Iraq*, p. 101. Lukitz, 'Axioms Reconsidered', p. 117. Hempshill, 'The Formation of the Iraqi Army', pp. 101, 103, 104. Silverfarb, *Informal Empire*, p. 64.

42 Ibid., pp. 77–85. Tarbush, *Military in Politics*, p. 160. Arbuthnott et al., *British Missions*, pp. 140–1.

43 Silverfarb, *Informal Empire*, pp. 65–73.

44 P.J. Vatikiotis, *Politics and the Military in Jordan* (London, 1967), p. 7. Wilson, *Abdullah*, pp. 3, 129.

45 Yoav Alon, *The Making of Jordan* (London, 2007), pp. 39, 43. Toby Dodge, *An Arabian Prince, English Gentlemen and the Tribes East of the River Jordan* (London, 1994), p. 11.

46 Ibid., p. 1. Klieman, *Foundations of British Policy*, p. 234. Kamal Salibi, *The Modern History of Jordan* (London, 1993), pp. 97–8. Ma'n Abu Nuwar, *The History of the Hashemite Kingdom of Jordan*, Vol. i (Oxford, 1989), pp. 40, 220. Meyer and Brysac, *Kingmakers*, p. 261.

47 Ibid., p. 30. Philip Robins, *A History of Jordan* (Cambridge, 2004), pp. 21–2. Alon, *Making*, pp. 47–8. Dodge, *An Arabian Prince*, pp. 16, 31.

48 Salibi, *Modern History*, p. 95. Uriel Dann, *Studies in the History of Transjordan* (Boulder, CO, 1984), p. 38.

49 Robins, *History*, p. 27.

50 Dann, *Studies*, p. 85.

51 Ibid., pp. 85–8. Nuwar, *History*, p. 126.

52 Ibid., pp. 69, 188. Salibi, *Modern History*, pp. 111, 113. Alon, *Making*, p. 50. Robins, *History*, p. 31.

53 Dann, *Studies*, pp. 88–9.

54 Alon, *Making*, p. 61. Nuwar, *History*, pp. 147–8. Robins, *History*, p. 31.

55 Leatherdale, *Britain and Saudi Arabia*, p. 52.

56 Nuwar, *History*, p. 206.

57 Wilson, *Abdullah*, p. 96, Robins, *History*, pp. 36–7.

58 Ibid., p. 25.

59 Ibid. Kirkbride, *A Crackle of Thorns*, p. 81. Alon, *Making*, pp. 91–2.

60 Trevor Royle, *Glubb Pasha* (London, 1992), pp. 165, 186.

61 Ibid., p. 176.

62 Glubb, *The Story of the Arab Legion*, p. 113. James Lunt, 'Sir John Glubb', *Dictionary of National Biography*, Vol. xxii (Oxford, 2004), pp. 503–4. C.S. Jarvis, *Arab Command* (London, 1943), p. 83.

63 Robins, *History*, p. 42. Royle, *Glubb*, pp. 176, 217. Glubb, *War*, p. 166.

64 Ricardo Bozeo and Tariq Tell, 'Pax Britannica in the Steppe', in Eugene Rogan and Tariq Tell (eds), *Village, Steppe and State* (London, 1994), p. 120. Alon, *Making*, pp. 128–9.

65 Ibid., pp. 134–5.

66 Michael Fishbach, 'British Land Policy in Transjordan', in Rogan and Tell, *Village, Steppe*, pp. 80, 107. Kingston, *Britain and the Politics of Modernisation*, p. 124.

67 Wilson, *Abdullah*, pp. 90, 106–7. Yoav Alon, 'Tribal Sheikhs and the Limits of British Imperial Rule in Transjordan', *JICH*, January 2004, p. 88.

68 Alon, *Making*, p. 6.

69 Ibid., pp. 5, 62. Dann, *Studies*, p. 16. Nuwar, *History*, p. 219.

Chapter Ten: 'Riding Two Horses at Once'

1 Douglas Hurd, *Choose Your Weapons* (London, 2010), p. 323.
2 Barr, *A Line in the Sand*, p. 157.
3 Ibid. Michael Cohen, *Retreat from the Mandate* (London, 1978), pp. 3–4. Kolinsky, *Britain's War in the Middle East*, p. 4.
4 Sahar Huneidi, 'Was the Balfour Policy Reversible?', *Journal of Palestine Studies*, winter 1998, p. 37.
5 Avi Shlaim, *The Iron Wall, Israel and the Arab World* (London, 2000), p. 18.
6 Martin Kolinsky, *Law, Order and Riots in Mandatory Palestine* (Basingstoke, 1993), p. 188.
7 *Palestine Royal Commission Report* (The Peel Commission) (London, 1937), pp. 24–5.
8 Marlowe, *The Seat of Pilate*, p. 62.
9 Kolinsky, *Law, Order and Riots*, p. 11. *Peel Commission*, p. 55.
10 Ibid., p. 131.
11 Bernard Wasserstein, *The British in Palestine* (London, 1979), p. 104.
12 Naomi Shepherd, *Ploughing Sand* (London, 1999), p. 82. *Peel Commission*, p. 124.
13 Ibid., pp.67–8.
14 Fieldhouse, *Western Imperialism*, pp. 179–80.
15 Sachar, *History of Israel*, pp. 136, 161–2.
16 Fieldhouse, *Western Imperialism*, p. 179.
17 Norman and Helen Bentwich, *Mandate Memories, 1914–1948* (London, 1965), p. 68. A.J. Sherman, *Mandate Days* (London, 1997), pp. 26–9, 73.
18 Ibid., p. 87.
19 Ibid., pp. 105–6.
20 Shepherd, *Ploughing Sand*, p. 226.
21 Ibid., pp. 105–6.
22 Ibid., p. 127. Humphrey Bowman, *Middle East Window* (London, 1942), p. 310.
23 Shepherd, *Ploughing Sand*, p. 126.
24 Evyatar Friesel, 'British Officials and the Situation in Palestine, 1923', *MES*, April 1987, p. 204.
25 Gabriel Sheffer, *Policy-Making and British Policies towards Palestine, 1929–39* (D.Phil, Oxford, 1970), p. 147.
26 Shepherd, *Ploughing Sand*, p. 136. Marlowe, *Seat of Pilate*, p. 134.
27 Norman Rose, *The Gentile Zionists* (London, 1973), p. 55. Kolinsky, *Law, Order and Riots*, pp. 5–6.
28 Friesel, 'British Officials and the Situation in Palestine', p. 200.
29 Sherman, *Mandate Days*, p. 85. Kolinsky, *Law, Order and Riots*, p. 82.
30 Ibid., p. 180.
31 Ibid., p. 176. Zvi Elpeleg, *The Grand Mufti* (London, 1993), p. 37.
32 *Peel Commission*, p. 279.
33 Sheffer, *Policy-Making and British Policies towards Palestine*, pp. 165–6, 179.
34 Elpeleg, *The Grand Mufti*, pp. 36–7.

35 Kolinsky, *Law, Order and Riots*, p. 188. Sachar, *History of Israel*, p. 199.

36 *Peel Commission*, pp. 2, 371.

37 Ibid., p. 370.

38 Cohen, *Retreat from Mandate*, p. 39.

39 Sachar, *History of Israel*, p. 205.

40 Ibid., pp. 209–11.

41 Kolinsky, *Law, Order and Riots*, p. 60.

42 Cohen, *Retreat from Mandate*, pp. 62, 64–6.

43 Nigel Hamilton, *Monty: The Making of a General, 1887–1942* (London, 1981), p. 296.

44 Sir Gawain Bell, *Shadows on the Sand* (London, 1983), p. 89.

45 Tom Bowden, 'The Politics of the Arab Rebellion in Palestine', *MES*, May 1975, p. 147.

46 Marlowe, *Seat of Pilate*, p. 151.

47 Sachar, *History of Israel*, p. 212.

48 Sherman, *Mandate Days*, p. 114.

49 Nicholas Bethell, *The Palestine Triangle* (London, 1979), p. 46. Bowden, 'The Politics of the Arab Revolt', pp. 170–3.

50 Ibid., p. 162.

51 Lawrence Pratt, *West of Suez, East of Malta* (Cambridge, 1975), p. 125. Morewood, *The British Defence of Egypt*, p. 164.

52 Bethell, *The Palestine Triangle*, p. 51.

53 Cohen, *Retreat from Mandate*, p. 84.

54 Marlowe, *Seat of Pilate*, pp. 155–7. Kolinsky, *Law, Order and Riots*, p. 227.

55 Rose, *Gentile Zionists*, p. 203.

56 Ibid., p. 207.

Chapter Eleven: Strong-men, Borders and Oil

1 Satia, *Spies in Arabia*, pp. 181–96. Riding, 'Travellers and Sitters', p. 61.

2 Joshua Teitelbaum, *The Rise and Fall of the Hashemite Kingdom of Arabia* (London, 2001), p. 279.

3 Randal Barker, *King Hussein and the Kingdom of the Hejaz* (Cambridge, 1979), pp. 167, 170–1.

4 Haifa Alangari, *The Struggle for Peace in Arabia* (Reading, 1998), p. 206.

5 Askar al-Enazy, *The Creation of Saudi Arabia* (Abingdon, 2010), p. 100.

6 Alangari, *Struggle*, pp. 206, 222.

7 Sir Andrew Ryan, *The Last of the Dragomans* (London, 1951), pp. 273–4.

8 Troeller, *The Birth of Saudi Arabia*, pp. 58–9.

9 Ibid., pp. 89–92.

10 Joseph Kostiner, *The Making of Saudi Arabia* (London, 1993), p. 54.

11 Troeller, *The Birth of Saudi Arabia*, p. 148.

12 Paris, *Britain, the Hashemites*, pp. 264–77. Teitelbaum, *Rise*, pp. 260–1, 266–7.

13 Kostiner, *Making*, pp. 60–1.

14 Al-Enazy, *Creation*, pp. 103–4.

15 Ibid., p. 134.

16 Alangari, *Struggle*, p. 241.

17 Al-Enazy, *Creation*, p. 155.

18 Leatherdale, *Britain and Saudi Arabia*, p. 113. Troeller, *The Birth of Saudi Arabia*, p. 236.

19 Daniel Silverfarb, 'Great Britain, Iraq and Saudi Arabia', *International History Review*, May 1982, pp. 222, 244–6. Harold Dickson, *Kuwait and its Neighbours* (London, 1956), p. 328. Leatherdale, *Britain and Saudi Arabia*, p. 117.

20 Ibid., pp. 147, 161. Sir George Rendel, *The Sword and the Olive* (London, 1957), p. 60.

21 Ryan, *The Last of the Dragomans*, p. 278. Dickson, *Kuwait*, p. 272.

22 Leatherdale, *Britain and Saudi Arabia*, p. 4.

23 Dickson, *Kuwait*, p. 274.

24 Leatherdale, *Britain and Saudi Arabia*, pp. 96–7. Silverfarb, 'Great Britain, Iraq and Saudi Arabia', p. 229.

25 Robert Collins (ed.), *An Arabian Diary* (Berkley, 1979), pp. 79, 126.

26 Joseph Kostiner, 'Britain and the Challenge of Axis Powers in Arabia', in Cohen and Kolinsky, *Britain and the Middle East in the 1930s*, pp. 132–3. John Wilkinson, *Arabia's Frontiers* (London, 1991), chapter 9. Leatherdale, *Britain and Saudi Arabia*, pp. 223–4.

27 Ibid., p. 275.

28 Sir Reader Bullard, *The Camels Must Go* (London, 1961), p. 197.

29 Kostiner, 'Britain and the Challenge of Axis Powers in Arabia', pp. 139–40.

30 Ibid., pp. 208–13. Troeller, *The Birth of Saudi Arabia*, pp. 240–1.

31 Silverfarb, 'Britain and Saudi Arabia on the Eve of the Second World War', *MES*, October 1983, p. 405.

32 Leatherdale, *Britain and Saudi Arabia*, pp. 139–40. Gavin, *Aden*, pp. 281–4. Harold Ingrams, *The Yemen* (London, 1963), p. 67.

33 Ibid., pp. 69–70. Gavin, *Aden*, pp. 296–7.

34 Ibid., pp. 252–3, 282, 286, 287, 290, 291–2.

35 Freya Stark, *A Winter in Arabia* (London, 1983 edn), p. 6.

36 Ibid., p. 9. Gavin, *Aden*, pp. 303–5. Doreen Ingrams, *A Time in Arabia* (London, 1970), p. 65.

37 Sir Kennedy Trevaskis, *Shades of Amber* (London, 1968), pp. 13–14.

38 Uriel Dann, 'Britain's Persian Gulf Concepts in the Light of Emerging Nationalism in the Late 1930s', in Uriel Dann, *The Great Powers in the Middle East* (New York, 1988), pp. 59–60.

39 Silverfarb, 'Great Britain, Iraq and Saudi Arabia', pp. 232, 237. Roderic Hill, *The Baghdad Air Mail* (Stroud, 2005 edn), pp. 12, 34.

40 Silverfarb, 'Britain and Saudi Arabia on the Eve of the Second World War', p. 420. R.W. Ferrier, *The History of the British Petroleum Company*, Vol. i (Cambridge, 1982), pp. 202, 634, 681. Dann, 'Britain's Persian Gulf Concepts', p. 56.

41 Yergin, *The Prize*, p. 283.

42 Ibid., p. 294.

43 Ibid., pp. 292–8. Leatherdale, *Britain and Saudi Arabia*, p. 239.

44 Balfour-Paul, *The End of Empire in the Middle East*, p. 106.

45 Ibid., p. 109. Leatherdale, *Britain and Saudi Arabia*, p. 323. Andrew Loewenstein, 'The Veiled Protectorate of Kuwait', *MES*, April 2000, p. 107. Simon Smith, *Britain's Revival and Fall in the Gulf* (London, 2004), p. 3.

46 Dann, 'Britain's Persian Gulf Concepts', p. 59.

47 Wright, *The English*, p. 183.

48 Ibid., pp. 181–4. Stephanie Cronin, 'Britain, the Iranian Military and the Rise of Reza Shah', in Martin (ed.), *Anglo-Iranian Relations*, pp. 119–24.

49 Houshany Sabahi, *British Policy* (London, 1990), pp. 162–3, 176, 195–6.

50 Ibid., pp. 76, 164–5, 195–6. Waterfield, *Professional Diplomat*, p. 75.

51 Ibid., pp. 75–7. Sabahi, *British Policy*, pp. 169–70.

52 Ibid., pp. 171, 172, 182, 188. Waterfield, *Professional Diplomat*, pp. 77, 94.

53 Bell, *Shadows in the Sand*, p. 228.

54 Yergin, *The Prize*, p. 269. Wright, *The English*, pp. 110–11. L.P. Elwell-Sutton, *Persian Oil* (London, 1955), pp. 93–4, 102. De Bellaigue, *Patriot of Persia*, pp. 5–6.

55 Ferrier, *History of the British Petroleum Company*, Vol. i, pp. 606, 629.

56 Elwell-Sutton, *Persian Oil*, p. 73. R.M. Burell (ed.), *Iran: Political Diaries*, Vol. xii (Chippenham, 1997), p. 491.

57 Ibid., Vol. ix, p. vii. Yergin, *The Prize*, pp. 270–1. Elwell Sutton, *Persian Oil*, pp. 80–7. De Bellaigue, *Patriot of Persia*, p. 98. Arbuthnott et al., *British Missions around the Gulf*, p. 30.

58 Frank Brenchley, *Britain and the Middle East* (London, 1989), p. 53.

59 Arbuthnott et al., *British Missions around the Gulf*, p. 31.

60 Burrell, *Iranian Diaries*, Vol. ix, p. 436.

61 FO371/11445, 'British Interests in Arabia', 26 November 1926.

Chapter Twelve: Egypt and World War II

1 Pratt, *West of Suez*, p. 108.

2 Callum MacDonald, 'Radio Bari', *MES*, May 1977, p. 195.

3 Morewood, *The British Defence of Egypt*, p. 27.

4 Denis Mack Smith, *Mussolini's Roman Empire* (London, 1976), pp. 33–4.

5 MacDonald, 'Radio Bari', pp. 195–6, 204. Caludio Segré, 'Liberal and Fascist Italy in the Middle East', in Dann, *The Great Powers in the Middle East*, pp. 208–9.

6 MacDonald, 'Radio Bari', p. 295.

7 Peter Partner, *Arab Voices* (London, 1988), p. 23.

8 Segré, 'Liberal and Fascist Italy in the Middle East', p. 205. Farnie, *East and West*, pp. 609–19.

9 Paul Harris, 'Egypt: Defence Plans', in Cohen and Kolinsky, *Britain and the Middle*

East in the 1930s, pp. 61, 74, 75. Pratt, *West of Suez*, p. 116. Morewood, *British Defence*, p. 401.

10 Ibid., p. 159. Farnie, *East and West of Suez*, p. 598.

11 Morewood, *British Defence*, p. 105.

12 Ibid., pp. 108–10. Rendel, *The Sword and the Olive*, p. 136.

13 Morewood, *Britain's Defence*, pp. 113–15, 122–3.

14 Harold Raugh, *Wavell and the Middle East* (London, 1993), p. 47.

15 Douglas Porch, *Hitler's Mediterranean Gamble* (London, 2004), pp. 132–4.

16 Winston Churchill, *The Grand Alliance* (London, 1950), p. 5.

17 Porch, *Mediterranean Gamble*, p. 26.

18 I.S.O. Playfair, *The Mediterranean and the Middle East*, Vol. ii (London, 1956), p. 249.

19 Martin Wilmington, *The Middle East Supply Centre* (Albany, 1971), p. 14.

20 Porch, *Mediterranean Gamble*, pp. 80–94. Raugh, *Wavell*, p. 64.

21 Ibid., pp. 139–41. Lukasz Hirsowica, *The Third Reich and the Arab East* (London, 1966), p. 98.

22 Ibid., pp. 100–1.

23 Playfair, *The Mediterranean and the Middle East*, Vol. ii, pp. 248–9, 60. Klaus-Michael Mallmann and Marti Cueppers, *Nazi Palestine* (New York, 2010), p. 115.

24 Ibid., p. 35. Porch, *Mediterranean Gamble*, pp. 277–8. Wilmington, *Middle East Supply Centre*, p. 55. Artemis Cooper, *Cairo in the War* (London, 1989), p. 195.

25 Ibid., pp. 218–19.

26 Freya Stark, *Dust in the Lion's Paw* (London, 1961), pp. 56–7.

27 Morewood, *British Defence*, p. 127. Raugh, *Wavell*, pp. 43, 54.

28 Ibid., p. 75.

29 Playfair, *The Mediterranean and the Middle East*, Vol. ii, pp. 226–7. George Kirk, *The Middle East in the War* (Oxford, 1952), p. 171. Cooper, *Cairo*, p. 112.

30 Wilmington, *Middle East Supply Centre*, pp. 39–40. Ahmed Gomma, *The Foundation of the League of Arab States* (London, 1977), p. 98.

31 Parsons, *They Say the Lion*, p. 2. Cooper, *Cairo*, pp. 114, 116–18.

32 Wilmington, *The Middle East Supply Centre*, pp. 25–6. Trefor Evans (ed.), *The Killearn Diaries* (London, 1972), p. 355.

33 Cooper, *Cairo*, pp. 102–3.

34 Kirk, *Middle East*, p. 34.

35 Laila Morsy, 'Britain's Wartime Policy in Egypt: 1940–42', *MES*, January, 1989, p. 84. Mallmann and Cueppers, *Nazi Palestine*, pp. 31, 106. Hirsowicz, *The Third Reich*, pp. 241–2.

36 Ibid., pp. 232–4.

37 Leila Morsy, 'Indicative Crises of British Wartime Policy in Egypt, 1942–4', *MES*, January 1994, p. 117.

38 Morewood, *British Defence*, p. 175.

39 Warburg, *Egypt and the Sudan*, p. 124.

40 Evans, *Killearn Diaries*, p. 123.

41 Ibid., pp. 132, 134.

42 Richmond, *Egypt*, p. 206.

43 Evans, *Killearn Diaries*, pp. 218–19.

44 Stadiem, *Too Rich*, p. 207.

45 Morsy, 'Indicative Crises', pp. 94, 99.

46 Warburg, *Egypt and the Sudan*, p. 142.

47 Morsy, 'Indicative Crises', p. 105.

48 Evans, *Killearn Diaries*, p. 290. Warburg, *Egypt and the Sudan*, p. 146. Terry, *Wafd*, p. 260.

49 Morsy, 'Indicative Crises', p. 117. Kolinsky, *Britain's War in the Middle East*, p. 186.

50 Cooper, *Cairo*, p. 172.

Chapter Thirteen: Holding the Middle East

1 Elpeleg, *The Grand Mufti*, p. 56.

2 Silverfarb, *Informal Empire*, p. 105.

3 Ibid., pp. 110–13. Hirsowicz, *The Third Reich and the Arab East*, p. 77. Kirk, *Short History*, pp. 57–9, 63.

4 Silverfarb, *Informal Empire*, pp. 120–1. Marr, *Modern History of Iraq*, p. 83.

5 Churchill, *The Grand Alliance*, p. 225.

6 Bell, *Shadows in the Sand*, p. 127.

7 Porch, *Mediterranean Gamble*, p. 574. Elie Kedourie, 'Wavell and Iraq, April–May 1941', *MES*, July 1966, pp. 382–3. Howard Sachar, *Europe Leaves the Middle East* (London, 1970), p. 175.

8 Mallman and Cueppers, *Nazi Palestine*, pp. 66–9. Playfair, *The Mediterranean and the Middle East*, Vol. iii, pp. 333–4.

9 De Gaury, *Three Kings*, p. 128. Kolinsky, *Britain's War in the Middle East*, p. 162.

10 Silverfarb, *Britain's Informal Empire*, pp. 133–40. Arbuthnott et al., *British Missions around the Gulf*, pp. 146–7. Daniel Silverfarb, *The Twilight of British Ascendency in the Middle East* (Basingstoke, 1994), pp. 11–13.

11 Ibid., pp. 11–16. Elliott, *Independent Iraq*, p. 43.

12 Ibid., pp. 20, 166–7.

13 Geoffrey Warner, *Iraq and Syria* (London, 1974), pp. 34–5.

14 Churchill, *Grand Alliance*, pp. 288–9.

15 Mallmann and Cueppers, *Nazi Palestine*, p. 72.

16 A.B. Gaunson, *The Anglo-French Clash in Lebanon and Syria* (London, 1987), p. 147.

17 Sir Llewelyn Woodward, *British Foreign Policy*, Vol. iv (London, 1975), p. 216.

18 Ibid., pp. 241, 262. François Kersuady, *Churchill and de Gaulle* (London, 1981), pp. 195–6.

19 Woodward, *British Foreign Policy*, Vol. iv, pp. 297–8.

20 Barr, *Line in the Sand*, p. 305.

21 Ibid., pp. 306–9. Charles de Gaulle, *Complete War Memoirs* (New York, 1972), pp. 878–94.

22 Hourani, *History*, p. 357.

23 Playfair, *The Mediterranean and the Middle East*, Vol. ii, p. 252. Alex Danchev and Daniel Todman (eds), *Alanbrooke War Diaries*, 1939–45 (London, 2001), p. 290.

24 Meyer and Brysac, *Kingmakers*, p. 319.

25 Burrell, *Iranian Political Diaries*, Vol. xi, p. 432.

26 Ibid., p. viii.

27 Ibid., p. 642. Vol. xii, p. 191.

28 Woodward, *British Foreign Policy*, Vol. iv, pp. 423, 427–8.

29 Ibid., pp. 444, 446, 447. Kirk, *Short History*, pp. 140, 150. Burrell, *Political Diaries*, Vol. xii, pp. 484–5.

30 Sherman, *Mandate Days*, p. 152. Silverfarb, *Twilight*, p. 11.

31 Sachar, *History of Israel*, p. 230.

32 Kolinsky, *Britain's War in the Middle East*, pp. 190–1.

33 Ronald Zweig, *Britain and Palestine during the Second World War* (London, 1986), p. 121.

34 Sachar, *History of Israel*, pp. 237–8.

35 Ibid., p. 247. Zweig, *Britain and Palestine*, p. 151. Bethell, *The Palestine Triangle*, p. 155.

36 Sachar, *History of Israel*, p. 246.

37 Cohen, *Retreat from Mandate*, p. 129. Zweig, *Britain and Palestine*, p. 110.

38 Ibid., p. 112.

39 Woodward, *British Foreign Policy*, Vol. iv, pp. 366–72.

40 Zweig, *Britain and Palestine*, p. 176.

41 Wilmington, *The Middle East Supply Centre*, p. 4.

42 Ibid., pp. 118–21, 127. Kirk, *Short History*, pp. 179, 180–5.

43 Wilmington, *Middle East Supply Centre*, p. 149.

44 Cohen, *Retreat from Mandate*, p. 142.

45 Gomma, *The Foundation of the Arab League of States*, p. 103. Stark, *Dust in the Lion's Paw*, p. 83.

46 Kolinsky, *Britain's War in the Middle East*, p. 214.

47 Ibid. Warburg, *Egypt and the Sudan*, p. 148.

48 Michael Thornhill, 'Britain and the Politics of the Arab League', in Cohen and Kolinksy, *Demise*, p. 50.

49 Woodward, *British Foreign Policy*, Vol. iv, pp. 385–6. Barry Rubin, *The Great Powers and the Middle East* (London, 1980), p. 50. Cooper, *Cairo*, pp. 224–6.

50 Christopher Thorne, *Allies of a Kind* (Oxford, 1978), p. xxiii.

51 Woodward, *British Foreign Policy*, Vol. iv, p. 400. Rubin, *Great Powers*, pp. 27, 34, 39, 42, 43, 54.

52 Ibid., p. 47.

53 Louis, *British Empire*, p. 192.

54 Rubin, *Great Powers*, pp. 77, 90.

55 Andrew Roberts, *Masters and Commanders* (London, 2008), p. 276.

Chapter Fourteen: Complex Adjustments

1 *Foreign Relations of the United States, 1961–3*, Vol. xiii (Washington, 1994), p. 1064.
2 Avi Shlaim, 'Britain and the Arab-Israeli War of 1948', *Journal of Palestine Studies*, summer 1987, p. 52.
3 Moshe Gat, *Britain and the Conflict in the Middle East* (Westport, CT, 2003), p. 2.
4 Steven Galpern, *Money, Oil and Empire in the Middle East* (Cambridge, 2009), p. 232. Peter Catterall (ed.), *The Macmillan Diaries*, Vol. i, *The Cabinet Years* (London, 2003), p. 492. David Goldsworthy (ed.), *The Conservative Government and the End of Empire, 1951–7*, Part 1, pp. 136, 139.
5 Galpern, *Money, Oil*, p. 260.
6 Ibid., pp. 3, 28, 178, 273.
7 Darwin, *Unfinished Empire*, p. 362. Charles Tripp, 'Egypt', in Cohen and Kolinsky, *Demise*, p. 144.
8 FO371/124968. Roger Makins, 'Some Notes on British Foreign Policy', August 1951.
9 Lord Franks, *Britain and the Tide of World Affairs* (London, 1955), p. 6.
10 Peter Mangold, *Success and Failure in British Foreign Policy* (Basingstoke, 2001), pp. 119–20.
11 Bullock, *Bevin*, pp. 49–50. Paul Kennedy, *The Realities behind Diplomacy* (London, 1981), pp. 317–18.
12 Kingston, *Britain and the Politics of Modernisation in the Middle East*, p. 19.
13 Goldsworthy, *Conservative Government*, p. 130.
14 Mostafa El-Feki, 'Britain and Egypt: Working Together', in Noel Brehony and Ayman El-Desouky, *British–Egyptian Relations* (London, 2007), p. 61.
15 Smith, *Britain's Revival and Fall in the Gulf*, p. 112.
16 Ivan Pearson, *In the Name of Oil* (Brighton, 2010), p. 52.
17 Heikal, *Cutting the Lion's Tail*, p. 41.
18 Ritchie Ovendale, *Britain, the United States and the Transfer of Power in the Middle East* (Leicester, 1996), pp. 44–5.
19 Ibid., p. 95.
20 Steve Marsh, *Anglo-American Relations and the Cold War* (Basingstoke, 2003), p. 46.
21 'British Interests in the Mediterranean and the Middle East', Royal Institute of International Affairs, 1958, p. 35.
22 Elliott, *Independent Iraq*, pp. 48–9. Kingston, *Britain and the Politics of Modernisation*, pp. 10–11. Louis, *Ends of British Imperialism*, p. 30. Louis, *British Empire*, pp. 17–18.
23 Ibid., pp. 317–18. Parsons, *They Say the Lion*, p. 9.
24 Sir Sam Falle, *My Lucky Life* (Lewes, 1996), p. 121.
25 Ibid., pp. 9, 20–1.
26 Corelli Barnett, *The Lost Victory* (London, 1995), p. 54.
27 Ovendale, *Britain, the United States*, p. 71. Bullock, *Bevin*, p. 243.
28 Ibid., pp. 242, 342–4.
29 Michael Ionides, *Divide and Lose* (London, 1960), pp. 253–4.

30 Letter, Lord Strang, 22 October 1959. Monroe papers, MECA.

31 Evelyn Shuckburgh, *Descent to Suez* (London, 1986), p. 17.

32 Stephen Dorrill, *MI6* (London, 2001), p. 682.

33 E.M. Forster, *Howard's End* (London, 1963 edn).

Chapter Fifteen: A Sea of Troubles

1 Bullock, *Bevin*, p. 167. Peter Clarke, *The Last Thousand Days of the British Empire* (London, 2007), p. 390. Motti Golani (ed.), *The End of the British Empire for Palestine* (Basingstoke, 2009), pp. 88, 128. Bruce Hoffman, *Anonymous Soldiers* (New York, 2015), pp. 281–2.

2 Louis, *British Empire*, p. 402.

3 Ibid., p. 427.

4 David Charteris, *The British Army and the Jewish Insurgency in Palestine* (Basingstoke, 1988), pp. 27–9. Bullock, *Bevin*, p. 305. Sachar, *History of Israel*, p. 205. Ritchie Ovendale, 'The Palestine Policy of the Labour Government, 1945–6, *International Affairs*, 1979, p. 413. Louis, *British Empire*, pp. 394, 421, 484.

5 Ibid., p. 174. Louis, *Ends of British Imperialism*, p. 433. Bethell, *Palestine Triangle*, p. 256. Ritchie Ovendale, 'The Palestine Policy of the British Labour Government, 1947', *International Affairs*, January 1980, pp. 277–8.

6 Hoffman, *Anonymous Soldiers*, pp. 356–8.

7 Sherman, *Mandate Days*, p. 187. Shepherd, *Ploughing Sand*, p. 228.

8 Hoffman, *Anonymous Soldiers*, pp. 235, 476–7.

9 Louis, *British Empire*, p. 467.

10 Charteris, The *British Army and the Jewish Insurgency in Palestine*, pp. 47, 140–9.

11 Ibid., p. 131.

12 Louis, *British Empire*, p. 390. Bullock, *Bevin*, pp. 167, 182–3. Sykes, *Crossroads to Israel*, pp. 328–30. Louis, *Ends of British Imperialism*, p. 426.

13 Ibid., p. 432.

14 Clarke, *Last Thousand Days*, p. 463.

15 Christopher Andrew, *The Defence of the Realm* (London, 2009), pp. 352–65. Calder Walton, 'British Intelligence and the Mandate in Palestine', *INS*, 2008, no. 4.

16 Clarke, *Last One Thousand Days*, pp. 463, 500. Sherman, *Mandate Days*, p. 187. Shepherd, *Ploughing Sand*, p. 225.

17 Louis, *Ends of British Imperialism*, p. 439.

18 Ovendale, 'The Palestine Policy of the British Labour Government, 1947', p. 91.

19 Louis, *British Empire*, pp. 538–9.

20 Wilson, *Abdullah*, p. 180.

21 Bradshaw, *Britain and Jordan*, pp. 152–3.

22 Wilson, *Abdullah*, p. 164. Royle, *Glubb*, pp. 332, 334. Alan Pappé, 'British Rule in Jordan', in Cohen and Kolinksy, *Demise*, p. 204.

23 Sherman, *Mandate Days*, pp. 211–12.

24 Ibid., p. 243.

25 Louis, *British Empire*, pp. 376, 557.

26 Ibid., pp. 565–7. Shlaim, 'Britain and the Arab-Israeli War of 1948', pp. 66–9.

27 Louis, *British Empire*, pp. 565–9.

28 Sherman, *Mandate Days*, pp. 228–9.

29 Shlaim, 'Britain and the Arab-Israeli War of 1948', p. 69.

30 Marlowe, *The Seat of Pilate*, p. 191.

31 Shlaim, 'Britain and the Arab-Israeli War of 1948', pp. 50–1.

32 Sherman, *Mandate Days*, p. 220.

33 Kenneth Harris, *Attlee* (London, 1982), p. 388.

34 Louis, *British Empire* (London, 1963 edn), pp. 27, 353.

35 Bradshaw, *Britain and Jordan*, p. 111.

36 Ibid., pp. 108–9, 142. Louis, *British Empire*, p. 355.

37 Ibid., p. 368.

38 Ibid., p. 327.

39 Ibid., pp. 335–40. Michael Eppel, 'The Decline of British Influence and the Ruling Elite in Iraq', in Cohen and Kolinsky, *Demise*, p. 191. De Gaury, *Three Kings*, pp. 150–5.

40 Simon Smith, 'An Empire Built on Sand', in Zach Levy and Elie Podeh (eds), *Britain and the Middle East* (Brighton, 2008), p. 51. Louis, *British Empire*, p. 721.

41 Ibid., pp. 247–8.

42 Ibid., p. 244.

43 Ibid., pp. 238–9.

44 Smith, 'An Empire Built on Sand', p. 52. John Kent, 'The Egyptian Base and the Defence of the Middle East', *JICH*, September 1993, p. 48.

45 Louis, *British Empire*, p. 715.

46 Ibid., pp. 609–21. Kingston, *Britain and the Politics of Modernisation*, pp. 20, 28.

47 De Bellaigue, *Patriot of Persia*, p. 56.

48 Louis, *British Empire*, p. 680.

49 De Bellaigue, *Patriot of Persia*, p. 134. Yergin, *The Prize*, p. 460.

50 Homa Katouzian, *Mussadiq and the Struggle for Power in Persia* (London, 1990), pp. 137–8.

51 Yergin, *The Prize*, pp. 453–4. Galpern, *Money, Oil and Empire*, pp. 81, 105, 107–8. George McGee, *Envoy to the World* (New York, 1983), p. 335.

52 James Cable, *Intervention at Abadan* (Basingstoke, 1991), p. 58.

53 Louis, *British Empire*, pp. 673–4.

54 Cable, *Intervention*, p. 38. Mary Ann Heiss, *Empire and Nationhood* (New York, 1997), pp. 225–6. Marsh, *Anglo-American Relations*, p. 63.

55 Cable, *Intervention*, p. 80.

56 Louis, *British Empire*, pp. 668–9.

57 Louis, *Ends of British Imperialism*, pp. 757–8. Dean Acheson, *Present at the Creation* (London, 1969), p. 507.

58 Ibid.

59 Yergin, *The Prize*, p. 464. Anabelle Sreberny and Massoumeh Torfeh, *Persian Service* (London, 2014), p. 74. Dorrill, *MI6*, p. 564.

60 Acheson, *Present*, p. 510.

61 Heiss, *Empire and Nationhood*, p. 223. Katouzian, *Mussadiq*, p. 144. De Bellaigue, *Patriot of Persia*, p. 165.

62 Ibid., p. 2. C.M. Woodhouse, *Something Ventured* (London, 1982), p. 121.

63 Brian Lapping, *End of Empire* (London, 1985), p. 214.

64 Woodhouse, *Something Ventured*, p. 121.

65 De Bellaigue, *Patriot of Persia*, p. 274.

66 FCO8/3601, 'British Policy in Iran, 1974–8'.

67 Ovendale, *Britain, the United States*, p. 74. Marsh, *Anglo-American Relations*, p. 167.

68 Ibid., p. 168. FO370/2694, Comments on 'British Policy on the Relinquishment of Abadan'.

69 FCO8/3359, Parsons Valedictory Despatch, 18 January 1979.

70 De Bellaigue, *Patriot of Persia*, p. 3. Marsh, *Anglo-American Relations*, p. 168. Heiss, *Empire and Nationhood*, pp. 215–16.

71 McGee, *Envoy*, p. 387.

Chapter Sixteen: The Road to Suez

1 Humphrey Trevelyan, *The Middle East in Revolution* (London, 1970), p. 7.

2 Robert McNamara, *Britain, Nasser and the Balance of Power in the Middle East* (London, 2003), p. 276.

3 Robert Stephens, *Nasser* (London, 1971), p. 29.

4 Rogan, *The Arabs*, pp. 282–3.

5 FCO8/3601, 'British Policy in Iran, 1974–8'. Scott Lucas and Alistair Morey, 'The "Hidden Alliance"', *INS*, no. 2, 2000, p. 98.

6 William Roger Louis, 'The Tragedy of the Anglo-Egyptian Settlement of 1954', in William Roger Louis and Roger Owen (eds), *Suez* (Oxford, 1989), pp. 52–5.

7 Laura James, *Nasser at War* (Basingstoke, 2006), p. 4.

8 John Kent, 'The Egyptian Base', p. 60. William Roger Louis, 'Churchill and Egypt, 1946–56', in Robert Blake and William Roger Louis (eds), *Churchill* (Oxford, 1993), p. 473.

9 Dorrill, *MI6*, p. 603. Sue Onslow, *Backbench Debate within the Conservative Party and its Influence on British Foreign Policy, 1948–57* (Basingstoke, 1997), pp. 120–2.

10 Louis, 'The Tragedy of the Anglo-Egyptian Settlement', p. 53.

11 Lucas and Morey, 'The "Hidden Alliance"', p. 99.

12 Heikal, *Cutting the Lion's Tail*, p. 49.

13 Mohammad Heikal, *Nasser: The Cairo Documents* (London, 1972), p. 77. Cf. Richard Thorpe, *Eden* (London, 2003), pp. 426–7.

14 Nutting, *Nasser*, p. 71. Colin Crowe, 'An Account of the Restoration of Relations between the UK and the UAR after the Suez Episode', MECA, p. 85. Heikal, *Nasser*, p. 87.

15 Richard Jasse, 'The Baghdad Pact', *MES*, January 1991, pp. 146–7.

16 Nutting, *Nasser*, pp. 77–8. James, *Nasser at War*, p. 10. Heikal, *Cutting*, p. 54. Patrick Seale, *The Struggle for Syria: A Study of Postwar Arab Politics* (London, 1963), p. 193. Ali E. Hillal Dessouki, 'Nasser and the Struggle for Independence', in Louis and Owen, *Suez*, pp. 35–6.

17 Raymond Cohen, 'Israeli Military Intelligence before the 1956 Sinai Campaign', *INS*, vol. 3, no. 1, 1988, pp. 117–18.

18 Catterall (ed.), *Macmillan Cabinet Diaries*, p. 500.

19 Trevelyan, *Middle East in Revolution*, pp. 33–5. Kyle, *Suez*, pp. 84, 102.

20 Rogan, *The Arabs*, p. 305. Brenchley, *Britain and the Middle East*, pp. 93–4. Balfour-Paul, *Ends of British Imperialism*, p. 148.

21 Selwyn Lloyd, *Suez* (London, 1978), p. 34.

22 Lord Trevelyan, 'Conversations with a Conspirator', *The Times*, 19 February 1977.

23 Heikal, *Nasser*, p. 36.

24 Ibid., p. 84.

25 Harold Macmillan, *Riding the Storm* (London, 1971), p. 656.

26 Nigel Ashton, *Eisenhower, Macmillan and the Problem of Nasser* (Basingstoke, 1996), p. 67. Pearson, *In the Name of Oil*, p. 88.

27 Royle, *Glubb*, pp. 453–4. Avi Shlaim, *Lion of Judah* (London, 2007), p. 104.

28 Shuckburgh, *Descent to Suez*, p. 347.

29 Edward Heath, *The Course of My Life* (London, 1998), p. 168.

30 Robert Rhodes James, *Anthony Eden* (London, 1986), pp. 372–3.

31 Galpern, *Money, Oil and Empire*, pp. 144, 166–7.

32 M.A. Fitzsimons, *Empire by Treaty* (Notre Dame, 1964), p. 148.

33 Kyle, *Suez*, p. 136. *Summary of World Broadcasts, Middle East and North Africa*, 2nd series, 1585, 22 June 1964.

34 Catterrall (ed.), *Macmillan Cabinet Diaries*, p. 590. Mangold, *Success and Failure in British Foreign Policy*, p. 104.

35 Ann Lane, 'The Past as Matrix: Sir Ivone Kirkpatrick', in Saul Kelly and Anthony Gorst (eds), *Whitehall and the Suez Crisis* (London, 2000), p. 209.

36 Goldsworthy, *Conservative Government*, 23 July 1956. Dorrill, *MI6*, pp. 616–17.

37 Alistair Horne, *Macmillan*, Vol. i (London, 1988), p. 447.

38 Trevelyan, *Middle East in Revolution*, pp. 105–6.

39 Horne, *Macmillan*, Vol. i, p. 443.

40 Christopher Goldsmith, 'In the Know?', in Kelly and Gorst, *Whitehall and the Suez Crisis*, p. 81.

41 Selwyn Lloyd, *Suez*, p. 42.

42 Lucas and Morey, 'The "Hidden Alliance"', p. 109.

43 Kyle, *Suez*, p. 465.

44 Goldsworthy, *Conservative Government*, p. 167.

45 Ibid., p. 154.

46 Dorrill, *MI6*, p. 649.

47 Sir Charles Johnston, *The Brink of Jordan* (London, 1972), p. 171.

48 Kyle, *Suez*, pp. 561–2. Margaret Thatcher, *The Downing Street Years* (London, 1993), p. 8.
49 P.M.H. Bell, *Britain and France*, Vol. ii (Harlow, 1997), pp. 154–5. General André Beaufre, *The Suez Expedition* (London, 1969), p. 127.

Chapter Seventeen: Still Fighting Nasser

1 Hourani, *History*, p. 368.
2 Crowe, 'An Account of the Restoration of Relations between the UK and the UAR after the Suez Episode', p. 4.
3 Pearson, *In the Name of Oil*, pp. 98–9. McNamara, *Britain, Nasser*, pp. 94–5.
4 Johnston, *The Brink of Jordan*, pp. 80–1, 124.
5 Dorrill, *MI6*, pp. 622, 636, 646–7.
6 Ashton, *Eisenhower, Macmillan and the Problem of Nasser*, p. 140. Macmillan, *Riding the Storm*, pp. 279–80.
7 Ibid., p. 281.
8 Matthew Jones, 'The "Preferred Plan"', *INS*, 2004, no. 3.
9 CAB 301/148 'Possible Reaction of the Soviet Union to the US Policy in Syria in Areas other than the Middle East', September 1957.
10 Horne, *Macmillan*, Vol. ii (London, 1989), p. 44. Lucas and Morey, 'The "Hidden Alliance"', p. 113.
11 Catterall (ed.), *The Macmillan Diaries*, Vol. ii, p. 103.
12 Rogan, *The Arabs*, pp. 310–11. Dorrill, *MI6*, p. 666.
13 Pearson, *In the Name of Oil*, p. 151. Richard Lamb, *The Macmillan Years, 1957–63* (London, 1995), p. 33.
14 PREM11/2373, 'State Visit of King Feisal to Britain', 16–19 July 1958.
15 Heikal, *Nasser*, pp. 97–8.
16 Falle, *My Lucky Life*, pp. 119–20, 129–31, 139.
17 Peter Sluglett, 'The Pan-Arab Movement and the Influence of Cairo and Moscow', in William Roger Louis and Roger Owen, *A Revolutionary Year in the Middle East* (London, 2002), p. 219.
18 Ashton, *Eisenhower, Macmillan*, p. 165. Parsons, *They Say the Lion*, p. 16. PREM11/2368, 'The Iraqi Revolution of 14 July, 1958'. Dorrill, *MI6*, pp. 667–8.
19 Falle, *My Lucky Life*, p. 149.
20 Macmillan, *Riding the Storm*, p. 511.
21 *Hansard*, Lords, Series 5, Vol. 210, col. 1313.
22 Lamb, *The Macmillan Years*, p. 35.
23 Ashton, *Eisenhower, Macmillan*, p. 170. Pearson, *In the Name of Oil*, p. 162.
24 Ibid., p. 163.
25 Mangold, *The Almost Impossible Ally* (London, 2006), pp. 104–6.
26 Ashton, *Eisenhower, Macmillan*, p. 228. David Easter, 'Spying on Nasser', *INS*, 2013, no. 6. Dorrill, *MI6*, p. 668.

27 Horne, *Macmillan*, Vol. ii, pp. 94–5. Orna Almog, *Britain, Israel and the United States* (London, 2003), pp. 185–6, 189–90, 195. Shlaim, *Lion of Judah*, p. 164. Ashton, 'A "Special Relationship"', p. 236. William Roger Louis, 'Britain and the Crisis of 1958', in Louis and Owen, *A Revolutionary Year*, p. 65. Johnston, *Brink of Jordan*, p. 104.

28 Ibid., p. 120.

29 Shlaim, *Lion of Judah*, p. 170.

30 Ibid., p. 168. Lawrence Tal, 'Britain and the Jordan Crisis of 1958', *MES*, January 1995, pp. 50–1.

31 Ashton, *Eisenhower, Macmillan*, p. 179.

32 Crowe, 'Account', p. 217.

33 Ibid., p. 50. McNamara, *Britain, Nasser*, p. 170.

34 Christopher Gandy, 'A Mission to the Yemen', *BJMES*, no. 2, 1998, pp. 265–6.

35 Ibid., pp. 263–4, 273. McNamara, *Britain, Nasser*, p. 179. James, *Nasser at War*, p. 73.

36 Asher Orkaby, 'The Yemen Civil War', *MES*, no. 2, 2015.

37 Jesse Ferris, *Nasser's Gamble* (Princeton, 2013), pp. 132–5. McNamara, *Britain, Nasser*, p. 200.

38 Clive Jones, *Britain and the Yemen Civil War* (Brighton, 2004), pp. 87, 97–8, 112. Cf. David Easter, 'Spying on Nasser', p. 841.

39 Ibid., pp. 18–19, 226. James, *Nasser at War*, p. 76. Dorrill, *MI6*, pp. 687, 691, 697.

40 Spencer Mawby, *British Policy in Aden and the Protectorates* (London, 2005), pp. 105, 117.

41 McNamara, *Britain, Nasser*, p. 200.

42 Ibid., p. 214.

43 James, *Nasser at War*, p. 87.

44 Ferris, *Nasser's Gamble*, p. 24.

45 Ibid., pp. 185–6.

46 Gat, *Britain and the Conflict in the Middle East*, p. 13.

47 Ibid., pp. 205–7. McNamara, *Britain, Nasser*, pp. 247–58.

48 Galpern, *Money, Oil and Empire*, pp. 268–9.

49 McNamara, *Britain, Nasser*, p. 275.

50 Brenchley, *Britain and the Middle East*, p. 154.

51 Ferris, *Nasser's Gamble*, p. 295.

52 Johnston, *The Brink of Jordan*, p. 20.

53 Rashid Khalidi, 'Perceptions and Reality: The Arab World and the West', in Louis and Owen, *A Revolutionary Year*, p. 187.

Chapter Eighteen: Oil, Force and Bases

1   Smith, *Britain's Revival and Fall*, pp. 15–16.

2   Simon Smith, *Kuwait* (Oxford, 1999), pp. 106–7.

3 Ibid., p. 66, Parsons, *They Say the Lion*, p. 132. Bernard Burrows, *Footnotes in the Sand* (Salisbury, 1990), p. 134. Sir James Craig, 'Dubai and the Other Trucial States', in Tempest (ed.), *Envoys*, Vol. ii, p. 158.

4 Balfour-Paul, *End of Empire*, p. 149. Peter Mangold, 'The Role of Force in British Policy in the Middle East', *1957–66* (PhD, London, 1973), pp. 173–4.

5 Matthew Parris and Andrew Bryson, *Parting Shots* (London, 2011), pp. 329–30.

6 Sir Donald Hawley, *The Emirates* (Norwich, 2007), p. 54.

7 Burrows, *Footnotes*, p. 56. Brenchley, *Britain and the Middle East*, pp. 133–4. Sir Rupert Hay, *The Persian Gulf States* (Washington, 1959), pp. 23–4.

8 Smith, *Britain's Revival and Fall*, p. 44.

9 Brenchley, *Britain and the Middle East*, pp. 80–1. Edward Henderson, *This Strange Eventful History* (London, 1978), pp. 53–4, 81–2.

10 Ibid., pp. 79–80.

11 Kyle, *Suez*, p. 100.

12 Pearson, *In the Name of Oil*, p. 49. Burrows, *Footnotes*, p. 109.

13 Sir Sam Falle, 'Under Threat of Invasion, 1958', in Tempest (ed.), *Envoys*, Vol. ii, pp. 111–14. Smith, *Kuwait*, pp. 85, 94.

14 Ibid., pp. 92–3. Ashton, *Eisenhower, Macmillan*, pp. 179–80. Ovendale, *Britain, the United States*, pp. 190–1. Macmillan, *Riding the Storm*, p. 523. R.A. Mobley, 'Deterring Iraq: The UK Experience', *INS*, no. 2, 2001, p. 61.

15 Smith, *Kuwait*, pp. 97, 106.

16 Richard Mobley, 'Gauging the Iraq Threat to Kuwait in the 1960s', https://www.cia.gov/library/center-for-the-study.../article03.html.

17 Ashton, 'Britain and the Kuwaiti Crisis', *Diplomacy and Statecraft*, no. 1, 1998, pp. 169–70. Sir Marrack Goulding, 'Kuwait, 1961', 'Britain and the Middle East', MECA. Mobley, 'Deterring Iraq', p. 63.

18 Ibid., Ashton, 'Britain and the Kuwaiti Crisis', p. 173.

19 Goulding, 'Kuwait, 1961'. Helen von Bismarck, *British Policy in the Persian Gulf* (Basingstoke, 2013), pp. 37–49.

20 Smith, *Kuwait*, p. 124.

21 Ibid., pp. 130–1.

22 Balfour-Paul, *End of Empire*, p. 149. Burrows, *Footnotes*, p. 143. Lucas, Papers, pp. 224–5.

23 Smith, *Revival and Fall*, p. 48.

24 Ibid., p. 3. Burrows, *Footnotes*, pp. 35–6.

25 Lucas, Papers, p. 225.

26 Smith, *Kuwait*, p. 49.

27 Catterall (ed.), *Macmillan Cabinet Diaries*, Vol. ii, pp. 50, 52. Macmillan, *Riding*, pp. 270–1. Sir David Lee, *Flight from the Middle East* (London, 1980), p. 126.

28 Ibid., pp. 130–6. Ovendale, *Britain, the United States*, pp. 187–8.

29 Abdel Razzak Takriti, *Monsoon Revolution* (Oxford, 2013), pp. 154–5. John Akenhurst, *We Won a War* (Salisbury, 1982), p. 15. Sir Gawain Bell, *Imperial Twilight* (London, 1989), pp. 175–6, 178, 182.

30 Takriti, *Monsoon Revolution*, pp. 148–50, 193, 195–206. Dorrill, *MI6*, pp. 730–3.

31 Miriam Joyce, 'On the Road towards Unity', *MES*, April 1999, p. 51. Bismarck, *British Policy in the Persian Gulf*, pp. 161–5.

32 Ibid., pp. 170–86. Glen Balfour-Paul, *Bagpipes in Baghdad* (London, 2005), pp. 203–5. Archie Lamb, 'The Shakhbut-Zayid Changeover', in Tempest (ed.), *Envoys*, Vol. ii, p. 150.

33 Lee, *Flight*, p. 264. Balfour-Paul, *Bagpipes*, pp. 198–9. Smith, *Britain's Revival and Fall*, pp. 22–4. Bismarck, *British Policy in the Persian Gulf*, pp. 148–53.

34 Ibid., p. 10. Burrows, *Footnotes*, pp. 36, 64–70.

35 Ibid., p. 65.

36 Lee, *Flight*, pp. 257–8.

37 Mangold, 'The Role of Force', p. 147.

38 Ronald Hyam and William Roger Louis, *The Conservative Government and the End of Empire* (London, 2000), pp. 287–8, 291.

39 Smith, *Britain's Revival and Fall*, p. 151. Burrows, *Footnotes*, p. 128.

40 Gat, *Britain and the Conflict in the Middle East*, p. 146. Tore Petersen, *The Decline of the Anglo-American Middle East* (Brighton, 2006), pp. 112–13.

41 Bismarck, *British Policy in the Persian Gulf*, pp. 194–5.

42 Patrick Gordon-Walker, *The Cabinet* (London, 1970), p. 129. Shohei Sato, 'Britain's Decision to Withdraw from the Persian Gulf', *JICH*, March 2009, p. 108.

43 Ibid., pp. 104–5. Gill Bennett, *Six Moments of Crisis* (Oxford, 2013), p. 106.

44 Bismarck, *British Policy in the Persian Gulf*, p. 210.

45 Louis, *Ends of British Imperialism*, pp. 892, 896–7.

46 Balfour–Paul, *End of the British Empire*, p. 132. Sir Denis Wright, 'Britain and the Withdrawal from the Persian Gulf', St Antony's College Conference, Oxford, 27 May 2000.

47 Louis, *Ends of British Imperialism*, pp. 899–900.

48 Hawley, *The Emirates*, pp. 46–7.

49 Bell, *Imperial Twilight*, chapter 16.

50 FCO8/1804, 'Annual Review, Persian Gulf, 1971'.

51 Sir Charles Johnston, *The View from Steamer Point* (London, 1964), p. 30. Trevaskis, *Shades of Amber*, p. 39. Hinchcliffe et al., *Without Glory in Arabia*, p. 10.

52 Lee, *Flight*, pp. 97, 149–53.

53 Sir William Jackson, *Withdrawal from Empire: A Military Review* (London, 1986), p. 173.

54 Trevaskis, *Shades of Amber*, p. 9.

55 Bell, *Imperial Twilight*, p. 155. Spencer Mawby, 'Britain's Last Imperial Frontier', *JICH*, March 2001, p. 79.

56 Balfour-Paul, *End of the British Empire*, pp. 69–70. Trevaskis, *Shades of Amber*, pp. 85–6.

57 Ibid., p. 135. Mawby, *British Policy in Aden and the Protectorates*, p. 54.

58 Ibid., p. 77. Hyam and Louis, *The Conservative Government and the End of Empire*, p. 559.

59 Catterall (ed.), *Macmillan Cabinet Diaries*, Vol. ii, p. 131. Hinchcliffe et al., *Without Glory*, pp. 40–1.

60 Mawby, 'Britain's Last Imperial Frontier', p. 91.

61 Ibid., pp. 89–91, 94–5. Ferris, *Nasser's Gamble*, pp. 74–5.

62 Trevaskis, *Shades of Amber*, pp. 33–4, 43, 44, 129, 133. Hinchcliffe et al., *Without Glory*, p. 14. Simon Smith, 'Rulers and Residents: Britain's Relations with the Aden Protectorates', *MES*, July 1995, p. 518.

63 Johnston, *View from Steamer Point*, p. 36. Trevaskis, *Shades of Amber*, p. 168.

64 Hyam and Louis, *The Conservative Government and the End of Empire*, pp. 557–69.

65 Mawby, *British Policy in Aden and the Protectorates*, p. 85.

66 S.R. Ashton and William Roger Louis, *East of Suez and the Commonwealth, 1964–71*, Part 1 (London, 2004), p. 278.

67 William Roger Louis, 'Aden: Britain's Withdrawal from the Persian Gulf', St Antony's College Conference, 27 May 2000.

68 Mawby, *British Policy in Aden and the Protectorates*, p. 68. Hinchcliffe et al., *Without Glory*, p. 273.

69 Ibid., pp. 53, 54, 92. Johnston, *View from Steamer Point*, pp. 38–49.

70 Trevaskis, *Shades of Amber*, p. 200.

71 Hyam and Louis, *The Conservative Government and the End of Empire*, p. 642.

72 Hinchcliffe et al., *Without Glory*, pp. 29–30.

73 Julian Paget, *Last Post* (London, 1969), p. 110.

74 Ibid., pp. 115–18. Hinchcliffe et al., *Without Glory*, pp. 43–5.

75 Mawby, *British Policy in Aden and the Protectorates*, p. 129. Bismarck, *British Policy in the Persian Gulf*, pp. 186–91.

76 Hinchcliffe et al., *Without Glory*, p. 273.

77 Ashton and Louis, *East of Suez*, p. 280.

78 Ibid., p. 248.

79 Paget, *Last Post*, p. 115.

80 Ashton and Louis, *East of Suez*, p. 239.

81 Ibid., p. 261.

82 Mawby, *British Policy in Aden and the Protectorates*, p. 174.

83 Ibid., p. 175.

84 Trevelyan, *The Middle East in Revolution*, p. 265.

85 Lapping, *End of Empire*, p. 310.

86 Hinchcliffe et al., *Without Glory*, pp. 243–57.

87 Glen Balfour-Paul, 'Britain and the Withdrawal from the Persian Gulf', St Antony's College Conference, 27 May 2000.

88 Sir Sam Falle, 'My Lucky Life – Withdrawal from Aden', in Tempest (ed.), *Envoys*, Vol. ii, p. 61.

89 Hinchcliffe et al., *Without Glory*, pp. 22–3. See also D.J. McCarthy, 'Lessons from South Arabia', in Ashton and Louis, *East of Suez*, pp. 275–82.

Chapter Nineteen: Just a Trading Nation

1 *Financial Times*, 14 September 1971.
2 David Rich, 'British Muslims and UK Foreign Policy', in Levy and Podeh, *Britain and the Middle East*, pp. 325–6.
3 Brenchley, *Britain and the Middle East*, pp. 211, 305, 310–11.
4 Sir James Craig, 'Britain and the Middle East', Seminar, St Antony's College, Oxford, 1999, MECA.
5 Sir Percy Cradock, *In Pursuit of British Interests* (London, 1997), p. 159.
6 Andrew, *The Defence of the Realm*, pp. 608–9, 648, 691.
7 Ibid., pp. 622–3.
8 Ibid., pp. 703, 746–8.
9 Mangold, *Success and Failure in British Foreign Policy*, p. 89.
10 Philip Ziegler, *Edward Heath* (London, 2010), p. 394. Shlaim, *Lion of Judah*, p. 328.
11 Henry Kissinger, *The White House Years* (London, 1979), p. 618.
12 Ashton, 'A "Special Relationship"', pp. 236–7.
13 Douglas Hurd, *Memoirs* (London, 2003), p. 268.
14 Ashton, 'A "Special Relationship"', pp. 222–3.
15 Sir John Coles, 'Britain and the Middle East', Seminar, St Antony's College, Oxford, 1999, MECA.
16 Thatcher, *The Downing Street Years*, pp. 326–8, 333–4.
17 Mathew Ferraro, *Tough Going* (New York, 2007), p. 67.
18 Ibid., pp. 10–11.
19 Howard Sachar, *Israel and Europe* (New York, 1999), p. 28. David Owen, *Time to Declare* (London, 1991), p. 391.
20 PREM15/1765, Minute, Sir A. Parsons, 12 October 1973.
21 PREM15/1765, Telegram. Washington, 12 October 1973.
22 Alistair Horne, *Kissinger's Year: 1973* (London, 2009), pp. 310–11. Richard Aldrich, *The Hidden Hand* (London, 2001), p. 262. Ferraro, *Tough Going*, p. 107.
23 Ibid., p. 49.
24 Aldrich, *The Hidden Hand*, pp. 289–90.
25 Ziegler, *Heath*, p. 305.
26 PREM15/1767, Carrington-Schlesinger.
27 PREM15/1767, Cromer-Schlesinger.
28 Craig, 'Britain and the Middle East'.
29 Jonathan Rynhold and Jonathan Spyer, 'British Policy in the Arab–Israeli Arena', *BJMES*, August 2007, pp. 148–9.
30 Jack Straw, *Last Man Standing* (London, 2012), pp. 444–5, 447. Lucas, Papers, pp. 110–11.
31 Dave Allen and Andrine Haus, 'The Euro–Arab Dialogue, the Venice Declaration and Beyond', in Daniel Moeckli and Victor Mauer (eds), *European–American Relations and the Middle East* (Abingdon, 2011), pp. 89–90.

32 Rynhold and Spyer, 'British Policy in the Arab–Israeli Arena', p. 150. www.publications.parliament.uk, accessed 6 August 2014.

33 Akenhurst, *We Won a War*, pp. 53–4, 55. Takriti, *Monsoon Revolution*, pp. 284–5, 301, 306.

34 Bell, *Imperial Twilight*, p. 188.

35 Sir Sherard Cowper Coles, *Ever the Diplomat* (London, 2013), p. 273.

36 CAB133/514. Briefs for Prime Minister's Visit to the Gulf, April 1981.

37 Hurd, *Memoirs*, p. 274.

38 Ivor Lucas, *A Road to Damascus* (London, 1997), pp. 141–2.

39 Valerie Yorke, *The Gulf in the 1980s* (London, 1980), p. 41. See chapter 4 for the security problems of the sheikhdoms and Saudi Arabia.

40 Ibid., p. 62.

41 Sir Alan Munro, *An Arabian Affair* (London, 1996), p. 74.

42 FCO8/2217. Secretary of State's Visit to Oman and Saudi Arabia, April 1973. CAB133/514. Brief for the Prime Minister's Visit to the Gulf, April 1981.

43 *Sandhurst and the Sheikhs*, Radio 4, 27 August 2014.

44 Munro, *An Arabian Affair*, pp. 74–5.

45 FCO8/3279. Papers for Incoming Ministers, 6 April 1979.

46 Coles, *Ever the Diplomat*, pp. 260–1.

47 Munro, *An Arabian Affair*, pp. 106–7. FCO8/3292, 'Defence Options Open to the UK in Contribution to the Gulf and Former Central Treaty Organisation Area'.

48 CAB133/514. Brief for the Prime Minister's Visit to the Gulf, April 1981.

49 Speech, Middle East Association, 22 May 1980.

50 FCO8/3739. Yamani-Howell, 20 June 1980. FCO8/3738. Telegrams. Jeddah, 14/15 May 1980. Lucas, *A Road to Damascus*, p. 150.

51 Lord Wright, 'Britain and the Middle East', Seminar, St Antony's College, Oxford, 1999, MECA.

52 Parris and Bryson, *Parting Shots*, p. 136.

53 FCO8/3601, 'Britain's Policy in Iran, 1974–78'.

54 Ibid. Sir A. Parsons, 5 August 1980.

55 FCO8/3601, 'Britain's Policy in Iran'.

56 Sreberny and Torfeh, *Persian Service*, pp. 78–81.

57 FCO8/3601, 'Britain's Policy in Iran'.

58 Mark Phythian, *The Politics of British Arms Sales since 1964* (Manchester, 2000), pp. 246–7.

59 Lucas, Papers, p. 430.

60 Phythian, *The Politics of British Arms Sales*, p. 28. FCO8/3285. Heads of Mission Conference, Arabia, 1979. Lucas, Papers, p. 430.

61 Rosemary Hollis, *Britain and the Middle East in the 9/11 Era* (London, 2010), p. 169.

62 *Financial Times*, 20 February 2014.

63 Lucas, Papers, p. 423.

64 FCO8/3601, 'Britain's Policy in Iran'.

65 FCO8/3601, Sir A. Parsons, 5 August 1980. Owen, *Time to Declare*, p. 391.

66 Ibid., p. 395. FCO8/3601, 'Britain's Policy in Iran'.

67 Sreberny and Torfeh, *Persian Service*, pp. 78, 94.

68 Arbuthnott et al., *British Embassies around the Gulf*, pp. 46–7.

69 Sreberny and Torfeh, *Persian Service*, p. 113.

70 Owen, *Time to Declare*, pp. 391–2.

71 *The Economist*, 24 January 2015. Timothy Garton Ash, 'Defying the Assassin's Veto', *New York Review of Books*, 19 February 2015.

Chapter Twenty: A Return to the Gulf

1 Roula Khalaf, 'The Spring has Ended but its Dreams Live on', *Financial Times*, 16 October 2014.

2 Cradock, *In Pursuit of British Interests*, p. 170.

3 Prince Khaled bin Sultan, *Desert Warrior* (London, 1995) p. 172. Richard Haas, *War of Necessity, War of Choice* (New York, 2009), p. 132.

4 George Bush and Brent Scowcroft, *A World Transformed* (New York, 1998), pp. 319–20.

5 Sir Alan Munro, 'Britain and the Middle East', Seminar, St Antony's College Oxford, 1999. John Major, *The Autobiography* (London, 1999), p. 220.

6 Thatcher, *The Downing Street Years*, p. 235.

7 James Baker, *The Politics of Diplomacy* (New York, 1995), p. 281.

8 Khaled bin Sultan, *Desert Warrior*, p. 261.

9 Munro, *An Arabian Affair*, pp. 98–9, 182, 187.

10 Ibid., pp. 223–4. Hurd, *Memoirs*, p. 410.

11 Munro, *An Arabian Affair*, pp. 169, 184. General Sir Peter de la Billière, *Storm Command* (London, 1992), pp. 80, 82, 100.

12 Ibid., pp. 81, 83, 143.

13 Cradock, *In Pursuit of British Interests*, pp. 173–4.

14 Bush and Scowcroft, *World Transformed*, p. 383.

15 Ibid., p. 430.

16 Ibid., p. 463. Cradock, *In Pursuit of British Interests*, p. 176.

17 Brian Jones, *Failing Intelligence* (London, 2010), pp. 24–5.

18 De la Billière, *Storm Command*, p. 304.

19 Bush and Scowcroft, *World Transformed*, pp. 443, 448, 463–4.

20 Major, *Autobiography*, p. 240.

21 Bush and Scowcroft, *World Transformed*, p. 463.

22 Radio 4, 27 January 2003. Haas, *War of Necessity, War of Choice*, pp. 129–31. Cradock, *In Pursuit of British Interests*, p. 179.

23 Ibid., pp. 181–2. Munro, *An Arabian Affair*, pp. 339–40, Anthony Seldon, *Major* (London, 1997), p. 163.

24 Evidence to Chilcot Enquiry (CE), Weapons of Mass Destruction, 24 November 2009.

25 Rogan, *The Arab*s, pp. 455–6.

26 Cradock, *In Pursuit of British Interests*, pp. 182–3. Kofi Annan, *Interventions* (New York, 2012), p. 320. 'Decade of Regrets', *The Economist*, 10 March 2013.

27 Tony Blair, *A Journey* (London, 2010), p. 222. Barry Lando, *Web of Deceit* (New York, 2007), p. 298. Jones, *Failing Intelligence*, pp. 48–9.

28 Parris and Bryson, *Parting Shots*, p. 139.

29 CE. Evidence. Sir John Sawers, 10 December 2009. Jonathan Powell, 15 December 2009. Geoffrey Hoon, 19 January 2010. Annan, *Interventions*, pp. 321, 324.

30 Jones, *Failing Intelligence*, p. 51.

31 David Rothkopf, *National Insecurity: American Leadership in an Age of Fear* (New York, 2014), p. 30. Mark Danner, 'Rumsfeld's War and its Consequences Now', *New York Review of Books*, 19 December 2013.

32 Andrew Rawnsley, *The End of the Party* (London, 2010), pp. 85–6.

33 Mark Danner, 'Rumsfeld: Why We Live in his Ruins', *New York Review of Books*, 6 February 2014.

34 George W. Bush, *Decision Points* (New York, 2010), p. 140.

35 Rawnsley, *End of the Party*, p. 89. Patrick Porter, 'Iraq, Afghanistan and the Special Relationship', *International Affairs*, December 2010, pp. 359–60.

36 BBC 2, 9 May 2013.

37 Ibid., p. 174. Jonathan Bailey, 'The Political Context', in Jonathan Bailey, Richard Iron and Hew Strachan, *British Generals in Blair's Wars* (Farnham, 2013), p. 7.

38 David Owen, *The Hubris Syndrome* (London, 2007).

39 Ibid., CE. Evidence, Tony Blair, 21 January 2011.

40 CE. Evidence, Tony Blair, 29 January 2010, 21 January 2011.

41 CE. Evidence, Weapons of Mass Destruction, 25 November 2009. Chris Mullen, *A View from the Foothills* (London, 2009), 15 January 2003.

42 David Reynolds, *Summits* (London, 2007), pp. 395–6. Owen, *The Hubris Syndrome*, pp. 32, 100, 103.

43 CE. Evidence, Sir John Scarlett, 8 December 2009.

44 John Morrison, 'British Intelligence Failure in Iraq', *INS*, 2011, no. 4.

45 CE. Evidence, Dame Eliza Manningham-Buller, 20 July 2010.

46 Jones, *Failing Intelligence*, pp. 48–9.

47 Rothkopf, *National Insecurity*, p. 30.

48 CE. Evidence, Geoffrey Hoon, 19 January 2010, p. 24, 12 January 2010. Clare Short, 2 February 2010. Tony Blair, 29 January 2010.

49 Charles Tripp, 'Trapped in the Vortex', *World Today*, February/March 2013, p. 24.

50 Max Rodenbeck, 'Iraq: The Outlaw State', *New York Review of Books*, 25 September 2014.

51 Ibid.

52 CE. Evidence, Sir Kevin Tebbit, 3 December 2009.

53 CE. Evidence, Sir David Manning, 30 November 2009. Donald Rumsfeld, *Known and Unknown* (New York, 2011), p. 487.

54 CE. Evidence, Lord Jay, 30 June 2010. Sir Jeremy Greenstock, 15 December 2009. Dominick Chilcott, 8 December 2009. Major-General Tim Cross, 7 December 2009.

55 CE. Evidence, Tony Blair, 29 January 2010.

56 Frank Ledwidge, *Losing Small Wars* (London, 2012), p. 17.

57 Rory Stewart, *Occupational Hazards* (London, 2007), p. 430.

58 'Run Out of Town: How the British Army Lost Basra', *Financial Times*, 21 August 2007.

59 Ledwidge, *Losing*, p. 34.

60 Stewart, *Occupational Hazards*, pp. 81–2, 169–70. Sir Hilary Synnott, *Bad Days in Basra* (London, 2008), pp. 48, 65.

61 CE. Evidence, Sir Jeremy Greenstock, 15 December 2009. Ledwidge, *Losing*, p. 5. 'Hoon Deploys One-Third of RAF Aircraft to the Gulf', *Financial Times*, 7 February 2003.

62 Geraint Hughes, 'Iraqnopobia', *RUSIJ*, December 2012, p. 57.

63 'Run Out of Town', *Financial Times*, 21 August 2007. Ledwidge, *Losing*, p. 57. Hughes, 'Iraqnopobia', p. 56.

64 Richard Iron, 'The Charge of the Knights', *RUSIJ*, February/March 2013, p. 55.

65 Ledwidge, *Losing*, p. 259.

66 Hughes, 'Iraqnopobia', p. 54.

67 Max Rodenbeck, 'Iraq'.

68 *More or Less*, Radio 4, 13 May 2011.

69 Tripp, 'Trapped in the Vortex', p. 24.

70 *Financial Times*, 9 September 2010, 16 June 2013.

71 'Imams Urge Restraint over Prophet Cartoon', *Financial Times*, 15 February 2015.

72 CE. Evidence, Dame Eliza Manningham–Buller, 20 July 2010.

73 Speech, Theresa May, BBC News, 24 November 2014. *National Security Strategy and 2015 Strategic and Defence Review*, Cm 9161; 'Cameron Steps Up UK's Fight Against ISIS', *Financial Times*, 3 July 2015; 'Cameron to Tell Putin to Focus on Fighting ISIS', *Financial Times*, 16 November 2015; 'Osborne Raises Spectre of ISIS Cyber Attacks', *Financial Times*, 18 November 2015.

74 Sir Nigel Scheinwald, Radio 4, 18 July 2014.

75 'Cameron Rules Out "Shock and Awe"' Strategy, *Financial Times*, 27/28 September 2014.

76 *Financial Times*, 10 February 2011.

77 Jon Moran, *From Northern Ireland to Afghanistan* (Farnham, 2013), p. 153.

78 'Keeping Up Appearances', *The Economist*, 11 March 2015.

79 'A Divided Land', *Financial Times*, 24 March 2015.

80 'Jihad by Social Media', *Financial Times*, 29/30 March 2014.

81 General Sir David Richards, *Taking Command* (London, 2014), pp. 320–1.

82 *The Economist*, 7 September 2013, Alistair Burt, 'Vote that Ties Britain's Hands', *The World Today*, February/March 2014, pp. 30–3.

83 Ramzy Mardini, 'Obama Revives the Failed Logic of the War on Terror', *Financial Times*, 25 September 2014.

84 *The Economist*, 31 December 2011.

85 'Cameron Rules Out "Shock and Awe" Strategy', *Financial Times*, 27/28 September 2014.

86 'House Sceptical, Even Fearful of Intervention', *Financial Times*, 27 August 2014.

87 'Isis Hones Foreign Policy to Expand Abroad'. *Financial Times*, 28 September 2015

88 Reynolds, *Summits*, p. 393.

89 *National Security Strategy and 2015 Strategic and Defence Review*, Cm 9161.

Chapter Twenty-One: Matters of Scruple

1 Louis, *British Empire*, pp. 469–70.

2 Hyam, *Britain's Imperial Century*, p. 49. Tuchman, *Bible and Sword*, p. 161.

3 Hourani, *History*, p. 301. Sherman, *Mandate Days*, p. 33.

4 Marston, *Britain's Imperial Role in the Red Sea Area*, p. 69.

5 Satia, *Spies in Arabia*, pp. 248, 252.

6 Boyle, *Boyle of Cairo*, pp. 49–51.

7 Ibid. Lloyd, *Egypt since Cromer*, Vol. i, p. 75.

8 Kazemzadeh, *Russia and Britain in Persia*, p. 340.

9 Rendel, *The Sword and the Olive*, p. 130.

10 Stephen Longrigg, 'The Decline of the West', *International Affairs*, July 1953, p. 333.

11 Tignor, *Modernisation and British Colonial Rule in Egypt*, p. 122.

12 Trevaskis, *Shades of Amber*, p. 12.

13 'Britain in Palestine', SOAS Exhibition, 2012.

14 Wright, *The English*, pp. 44–6.

15 Jones, *Britain and the Yemen Civil War*, p. 68.

16 Paris, *Britain, the Hashemites and Arab Rule*, p. 290.

17 Parris and Bryson, *Parting Shots*, p. 239.

18 Al-Enazy, The *Creation of Saudi Arabia*, p. 34.

19 Sabahi, *British Policy in Persia*, p. 191. Meyer and Brysac, *Kingmakers*, p. 316. Waterfield, *Professional Diplomat*, p. 164.

20 Burrows, *Footnotes in the Sand*, p. 16.

21 *Peel Report*, pp. 147, 379.

22 Trevaskis, *Shades of Amber*, pp. 65–6, 132, 133.

23 Hinchcliffe et al., *Without Glory*, p. 209.

24 Ibid., pp. 75, 160–4. Mawby, *British Policy in Aden and the Protectorates*, p. 152.

25 Louis, *Ends of British Imperialism*, p. 877.

26 Alex Stirling, 'The End of British Protection', in Tempest (ed.), *Envoys*, Vol. ii, p. 124.

27 Lawrence, *Seven Pillars of Wisdom*, pp. 282–3.

28 Wilson, *Lawrence of Arabia*, p. 404. Kedourie, *In the Anglo-Arab Labyrinth*, p. 252.

29 Friesel, 'British Officials and the Situation in Palestine', p. 200.

30 Peter Hennessy, *Having it So Good* (London, 2006), p. 438.

31 Ibid., p. 438.

32 Bell, *Britain and France*, Vol. ii, p. 153.

33 Steiner, *Britain and the Origins of the First World War*, p. 83.

34 Dickson, *Kuwait and her Neighbours*, p. 276.

35 Hoffman, *Anonymous Soldiers*, pp. 398–9.
36 William Roger Louis, 'Britain and the Crisis of 1958', in Louis and Owen, *A Revolutionary Year*, p. 66.
37 Smith, *Kuwait*, p. 44.
38 Ivor Lucas, Papers, p. 430.
39 David Gardner, *Last Chance in the Middle East* (London, 2009), pp. 172–3.
40 Catterall (ed.), *The Macmillan Cabinet Diaries*, Vol. ii, p. 292.
41 Trevelyan, *The Middle East in Revolution*, p. 129.
42 Lewis Johnman, 'Playing the Role of Cassandra', in Kelly and Gorst, *Whitehall and the Suez Crisis*, p. 47.
43 Ibid., pp. 46–62.
44 Hennessy, *Having it So Good*, p. 428.
45 Catterall (ed.), *Macmillan Cabinet Diaries*, Vol. ii, 16 July 1958.
46 Hennessy, *Having it So Good*, p. 426.
47 CE. Evidence, Lord Boyce, 13 December 2009. Tony Blair, 14 January 2011.
48 Philippe Sands, *Lawless World* (London, 2006), p. 175.
49 Ibid., pp. 187–93. CE. Summary by Sir Roderick Lyne, 29 January 2010. Tom Bingham, *The Rule of Law* (London, 2010), pp. 123–6.
50 Ibid., p. 110.
51 Naguib Mahfouz, *Sugar Street* (London, 1994 edn), p. 175.
52 Jacob Norris, 'Repression and Rebellion: Britain's Response to the Arab Revolt in Palestine', *JICH*, no. 1, 2008. Matthew Hughes, 'Lawlessness was the Law', in Rory Miller (ed.), *Britain, Palestine and Empire* (Farnham, 2010), p. 145.
53 Ibid., pp. 147–8. Ian Cobain, *Cruel Britannia* (London, 2012), pp. 102–3.
54 Ibid., p. 103.
55 Ibid., pp. 148–9.
56 Ibid., p. 156.
57 Mawby, *British Policy in Aden and the Protectorates*, p. 169.
58 Owen, *Cromer*, pp. 301–3.
59 Shepherd, *Ploughing Sand*, pp. 211–14.
60 Terry, *The Wafd*, p. 171.
61 Victoria Schofield, *Wavell* (London, 2006), p. 188.
62 Eric Grove and Sally Rohan, 'The Limits of Opposition', in Kelly and Gorst, *Whitehall and the Suez Crisis*, pp. 101, 106, 110, 112.
63 Satia, *Spies in Arabia*, p. 303.
64 Towle, *Pilots and Rebels*, pp. 20–1. Omissi, *Air Power*, p. 163.
65 Olson, *Anglo-Iranian Relations during the First World War*, pp. 70–1.
66 Joseph Nero, 'Al-Haji Amin and the British during the Second World War', *MES*, June 1984, p. 11. Jones, *Britain and the Yemen Civil War*, p. 95.
67 Dorrill, *MI6*, pp. 610, 613–14.
68 Jones, 'The Preferred Plan', p. 409.
69 Ward Thomas, *The Ethics of Destruction* (Ithaca, 2001), pp. 47, 78. Dorrill, *MI6*, pp. 735–7, 793.

70 Bonakdarian, *Britain and the Iranian Constitutional Revolution*, p. 175.

71 Gilmour, *Curzon*, p. 79.

72 Johnston, *Brink of Jordan*, p. 78.

73 Rashid Khalidi, 'Perceptions and Reality', in Louis and Owen, *A Revolutionary Year in the Middle Eas*t, pp. 192–3, 198–9.

74 *Financial Times*, 23 February 2011.

75 McLean, *Britain and her Buffer State*, p. 91.

76 Hollis, *Britain and the Middle East in the 9/11 Era*, p. 176.

77 Coles, *Ever the Diplomat*, p. 283. Philip Hammond, BBC News, 6 December 2014.

78 Mustapha Kamel al-Sayyid. 'The UK and the Question of Democracy Promotion in Egypt', in Brehony and El-Desouky, *British–Egyptian Relations*, pp. 85–7.

79 'Cameron Ardent in Support of Rebels in Libya', *Financial Times*, 10 March 2011.

80 Philip Stephens, *Financial Times*, 22 March 2011.

81 Bonakdarian, *Britain and the Iranian Constitutional Revolution*, pp. 91–6.

82 *The Iraq War*, BBC 2, 29 May 2013.

83 *Any Questions*, Radio 4, 13 May 2011.

84 BBC 4, 15 July 2011.

85 John Fisher, 'Man on the Spot', *MES*, March 2008, p. 227.

86 Bonakdarian, *Britain and the Iranian Constitutional Revolution*, p. 196.

87 Steiner, *Britain and the Origins of the First World War*, pp. 142–3.

88 Kyle, *Suez*, p. 563.

89 Owen, *Time to Declare*, p. 401.

90 John Young, 'Conclusion', in Kelly and Gorst, *Whitehall and the Suez Crisis*, pp. 226–7. Burrows, *Footnotes*, pp. 85–6. Jones, *Failing Intelligence*, p. 95. Falle, *My Lucky Life*, p. 98.

91 Sands, *Lawless World*, pp. 175–6.

92 Mansfield, *Britain in Egypt*, p. 324. Hopwood, 'Earth's Proud Empires Pass Away', p. 120.

Chapter Twenty-Two: How Did the British Do?

1 Crowe, 'Account'.

2 Bell, *Shadows on the Sand*, pp. 247–8.

3 Peter Mangold, *Superpower Intervention in the Middle East* (Abingdon, 2013 edn), p. 115.

4 Philip Stephens, 'The Half-hearted Threat to the US Superpower', *Financial Times*, 28 November 2014.

5 Jonathan Bailey, 'The Political Context', in Bailey et al., *Britain's Generals in Blair's Wars*, p. 24.

6 Falle, *My Lucky Life*, pp. 135–8.

7 Easter, 'Spying on Nasser', p. 827.

8 'A Missed Moment', *Financial Times*, 15 December 2010.

9 'Britain's Withdrawal from the Persian Gulf', Conference, St Antony's College, Oxford, 27 May 2000. Monroe, *Britain's Moment*, pp. 317–19.

10 Parsons, *They Say the Lion*, p. 54.

11 Straw, *Last Man Standing*, p. 442.

12 Mostafa El-Feki, 'Britain and Egypt', in Brehony and El-Desouky, *British–Egyptian Relations*, p. 59.

13 Galpern, *Money, Oil and Empire*, p. 83.

14 Hopwood, 'Earth's Proud Empires Pass Away', p. 118. Longrigg, 'The Decline of the West', pp. 328–9.

15 Michael Fry and Itamar Rabinovich, *Despatches from Damascus* (Tel Aviv, 1985), p. 136.

16 Klieman, *Foundations of British Policy in the Arab World*, p. 253.

17 Kwarteng, *Ghosts of Empire*, p. 262.

18 Louis, *Ends of British Imperialism*, pp. 21–2.

19 Michael Peel, 'Complex Roots of Nigeria's Deadly Insurgency', *Financial Times*, 23 March 2015.

20 Sluglett, *Britain in Iraq*, p. 211.

21 David Runciman, 'Unsafe for Democracy', *Financial Times*, 27 August 2014.

22 De Bellaigue, *Patriot of Persia*, pp. 273–4.

Select Bibliography

Diaries, Memoirs, Papers

Akenhurst, Brigadier John, *We Won a War: The Campaign in Oman, 1965–75* (Salisbury, 1982).

Ashton, S.R. and William Roger Louis (eds), *East of Suez and the Commonwealth, 1964–1971: British Documents on the End of Empire*. Part 1: *East of Suez Series A*, Vol. v (London, 2004).

Balfour-Paul, Glen, *Bagpipes in Baghdad* (London, 2005).

Bell, Sir Gawain, *Shadows on the Sand* (London, 1983).

——, *An Imperial Twilight* (London, 1989).

Bentwich, Norman and Helen, *Mandate Memories, 1918–1948* (London, 1965).

Billière, Sir Peter de la, *Storm Command: A Personal Account of the Gulf War* (London, 1992).

Blair, Tony, *A Journey* (London, 2011).

'Britain and the Middle East', Seminar Series, 1999, Middle East Centre Archive, St Antony's College, Oxford.

'British Diplomatic Oral History Programme', Churchill College, Cambridge.

Burrell, R.M. (ed.), *Iran Political Diaries, 1881–1965*, Vols viii–xiv (Chippenham, 1997).

Burrows, Sir Bernard, *Footnotes in the Sand: The Gulf in Transition* (Salisbury, 1990).

Catterall, Peter (ed.), *The Macmillan Diaries: The Cabinet Years, 1950–57* (London, 2003), Vol. ii (London, 2011).

Cecil, Lord Edward, *The Leisure of an Egyptian Official* (London, 1921).

Chirol, Sir Valentine, *Fifty Years in a Changing World* (London, 1927).

Coles, Sir Sherard Cowper, *Ever the Diplomat* (London, 2013).

Collins, Robert (ed.), *An Arabian Diary: Sir Gilbert Clayton* (Berkley, 1969).

Evans, Trefor (ed.), *The Killearn Diaries, 1934–1946* (London, 1972).

Falle, Sir Sam, *My Lucky Life: In War, Revolution, Peace and Diplomacy* (Lewes, 1996).

Glubb, Sir John, *War in the Desert: An RAF Frontier Campaign* (London, 1960).

Goldsworthy, David (ed.), *The Conservative Government and the End of Empire, 1951–1957*, Part 1: *International Relations* (London, 1994).

Grafftey-Smith, Sir Lawrence, *Bright Levant* (London, 1970).

Hill, Roderic, *The Baghdad Airmail* (Stroud, 2005 edn).

Hyam, Ronald and William Roger Louis (eds), *The Conservative Government and the End of Empire: British Documents on the End of Empire*, Part 1: *High Policy, Political and Constitutional Change* (London, 2000).

Johnston, Sir Charles, *The View from Steamer Point* (London, 1964).

——, *The Brink of Jordan* (London, 1972).

Kirkbride, Sir Alex, *A Crackle of Thorns: Experiences in the Middle East* (London, 1956).

Lucas, Ivor, *A Road to Damascus: Mostly Diplomatic Memoirs from the Middle East* (London, 1997).

——, Collected Papers, 1947–1999 (no publisher).

Macmillan, Harold, *Memoirs*, Vols iii–vi (London, 1969–73).

McGhee, George, *Envoy to the World: Adventures in Diplomacy* (New York, 1983).

Munro, Sir Alan, *An Arabian Affair: Politics and Diplomacy behind the Gulf War* (London, 1996).

Owen, David, *Time to Declare* (London, 1991).

Palestine Royal Commission Report (London, Cmnd. 5749, 1937).

Parris, Matthew and Andrew Bryson, *Parting Shots* (London, 2011).

Parsons, Sir Anthony, *They Say the Lion: Britain's Legacy to the Arabs* (London, 1986).

Rendel, Sir George, *The Sword and the Olive: Recollections of Diplomacy and the Foreign Service, 1913–54* (London, 1957).

Ryan, Sir Alan, *The Last of the Dragomans* (London, 1951).

Selwyn Lloyd, Lord, *Suez, 1956: A Personal Account* (London, 1978).

Shuckburgh, Sir Evelyn, *Descent to Suez: Diaries 1951–1956* (London, 1986).

Sonbel, Amira El-Azhary, *The Last Khedive of Egypt: Memoirs of Abbas Hilmi II* (Reading, 1998).

Stark, Freya, *Dust in the Lion's Paw: Autobiography, 1939–46* (London, 1961).

Stewart, Rory, *Occupational Hazards: My Time Governing in Iraq* (London, 2007).

Storrs, Sir Ronald, *Orientations* (London, 1937).

Straw, Jack, *Last Man Standing: Memoirs of a Political Survivor* (London, 2012).

Trevaskis, Sir Kennedy, *Shades of Amber: A South Arabian Episode* (London, 1968).

Trevelyan, Lord, *The Middle East in Revolution* (London, 1979).

Weizmann, Chaim, *Trial and Error: The Autobiography of Chaim Weizmann* (London, 1949).

Woodhouse, C.M., *Something Ventured* (London, 1982).

Yapp, Malcolm (ed.), *Politics and Diplomacy in Egypt: The Diaries of Sir Miles Lampson, 1935–37* (Oxford, 1987).

Secondary Sources

Adelson, Roger, *Mark Sykes: Portrait of an Amateur* (London, 1975).

——, *London and the Invention of the Middle East: Money, Power and War, 1902–1922* (New Haven, 1995).

Ahmad, Ishtiaq, *Anglo-Iranian Relations, 1905–1919* (London, 1974).

Alangari, Haifa, *The Struggle for Power in Arabia: Ibn Sa'ud, Hussein and Great Britain, 1914–1924* (Reading, 1998).

Allawi, Ali, *Faisal I of Iraq* (New Haven, 2014).

Almog, Orna, *Britain, Israel and the United States, 1955–58* (London, 2003).

Alon, Yoav, *The Making of Jordan: Tribes, Colonialism and the Modern State* (London, 2007).

Anderson, M.S., *The Eastern Question, 1774–1923: A Study in International Relations* (London, 1966).

Andrew, Christopher, *Defence of the Realm: The Authorized History of MI5* (London, 2009).

Antonius, George, *The Arab Awakening: The Story of the Arab National Movement* (London, 1938).

Arbuthnott, Hugh, Terence Clark and Richard Muir, *British Missions Around the Gulf: Iran, Iraq, Kuwait, Oman, 1575–2005* (Folkestone, 2008).

Ashton, Nigel, *Eisenhower, Macmillan and the Problem of Nasser: Anglo-American Relations and Arab Nationalism, 1955–1959* (Basingstoke, 1996).

Avery, Peter, *Modern Iran* (London, 1965).

Bailey, Jonathan, Richard Iron and Hew Strachan, *Britain's General in Blair's Wars* (Farnham, 2013).

Balfour-Paul, Glen, *The End of Empire in the Middle East: The Relinquishment of Power in Her Last Three Arab Dependencies* (Cambridge, 1991).

Barr, James, *Setting the Desert on Fire: T.E. Lawrence and Britain's Secret War in Arabia, 1916–1918* (London, 2007).

——, *A Line in the Sand: Britain, France and the Struggle for the Mastery of the Middle East* (London, 2011).

Bell, P.M.H., *France and Britain, 1900–1940: Entente and Estrangement* (Harlow, 1996).

——, *1940–1994: The Long Separation* (Harlow, 1997).

Bethell, Nicholas, *The Palestine Triangle: The Struggle between the British, the Jews and the Arabs, 1935–1945* (London, 1979).

Biger, Gideon, *An Empire in the Holy Land: Historical Geography of the British Administration in Palestine, 1917–39* (Jerusalem, 1994).

Bonakdarian, Mansour, *Britain and the Iranian Constitutional Revolution of 1906–1914: Foreign Policy, Imperialism and Dissent* (New York, 2006).

Bradshaw, Tancred, *Britain and Jordan: Imperial Strategy, King Abdullah I and the Zionist Movement* (London, 2012).

Brehony, Noel and Ayman El-Desouky (eds), *British–Egyptian Relations: From Suez to the Present Day* (London, 2007).

Brenchley, Frank, *Britain and the Middle East: An Economic History, 1945–1987* (London, 1989).

Bullock, Alan, *Ernest Bevin: Foreign Secretary* (Oxford, 1983).

Busch, Briton Cooper, *Britain and the Persian Gulf, 1894–1914* (Berkley, 1967).

——, *Britain, India and the Arabs: 1914–21* (Berkley, 1971).

Butt, Gerald, *The Lion in the Sand: The British in the Middle East* (London, 1995).

Cable, James, *Intervention at Abadan* (Basingstoke, 1991).

Catherwood, Christopher, *Churchill's Folly: How Winston Churchill Created Modern Iraq* (New York, 2004).

Charmley, John, *Lord Lloyd and the Decline of the British Empire* (London, 1987).

Charteris, David, *The British Army and the Jewish Insurgency in Palestine, 1945–1947* (Basingstoke, 1989).

Cobain, Ian, *Cruel Britannia: A Secret History of Torture* (London, 2012).

Cohen, Michael, *Retreat from the Mandate: The Making of British Policy, 1936–1945* (London, 1978).

Cohen, Michael and Martin Kolinsky (eds), *Britain and the Middle East in the 1930s: Security Problems, 1935–1939* (Basingstoke, 1992).

——, *Demise of the British Empire in the Middle East: Britain's Response to the Nationalist Movements, 1943–1955* (London, 1998).

Cohen, Stuart, *British Policy in Mesopotamia, 1903–1914* (London, 1976).

Cooper, Artemis, *Cairo in the War, 1939–1945* (London, 1989).

Cradock, Sir Percy, *In Pursuit of British Interests: Reflections on Foreign Policy under Margaret Thatcher and John Major* (London, 1997).

Craig, Sir James, *Shemlan: A History of the Middle East Centre for Arab Studies* (Basingstoke, 1998).

Cromer, Lord, *Abbas II* (London, 1915).

Daly, M.W. (ed.), *The Cambridge History of Egypt*, Vol. ii (Cambridge, 1998).

Dann, Uriel (ed.), *Studies in the History of Transjordan: The Making of a State, 1920–1924* (Boulder, CO and London, 1984).

——, *The Great Powers in the Middle East, 1919–1939* (New York and London, 1988).

Darwin, John, *Britain, Egypt, and the Middle East: Imperial Policy in the Aftermath of War* (London, 1981).

——, *The Empire Project: The Rise and Fall of the British World System* (Cambridge, 2009).

——, *Unfinished Empire: The Global Expansion of Britain* (London, 2012).

De Bellaigue, Christopher, *Patriot of Persia: Muhammad Mossadegh and a Very British Coup* (London, 2012).

Deeb, Marius, *Party Politics in Egypt: The Wafd and its Rivals, 1919–1939* (London, 1979).

Dickson, H.R.P., *Kuwait and its Neighbours* (London, 1956).

Dodge, Toby, *An Arabian Prince, English Gentlemen and the Tribes East of the River Jordan: Abdullah and the Creation and Consolidation of the Trans-Jordanian State* (London, 1994).

——, *Inventing Iraq: The Failure of Nation-Building and a History Denied* (London, 2003).

Dorrill, Stephen, *MI6: Fifty Years of Special Operations* (London, 2000).

Elliott, Major-General Christopher, *High Command: British Military Leadership in the Iraq and Afghanistan Wars* (London, 2015).

Elliot, Matthew, *Independent Iraq: The Monarchy and British Influence, 1941–1958* (London, 1996).

Elpeleg, Zvi, *The Grand Mufti: Haj Amin al-Hussaini, Founder of the Palestine National Movement* (London, 1993).

Elwell-Sutton, L.P., *Persian Oil: A Study in Power Politics* (London, 1955).

Al-Enazy, Askar, *The Creation of Saudi Arabia: Ibn Sa'ud and British Imperial Policy, 1914–1927* (Abingdon, 2010).

Farnie, D.A., *East and West of Suez: The Suez Canal in History, 1854–1956* (Oxford, 1969).

Ferraro, Matthew, *Tough Going: Anglo-American Relations and the Yom Kippur War of 1973* (New York, 2007).

Ferrier, R.W., *The History of the British Petroleum Company*, Vol. i: *The Developing Years, 1901–1932* (Cambridge, 1982).

Ferris, Jesse, *Nasser's Gamble: How Intervention in Yemen Caused the Six Day War and the Decline of Egyptian Power* (Cambridge, 2013).

Fieldhouse, D.K., *Western Imperialism in the Middle East, 1914–1958* (Oxford, 2006).

Fisher, John, *Curzon and British Imperialism in the Middle East, 1916–1919* (London, 1999).

Fitzsimon, M.A., *Empire by Treaty: Britain and the Middle East in the Twentieth Century* (Notre Dame, 1964).

Fromkin, David, *A Peace to End all Peace: Creating the Modern Middle East, 1914–1922* (London, 1991 edn).

Galpern, Steven, *Money, Oil and Empire in the Middle East: Sterling and Post-War Imperialism, 1944–1971* (Cambridge, 2009).

Gat, Moshe, *Britain and the Conflict in the Middle East, 1964–1967* (Westport, CT, 2003).

Gaury, Gerald de, *Three Kings in Baghdad: The Tragedy of Iraq's Monarchy* (London, 2008 edn).

Gavin, R.J., *Aden Under British Rule, 1839–1967* (London, 1965).

Gifford, Prosser and William Roger Louis (eds), *Britain and France in Africa* (Yale, 1971).

Gilmour, Ian, *Curzon* (London, 1994).

Glubb, Sir John, *The Story of the Arab Legion* (London, 1948).

——, *Britain and the Arabs* (London, 1959).

Gomma, Ahmed, *The Foundation of the League of Arab States: Wartime Diplomacy and Inter-Arab Politics, 1941–1945* (London, 1977).

Greaves, Rose, *Persia and the Defence of India, 1884–1892: A Study in the Foreign Policy of the Third Marquess of Salisbury* (London, 1959).

Grigg, John, *Lloyd George: War Leader, 1916–18* (London, 2002).

Harrison, Robert, *Gladstone's Imperialism in Egypt: Techniques of Domination* (Westport, CT, 1995).

Hay, Sir Rupert, *The Persian Gulf States* (Washington, 1959).

Heikal, Mohammad, *Nasser: The Cairo Documents* (London, 1972).

——, *Cutting the Lion's Tail: Suez through Egyptian Eyes* (London, 1986).

Heiss, Mary Ann, *Empire and Nationhood: The United States, Great Britain and Iranian Oil* (New York, 1997).

Hennessy, Peter, *Having it So Good: Britain in the Fifties* (London, 2006).

Hinchcliffe, Peter, John Ducker and Maria Holt, *Without Glory in Arabia: The British Retreat from Aden* (London, 2006).

Hirsowicz, Lukasz, *The Third Reich and the Arab East* (London, 1966).

Holland, Robert, *Blue Water Empire: The British in the Mediterranean since 1800* (London, 2011).

Hollis, Rosemary, *Britain and the Middle East in the 9/11 Era* (London, 2010).

Hopwood, Derek, *Tales of Empire: The British in the Middle East, 1880–1952* (London, 1989).

Horne, Alistair, *Macmillan*, Vols i and ii (London, 1988, 1989).

Hoskins, Halford, *British Routes to India* (London, 1966 edn).

Hourani, Albert, *A History of the Arab Peoples* (London, 1991 edn).

Hughes, Matthew, *Allenby and British Strategy in the Middle East, 1917–1919* (London, 1999).

Huneidi, Sahar, *A Broken Trust: Herbert Samuel, Zionism and the Palestinians, 1920–25* (London, 2001).

Hunter, Archie, *Power and Passion in Egypt: A Life of Sir Eldon Gorst* (London, 2007).

Hyam, Ronald, *Britain's Imperial Century, 1815–1914: A Study of Empire and Expansion* (London, 1976).

Ibrahim, Hassan Ahmed, *The 1936 Anglo-Egyptian Treaty* (Khartoum, 1976).

Ingram, Edward, *In Defence of British India, 1775–1882* (London, 1984).

Ireland, Philip, *Iraq: A Study in Political Development* (London, 1937).

James, Laura, *Nasser at War: Arab Images of the Enemy* (Basingstoke, 2006).

James, Lawrence, *The Rise and Fall of the British Empire* (London, 1998 edn).

Jarvis, C.S., *Arab Command: The Biography of Lieut.-Col. F.G. Peake Pasha* (London, 1943).

Jones, Brian, *Failing Intelligence: The True Story of How We Were Fooled into Going to War in Iraq* (London, 2010).

Jones, Clive, *Britain and the Yemen Civil War, 1962–1965: Foreign Policy and the Limits of Covert Action: Ministers, Mercenaries and Mandarins* (Brighton, 2004).

Joyce, Miriam, *Kuwait: 1945–1956 – An Anglo-American Perspective* (London, 1998).

Kampfner, John, *Blair's Wars* (London, 2003).

Karsh, Efraim and Inari, *Empires of the Sand: The Struggle for Mastery of the Middle East, 1789–1923* (Cambridge, MA, 1999).

Katouzian, Homa, *Mussadiq and the Struggle for Power in Iran* (London, 1990).

Kazemzadeh, Firuz, *Russia and Britain in Persia, 1864–1914* (New Haven, 1968).

Kedourie, Elie, *The Chatham House Version and Other Middle Eastern Studies* (London, 1970).

——, *In the Anglo-Arab Labyrinth: The McMahon-Husayn Correspondence and its Interpretations, 1914–1939* (Cambridge, 1976).

——, *England and the Middle East: The Destruction of the Ottoman Empire* (London, 1987).

Kelly, J.B., *Britain and the Persian Gulf, 1798–1880* (Oxford, 1968).

Kelly, Saul and Anthony Gorst (eds), *Whitehall and the Suez Crisis* (London, 2000).

Kent, Marian (ed.), *The Great Powers and the End of the Ottoman Empire* (London, 1984).

——, *Moguls and Mandarins: Oil, Imperialism and the Middle East in British Foreign Policy, 1900–1940* (London, 1993).

Kingston, Paul, *Britain and the Politics of Modernization in the Middle East, 1945–1958* (Cambridge, 1996).

Kirk, George, *A Short History of the Middle East: From the Rise of Islam to Modern Times* (London, 1948).

——, *The Middle East in the War* (Oxford, 1952).

Klieman, Aaron, *Foundations of British Policy in the Arab World: The Cairo Conference of 1921* (Baltimore, 1970).

Kolinsky, Martin, *Law, Order and Riots in Mandatory Palestine, 1928–1935* (London, 1993).

——, *Britain's War in the Middle East, Strategy and Diplomacy, 1936–1942* (Basingstoke, 1999).

Kostiner, Joseph, *The Making of Saudi Arabia, 1916–36: From Chieftaincy to Monarchical State* (Oxford, 1993).

Kumar, Ravinder, *India and the Persian Gulf Region, 1858–1907* (London, 1965).

Kwateng, Kwasi, *Ghosts of Empire: Britain's Legacy in the Modern World* (London, 2011).

Kyle, Keith, *Suez* (London, 1991).

Landes, David, *Bankers and Pashas: International Finance and Economic Imperialism in Egypt* (Cambridge, MA, 1979 edn).

Lapping, Brian, *End of Empire* (London, 1985).

Leatherdale, Clive, *Britain and Saudi Arabia, 1925–1939: The Imperial Oasis* (London, 1983).

Ledwidge, Frank, *Losing Small Wars: Britain's Military Failure in Iraq and Afghanistan* (New Haven and London, 2012).

Lee, Air Chief Marshal Sir David, *Flight from the Middle East: A History of the RAF in the Arabian Peninsula and Adjacent Territories, 1945–72* (London, 1980).

Levey, Zach and Elie Podeh (eds), *Britain and the Middle East: From Imperial Power to Junior Partner* (Brighton, 2008).

Lloyd, Lord, *Egypt since Cromer*, Vols i and ii (London, 1933 and 1934).

Longrigg, Stephen, *Iraq, 1900–1950* (London, 1953).

Louis, William Roger, *The British Empire in the Middle East, 1945–51: Arab Nationalism, the United States and Post-War Imperialism* (Oxford, 1984).

——, *Ends of British Imperialism: The Scramble for Empire, Suez and Decolonization* (London, 2006).

Louis, William Roger and Roger Owen (eds), *Suez 1956: The Crisis and its Consequences* (Oxford, 1989).

——, *A Revolutionary Year: The Middle East in 1958* (London, 2002).

Lukitz, Liora, *Iraq: The Search for National Identity* (London, 1995).

Macmillan, Margaret, *Peacemakers: Six Months that Changed the World* (London, 2002).

Mallmann, Klaus-Michael and Martin Cueppers, *Nazi Palestine: The Plan for the Extermination of the Jews in Palestine* (New York, 2010).

Mangold, Peter, *Success and Failure in British Foreign Policy, 1900–2000* (Basingstoke, 2001).

Mansel, Peter, *Levant: Splendour and Catastrophe on the Mediterranean* (London, 2010).

Mansfield, Peter, *Britain in Egypt* (London, 1971).

Marlowe, John, *The Seat of Pilate: An Account of the Palestine Mandate* (London, 1959).

——, *Anglo-Egyptian Relations, 1820–1956* (London, 1965 edn).

——, *Late Victorian: The Life of Sir A. Talbot Wilson* (London, 1967).

——, *Perfidious Albion: The Origins of Anglo-French Rivalry in the Levant* (London, 1971).

Marr, Phoebe, *The Modern History of Iraq* (Boulder, CO, 1985).

Marsh, Steve, *Anglo-American Relations and Cold War Oil* (Basingstoke, 2003).

Marston, Thomas, *Britain's Imperial Role in the Red Sea Area, 1800–78* (Hamden, CT, 1961).

Martin, Vanessa (ed.), *Anglo-Iranian Relations since 1800* (London, 2005).

Mawby, Spencer, *British Policy in Aden and the Protectorates, 1955–1967: Last Outpost of Empire* (London, 2005).

McDowell, David, *A Modern History of the Kurds* (London, 1996).

McKale, Donald, *War by Revolution: Germany and Great Britain in the Middle East in the Era of World War One* (Kent, Ohio, 1998).

McLean, David, *Britain and her Buffer State: The Collapse of the Persian Empire, 1890–1914* (London, 1979).

Mcloughlin, Leslie, *In a Sea of Knowledge: British Arabists in the Twentieth Century* (Reading, 2002).

McMeekin, Sean, *The Berlin-Baghdad Express: The Ottoman Empire and Germany's Bid for World Power, 1898–1918* (London, 2010).

McNamara, Robert, *Britain, Nasser and the Balance of Power in the Middle East, 1952–1967* (London, 2003).

Mejcher, Helmut, *Imperial Quest for Oil: Iraq, 1910–1928* (London, 1976).

Meyer, Karl and Shareen Brysac, *Kingmakers: The Invention of the Middle East* (New York, 2008).

Milner, Alfred, *England in Egypt* (London, 1893).

Mishra, Pankaj, *The Revolt against the West and the Remaking of Asia* (London, 2012).

Moeckli, Daniel and Victor Mauer (eds), *European–American Relations in the Middle East: From Suez to Iraq* (Abingdon, 2011).

Mohs, Polly, *Military Intelligence and the Arab Revolt: The First Modern Intelligence War* (London, 2008).

Monroe, Elizabeth, *Britain's Moment in the Middle East, 1914–71* (London, 1963 and 1981).

Morewood, Steven, *The British Defence of Egypt, 1935–40: Conflict and Crisis in the Eastern Mediterranean* (London, 2005).

Nasser, Hoda Gamal Abdel, *Britain and the Egyptian Nationalist Movement, 1936–1956* (Reading, 1994).

Nevakivi, Jukka, *Britain, France and the Arab Middle East, 1914–21* (London, 1968).

Nuwar, Abu Ma'n, *The History of the Hashemite Kingdom of Jordan*, Vol. i, *The Creation and Development of Transjordan, 1920–1929* (Oxford, 1989).

Olson, William, *Anglo-Iranian Relations during World War One* (London, 1984).

Omissi, David, *Airpower and Colonial Control* (Manchester, 1990).

Onley, James, *The Arabian Frontier of the British Raj: Merchants, Rulers and the British in the Nineteenth-Century Gulf* (Oxford, 2007).

Ovendale, Ritchie, *Britain, the United States and the Transfer of Power in the Middle East* (Leicester, 1996).

Owen, David, *The Hubris Syndrome: Bush, Blair and the Intoxication of Power* (London, 2007).

Owen, Roger, *Lord Cromer: Victorian Imperialist, Edwardian Proconsul* (Oxford, 2004).

Paget, Julian, *Last Post: Aden, 1964–1967* (London, 1969).

Paris, Timothy, *Britain, the Hashemites and Arab Rule, 1920–1925* (London, 2003).

Partner, Peter, *Arab Voices: The BBC Arabic Service, 1938–88* (London, 1988).

Pearson, Ivan, *In the Name of Oil: Anglo-American Relations in the Middle East, 1950–58* (Brighton, 2010).

Petersen, Tore, The *Decline of the Anglo-American Middle East, 1961–1969: A Willing Retreat* (Brighton, 2006).

Phythian, Mark, *The Politics of British Arms Sales since 1964* (Manchester, 2000).

Playfair, I.S.O., *The Mediterranean and the Middle East*, Vols i and ii (London, 1954 and 1956).

Porch, Douglas, *Hitler's Mediterranean Gamble: The North African and Mediterranean Campaigns in World War II* (London, 2004).

Porter, Andrew (ed.), *The Oxford History of the British Empire*, Vol. ii: *The Nineteenth Century* (Oxford, 1999).

Pratt, Lawrence, *West of Suez, East of Malta* (Cambridge, 1975).

Raugh Jr, Harold, *Wavell and the Middle East, 1939–1941: A Study in Generalship* (London, 1993).

Rawnsely, Andrew, *The End of the Party: The Rise and Fall of New Labour* (London, 2010).

Richmond, Sir John, *Egypt 1798–1952: Her Advance towards a Modern Identity* (London, 1977).

Ridley, Jasper, *Lord Palmerston* (London, 1970).

Rizk, Younan Labib, *Britain and Arab Unity: A Documentary History from the Treaty of Versailles to the End of World War Two* (London, 2009).

Roberts, Andrew, *Salisbury: Victorian Titan* (London, 1999).

Robins, Philip, *A History of Jordan* (Cambridge, 2004).

Robinson, Ronald, John Gallagher and Alice Denny, *Africa and the Victorians: The Official Mind of Imperialism* (London, 1967).

Rogan, Eugene, *The Arabs: A History* (London, 2009).

——, *The Fall of the Ottomans: The Great War in the Middle East* (London, 2015).

Rose, N.A., *The Gentile Zionists: A Study in Anglo-Zionist Diplomacy, 1929–1939* (London, 1973).

Royle, Trevor, *Glubb Pasha* (London, 1992).

Rubin, Barry, *The Great Powers and the Middle East, 1941–1947* (London, 1980).

Sabahi, Houshang, *British Policy in Persia, 1918–1925* (London, 1990).

Sabit, Adel, *A King Betrayed: The Ill-fated Reign of King Farouk of Egypt* (London, 1989).

Sachar, Howard, *The Emergence of the Middle East, 1914–24* (London, 1970).

——, *Europe Leaves the Middle East* (London, 1970).

——, *A History of Israel: From the Rise of Zionism to Our Time* (Oxford, 1977).

Salibi, Kamal, *The Modern History of Jordan* (London, 1993).

Satia, Priya, *Spies in Arabia: The Great War and the Cultural Foundations of Britain's Covert Empire in the Middle East* (Oxford, 2008).

Al-Sayyid-Marsot, Afaf Lutfi, *Egypt and Cromer: A Study in Anglo-Egyptian Relations* (London, 1968).

——, *Egypt's Liberal Experiment, 1922–36* (Berkley, 1977).

Schneer, Jonathan, *The Balfour Declaration: The Origins of the Arab–Israeli Conflict* (London, 2010).

Searight, Sarah, *The British in the Middle East* (London, 1979).

Shepherd, Naomi, *Ploughing Sand: British Rule in Palestine, 1917–1948* (London, 1999).

Sherman, A.J., *Mandate Day: British Lives in Palestine, 1918–1948* (London, 1997).

Shlaim, Avi, *Lion of Judah: The Life of King Hussein in War and Peace* (London, 2007).

Silverfarb, Daniel, *Britain's Informal Empire in the Middle East: A Case Study of Iraq, 1929–1941* (Oxford, 1986).

——, *The Twilight of British Ascendency in the Middle East: A Case Study of Iraq, 1941–1950* (Basingstoke, 1994).

Sluglett, Peter, *Britain and Iraq: Contriving King and Country* (London, 2007 edn).

Smith, Simon, *Kuwait, 1950–65: Britain, the al-Sabah and Oil* (Oxford, 1999).

——, *Britain's Revival and Fall in the Gulf: Kuwait, Bahrain, Qatar and the Trucial States, 1950–71* (London, 2004).

——, *Ending Empire in the Middle East* (London, 2012).

Sreberny, Anabelle and Massoumeh Torfeh, *Persian Service: The BBC and British Interests in Iran* (London, 2014).

Stadiem, William, *Too Rich: The High Life and Tragic Death of King Farouk* (London, 1992).

Stephens, Robert, *Nasser: A Political Biography* (London, 1971).

Sykes, Christopher, *Crossroads to Israel* (London, 1965).

Takriti, Abdel Razzaq, *Monsoon Revolution: Republicans, Sultans and Empire in Oman, 1965–76* (Oxford, 2013).

Tarbush, Mohammad, *The Role of the Military in Politics: A Case Study of Iraq to 1941* (London, 1982).

Teitelbaum, Joshua, *The Rise and Fall of the Hashemite Kingdom of Arabia* (London, 2001).

Tempest, Paul (ed.), *Envoys to the Arab World*, Vol. ii, *MECAS Memoirs, 1944–2009* (London, 2009).

Terry, Janice, *The Wafd, 1919–1952* (London, 1982).

Thomas, Hugh, *The Suez Affair* (Harmondsworth, 1970 edn).

Tidrick, Kathryn, *Heart-Beguiling Araby* (Cambridge, 1981).

Tignor, Robert, *Modernisation and British Colonial Rule in Egypt, 1882–1914* (Princeton, 1966).

Tombs, Robert and Isabelle, *That Sweet Enemy: The French and the British from the Sun King to the Present* (London, 2006).

Towle, Philip, *Pilots and Rebels: The Use of Aircraft in Unconventional Warfare* (London, 1989).

Townsend, John, *Proconsul in the Middle East: Sir Percy Cox and the End of Empire* (London, 2010).

Townshend, Charles, *When God Made Hell: The British Invasion of Mesopotamia and the Creation of Iraq, 1914–1922* (London, 2010).

Tripp, Charles, *A History of Iraq* (Cambridge, 2000).

Troeller, Gary, *The Birth of Saudi Arabia: Britain and the Rise of the House of Sa'ud* (London, 1976).

Tuchman, Barbara, *Bible and Sword: England and Palestine from the Bronze Age to Balfour* (London, 1956).

Ulrichsen, Kristian Coates, *The First World War in the Middle East* (London, 2014).

Vatikiotis, P.J., *Politics and the Military in Jordan: A Study of the Arab Legion, 1921–1957* (London, 1967).

——, *The History of Egypt from Muhammad Ali to Mubarak* (London, 1985 edn).

Von Bismarck, Helene, *British Policy in the Persian Gulf, 1961–68* (Basingstoke, 2013).

Warburg, Gabriel, *Egypt and the Sudan* (London, 1985).

Wasserstein, Bernard, *The British in Palestine: The Mandatory Government and the Arab–Jewish Conflict, 1917–1929* (London, 1979).

Waterfield, Gordon, *Professional Diplomat: Sir Percy Loraine* (London, 1973).

Westrate, Bruce, *The Arab Bureau: British Policy in the Middle East, 1916–20* (University Park, PA, 1992).

Wilkinson, John, *Arabia's Frontiers: The Story of Britain's Boundary Drawing in the Desert* (London, 1991).

Wilmington, Martin, *The Middle East Supply Centre* (Albany, 1971).

Wilson, Sir Arnold, *The Persian Gulf: An Historical Sketch from the Earliest Times to the Beginning of the Twentieth Century* (Oxford, 1928).

Wilson, Jeremy, *Lawrence of Arabia: The Authorised Biography of T.E. Lawrence* (London, 1989).

Wilson, Keith (ed.), *Imperialism and Nationalism in the Middle East: The Anglo-Egyptian Experience, 1882–1982* (London, 1982).

Wilson, Mary, *King Abdullah, Britain and the Making of Jordan* (Cambridge, 1987).

Woodward, Sir Llewelyn, *British Foreign Policy in the Second World War*, Vol. iv (London, 1962 and 1975).

Wright, Sir Denis, *The English amongst the Persians: Imperial Lives in Nineteenth-Century Iran* (London, 1997).

Yapp, Malcolm, *Strategies of British India: Britain, Iran and Afghanistan, 1798–1850* (Oxford, 1980).

Yergin, Daniel, *The Prize: The Epic Quest for Oil, Money and Power* (New York, 2003 edn).
Yorke, Valerie, *The Gulf in the 1980s* (London, 1980).
Zweig, Ronald, *Britain and Palestine during the Second World War* (London, 1986).

Articles

Alon, Yoav, 'Tribal Sheikhs and the Limits of British Imperial Rule in Transjordan, 1920–46', *JICH*, January 2004.

Ashton, Nigel, 'Kuwait 1961: Britain and the Kuwaiti Crisis', *Diplomacy and Statecraft*, 1998, no. 1.

——, 'A "Special Relationship" Sometimes in Spite of Ourselves: Britain and Jordan, 1957–1963', *JICH*, 2005, no. 2.

Balfour-Paul, Glen, 'Britain's Informal Empire in the Middle East', in Brown and Louis (eds), *Oxford History of the British Empire*, Vol. v (Oxford 1999).

Bowden, Tom, 'The Politics of the Arab Rebellion in Palestine, 1936–1939', *MES*, May 1975.

Burrell, R.M., 'Britain, Iran and the Persian Gulf: Some Aspects of the Situation in the 1920s and 1930s', in Derek Hopwood et al., *The Arabian Gulf: Society and Politics* (London, 1972).

Chamberlain, M.E., 'The Alexandria Massacre of 11 June 1982 and the British Occupation of Egypt', *MES*, January 1977.

Cox, Jafna, 'A Splendid Training Ground: The Importance to the RAF of its Role in Iraq, 1919–32', *JICH*, January 1985.

Darwin, John, 'An Undeclared Empire: The British in the Middle East, 1918–39', *JICH*, May 1999.

Easter, David, 'Spying on Nasser: British SIGINT in Middle East Crises and Conflicts', *INS*, 2013, no. 6.

Eshragi, F, 'The Anglo-Soviet Occupation of Iran, 1941', *MES*, January 1984.

Friesel, Evyatar, 'British Officials on the Situation in Palestine, 1923', *MES*, April 1987.

Galbraith, Jonathan and Afaf Lutfi al-Sayyid-Marsot, 'The British Occupation of Egypt: Another View', *BJMES*, 1973, no. 4.

Gandy, Christopher, 'A Mission to Yemen: August 1962–January 1963', *BJMES*, 1998, no. 2.

Gillon, D.Z., 'The Antecedents of the Balfour Declaration', *MES*, May 1969.

Goldstein, Erik, 'British Peace Aims and the Eastern Question: The Political Intelligence Department and the Eastern Question, 1918', *MES*, October 1987.

Greaves, Rose, 'Iran's Relations with Great Britain and India, 1798–1921', in Peter Avery et al. (eds), *The Cambridge History of Iran*, Vol. vi (Cambridge, 1986).

Hopkins, A.G., 'The Victorians and Africa: A Reconsideration of the Occupation of Egypt, 1882', *Journal of African Studies*, 1986, no. 2.

Hopwood, Derek, 'Earths Proud Empires Pass Away: Britain's Moment in the Middle East', *BJMES*, November 2002.

Hourani, Albert, 'The Decline of the West in the Middle East I', *International Affairs*, January 1953.

——, 'The Decline of the West in the Middle East II', *International Affairs*, July 1953.

Hughes, Geraint, 'Iraqnophobia: The Danger of Forgetting Operation Telic', *RUSIJ*, December 2012.

Jasse, Richard, 'The Baghdad Pact: Cold War or Colonialism', *MES*, January 1991.

Jones, Matthew, 'The "Preferred Plan": The Anglo-American Working Group Report on Covert Action in Syria', *INS*, 2004, no. 33.

Joyce, Miriam, 'On the Road towards Unity: The Trucial States from a British Perspective, 1960–6', *MES*, April 1999.

Katouzian, Homa, 'The Campaign against the Anglo-Iranian Treaty of 1919', *BJMES*, May 1998.

Kelly, Saul and Gareth Stansfield, 'Britain, the United Arab Emirates and the Defence of the Gulf Revisited', *International Affairs*, September 2013.

Kent, John, 'The Egyptian Base and the Defence of the Middle East, 1945–1954', *JICH*, September 1993.

Klein, Ira, 'British Intervention in the Persian Revolution, 1905–1909', *The Historical Journal*, December 1972.

Loewenstein, Andrew, '"The Veiled Protectorate of Kuwait": Liberalized Imperialism and British Efforts to Influence Kuwaiti Domestic Policy during the Reign of Sheikh Ahmed al-Jaber, 1939–50', *MES*, April 2000.

Longrigg, Stephen, 'The Decline of the West: An Alternative View', *International Affairs*, July 1953.

Louis, William Roger, 'Churchill and Egypt, 1946–56', in Robert Blake and William Roger Louis, *Churchill* (Oxford, 1993).

Lucas, W. Scott, 'Redefining Suez Collusion', *MES*, January 1990.

Lucas, W. Scott and Alistair Morey, 'The "Hidden Alliance": The CIA and MI6 Before and After Suez', *INS*, 2000, no. 2.

MacDonald, Callum, 'Radio Bari: Italian Wireless Propaganda in the Middle East and British Counter-Measures, 1934–1938', *MES*, May 1977.

Mejcher, Helmut, 'Oil and British Policy towards Mesopotamia: 1914–18', *MES*, October 1972.

——, 'British Middle East Policy, 1917–21: The Interdepartmental Level', *Journal of Contemporary History*, October 1973.

Mobley, Richard, 'Gauging the Iraq Threat to Kuwait in the 1960s', https://www.cia.gov/library/center-for-the-study.../article03.html.

Morsy, Leila, 'Farouk in British Policy', *MES*, October 1984.

——, 'Britain's Wartime Policy in Egypt, 1940–1942', *MES*, January 1989.

——, 'Indicative Cases of Britain's Wartime Policy in Egypt, 1942–1944', *MES*, January 1994.

O'Connor, Damian, 'The Suez Crisis, 1871–82', *RUSIJ*, June 2001.

Omissi, David, 'Britain, the Assyrians and the Iraqi Levies, 1919–32', *JICH*, May 1989.

⌐nley, James, 'The Politics of Protection in the Gulf: The Arab Rulers and the British Resident in the Nineteenth Century', *New Arabian Studies*, no. 6.

Pearson, William, 'The Syrian Crisis of 1957: The Anglo-American "Special Relationship" and the 1958 Landings in Jordan and Lebanon', *MES*, January 2007.

Porter, Patrick, 'Last Charge of the Knights? Iraq, Afghanistan and the Special Relationship', *International Affairs*, March 2010.

Rabi, Uzi, 'Britain's Special Position in the Gulf: Its Origins, Dynamics and Legacy', *MES*, May 2006.

Roberts, David, 'British National Interests in the Gulf: Rediscovering a Role?', *International Affairs*, May 2014.

Rudd, Jeffery, 'The Origins of the Transjordan Frontier Force', *MES*, April 1990.

Rynhold, Jonathan and Jonathan Spyer, 'British Policy in the Arab–Israeli Arena, 1973–2004', *BJMES*, April 2007.

Sato, Shohei, 'Britain's Decision to Withdraw from the Persian Gulf, 1964–8', *JICH*, March 2009.

Sheffer, Gabriel, 'British Colonial Policy-making towards Palestine, 1929–39', *MES*, October 1978.

Shlaim, Avi, 'Britain and the Arab–Israeli War of 1948', *Journal of Palestine Studies*, summer 1987.

Silverfarb, Daniel, 'Great Britain, Iraq and Saudi Arabia: The Revolt of the Ikhwan', *International History Review*, May 1982.

——, 'Britain and Saudi Arabia on the Eve of the Second World War', *MES*, October 1983.

Smith, Simon, 'Rulers and Residents: British Relations with the Aden Protectorates, 1937–1959', *MES*, July 1995.

Standish, J.F., 'British Maritime Policy in the Persian Gulf', *MES*, July 1967.

Syk, Andrew, 'The 1917 Mesopotamia Commission: Britain's First Iraq Inquiry', *RUSIJ*, 2009, no. 4.

Thornton, A.P., 'British Policy in Persia, 1858–90', *English Historical Review*, October 1954 and January 1955.

Warburg, Gabriel, 'Lampson's Ultimatum to Faruq, 4 February, 1942', *MES*, January 1975.

Theses

Innes, Mary, 'In Egyptian Service: The Role of British Officials in Egypt, 1911–1936' (D.Phil, Oxford, 1981).

Mangold, Peter, 'The Role of Force in British Policy in the Middle East, 1957–66' (PhD, London, 1973).

Sandall, Alan, 'The Involvement of the United Kingdom in the Domestic Politics of Egypt, 1922–31' (B.Litt, Oxford, 1975).

Sheffer, Gabriel, 'Policy-Making and British Policy towards Palestine, 1929–39' (D.Phil, Oxford, 1970).

Index